Intergovernmental Relations in the UK

Intergovernmental Relations in the UK provides a timely and up-to-date analysis of a turbulent decade in British politics and presents a fascinating case study of intergovernmental relations and territorial power in a devolved unitary state.

As over time a widening range of powers has been transferred from the Westminster Parliament to the devolved legislatures in Scotland, Wales and Northern Ireland, intergovernmental relations have become increasingly important to deal with the corresponding overlaps of legislative and fiscal authority. However, leaving the European Union has exposed the weakness of the intergovernmental architecture and challenged the functionality of the UK's multilevel polity. Until now, the question of how powerful the devolved administrations really are has not been satisfactorily answered. The author uses insights from comparative studies of federations to develop a systematic account of shared rule and intergovernmental relations. This book examines how informal institutions and practices can provide political influence beyond formal structures, with reference to an extensive range of institutions, practices, policies and political decisions. Unlike other studies focused predominantly on the state of the Union, this volume points to the interplay between conflict and cooperation and demonstrates that the proclaimed 'break-up of the Union' is accompanied by efforts to integrate the different jurisdictions.

This book will be of interest to scholars and postgraduate students of comparative politics, political systems, multilevel governance, regional and federal studies, British politics and public administration. It will also appeal to politicians, government advisers, civil servants and other practitioners, who seek a better, more nuanced understanding of the UK's multilevel constitution and politics, and the nature of intergovernmental relations in the UK.

Marius Guderjan is Postdoctoral Researcher at the Freie Universität Berlin, Germany. Until July 2022, he worked as Researcher and Lecturer at the Centre for British Studies at Humboldt-Universität zu Berlin, Germany, where he co-chaired the Berlin-Britain Research Network. He is also Co-Chair of the German Association for British Studies. Previous publications include *Local Government in the European Union: Completing the Integration Cycle* (2021, with Tom Verhelst), and *Contested Britain: Brexit, Austerity and Agency* (2020, edited with H. Mackay and G. Stedman).

Federalism Studies
Series Editor: Soren Dosenrode

The end of the Cold War profoundly altered the dynamics between and within the various states in Europe and the rest of the World, resulting in a resurgence of interest in the concept of federalism. This shift in balance has been further fuelled by the increase in the number of conflicts arising from the disaffection of the diverse ethnic or religious minorities residing within these states (e.g. Sudan, Iraq). Globalization is forcing governments not only to work together, but also to reconsider their internal roles as guarantors of economic growth, with regions playing the major part. Federalism Studies offers academics a complete and in-depth understanding of federalism and intergovernmental relations in historical, theoretical and comparative contexts. Intended to be international and interdisciplinary in scope, the books in the series are designed to build a common framework for the constructive analysis of federalism. Contributions are welcome on topics which explore federalism as a theory; as a political system and as a form of conflict management.

Federalism, Secession and International Recognition Regime
Iraqi Kurdistan
Edited by Alex Danilovich

Comparative Paradiplomacy
Jorge A. Schiavon

Tensions of American Federal Democracy
Fragmentation of the State
Jared Sonnicksen

Intergovernmental Relations in the UK
Cooperation and Conflict in a Devolved Unitary State
Marius Guderjan

For more information about this series, please visit: https://www.routledge.com/Federalism-Studies/book-series/FEDSTUD

Intergovernmental Relations in the UK

Cooperation and Conflict in a Devolved Unitary State

Marius Guderjan

LONDON AND NEW YORK

First published 2023
by Routledge
4 Park Square, Milton Park, Abingdon, Oxon OX14 4RN

and by Routledge
605 Third Avenue, New York, NY 10158

Routledge is an imprint of the Taylor & Francis Group, an informa business

© 2023 Marius Guderjan

The right of Marius Guderjan to be identified as author of this work has been asserted in accordance with sections 77 and 78 of the Copyright, Designs and Patents Act 1988.

All rights reserved. No part of this book may be reprinted or reproduced or utilised in any form or by any electronic, mechanical, or other means, now known or hereafter invented, including photocopying and recording, or in any information storage or retrieval system, without permission in writing from the publishers.

Trademark notice: Product or corporate names may be trademarks or registered trademarks, and are used only for identification and explanation without intent to infringe.

British Library Cataloguing-in-Publication Data
A catalogue record for this book is available from the British Library

ISBN: 978-1-032-39485-5 (hbk)
ISBN: 978-1-032-39488-6 (pbk)
ISBN: 978-1-003-34995-2 (ebk)

DOI: 10.4324/9781003349952

Typeset in Times New Roman
by KnowledgeWorks Global Ltd.

To Polly Eleanor

Contents

Preface and Acknowledgements		viii
List of Acronyms and Abbreviations		x
1	Introduction	1
2	Theoretical and Methodological Perspectives	15
3	Self-rule and the Devolution of Political, Legislative and Fiscal Authority	50
4	Formal and Informal Intergovernmental Institutions and Practices	84
5	Patterns of Interaction and Political Influence	148
6	Comparing Scotland and Wales	250
7	Lessons from and for Comparative Federalism	286
	Index	306

Preface and Acknowledgements

The origins of this study date back to 2014, when I had just moved from Manchester to Berlin to become a lecturer and researcher at the Centre for British Studies at Humboldt-Universität zu Berlin. By default, my new long-term research project had to be about the UK and was part of my habilitation thesis. British politics has been an exciting and fast-moving subject. Being politically socialised in the Federal Republic of Germany, the British way of muddling through messy terrains is full of wonders. My new job started shortly after Scotland had held its independence referendum, and two years later the UK's withdrawal from the EU was decided in another referendum.

A long time has passed since the early days of this project, during which I have engaged intensively with territorial politics, especially with devolution, and, of course, Brexit. I got to know a number of great colleagues who helped me to shape my research objective and approach. Among them, Arjan Schakel, Neil McGarvey, Paul Carmichael and, especially, Klaus Stolz were particularly supportive, and I would like to thank them for all their advice.

After I was awarded a scholarship by the German Research Foundation to go to the UK and conduct the in-depth field work necessary for this study, I spent several weeks in Edinburgh, Cardiff and London in 2019 and 2020. I genuinely enjoyed learning more about these places and their culture, and I visited excellent research hubs, such as the Centre on Constitutional Change, the Wales Governance Centre and the Institute for Government, where I once again benefitted from the advice of members. Many thanks to Michael Keating, Dan Wincott, Richard Wyn Jones, Jo Hunt, Ed Poole, Guto Ifan, Akash Paun and Jess Sargeant for their hospitality and expertise. My special thanks also to Paul Cairney, who did not only share his knowledge about Scottish politics but also invited me to the University of Stirling, where my fellowship was based.

The pandemic abruptly ended my research time abroad in March 2020, and I had to return to Berlin. I was still able to conduct some interviews with UK officials online. However, circumstances were such that I was unfortunately unable to travel to Belfast and this meant I had to make the difficult choice of excluding Northern Ireland from my study. Luckily, I got to visit Belfast on another occasion, and I can now say that I have been to all four capitals and inside all four legislatures of the UK.

I am immensely grateful for the members of the different legislatures and the government officials who spoke to me and provided crucial insights on which this book is based. Due to the confidentiality of our interviews, I will not disclose any names but perhaps some interviewees may recognise themselves in some quotes or statements in this book. I would also like to express my deep gratitude to the civil servants from the Scottish, Welsh and UK Governments who connected me with their colleagues from other departments.

My colleagues also played an important part in contributing to my work at the Centre for British Studies. My dearest thanks to Catherine Smith (especially for proofreading my texts!), Corrina Radke, Sylvena Zöllner, Christine Seuring, Sam McIntosh, Johanna Zinecker, Felicia Kompio, Sonya Permiakova, Gesa Stedman, Christiane Eisenberg, and, of course, Gerhard Dannemann for supporting my research endeavours. Lastly, I would like to thank the student assistants at the Centre for British Studies for successfully handling the various tasks I threw at them. Particular thanks to David Bell who did an excellent job of proofreading to complete manuscript.

Over the last few years, my personal situation has changed significantly. I am now married to my wonderful wife Katharina and I have become the humble father of an adorable daughter. During the time working on this book I could always rely on the love of my friends and family. I am very fortunate to have them in my life.

With all this in mind, I hope you enjoy reading this book as much as I did writing it.

Gefördert durch die Deutsche Forschungsgemeinschaft (DFG) – 427941795.

Funded by the Deutsche Forschungsgemeinschaft (DFG, German Research Foundation – 427941795.

Acronyms and Abbreviations

AM	Assembly Member
APD	Air Passenger Duty
APNI	Alliance Party of Northern Ireland
AS	Ascription
BBC	British Broadcasting Corporation
BEIS	Department for Business, Energy and Industrial Strategy
CAFCASS	Children and Family Courts Advisory and Support Service
CAP	Common Agriculture Policy
CMA	Competition and Markets Authority
COBR	Civil Contingencies Committee
DAERA	Department for Agriculture, Environment and Rural Affairs
DEFRA	Department for Environment, Food and Rural Affairs
DfT	Department for Transport
DIT	Department for International Trade
DUP	Democratic Unionist Party
DWP	Department for Work and Pensions
EAR	Ergo-Perception/Alter-Perception/Researcher's Analysis
EEA	European Economic Area
EU	European Union
EUPFN	European Union Protected Food Name
F:ISC	Finance Interministerial Standing Committee
FCO	Foreign and Commonwealth Office
GA	Goal-achievement
HM	Her/His Majesty
HSE	Health and Safety Executive
IC	Interministerial Committee
IGR	Intergovernmental relations
IMG	Interministerial Group
IMG EFRA	Interministerial Group for Environment, Food and Rural Affairs
IMSC	Interministerial Standing Committee
IPR	Interparliamentary relations
IRA	Irish Republican Army

IV	Independent variable
JEC	Joint Exchequer Committee
JMC	Joint Ministerial Committee
JMC EN	JMC European Negotiations
MIG	Ministerial implementation group
MLS	Member of the Legislative Assembly
MoJ	Ministry of Justice
MoU	Memorandum of Understanding
MP	Member of Parliament
MS	Member of the Senedd
MSP	Member of the Scottish Parliament
NHS	National Health Service
OEP	Office for Environmental Protection
OIM	Office for the Internal Market
PI	Political influence
PM	Prime Minister
PR	Political relevance
SDLP	Social Democratic and Labour Party
SNP	Scottish National Party
TEU	Treaty on European Union
TRA	Trade Remedies Authority
UK	United Kingdom
UKGI	United Kingdom Geographical Indication Scheme
US	United States
UUP	Ulster Unionist Party
VAT	Value-added tax
WTO	World Trade Organisation

1 Introduction

Territorial politics, intergovernmental relations and federalism

Territorial politics has become a field of study that covers a diverse range of disciplines, including geography, economics, sociology, law and of course politics, to study social and political communities as well as the multilevel structures within and also beyond state boundaries (Hepburn and Detterbeck 2018, 2–3).[1] This book is particularly interested in the constitutional and institutional design of territorial politics, the allocation of power and the relations between central and decentralised levels of government within states. Looking at legislative, fiscal and administrative competences and authority seems a legitimate starting point to understand how powerful or autonomous substate or regional governments are. Yet, even though many scholars have found a growing decentralisation of power in multilevel polities (see e.g. Hutchcroft 2001; Schneider 2003; Agranoff 2004; Gerber and Kollman 2004; Rodden 2004; Marks et al. 2008; Mueller 2011; Falleti 2013; Hooghe et al. 2016), merely examining levels of decentralisation does not allow for a sufficiently complex analysis of territorial power (Behnke 2018, 31). The extent to which regions can rule autonomously depends also on the degree to which different governmental levels interfere with each other's activities and on the structures that incentivise their interactions. A study of territorial politics is therefore flawed if it looks only at the powers regional governments can exert autonomously (Bolleyer and Thorlakson 2012, 566–567). Only a perspective that accounts for self-rule capabilities in combination with the exercise of shared rule can deliver a truthful picture of territorial power and autonomy (cf. Hooghe et al. 2016; Behnke 2018, 36). Whereas in federations, formal power-sharing arrangements are a natural subject and have been studied comprehensively (cf. Wright 1988; Watts 2008; Bolleyer 2009; Hueglin and Fenna 2010; Broschek 2011; Bolleyer and Thorlakson 2012; Poirier et al. 2015), in unitary polities, where power-sharing is not an obvious part of the constitutional architecture, this has only fairly recently attracted the attention of scholars. If we direct our analysis away from the constitutional distribution of legislative authority (self-rule) towards the relations between levels of government (shared rule),

DOI: 10.4324/9781003349952-1

new opportunities for comparative studies open up (Burgess 2006, 138). Furthermore, relations of power and influence depend not only on formal provisions but also on informal interactions (Behnke 2015, 16; Poirier and Saunders 2015a, 1). While formalised forms of shared rule have traditionally enjoyed high levels of attention in comparative research (Helmke and Levitsky 2004, 725; Lauth 2016, 191), to learn how political systems work in practice it is vital to examine the interplay between formal and informal arrangements (Lauth 2014, 20 et seq.). In particular, the absence of any deeply formalised power-sharing, or any institutionalised power-sharing at all, requires the focus to be on the informal intergovernmental relations between different levels of government.

Since the 1950s, intergovernmental relations have become increasingly important for coordination, cooperation and joint decision-making across multilevel polities, and consequently have attracted growing scholarly interest (cf. Agranoff 2004; Benz and Broschek 2013, 7; Poirier and Saunders 2015b, 442; Hooghe et al. 2016; Behnke and Mueller 2017, 508; Hamilton and Stenberg 2018, 1). Nowadays, flexible and informal patterns of interactions have become an essential element of multidimensional regimes and an "indispensable tool of political practice" (Hueglin and Fenna 2010, 50) which have developed their own dynamics – also within federations (op. cit., 219). Focusing on intergovernmental relations allows us to overcome a static perspective on territorial power (Behnke 2018, 37), meanwhile constitutional settings remain crucial in determining the role of territorial governments in decision-making at the centre of the state. A federal lens is therefore useful to make sense of the legal and institutional structures in which intergovernmental interactions take place (Wright 1988, 31 et seq.; cf. Poirier and Saunders 2015a, 5–6) and to develop a systematic account of both self and shared rule and intergovernmental relations (cf. Benz 2002, 11). Importantly, comparative federalism should be seen as an evolving body of research that has expanded its initial focus on classical federations to a wide range of emerging multilevel polities that have decentralised power downwards to territorial governments (Behnke 2015, 9). Such hybrid models have challenged the dichotomy between unitary and federal polities (von Beyme 2010, 208; cf. Broschek 2016, 338), and according to Behnke (2018, 30), "[t]he blurring of boundaries between federal and non-federal states is most impressively illustrated with the examples of the United Kingdom [...] or Spain [...], states that have begun only in the past decades to allocate competences to different levels of government".

A devolved unitary state

Since 1999, the formerly highly centralised UK has gradually devolved a wide range of powers to administrations[2] and legislatures in Scotland, Wales and Northern Ireland. After the Scottish independence referendum in 2014, former Prime Minister David Cameron (2015) even promised to make the

Scottish Parliament "one of the most powerful devolved parliaments in the world." Yet, the devolution of legislative and fiscal responsibilities to the parliaments and assemblies of Scotland, Wales and Northern Ireland has never followed a comprehensive strategy to ensure effective governance, but has throughout been a matter of traditional statecraft to accommodate demands for self-rule and to save the Union (cf. Stolz 2010, 6) – what Watts (2008, 8) would call "a pragmatic search for workable political arrangements". The difference between unitary and federal states is not necessarily whether power is decentralised or not but whether political sovereignty is allocated and shared across different levels of government. As the different levels operate largely independently within their jurisdictions, flexibility and informality are the predominant characteristics of intergovernmental exchange in the UK (Broschek 2016, 331–332). Unlike federalism, devolution represents a "piecemeal approach to constitutional change" rooted in the British constitutional tradition. By taking a top-down approach to decentralising political authority the UK adopted some federal characteristics without fundamentally altering the unitary hierarchies (Jeffery 2009, 291–292). Whereas the "genius [of federations] lies in their capacity, via constitutional entrenchment, to accommodate and reconcile different forms of unity with different forms of diversity" (Burgess 2006, 156), constitutional sovereignty in the UK lies solely with the Westminster Parliament and not with other legislative bodies.[3] Westminster and Whitehall have made little effort to adapt to devolution. No mechanisms were introduced to coordinate policies vertically and horizontally between the different administrations and legislatures, and conflict-resolution, decision-making and policy-implementation have remained unsystematic. The relations between the different governments are dependent on goodwill and mutual trust that neither centre nor periphery disrespect their boundaries by pushing their powers too far and instead cooperate in the pursuit of common interests (O'Neill 2004, 191; McEwen and Petersohn 2015, 195–196).

When New Labour introduced the devolved legislatures, the same party was in government in Westminster, Scotland and Wales, and intergovernmental business was largely channelled through intra-party channels. After 2007, when the Scottish National Party (SNP) came to power in Scotland and in 2010 the Conservative Party won the UK elections, intergovernmental relations had to turn to extra-party engagements. Although there was no urgent need to work together and manage policy divergence, as more competences were devolved, their allocation across different levels has in practice often become blurred (Cairney 2011, 87–88). This has created challenges for the coordination of policies, as well as ongoing conflict over responsibilities. The UK's withdrawal from the European Union (EU) has triggered further constitutional tensions exacerbated by the repatriation of powers to the UK. The different positions towards EU membership have severely constrained the relationships between the governments, which were at a low when this study was conducted.[4] Taking away the EU's regulatory and governance framework, in which the devolution settlement unfolded over the course of two decades, has not only exposed the weaknesses of the lightweight intergovernmental architecture but has made the representation of territorial interests at UK level ever more relevant (cf. Hunt and Minto 2017). The volatility of the UK's devolution process stands in stark contrast to the relatively stable arrangements of federal political systems and has over time threatened the British Union. The cultivation of different nationalisms, which have in the past been reconciled under a common British identity, is most clearly reflected in the Scottish secessionist movement. But public support for Welsh independence too has grown considerably, particularly since the 2019 General Election and the outbreak of the COVID-19 pandemic (Paun and Hall 2021). The Welsh Labour-led Government, which unlike the Scottish Government advocates staying part of the UK, has repeatedly expressed its doubts about the sustainability of the Union without more federal-like provisions.[5]

As the UK's unitary state faces substantial and growing pressures, this book provides a timely and up-to-date analysis of a turbulent decade in British politics. The devolution of further powers as well as EU withdrawal accelerated the need for more interaction between governments, which is why the time frame of this research covers the decade between 2011 and 2020. Prior to 2010, intergovernmental relations had not been particularly developed. Since then, political dynamics have provided great potential for cooperation and conflict between the different levels of government, which makes the UK a pressing and fascinating case for the study of territorial politics and power. This is even more so the case in light of the informality of intergovernmental exchange in the UK. Unlike other research that focuses predominantly on the state of the Union and highlights the tensions between governments, this study points to the interplay between conflict and cooperation, and demonstrates that the proclaimed 'break-up of the Union' is accompanied by an evolving web of institutions and practices integrating the different jurisdictions. Furthermore, at the start of 2022, the central and devolved governments introduced a review of intergovernmental relations, which introduced substantive reforms with the potential to install a more coherent structure to the UK multilevel polity and to facilitate greater engagement between the different levels in light of the common challenges ahead.

Research objectives

Since the question of how powerful the devolved legislatures and governments really are has not been answered in satisfactory detail until today, the idea for this study is to examine their power and decision-making autonomy in the UK's non-federal multilevel polity. Due to reasons given earlier, such an endeavour needs to look beyond the self-rule capacities of individual levels and be attuned to the relational power between different jurisdictions. Though this study accounts for the legislative and fiscal authority allocated across the different levels, engaging solely with the devolved competences would be neither sufficient to grasp their political power nor likely lead to particularly new insights. Therefore, the main objective is to shed light on the nature of intergovernmental relations in a unitary political system based on a high degree of informality and flexibility instead of an explicitly codified constitutional architecture. For this purpose, the research objective is divided into three guiding questions, which will be briefly outlined in the following: How are intergovernmental relations structured and organised? How do different governments engage with each other to achieve their policy objectives? How capable are subnational governments at influencing decisions of the centre?

How are intergovernmental relations structured and organised?

The UK is a prominent example of a majoritarian democracy that relies heavily on informal institutions to guide political actions, in which an effective formalisation of intergovernmental relations would undermine the supremacy of the UK Parliament and the Government's ability to act unilaterally (cf. Jeffery 2009, 304; Cairney 2011, 114; Gallagher 2012, 200).[6] As shared rule depends by and large on informal interaction typically dealt with on an ad hoc basis by government officials not on the public's radar, focusing merely on formal provisions will not fully explain the structures that enable or constrain actors' behaviour and interactions (Helmke and Levitsky 2004, 725–727). Following a neo-institutionalist approach (cf. Lowndes and Roberts 2013, 46–47), this study will take stock of various arrangements through which governments interact with each other and examine the formality and institutional depth of intergovernmental *institutions* and *practices* (Bolleyer 2009; 2013, 324–325; Bröchler and Lauth 2014, 3 et seq.; Lauth 2014, 20 et seq.; Bolleyer 2018, 48). These can include intergovernmental institutions, forums, agencies, agreements, decision-making processes and mechanisms for dispute resolution (cf. Watts 2008, 118 et seq.; Hueglin and Fenna 2010, 57 et seq.; Poirier et al 2015). Apart from *intra-institutional* arrangements through which different levels of government participate in joint decision-making and formally share the exercise of power (cf. Broschek 2011, 545), multilateral bodies that bring together heads of governments or sectoral ministers, legislatures, courts and political parties are important arenas for intergovernmental exchange. In addition, compacts, concordats, constitutional conventions, protocols, memorandums of understanding and treaties play a vital role for the cooperation of governments (Poirier and Saunders 2015b, 442 et seq.).

How do different governments engage with each other to achieve their policy objectives?

The question of how governments engage with each other to achieve their policy objectives is central to the nature of intergovernmental relations and presents a behavioural continuum (cf. Bolleyer 2009, 14); including either consultation, co-decision and coordination, or tension, collusion, competition, control and even coercion (Poirier and Saunders 2015a, 1). Based on Michael Tatham's (2016, 16 et seq.) research on regional engagement in EU affairs, the second stage of this study will analyse patterns of *(non-) interaction, cooperation* and *conflict* between governments. It will explain why governments do or do not attempt to coordinate their policies, work together to achieve common policy goals, or compete to achieve oppositional outcomes. In order to do so, this research will investigate a set of four variables that inform these patterns of intergovernmental exchange: functional and political interdependence, preference intensity, party congruency and strategic power.

Functional and political interdependence: The more closely different levels are interlinked, the more they are subject to intergovernmental bargaining (Watts 2008, 123; Bolleyer 2009, 43; Broschek 2011, 545). *Loosely coupled* multilevel polities that allocate power to independently operating institutions provide little incentive to cooperate and enable governments to act unilaterally. While this increases the likeliness of either non-interaction or conflict (Lehmbruch 1998, 30; cf. Scharpf 2006, 289; Broschek 2011, 545; Bolleyer and Thorlakson 2012, 571–573), even loosely integrated polities engage in voluntary, non-hierarchical coordination (Bolleyer 2018, 45). Though the UK has strived for a dual allocation of power, devolved and reserved powers are increasingly overlapping and their allocation across different levels has in practice become blurred (Cairney 2011, 87–88). In particular, the implementation of EU legislation and policies has required the different governments to work together (Gallagher 2012, 200; Keating 2012, 225–226; McEwen and Petersohn 2015, 195; Tatham 2016, 156 et seq.), which has further intensified in the course of leaving the EU. As a consequence, different levels are expected to cooperate in order to avoid costly conflicts or political crises (McEwen and Petersohn 2015, 193 et seq.).

Preference intensity: In case of opposing interests across governments, the political salience of the matter determines whether devolved actors cooperate or engage in conflict with central government. To learn about the impact of preference intensity on patterns of interaction, it is crucial to examine a broad range of areas and policy fields. Constitutional issues, the allocation of powers and Brexit have been highly salient issues for the devolved administration. Fiscal policy is typically another high-conflict area, as all multilevel systems bargain for financial resources (Bolleyer 2009, 51; Gallagher 2012, 206).

Party congruency: Much of the exchange between governments is channelled through political parties that are operating at multiple levels. Informal partisan lines provide convenient and effective ways to coordinate their positions. However, as McEwen (2017, 670) argues, "when governments are led by parties that compete against each other, there may be more competition than cooperation between governments. This can result in less willingness to cooperate or make concessions, and less confidence in sharing privileged information." Especially in majoritarian systems, parties compete with each other for electoral support in order to shift blame for political failures onto governments ruled by different parties (Scharpf 1997, 183 et seq.; Bolleyer 2009, 35–37; 2018, 51; Poirier and Saunders 2015b, 451). Though a number of scholars (cf. Cairney 2012, 232 et seq.; Deacon 2012, 244; McEwen et al. 2012, 324) had suggested that party incongruency would only have a modest impact on how different levels in the UK settle disputes, the situation has over the last decade changed significantly and requires re-evaluation. Despite the fact that the time frame of this study does not cover periods of party congruency, it will examine to what extent cooperation and conflict have become more prominent under changing party constellations.

Strategic power: Governments' perception and evaluation of political leverage and achievable objectives are not only informed by the self- and shared-rule capacities of governments, but also by their popularity and electoral strength (Petersohn et al. 2015, 631–632). The fourth variable is informed by Scharpf's (1997) actor-centred institutionalism and accounts for governments' strategic preferences, negotiation power and the prevailing negotiation mode. As part of their strategic power, the devolved governments are assumed to reflect on their perceived leverage when faced with the choice between cooperation and conflict. For instance, unitary polities allow the centre to exit negotiation systems and avoid decisions by majority vote as instead they can act unilaterally and hierarchically. Still, all governments operate within wider strategic constellations which limit their scope of choice (cf. Scharpf 1997, 45; Benz 2009, 85 et seq.).

How capable are subnational governments at influencing decisions of the centre?

An understanding of patterns of interactions will help us to comprehend the strategic choices of actors but it does not tell us how effective the devolved administrations are in influencing the UK Government. Existing studies have not systematically examined the political influence of the devolved administrations across a wider range of policy areas and the question of how powerful the devolved administrations really are has not been satisfactorily answered yet. The third research question is therefore about the ability of the devolved administrations to influence political decisions of the centre that affect their jurisdictions. Measuring actual political influence beyond a legalistic analysis of political, legislative and fiscal authority is not an easy undertaking as it involves multiple actors with diverging or converging preferences who deploy different means within varying contexts to achieve their goals. This study applies the so-called *EAR instrument*, introduced by Bas

Arts and Piet Verschuren (1999) as a tool to qualitatively assess complex decision-making. The triangulation of different perspective aims to provide a transparent measurement within decision-making procedures involving multiple stakeholders who use formal and informal bargaining to promote their interests. The EAR instrument uses ego-perception (E) to capture key player A's own perception of their level of influence; alter-perception (A) to compare A's perception with key players B-to-Z's perceptions of A's level of influence and the researcher's analysis (R) to validate these perceptions. If the exercise of influence can be repeatedly observed for various cases, the findings enable conclusions on territorial power, as the general ability to produce intended or to prevent undesired effects.

The selection of different decisions corresponds with examples of cooperation and conflict and covers the development and passage of Westminster legislation, wider constitutional and governance matters, international affairs and, in particular, EU withdrawal and relations, and policy agreement in areas such as fiscal policy and economic development. The channels and forums used to have an impact on these decisions vary across the different examples and include the executives, legislatives and judicial branches at the central level. All devolved governments operate under the 'shadow of hierarchy' of a unitary state and can be excluded more easily from decision-making. De jure the UK Government ultimately has the upper hand and can address them bilaterally or overrule them (Keating 2012, 223; McEwen et al. 2012, 332–333). Nevertheless, power is less top-down and concentrated in the centre than is usually asserted (Cairney 2012, 232–235). A clear and nuanced picture of the devolved governments' impact on central decisions will make a profound contribution to understanding the effectiveness of shared rule and intergovernmental relations in the UK.

Methodological and practical considerations

As existing works are skewed towards formal institutions, a major aim of this research is to make the unrecorded visible, and to find out how informal institutions and practices can provide political influence beyond formal structures. The informality of the UK's intergovernmental set-up, insights into the rationales behind cooperation and conflict, and the complexity of decision-making can only be adequately captured through a comparison of small-n case studies and intensive field work (Helmke and Levitsky 2004, 733). This study seeks to explain the commonalities in the operation of intergovernmental relations across different administrations and policy fields and to reflect on the structural linkages between the macro-level dynamics of institutional configurations and micro-level analysis of specific policies (cf. Bolleyer 2009, 16–17). Insights from wider theoretical approaches will ensure a broader perspective feeding back into conceptual debates (cf. Bukve 2019, 121; 163). The comparative merit of this case study is provided by the UK's critical nature as a decentralised unitary state and its links to comparative federalism.

The two cases covered by the study are the Scottish and Welsh Governments. While the initial scope of this study sought to include Northern Ireland, conducting interviews with respondents from the Northern Ireland Executive and Assembly was frustrated by the COVID-19 travel restrictions during 2020. Considering the particular circumstances in Northern Ireland and the suspension of the Northern Ireland Executive and Assembly between 2017 and 2019, a comparison with Scotland and Wales would have been challenging to begin with. Qualitative, semi-structured interviews were conducted throughout 2019 and 2020 with policymakers, parliamentarians and civil servants in Edinburgh, Cardiff and London. These are triangulated with a documentary analysis to provide thorough and balanced conclusions.

Outline of the book

Following this introduction, Chapter 2 will present relevant theoretical approaches and the overall conceptual framework guiding this research. It will draw on insights into the study of territorial politics and power, self-rule and shared rule, and comparative federalism, and subsequently explain the relationship between federalism and intergovernmental relations. The research objectives will be set out in detail and operationalised with the help of existing works on formal and informal institutions, intergovernmental relations and political influence. Chapter 2 will also elaborate on the case-study approach and the qualitative methodology applied to the collection and analysis of empirical data. Before the actual empirical analysis, Chapter 3 will turn to the UK's devolution settlement and outline the evolution of the UK's multilevel polity. It will discuss the allocation and distribution of political, legislative and financial authority at the central and constituent levels. Focusing on the self-rule capacities for autonomous decision-making in light of the emerging overlap of responsibilities across different levels will provide the necessary context for the following analysis.

The presentation of research findings starts in Chapter 4 with an explanation of the formal and informal intergovernmental institutions and practices in the UK and identifies their institutional depth. These include Whitehall departments; the Supreme Court; the Sewel Convention; memorandums of understanding, intergovernmental agreements, concordats and the UK Common Frameworks programme; the Joint Ministerial Committee; the Joint Exchequer Committees; the British-Irish Council and ministerial, officials and interparliamentary arrangements and working groups. The chapter examines the purpose of these institutions and practices and how actors from different levels use them. As the different policy issues analysed in this study are typically a story of both cooperation and conflict, and allow for conclusions on the impact of the devolved administrations on central decision-making, Chapter 5 presents both the findings of patterns of interaction and political influence. The policies and decisions covered in this chapter include constitutional reforms; various issues around the UK's withdrawal from the EU; foreign and trade policies; immigration; fiscal policy; agriculture and food; environment, climate change and energy; economic development; transport; public health care and justice and policing. The analysis is guided by three dependent variables (non-interaction, cooperation, conflict) and four independent variables (functional and political interdependence, preference intensity, party congruency, strategic power); and the EAR-instrument to conclude whether the Scottish and Welsh Governments exercise great, substantial, some or no influence on the UK Government.

Chapter 6 will compare the differences across Scotland and Wales in terms of the usage of the intergovernmental institutions and practices available to them; the relationship between the independent and dependent variables shaping their patterns of interaction; and the political influence they exert on the UK Government. Finally, Chapter 7 will return to the theoretical perspective and place the findings of this study into wider debates about self-rule, shared rule and territorial sovereignty. It will draw lessons from comparative federalism to reflect on the UK's nature as a devolved unitary state in transition. In turn, the chapter will also elaborate how the insights from the UK contribute to our understanding of federalism.

Notes

1 Existing research extends to a long list of relevant issues covering questions of space, identity, culture, history, norms, nationalisms, sovereignty, autonomy, in- and interdependence, representation, democracy, legitimacy, accountability, policymaking, political behaviour, voting, elections, political parties, public policy, policy innovation, fiscal resources, economic performance and gender issues.
2 While the term 'devolved administration' politically, either intentionally or unintentionally, implies that the Scottish and Welsh executives are inferior to the UK Government (cf. McEwen 2022), the author has no intention to deny their status as fully-fledged governments. Even though 'devolved administration' is used more often in relation to the Scottish and Welsh Governments, this study will also refer to the UK Government as administrations; for instance, as in the "Johnson administration".
3 Parliament is the highest legislative authority in the UK and the Crown is constitutionally part of Parliament (UK Parliament 2021).
4 It is well known that majorities in Scotland and in Northern Ireland voted to remain in the EU, and that the Welsh Government has also expressed a desire to remain in the EU.
5 In March 2021, the First Minister of Wales, Mark Drakeford, highlighted before the Welsh Affairs Committee (2021) of the House of Commons: "There is no institutional architecture to make the United Kingdom work. It is all ad hoc, random, and made up as we go along. And I'm afraid that really is not a satisfactory basis to sustain the future of the UK."
6 Under the principle of parliamentary sovereignty, the Westminster Parliament can make or unmake any law, and there are no constitutional guarantees that will in theory prevent it from reforming or even ending the devolution settlement without consent from the devolved administrations.

Bibliography

Agranoff, Robert (2004) *Autonomy, Devolution and Intergovernmental Relations*. Regional and Federal Studies, Volume 14, Issue 1, pp. 26–65.

Arts, Bas and Verschuren, Piet (1999) *Assessing Political Influence in Complex Decision-Making: An Instrument Based on Triangulation*. International Political Science Review, Volume 20, Issue 4, pp. 411–424.

Behnke, Nathalie (2015) *Stand und Perspektiven der Föderalismusforschung*. Aus Politik und Zeitgeschichte, Volume 65, pp. 28–30.

Behnke, Nathalie (2018) *Federal, Devolved or Decentralized State: On the Territorial Architecture of Power*. In: Detterbeck, Klaus and Hepburn, Eve (eds.) *Handbook of Territorial Politics*. Cheltenham: Edward Elgar Publishing, pp. 30–44.

Behnke, Nathalie and Mueller, Sean (2017) *The Purpose of Intergovernmental Councils: A Framework for Analysis and Comparison*, Regional and Federal Studies, Volume 27, Issue 5, pp. 507–527.

Benz, Arthur (2002) *Themen, Probleme und Perspektiven der vergleichenden Föderalismusforschung*. In: Benz, Arthur and Lehmbruch, Gerhard (eds.) *Analysen in entwicklungsgeschichtlicher und vergleichender Pespektive*. Wiesbaden: Westdeutscher Verlag, pp. 9–50.

Benz, Arthur (2009) *Politik in Mehrebenensystemen*. Wiesbaden: Springer VS.

Benz, Arthur and Broschek, Jörg (eds.) (2013) *Federal Dynamics: Introduction*. In: *Federal Dynamics: Continuity, Change, and the Varieties of Federalism*. Oxford: Oxford University Press, pp. 1–23.

Beyme, Klaus von (2010) *Vergleichende Politikwissenschaft*. Wiesbaden: Springer VS.

Bolleyer, Nicole (2009) *Intergovernmental Cooperation: Rational Choices in Federal Systems and Beyond*. Oxford: Oxford University Press.

Bolleyer, Nicole (2013) *Paradoxes of Self-Coordination in Federal Systems*. In: Benz, Arthur and Broschek, Jörg (eds.) *Federal Dynamics: Continuity, Change, and the Varieties of Federalism*. Oxford: Oxford University Press, pp. 321–342.

Bolleyer, Nicole (2018) *Challenges of Interdependence and Coordination in Federal Systems*. In: Detterbeck, Klaus and Hepburn, Eve (eds.) *Handbook of Territorial Politics*. Cheltenham: Edward Elgar Publishing, pp. 45–60.

Bolleyer, Nicole and Thorlakson, Lori (2012) *Beyond Decentralization – The Comparative Study of Interdependence in Federal Systems*. The Journal of Federalism, Volume 42, Issue 4, pp. 566–591.

Bröchler, Stephan and Lauth, Hans-Joachim (2014) *Die Lokalisierung von Schneisen im Dickicht – Konzeptionelle Grundlegungen und empirische Befunde informaler Governance*. Zeitschrift für Vergleichende Politikwissenschaft, Volume 8, Issue 1 (Supplement), pp. 1–33.

Broschek, Jörg (2011) *Conceptualizing and Theorizing Constitutional Change in Federal Systems: Insights from Historical Institutionalism*. Regional and Federal Studies, Volume 21, Issue 4–5, pp. 539–559.

Broschek, Jörg (2016) *Staatsstrukturen in der Vergleichenden Politikwissenschaft: Förderal-und Einheitsstaat*. In: Lauth, Hans-Joachim, Kneuer, Marianne and Pickel, Gert (eds.) *Handbuch Vergleichende Politikwissenschaft*. Wiesbaden: Springer VS, pp. 331–343.

Bukve, Oddbjorn (2019) *Designing Social Science Research*. Cham: Palgrave Macmillan.

Burgess, Michael (2006) *Comparative Federalism: Theory and Practice.* London: Routledge.

Cairney, Paul (2011) *The Scottish Political System Since Devolution: From New Politics to the New Scottish Government.* Exeter: Imprint Academic.

Cairney, Paul (2012) *Intergovernmental Relations in Scotland: What Was the SNP Effect?* British Journal of Politics and International Relations, Volume 14, Issue 2, pp. 231–249.

Cameron, David (2015) *Scottish Parliament New Powers: David Cameron Speech.* Speech. 22 January. https://www.gov.uk/government/speeches/scottish-parliament-new-powers-david-cameron-speech

Deacon, Russell (2012) *Devolution in the United Kingdom.* Edinburgh: Edinburgh University Press.

Falleti, Tulia G. (2013) *Decentralization in Time: A Process-Tracing Approach to Federal Dynamics of Change.* In: Benz, Arthur and Broschek, Jörg (eds.) *Federal Dynamics: Continuity, Change, and the Varieties of Federalism.* Oxford: Oxford University Press, pp. 141–166.

Gallagher, Jim (2012) *Intergovernmental Relations in the UK: Co-Operation, Competition and Constitutional Change.* British Journal of Politics and International Relations, Volume 14, Issue 2, pp. 198–213.

Gerber, Elisabeth R. and Kollman, Kenneth (2004) *Introduction – Authority Migration: Defining an Emerging Research Agenda.* Political Science and Politics, Volume 37, Issue 3, pp. 397–401.

Hamilton, David K. and Stenberg, Carl W. (2018) *Introduction: Intergovernmental Relations in Transition.* In: Stenberg, Carl W. and Hamilton, David K. (eds.) *Intergovernmental Relations in Transition.* New York, NY: Routledge, pp. 1–12.

Helmke, Gretchen and Levitsky, Steven (2004) *Informal Institutions and Comparative Politics: A Research Agenda.* Perspectives on Politics, Volume 2, Issue 4, pp. 725–740.

Hepburn, Eve and Detterbeck, Klaus (eds.) (2018) *Introduction to the Handbook of Territorial Politics.* In: *Handbook of Territorial Politics.* Cheltenham: Edward Elgar Publishing, pp. 1–14.

Hooghe, Liesbet, Marks, Gary, Schakel, Arjan H., Chapman Osterkatz, Sandra, Niedzwiecki, Shair-Rosenfield, Sarah (2016) *Measuring Regional Authority: A Postfunctionalist Theory of Governance*, Volume I. Oxford: Oxford University Press.

Hueglin, Thomas O. and Fenna, Alan (2010) *Comparative Federalism: A Systematic Inquiry.* Peterborough: Broadview Press.

Hunt, Jo and Minto, Rachel. (2017) *Between Intergovernmental Relations and Paradiplomacy: Wales and the Brexit of the Regions.* The British Journal of Politics and International Relations, Volume 19, Issue 4, pp. 647–662.

Hutchcroft, Paul D. (2001) *Centralization and Decentralization in Administration and Politics: Assessing Territorial Dimension of Authority and Power.* Governance, Volume 14, Issue 1, pp. 23–53.

Jeffery, Charlie (2009) *Devolution in the United Kingdom: Problems of a Piecemeal Approach to Constitutional Change.* Publius, Volume 39, Issue 2, pp. 289–313.

Keating, Michael (2012) *Intergovernmental Relations and Innovation: From Co-Operative to Competitive Welfare Federalism in the UK.* British Journal of Politics and International Relations, Volume 14, Issue 2, pp. 214–230.

Lauth, Hans-Joachim (ed.) (2014) *Analytische Konzeption für den Vergleich politischer Systeme.* In: *Politische Systeme im Vergleich: Formale und informelle Institutionen im politischen Prozess.* Oldenbourg: De Gruyter, pp. 3–50.

Lauth, Hans-Joachim (2016) *Formale und informelle Institutionen in der vergleichenden Politikwissenschaft*. In: Lauth, Hans-Joachim, Kneuer, Marianne and Pickel, Gert (eds.) *Handbuch Vergleichende Politikwissenschaft*. Wiesbaden: Springer VS, pp. 181–195.

Lehmbruch, Gerhard (1998) *Parteienwettbewerb im Bundesstaat: Regelsysteme und Spannungslagen im Institutionengefüge der Bundesrepublik Deutschland*. 2nd edition. Wiesbaden: Westdeutscher Verlag.

Lowndes, Vivien and Roberts, Mark (2013) *Why Institutions Matter*. 4th edition. London: Palgrave Macmillan.

Marks, Gary, Hooghe, Liesbet and Schakel, Arjan H. (2008) *Measuring Regional Authority*. Regional and Federal Studies, Volume 18, Issue 2–3, pp. 111–121.

McEwen, Nicola (2017) *Still Better Together? Purpose and Power in Intergovernmental Councils in the UK*. Regional and Federal Studies, Volume 27, Issue 5, pp. 667–690.

McEwen, Nicola (2022) *Intergovernmental Relations Review: Worth the Wait?* Commentary. 17 January. UK in a Changing Europe. https://ukandeu.ac.uk/intergovernmental-relations-review/

McEwen, Nicola and Petersohn, Bettina (2015) *Between Autonomy and Interdependence: The Challenges of Shared Rule after the Scottish Referendum*. The Political Quarterly, Volume 86, Issue 2, pp. 192–200.

McEwen, Nicola, Swenden, Wilfried and Bolleyer, Nicole (2012) *Intergovernmental Relations in the UK: Continuity in a Time of Change?* British Journal of Politics and International Relations, Volume 14, Issue 2, pp. 323–343.

Mueller, Sean (2011) *The Politics of Local Autonomy: Measuring Cantonal (De) Centralisation in Switzerland*. Space and Polity, Volume 15, Issue 3, pp. 213–239.

O'Neill, Michael (2004) *Devolution and British Politics*. London: Routledge.

Paun, Akash and Hall, Dan (2021) *Election 2021: Welsh Independence*. Explainer. 22 April. Institute for Government. https://www.instituteforgovernment.org.uk/explainers/welsh-independence

Petersohn, Bettina, Behnke, Nathalie and Rhode, Eva Maria (2015) *Negotiating Territorial Change in Multinational States: Party Preferences, Negotiating Power and the Role of the Negotiation Mode*. Publius, Volume 45, Issue 4, pp. 626–652.

Poirier, Johanne and Saunders, Cheryl (eds.) (2015a) *Comparing Intergovernmental Relations in Federal Systems: An Introduction*. In: *Intergovernmental Relations in Federal Systems*. Oxford: Oxford University Press, pp. 1–13.

Poirier, Johanne and Saunders, Cheryl (eds.) (2015b) *Conclusion: Comparative Experience of Intergovernmental Relations in Federal Systems*. In: *Intergovernmental Relations in Federal Systems*. Oxford: Oxford University Press, pp. 440–498.

Poirier, Johanne, Saunders, Cheryl and Kincaid, John (2015) *Intergovernmental Relations in Federal Systems*. Oxford: Oxford University Press.

Rodden, Jonathan (2004) *Comparative Federalism and Decentralization – On Meaning and Measurement*. Comparative Politics, Volume 36, Issue 4, pp. 481–500.

Scharpf, Fritz (1997) *Games Real Actors Play – Actor-Centered Institutionalism in Policy Research*. Boulder, CO: Westview Press.

Scharpf, Fritz (2006) *Interaktionsformen – Akteurzentrierter Institutionalismus in der Politikforschung*. Wiesebaden: Springer VS.

Schneider, Aaron (2003) *Decentralization: Conceptualization and Measurement*. Studies in Comparative International Development, Volume 38, Issue 3, pp. 32–56.

Stolz, Klaus (2010) *Devolution – A Balance after Ten Years*. In: *Ten Years of Devolution in the United Kingdom: Snapshot at a Moving Target*. Augsburg: Wißner-Verlag, pp. 6–12.

Tatham, Michael (2016) *With, Without, or Against the State? How European Regions Play the Brussels Game*. Oxford: Oxford University Press.

UK Parliament (2021) *Parliament and Crown*. https://www.parliament.uk/about/how/role/relations-with-other-institutions/parliament-crown/

Watts, Ronald L. (2008) *Comparing Federal Systems*. Montreal and Kingston: McGill-Queen's University Press.

Welsh Affairs Committee (2021) *Meeting Thursday 4 March 2021, 2.30 pm*. 4 March. UK Parliament Live TV. https://parliamentlive.tv/event/index/dd4121c8-de6d-4ac7-ad9c-aea7d71c1510

Wright, Deil S. (1988) *Understanding Intergovernmental Relations*. 3rd edition. Belmont, CA: Brooks/Cole Publishing.

2 Theoretical and Methodological Perspectives

Though it is widely acknowledged that the devolution settlement is characterised by a high degree of *self-rule* and little capacity for *shared rule*, intergovernmental relations have become increasingly relevant in the UK. Especially in the aftermath of the Scottish independence and the EU referendums, scholars have turned to the constitutional and political controversies shaping the Union between England, Scotland, Wales and Northern Ireland. Thereby, the UK is often examined rather introspectively as an idiosyncratic case without putting it in a wider theoretical perspective that allows for a systematic comparison with other multilevel polities. At the same time, detailed empirical analysis of the mechanisms and areas relevant to interactions between governments is rare. To obtain a new and holistic picture of territorial politics in the UK and beyond, this research builds on a synthesis of different theoretical and methodological concepts. Combining insights from comparative studies of federations and intergovernmental relations offers a global, yet dynamic approach to capture the formal and informal structures and constellations of a political multilevel system that has been undergoing a substantial transformation over the last decade.

This research deploys a mix of selected studies and approaches suitable to answer how intergovernmental relations are organised; how different governments engage with each other to achieve their policy objectives and how capable subnational governments are at influencing political decisions of the centre. The intergovernmental institutions and practices and patterns of interaction between governments have not been examined to the same scope and extent by other works. Further, this book makes an unprecedented contribution to understanding how powerful the devolved administrations really are by assessing their political influence beyond their self-rule capacities. The findings will not only enhance our empirical knowledge of territorial politics in the UK, but also feed back into theoretical perspectives on multilevel systems. The conceptual discussion starts with the decentralisation or devolution of territorial power and authority, and how this relates to notions of self-rule and shared rule. It then turns to the relevance of comparative federalism and intergovernmental relations for the UK before continuing to introduce the operational approaches informing the analysis of

DOI: 10.4324/9781003349952-2

16 *Theoretical and Methodological Perspectives*

formal and informal institutions and practices, patterns of interaction and political influence. The last part of this chapter sets out the research design and methodology.

Decentralisation, self-rule and shared rule

Until the beginning of the 1980s, central governments were the principal decision-maker and holder of sovereignty in unitary states. Since then, economic, social and political globalisation has challenged the traditional allocation of responsibilities for policy outcomes and the role of the centre. International regimes started to promote decentralisation and subnational policymakers and civil society actors seized opportunities to acquire new resources and powers (Schneider 2003, 33–34; Cheema and Rondinelli 2007, 1, 5):

> As globalization pushed more countries to adopt market or quasi-market economies, and as technology drove the growth and integration of worldwide communication and transportation networks, demands for political and economic participation grew even in countries that had totalitarian, authoritarian, or dictatorial governments and in which the state traditionally played the dominant or controlling role in managing national affairs. Good governance came to be seen as transparent, representative, accountable, and participatory systems of institutions and procedures for public decisionmaking.
> (Cheema and Rondinelli 2007, 2)

Consequently, many formerly highly centralised states in Western Europe have experienced a downwards shift of authority to territorial governments (Behnke 2015, 9). Despite some variations across academic works,[1] decentralisation generally means the transfer of power, authority and resources from the centre to lower levels of government (Hutchcroft 2001, 29; Keuffer and Ladner 2021, 21).[2] The level of decentralisation then determines to what extent authority is dispersed across multiple levels or monopolised by central government (Schimmelfennig et al. 2015, 766). Unlike the *deconcentration* or *delegation* of specific functions and tasks from the centre to constituent units, *decentralisation* describes an extensive shift of authority over public policy and services. Subnational institutions remain to some extent accountable to central government but are provided with a strong degree of autonomy (Hutchcroft 2001, 30; Schneider 2003, 32 et seq.; Petak 2004, 2–3; Dickovick 2005, 186; Cheema and Rondinelli 2007, 3; Keil and Anderson 2018, 90; Sturm 2020, 175). Authority can be dispersed in multiple ways and take the form of administrative, political and fiscal decentralisation (cf. Schneider's 2003, 33; Bolleyer and Thorlakson 2012, 569; Keil and Anderson 2018, 91). Whereas an administrative decentralisation of government structures, bureaucracies and resources does not necessarily result in autonomous decision-making, political decentralisation enhances citizen participation and empowers subnational elected bodies and executives through the devolution of legislative authority and decision-making over a defined territorial jurisdiction (Cheema and Rondinelli 2007, 6–7). Political decentralisation thus reconfigures the constitution of a state (Pasquier 2021, 59),[3] whereby the scope of policy areas which are decentralised determines how powerful subnational governments are (Schimmelfennig et al. 2015, 766). Lastly, fiscal decentralisation refers to the extent to which each level of government can decide over revenues and expenditure.[4] Without a transfer of adequate resources subnational authorities would struggle in meeting their new responsibilities and realising local policies (Cheema and Rondinelli 2007, 6–7). Even though in unitary states the legislative competences are transferred downwards by the central legislature and can in principle be taken back again (Sturm 2020, 176), devolution in the UK means not merely an administrative deconcentration or delegation but the decentralisation in particular of political and fiscal authority (Keil and Anderson 2018, 90).

At the beginning of the new millennium, Rodden (2004, 494) highlighted the need to focus beyond the common indicators for public expenditure and tax revenues,[5] as attempts to engage with a robust methodology and empirical data to study the decentralisation – or migration[6] (Gerber and Kollman 2004) – of political authority in multilevel polities were rare at the time (cf. Hutchcroft 2001, 24). In response, new research has emerged during the last two decades (see Hutchcroft 2001; Schneider 2003; Gerber and Kollman 2004; Rodden 2004; Dickovick 2005; Mueller 2011; Falleti 2013; Petersohn et al. 2015), among which the *Regional Authority Index* (Marks et al. 2008; Hooghe et al. 2016)[7] is one of the most comprehensive attempts to analyse regional autonomy.[8] The Regional Authority Index accounts for the degree of autonomy of subnational governments (institutional depth);[9] the range of policy areas subject to subnational decision-making (policy scope);[10] their tax powers (fiscal autonomy);[11] ability to borrow money (borrowing autonomy)[12] and the independence of regional legislatures and executives (representation)[13] (Hooghe et al. 2008, 125–129; Hooghe et al. 2016, 25–28). While the Regional Authority Index is certainly a useful means to compare the decentralisation or regionalisation of authority, it can only provide a broad picture of territorial power without capturing the full complexities the power relations between centre and periphery.

Schneider (2003, 33–34) suggested that decentralisation is a zero-sum game and can be measured as either an increase or a reduction of authority at the territorial or central level of government. Similarly, for Bolleyer and Thorlakson (2012, 569) the decentralisation of authority "implies a trade-off across levels: the reduction of federal power leads to an increase of subnational power". Others have challenged this view, and do not think of the reallocation of power as simply a matter of a zero-sum logic whereby a win for one level means a loss for the other (Benz 2002, 25–26; 2009b, 35). The authors of the Regional Authority Index have also argued against measuring the relationship between subnational government and central governmental against a centralisation-decentralisation dichotomy (Marks et al. 2008, 112). In reality, modern policy challenges do not only affect the responsibilities of one jurisdiction but spill over across different levels. In order to manage such overlaps of competences, governments need to coordinate their policies to some extent (McEwen and Petersohn 2015, 193–195). Pasquier (2021, 60), for instance, has observed that emergence of territorial governance creates new political spaces with additional functions and competences, not automatically at the cost of central authority. Decentralisation may even be a positive-sum game when authority is shared across different levels and central government can introduce coordination and control mechanisms to compensate for their loss (Jensen et al. 2014, 1249). Empowering constituent units adds complexity to existing state structures (Behnke and Mueller 2017, 507), which can increase democratic legitimacy but also slow down decision-making and lead to conflicts (Watts 2008, 117; Behnke 2015). As Marks et al. (2008, 112) point out:

> Such measures tap the extent to which the national state monopolizes authority, but they do not tell us how government below the national level is structured. They conceive government within countries in unidimensional terms as the 'other', the 'not central state'. Centralization/decentralization measures, no matter how accurate, are ill-suited for inquiry into the scale and structure of government below the national state.

Because decentralisation hardly means complete autonomy for subnational governments (cf. Rodden 2004, 486; Cheema and Rondinelli 2007), power relations in multilevel systems depend on the interference from the centre on subnational decisions (Dickovick 2005, 186), the division of tasks in areas of shared and concurrent responsibility (Poirier and Saunders 2015b, 445), as well as on institutional incentives to deal with occurring interdependencies (Bolleyer and Thorlakson 2012, 566–567). In essence, the way decentralisation or centralisation dynamics empower or disempower government depends on the interdependence and autonomy of the different levels in exercising these powers (Bolleyer 2018, 47). This is why it is crucial to consider not only the authority of individual governments (self-rule) but also governance arrangements between levels of government (shared rule) (cf. Burgess 2006, 138; McEwen and Petersohn 2015, 192; Hooghe et al. 2016; Behnke 2018, 36).

Shared rule captures the capacity of subnational government to influence decisions made for the whole state (Marks et al. 2008, 115).[14] It can be institutionalised through subnational representation in bicameral legislatures and other intergovernmental arrangements to co-decide on state-wide policies (McEwen and Petersohn 2015, 192). Formal power-sharing arrangements are at the core of a federal architecture and have been studied comprehensively (cf. Wright 1988; Watts 2008; Bolleyer 2009; Hueglin and Fenna 2010; Broschek 2011; Bolleyer and Thorlakson 2012; Poirier et al. 2015), but in unitary polities, where power-sharing is not necessarily enshrined in the constitutional design, this has only fairly recently attracted the attention of scholars. The Regional Authority Index makes an important contribution to systematic examination of shared rule. It considers direct participation in central decision-making and the ability to veto legislation by national legislatures, typically in the upper or second chamber of parliaments (law making);[15] sharing executive responsibility for the implementation of policies with central governments (executive control);[16] influence over the distribution of tax revenues across the whole state (fiscal control);[17] co-determination of national and regional borrowing constraints (borrowing control);[18] and exercising constitutional authority (constitutional reform)[19] (Hooghe et al. 2008, 131–135; Hooghe et al. 2016, 26–29).

Potent power-sharing capacities can not only empower governments (cf. Tomkins 2018, 99) but also offer a way to counter unintended effects of decentralisation. As Benz (2013, 73) has argued: "Decentralization and self-rule enables groups to pursue their particular common goals, while it limits opportunities to deal with problems requiring coordination across boundaries of jurisdictions and between levels." Even though decentralising authority may help to resolve conflicts and to prevent secessionist ambitions in multinational states, when regional and pro-secessionist parties grow and can demonstrate their ability and legitimacy to rule in government, rather than being governed by the centre, demands for even greater autonomy and further conflict with the centre are likely to follow. Instead of settling questions of territorial autonomy, transferring competences can then cause the opposite effect and worsen territorial tensions (Keil and Anderson 2018, 96–99). This brings us inevitably to federal principles, which "are concerned with the combination of self-rule and shared rule" (Elazar 1987, 5) and provide an alternative, polycentric perspective to the central-peripheral model by looking at integrated linkages between different focal points rather than merely at the allocation of power (op. cit., 13).

Comparative federalism

The distribution of authority across multiple levels of government does not refer to a particular type of state, or vice versa.[20] Neither is power-sharing exclusive to federal systems, as Gerber and Kollman (2004, 397) point out:

> In every modern political system, power is shared to a greater or lesser extent between levels of government. These power sharing arrangements are perhaps most explicit in formal federal systems like the United States and Canada, where federal constitutions define the relative powers of central and subnational governments. They are no less important, however, in unitary democracies and even authoritarian

regimes where central governments require local actors to implement policy on the ground and often delegate significant authority to them.

Nevertheless, unitary polities and federations differ fundamentally in their approach to conciliating the collective identity of a state with the individual identity of subordinated states.[21] Unitary states transfer authority through legal acts by central government and parliament without providing legal safeguards that it will not abolish or reform territorial arrangements without consent from the constituent entities. Federalism, in contrast, incorporates the "territorial dimension into the very architecture of the state" (O'Neill 2004, 179), and supports a particular form of state "to accommodate the constituent units of a union in the decision-making procedure of the central government by means of constitutional entrenchment." (Burgess 2006, 2–3) Federal constitutions aim to guarantee the sovereignty of the lower level, protect territorial autonomy against unilateral amendments and disperse power between more than one level[22] (as well as between the executive, legislature and judiciary) (Hueglin and Fenna 2010, 31–33; Hueglin 2013, 44).[23] This does not mean that federalism provides absolute autonomy to regional units. In Rodden's (2004, 493) words:

> Federalism does not necessarily entail greater independent authority for subnational governments over taxes, expenditure, or anything else. Federalism does not imply that the centre and states are sovereigns, each protected from the interference of the other. On the contrary, federations have evolved as ongoing incomplete contracts and by their very nature are under constant renegotiation. In most federations the center often depends on the provinces to implement and enforce many of its decisions, and the center can not change the status quo in certain areas without the consent of the constituent units.

The essence of the 'federal genius' is then to complement the sovereignty and autonomy of different territories, not only by vertically allocating powers to them but also by sharing powers for common purposes (Watts 2008, 23; Benz 2013, 72). Shared institutions which represent both the federal government and the federated states are essential for common action and "provide the glue to hold the federation together" (Watts 2008, 135). Such built-in mechanisms allow federal states to balance central dominance and to resolve conflicts between levels of government that could block policies (O'Neill 2004, 179).

Federalism presents not a fully-fledged but at best a partial theory dealing with a wide range of issues, including constitutional, political, social, economic, cultural, legal, philosophical and ideological questions (Burgess 2006, 1). Like unitary states, federations come in different forms and shapes and vary in regard to the number of constituent units, size, resources, status, powers, influence at the federal level, and cooperation and conflict-resolution mechanisms (Benz 2002, 12; Watts 2008, 1; 18–19). Such asymmetries produce de facto differences in the political importance of each part for the whole of the federation (Requejo 2011, 5). As Burgess (2006, 222) argues:

> There is no perfectly symmetrical or asymmetrical federation in the world. Consequently, it is better to see in asymmetrical federation an instrumental device for accommodating difference in a way that adds to the overall political stability of federations. Both de facto and de jure asymmetries suggest flexibility in federations in the general search for consensus among political elites and mass publics. Consensus is not something that can be taken for granted; it is something that is forged via hard bargaining and negotiations between competing and sometimes conflicting elites.

Despite their emphasis on a constitutional dispersion of authority, federalism does not describe a static distribution of power but a process through which power is distributed via a set of institutional structures and that requires consent and active cooperation between national and subnational governments (Rodden 2004, 289). In fact, it is common in modern federations to centralise powers without explicitly changing the allocation of authority. The provision of general competences over policies by national governments (e.g. welfare) and constitutional interpretations by courts have over time widened the scope of action at the central level (Hueglin and Fenna 2010, 42).

All federations combine cooperative and competitive elements and rely on intra- and inter-institutional mechanisms to resolve conflicts and negotiate compromise. These interactions are dependent on whether the allocation of competences across jurisdictions is dualistic or functionally integrated (Broschek 2011, 545; Poirier and Saunders 2015b, 446). In federations applying a dual allocation of power constituents and centre enjoy high levels of self-rule and exclusive jurisdictions over legislation policymaking and implementation. Typical examples hereof are the US, Canada and Australia (Hueglin and Fenna 2010, 219; Kropp 2011, 15; Hueglin 2013, 44; Lauth 2014, 7–8; McEwen and Petersohn 2015, 194). Such *divided* or *interstate federations* with dual competence structures do not aim at joint decision-making but resemble diplomatic negotiations (Behnke 2018, 38). The need for close cooperation and regional participation in national policymaking is limited and each jurisdiction holds sovereignty over discrete policy areas and tends to operate 'in splendid isolation'. The federal government is typically exclusively responsible for foreign affairs, while the constituent units have the full capacities to make, implement and administer their areas of jurisdiction, such as education and culture policy (Hueglin and Fenna 2010, 146 et seq.).[24] In contrast to an exclusive or dual allocation of power, under a functional distribution of competences, different levels hold the authority to either legislate on or implement policies and are therefore highly interdependent (Bolleyer 2018, 47–48). In such *integrated federations* – or *intrastate federalism* (Behnke 2018, 41) – multilateral negotiations are a compulsory part of intra-governmental institutions (Benz 2013, 82)[25] through which power is exercised together[26] and complex challenges and conflict can be dealt with on an inclusive and ongoing basis. Hence, they rely on an *intra-institutional* instead of an *inter-institutional* set-up. Whereas *inter-institutional* arrangements provide scope for governments to act without being constrained by other levels and allow for exit strategies (Broschek 2011, 545; Hueglin 2013, 39), *intra-institutional* mechanisms (typically a federal chamber of the legislature) produce a distinct federal loyalty by giving constituent units the right to participate in the making of federal laws and policies, which they then have to administer and implement (Poirier and Saunders 2015a, 6–7; 2015b 446).[27] In their work on *federal dynamics*, Benz and Broschek (2013, 4–8) have researched causes, processes and consequences of changes at different levels and suggested that federations develop either towards a *loosely coupled* federalism by decentralising political authority or towards a *tightly coupled* federalism relying on institutional arrangements for joint decision-making across different levels of government. The direction federal dynamics take depends on the intra- and inter-institutional configuration shaping the interactions of different tiers; the formal institutions and informal routines establishing authority relationships between tiers; normative and ideational constructs providing orientation, legitimacy and justifications for the actions of tiers; and the constellation of political actors (particularly territorial government and parties) which are dependent on their resources, capacities and competences. The following sections cover these dynamics and adapt them to the purpose of this study.

In regular intervals, academics and politicians have debated the UK's potential as a federal state (see for instance, Dardanelli and Kincaid 2016; Lee 2017; Ackerman 2018; Keating and Laforest 2018; Tierney 2018; Dickson 2019, 74 et seq.; Hunt 2021; Keating 2021; Martin 2021, 19–24). Among the political parties, Labour has recently initiated debates about a federal Britain – for instance by party leaders, such as Jeremy Corbyn, Keir Starmer (Mason 2020; Carrell 2021), Mark Drakeford and the Radical Federalism group (2021). Nevertheless, political attitudes towards federalism have generally been hostile or apathetic – not only internally within the UK but also externally in relation to the EU (Tierney 2018, 106; Dickson 2019, 85). When the devolved administrations were established, there were voices calling for the UK to be turned into a federation, but they had little influence over the constitutional reforms under New Labour (Bradbury 2021, 275). As a result, the devolved administrations have enjoyed growing powers without fundamentally altering the UK's unitary structures. Scotland, Wales and Northern Ireland are not sovereign states provided with joint decision-making and constitutional guarantees protecting the autonomy of their legislatures and executives. The constituent parts were incorporated and subordinated to the supremacy of the Westminster Parliament, which has ever since obstructed the idea of shared sovereignty under a federal constitutional order (cf. Dardanelli and Kincaid 2016, 14; Schütze 2018 1–3; 17). As Flinders (2009, 181) suggested: "the logic and principles of federalism have been rejected and the shadow of majoritarianism hangs over the devolved state". Importantly, the concept of a union, outside of the unitary-federal dichotomy, has gained momentum among scholars (see for instance, Andrews 2021; Bradbury 2021; Keating 2021; Kenny et al. 2021; Martin 2021; Wincott et al. 2021), as well as politicians from Scotland and Wales (Wincott et al. 2021, 689)[28] who argue for the voluntary nature of the UK.

Looking at multilevel states around the globe, the distinction between unitary and federal states has become somewhat blurred and the relationship between territory and power is increasingly complex (Keating and Laforest 2018, 2–3), and hybrid models, like the UK, have increasingly challenged the idea of a clear-cut unitary and federal dichotomy (von Beyme 2010, 208; cf. Broschek 2016, 338; Behnke 2018, 30). Hence, by expanding its initial focus to decentralised states comparative federalism has evolved as a framework to also study non-federal multilevel polities (Behnke 2015, 9). The processual nature of federalism is particularly important to understand the direction that the UK's multilevel state has taken over the last decade. The allocation of self-rule and shared rule is neither static nor immune to adjustments but undergo regular transformations in response to functional and political demands from different tiers (Benz 2013, 73). As mentioned earlier, federalism has often been used as a means to preserve the integrity of the state against secessionist ambitions. Such 'holding-together federalism' follows the idea that in order to maintain a political union, fiscal and legislative powers are devolved outside of a symmetrical constitutional framework (Eccleston et al. 2017b, 17–19). At the same time, however, the idea behind federations is to reconcile and entrench territorial and other forms of diversity under a common constitutional framework (Burgess 2006, 156) and to "create[s] a balance between national and subnational units." (Hueglin and Fenna 2010, 34) In light of the looming prospect of Scottish independence and growing public support for political autonomy in Wales, federalism offers valuable insights for academics and practitioners alike.

Intergovernmental relations

All multilevel systems are characterised by the interplay of formal and informal institutions and practices (cf. Benz 2009b, 51; Hueglin and Fenna 2010, 50; Benz and Broschek 2013, 7). *Intergovernmental relations* refer to political actions and interactions within the constitutional and legal settings of a polity comprising two or more levels of government for the purpose of producing and delivering public policies. This naturally relates to notions of federalism (Poirier and Saunders 2015a, 5–6). Elazar (1987, 15) described

24 Theoretical and Methodological Perspectives

the relationship between intergovernmental relations and federalism as the following:

> Federalism is the generic term for what may be referred to as self-rule/shared-rule relationships; "intergovernmental relations" has to do with particular ways and means of operationalizing a system of government [...] ways and means that involve extensive and continuing relations among the federal state, and local governments or any combination thereof.

Comparative federalism allows us to place the relationships between different governmental levels within a wider configuration of political authority, rules, institutions and practices (cf. Wright 1988, 31 et seq.; Benz and Broschek 2013, 4 et seq.; Poirier and Saunders 2015a, 5–6). But even in multilevel polities with highly institutionalised intergovernmental arrangements, an essential part of interaction is hidden (McEwen et al. 2015, 16). Since the 1950s, the relevance of intergovernmental relations has grown for coordination, cooperation and joint decision-making across multilevel polities, which has attracted more and more scholarly interest (cf. Agranoff 2004; Hueglin and Fenna 2010, 50; Benz and Broschek 2013, 7; Poirier and Saunders 2015b, 442; Hooghe et al. 2016; Behnke and Mueller 2017, 508; Hamilton and Stenberg 2018, 1). By focusing on intergovernmental relations, we can overcome a static perspective on territorial power and gain a more dynamic account of how different levels of government interact with each other (Behnke 2018, 37) – in particular when formalised power-sharing or any other institutionalised power-sharing is missing. Yet, there is still relatively little research on how such interactions are channelled, structured and institutionalised (Bolleyer 2009, 1). Eccleston et al. (2017a, 2) have therefore argued: "Our focus on the future of federalism in the twenty-first century is significant, because despite the increasingly ubiquitous nature of devolution and multilevel governance regimes in the early years of this century, there is relatively little research on contemporary trends in intergovernmental relations and their consequences." Because the relationship between governments depends on the formal constitutional framework, as well as on the socio-historical context (Eccleston et al. 2017b, 16–18), cultures and norms (Bolleyer and Thorlakson 2012, 569) and informal interactions (Behnke 2015, 16; Poirier and Saunders 2015a, 1), this study combines the federal account of shared rule with the flexible dynamics of intergovernmental relations.

In his work *Territory and Power in the United Kingdom*, which was first published in 1983, Jim Bulpitt (2008, 59) examined the informal dynamics, strategies, values and interests within the relations between the centre and peripheral governmental bodies, organisations, communities and interests pre-devolution. Although at the time, research on central-local relations focused primarily on formal institutions, John (2009, 429) described Bulpitt's understanding of territorial politics as "about how spatially located decision makers play out their strategies and realise their values and interests. Institutions may give central and peripheral elites their formal roles, but territorial politics is more often about the informal and political relationships." Bulpitt thought of the UK as a dual polity consisting of *high politics* (foreign and state affairs, economy) reserved to the *centre* (primarily London) and *low politics* (administration and public services) dealt with by the *periphery* (the rest of the country) (John 2008, 4; 2022, 249). Among the different strategies to control territorial politics and to achieve its aims, the centre can rely on either coercion, its legitimate authority and bargaining, or to seek autonomy from territorial demands particularly in areas of high politics (Bulpitt 2008, 67–68). While Bulpitt's ideas offer considerable occasions to reflect on today's territorial politics in the UK, his outlook was essentially top-down and concerned about the management of territorial demands by the central government. More recent research on territorial politics, regionalism and federalism has rejected such a purely state-centric view and turned to bottom-up perspectives of substate actors (Hepburn and Detterbeck 2018, 3). After the establishment of the devolved administrations in the late 1990s, it took some time before scholars started to focus on the relationship between central and decentralised governments. Mitchell (2010, 57) argued that despite the interdependencies of government, the devolution settlement sought to create clear separations of responsibilities, relied on intra-party channels and "borrowed heavily from Intra-Governmental relations pre-devolution". Even with the SNP coming to power in Scotland in 2007, administrations continued to cooperate on day-to-day issues, while highly salient issues, such as economics, tax issues and nuclear defence, were subject to more adversarial relations (op. cit., 59–66). The role of interdependencies, issue salience and party congruency will also inform the analysis of patterns of interaction between governments.

Since 2010, with different parties in government across all four legislations, research on their mutual engagement has gained more prominence. In his book *Comparing Devolved Governance*, Derek Birrell (2012a) dedicated a chapter to describing the intergovernmental and external relations of the devolved executives. In the same year, after the 2010 Coalition Government came to power in Westminster, the *British Journal of Politics and International Relations* published a special issue to analyse the impact of party incongruence on the UK's intergovernmental relations (McEwen et al. 2012a; 2012b). The special issue features chapters on the evolution of intergovernmental relations (Gallagher 2012); welfare federalism in the UK (Keating 2012); Scotland (Cairney 2012); Wales (Wyn Jones and Royles 2012); Northern Ireland (Birrell 2012b); the roles of the civil service (Parry 2012); and the courts (Trench 2012) to facilitate the exchange between governments and manage disputes. More recent works on the UK have appeared in the aftermath of the 2014 Scottish independence referendum (McEwen and Petersohn 2015) and the 2016 EU referendum (Hunt and

Minto 2017; Deacon 2018; McEwen et al. 2020; McEwen 2021), and include a comparison with Canada's federalism (Anderson and Gallagher 2018), as well as reports by the Centre on Constitutional Change on parliamentary scrutiny (McEwen et al. 2015) and potential reforms (McEwen et al. 2018) of intergovernmental relations. Notwithstanding these works, predominantly written by scholars from within the UK, compared with the wealth of comprehensive studies which have engaged with formal power-sharing arrangements in federations (cf. Wright 1988; Watts 2008; Hueglin and Fenna 2010; Broschek 2011; Bolleyer and Thorlakson 2012) systematic and comparative research on informal intergovernmental relations in unitary polities is still in its infancy. In light of the ongoing, fast-paced and radical changes to the UK's multilevel system around the Scotland's potential secession and Brexit, there remains great potential for in-depth investigations.

The collected volume on *Intergovernmental Relations in Federal Systems* (Poirier et al. 2015) provides a comparison of different federations against a comprehensive list of intergovernmental arenas and arrangements. At the top of the intergovernmental machinery stand intra-institutional arrangements through which different levels of government participate in joint decision-making and formally share the exercise of power. Also high up in the intergovernmental order are multilateral bodies that bring together heads of governments or sectoral ministers. Legislatures, courts, agencies and political parties represent other important institutions and actors, as well as expert committees that sort out technical questions and prepare high-profile summits. Central to the cooperation of governments are intergovernmental agreements, in the form of compacts, concordats, constitutional conventions, protocols, memorandums of understanding and treaties, that can to varying degrees bind participants vertically, horizontally, unilaterally or multilaterally (Poirier and Saunders 2015b, 442 et seq.). Though the outset of the book offers a useful initial orientation, it does not engage with a sufficiently explanatory account to inform the design of this research. *Regional and Federal Studies* published a special issue on the purpose and effectiveness of intergovernmental councils in federations (Behnke and Mueller 2017), which provides a set of helpful explanatory factors and propositions[29] and includes an article on intergovernmental councils in the UK (McEwen 2017). While these factors are closely related to this study's variables explaining the patterns of interactions, in the UK only a fairly small part of interactions take place within such bodies.

A significant, yet often underrated perspective is accounted for by Nathalie Behnke (2019), who has highlighted the importance of civil servants to *bridge* intergovernmental divisions and conflict. Because bureaucrats are typically less or not dependent on or accountable to an electorate than politicians, they tend to focus on problem-solving rather than on political ideologies. Many intergovernmental negotiations start at official level before they move up for approval or in the case of sensitive issues escalate to the political level. Regular interactions between civil servants are therefore vital to maintain trust across government and to depoliticise contested matters. Their long-term expertise and supposed *neutrality*, as well as the sharing of similar experiences and perspectives, enable them to *bond* with their counterparts from other administrations and to anticipate and mediate between different positions and arguments. Although – in line with comparative federalism (op. cit., 42) – this study treats the different governments largely as unified actors,[30] the empirical analysis will account for the impact of officials' relations and networks between the different organisations depending on different policy areas.

Finally, Nicole Bolleyer's (2009) book *Intergovernmental Cooperation* made a major contribution to the study of intergovernmental relations in federal polities. She investigated how the horizontal relations between executives and legislatures inform institutional choices in Canada, Switzerland and the United States hypothesising that "power-concentrating governments undermine the institutionalization of intergovernmental arrangements, while power-sharing governments support it." (op. cit., 34) According to Bolleyer, consensus democracies incentivise a stronger integration of intergovernmental exchange, because power-sharing coalition governments make complete turnovers of the ruling parties less likely than in single-party governments. In majoritarian systems, governments are assumed to prefer ad hoc coordination over an institutionalisation of intergovernmental relations because it enables politicians to adapt more flexibly to new interest configurations when governments are changing (op. cit., 34–35). As the Westminster model of democracy has been widely acknowledged as the prototype of a majoritarian system (foremost by Lijphart 2012, 9 et seq.) and associated with the domination of the executive over the legislative branches of government (King 2001; Bogdanor 2009, 15; Flinders 2009; Russell 2016, 100),[31] the relation between majoritarianism and the nature of intergovernmental relations is highly relevant for this study.

Formal and informal institutions and practices

The institutional design of federal and multilevel states and its impact on policymaking has attracted a strong interest in comparative research (Bolleyer and Thorlakson 2012, 566). Formal institutional and informal routines structure power relations, enable or constrain actors' behaviour and interaction (Helmke and Levitsky 2004, 727; Benz and Broschek 2013, 6), and embody the rules and norms linked to the making and enforcement of binding decisions (Lauth 2016, 182). Institutional incentives are crucial determinants for cooperation between governments (Bolleyer and Thorlakson 2012, 570), they inform actors' strategies to deal with conflict (Benz 2009b, 51). Knowing about formalisation and institutionalisation of intergovernmental relations therefore provides an essential basis to examine how different governments engage with each other and under which conditions subnational governments are able to influence political decisions of the centre. Looking merely at formal institutions cannot fully explain the incentives informing political behaviour (Helmke and Levitsky 2004, 725–726), as Lowndes and Roberts (2013, 62) put it: "Recognizing the role played by informal practices, alongside formal rules, is vital for both interpreting institutional dynamics and developing robust approaches to institutional design and reform." The UK, due to the absence of a codified constitution, is a prominent example of a political system resting on informal institutions in the form of conventions which complement formal institutions to guide political actions (Lauth 2016, 184). In order to gain a theoretically informed understanding of how intergovernmental relations are organised in the UK, this study thus takes a neo-institutional perspective by focusing on power relations, norms, constraints and opportunities provided by both formal constitutional orders and informal conventions, as well as on the interaction between institutions and actors (Lowndes 2018, 55 et seq.).[32]

For the purpose of identifying the formalisation and consistent patterns of intergovernmental mechanisms, this study draws on definitions of formal and informal institutions and practices by Lauth (2014) who distinguishes between irregular and spontaneous exchange, and regular and consistent patterns. The latter cover *formal institutions* that are legally binding; *informal institutions* that are not legally codified but encompass persistent obligations that can be socially and politically sanctioned;[33] and informal *practices* that can, unlike informal institutions, not be sanctioned at all. In contrast to spontaneous exchange, practices are consistent patterns shaping political processes (Bröchler and Lauth 2014, 3 et seq.; Lauth 2014, 20 et seq.). Practices do not refer to personal habits but "they are specific to a particular political and government setting, they are recognized by actors (if not always adhered to), have a collective (rather than personal) effect, and can be described and explained to the researcher." (Lowndes and Roberts 2013, 47). It is important to note that practitioners, as well as other scholars, then often describe what this research defines as informal as 'formal'. Parker (2015, 2–4), for instance, has considered intergovernmental agreements which guide the cooperation between national and subnational governments as formal institutions. However, if they are not legally binding, they represent codified, yet informal institutions, while working arrangements that are not politically binding qualify as practices.[34] Rules to resolve conflict, for instance, are usually not codified but part of a mutual understanding practised by actors (Lehmbruch 1998, 14).

The impact of informal rules and practices can vary profoundly across countries, and either support, complement, undermine, have no effect, or stand in contrast to the formal structures of a political system (Lauth 2014, 22 et seq.). Helmke and Levitsky (2004, 728–731) distinguish between informal institutions that are *complementing* and enhance the efficiency of effective formal institutions; *accommodating* by altering the intention and effects of ineffective formal institutions without violating them; *competing* and violating ineffective formal institutions; or *substantive* to achieve what ineffective formal institutions fail to do. Clarity about the nature of intergovernmental relations will allow us to explain why formal or informal institutions and practices have emerged and under what circumstances actors from different levels rely on them. What are the power and interest constellations behind the introduction of informal institutions? Have informal institutions been set up because formal rules are ineffective, undesirable, too costly, or publicly or internationally unacceptable? In addition to identifying the formalisation of institutions and practices, this study also reflects on the institutional depth of intergovernmental relations. According to Bolleyer (2009; 2013, 324–325; 2018, 48), regular meetings without a separate intergovernmental body show only *weak* institutional depth. A *medium* institutionalisation is provided by an autonomous institution with statutory functions and its own resources and infrastructure (collectively financed staff, secretariat) that provide bureaucratic support and ensure frequent meetings. Intergovernmental arrangements are *highly* institutionalised, when at least two of the following four criteria applying: (a) majority rule which deviates from unanimity; (b) an internal differentiation of the coordinating body into offices and organs with policy-specific tasks; (c) the legal status to produce binding agreements and (d) the formulation of precise arrangements. While formal institutions are then likely to show a *high* institutional depth, informal institutions can be further differentiated into *weak* and *medium* informal institutions.

Patterns of interaction

Intergovernmental relations "oscillate between conflict and cooperation" (Hueglin and Fenna 2010, 215). According to Poirier and Saunders (2015a, 1): "Modalities of interaction between orders of government in a federation include co-operative institutions and processes (e.g. consultation, co-decision and coordination) as well as more conflictual processes of tension, collusion, competition, control, and even coercion." Based on Michael Tatham's (2016, 16 et seq.) book *With, Without or Against the State*, which focuses on state and substate interest representation in EU affairs, this study distinguishes between three types of interaction, as dependent variables:[35] *Non-interaction* (DV1) refers to a state where levels of government do not attempt to coordinate their policies or are indifferent and unconcerned about policymaking at the other level regardless of whether their objectives are similar or not. *Cooperation* (DV2) takes place when governments work together to achieve common policy goals through collective actions by exchanging information, pooling resources or by coordinating their legislation and policy implementation. *Conflict* (DV3) describes a situation where governments pursue diverging outcomes contrary to the other's interests, leading to a competition between them.[36] Whereas Tatham (op. cit., 18) looked at the final outcome to evaluate under what conditions interest representation of states and substates at EU level is characterised by non-interaction, cooperation or conflict, this research considers the patterns of interaction as processes that can change over time.

Tatham (op. cit., 19 et seq.) further identified three independent variables explaining the pattern of interaction between central governments and regions in interest representation at the EU level: devolution of powers, preference intensity and party-political configurations. However, not all are equally suitable for the purpose of this study. To understand the circumstances under which devolved and central governments in the UK either cooperate, engage in conflict or do not interact, the independent variables tested here are modified and expanded to *functional and political interdependence* (IV1), *preference intensity* (IV2), *party congruency* (IV3) and *strategic power* (IV4). Other factors, such as history, geography, culture, ethnic diversity (cf. Poirier and Saunders 2015a, 1), skills, ambitions and personalities, also inform the nature of cooperation and confrontation, but these are difficult to compare as systematic patterns (Tatham 2016, 19).

Tatham (2016, 21) hypothesised that a decentralisation of authority to substate entities leads to a greater mobilisation to influence EU policies independently without interacting with central government. This assumption is slightly adapted to this study. The first independent variable suggests that functional and political interdependence (IV1) of different executives (and legislatures) requires more intergovernmental bargaining as they seek to prevent the negative impact of disruptive decisions by the other government. Different levels are then expected to cooperate (DV2) in order to avoid costly conflicts or political crises (McEwen and Petersohn 2015, 193 et seq.). At the same time, functional and political interdependence (IV1) can also be a source of conflict (DV3) when governments want to take decisions that have consequences with an unwelcomed impact on the other jurisdiction. When devolution promotes a dual allocation of powers with little need for close coordination of policies, non-interaction (DV1) is the most likely pattern of interaction (cf. Lehmbruch 1998, 30; cf. Scharpf 2000, 289; Broschek 2011, 545; Bolleyer and Thorlakson 2012, 571–573).

According to Tatham (2016, 22), preference intensity (IV2) determines the pattern of interaction. When governments share similar objectives high preference intensity leads to cooperation (DV2). In turn, diverging interests around issues of high priority is likely to cause conflict (DV3). When preference intensity is high for one side but low for the other, cooperation (DV2) and non-interaction (DV1) rather than conflict (DV3) are expected outcomes. Issues of great salience typically include, for instance, economic prosperity, cultural identity, political autonomy and fiscal policy (Bolleyer 2009, 51; Gallagher 2012, 206).

Tatham's (2016, 24) third variable accounts for different party-political configurations and tests whether party congruence (IV3) is a source of cooperation (DV2) rather than of conflict (DV3). Much intergovernmental exchange is channelled through political parties that are operating at multiple levels and provide an important arena for strategic interaction, negotiations and coordination (Behnke 2018, 37–38). When governments run by the same party share common ideologies, agendas and policy objectives, parties provide convenient and effective opportunities and access points to coordinate their positions (McEwen et al. 2012b, 323; Weissert and Fahey 2018, 345). When different parties are at power at different levels, governments are less likely to cooperate (DV2), share information and make concessions but rather compete with each other (McEwen 2017, 670). While conflict (DV3) between incongruent governments may intensify in the course of election campaigns, congruent governments may downplay divergence (Poirier and Saunders 2015b, 451; cf. Tatham 2016, 24 et seq.). This is particularly the case for majoritarian two-party systems, which create strong pressures for parties to compete with each other for electoral support and to shift blame for political failures onto governments ruled by different parties. Proportional election and power-sharing systems, in turn, generate more stable interest configurations and a continuous need to work together through government coalitions at different levels (Scharpf 1997, 183 et seq.; Bolleyer 2009, 35–37; 2018, 51; Poirier and Saunders 2015b, 451).[37] Since 2010, all four governments in the UK have been led by different parties, this study does not aim for a strict comparison of patterns of interaction between government run by the same or different parties. Nevertheless, it will reflect on the role of party congruency (IV3) on cooperation (DV2) and conflict (DV3) between administrations.

Strategic power (IV4) was not addressed by Tatham but is based on the research of negotiations about territorial change by Petersohn, Behnke and Rhode (2015), which draws on Scharpf's (1997) *actor-centred institutionalism*. They highlight the importance of the strategic power (IV4) of actors to pursue their interests within negotiation processes in relation to the opportunities and constraints of institutional settings, the competences and recourses of governments, and actors' interests (Petersohn, Behnke and Rhode 2015, 627). The focus of this study is not primarily on political parties, though, of course, they form governments.[38] Therefore, Petersohn, Behnke and Rhode's (2015, 628–632) framework is slightly modified but takes into account governments' *strategic preferences* for territorial change and other policies; *negotiation power* based on their electoral strength and public support;[39] and the prevailing *mode of interaction*.[40] The availability of different preferences (hierarchically ranked according to their preference intensity) provides governments with a range of strategic options by which to use cooperation (DV2) and conflict (DV3) to their advantage. High electoral support further provides them with a strong political mandate and democratic legitimacy to fight for their advocated objectives. Conflict (DV3) becomes more 'affordable' when public support is strong and cooperation (DV2) more likely when governments enjoy less negotiation power – albeit established norms may restrain actors from egoistically blocking decisions, for instance, in times of crisis (Benz 2009b,

168). In relation to interest representation at the EU level, for instance, Tatham (2016, 33) argued:

> [...] it is always to the players' a priori advantage to coordinate interest representation rather than non-interacting or suffering from a conflicting pattern of interaction. Indeed, it is through cooperation that interest representation is likely to be most efficient and has the highest likelihood of achieving its stated objective: influencing the policy process closer to one's policy preferences.

Caught in the dilemma of finding compromises to coordinate policies and decisions with other administrations while appealing to their voters at home, multilevel politics becomes a strategic game with its own dynamics beyond the institutionalised rules (Benz 2009b, 82–83). As Bolleyer (2018, 51) suggested: "Whether governments prioritize autonomy protection over problem-solving in IGR (or vice versa) is at least partially linked to the political pressures they are exposed to in their home arenas." According to Scharpf (1997, 44–49), the combination of *actor constellation* (strategic options in consideration of the preferences of involved actors and their evaluation of possible outcomes) and *mode of interaction* define the negotiation game. He distinguishes between *unilateral action, negotiated agreement, majority vote* and *hierarchical direction*. The institutional framework of unitary states typically enables the centre to legislate and allocate finances unilaterally by hierarchical direction instead of decisions by majority vote as the applied norms and practices. And yet, even hierarchical relations are embedded in wider strategic constellations that limit individual actions and decision-making by the higher authority (cf. Scharpf 1997, 45; Benz 2009b, 85 et seq.). Most intergovernmental decisions are made by *negotiations* or *competition* but can be complemented by *hierarchical direction* and *networks* (Benz 2009b, 85–86). While competition is typically not subject to intergovernmental coordination,[41] negotiations can involve *bargaining*, which includes manipulation of information and threats to withdraw from talks or *arguing* through the exchange of rational views to create a mutual understanding. Both strategies can be used simultaneously (op. cit., 88–90). Negotiations depend on the nature of the institutional framework, and in the context of this study, in particular on the availability of and involvement of actors in *negotiation systems*. Whereas *voluntary negotiation systems* are informal *self-organising networks* or formalised *normative regimes* with terms of references setting out participating actors, objectives and procedures, *compulsory negotiation systems* describe constellations where actors have to work together on the basis of unanimity or consensus because unilateral actions are legally or practically not possible (Scharpf 2000, 241–245). The latter "may arise naturally from physical adjacency or functional interdependence", for instance, to realise common infrastructure projects across shared borders (Scharpf 1997, 143). Voluntary negotiation systems are also based on functional interdependence but they are more prone to exit strategies and autonomous actions, and therefore only provide loose structural coupling (Benz 2009b, 87). Whether governments engage in conflict (DV3) depends heavily on the willingness and appetite of the political leadership to risk or foster open confrontation, which is usually limited. As a result, they tend only to engage in a negative coordination to prevent decisions by their counterpart that would have a detrimental impact on themselves or they bargain about the allocation of resources. Most conflicts do not therefore reach the ministerial level but are solved in negotiations among non-political civil servants. While decisions can then be hierarchically taken, policy formation is subject to more cooperative modes of interaction (Scharpf 2000, 292), which relies on mutual willingness and recognition of each other's concerns (op. cit., 226).[42] In summary, strategic preferences and negotiation power in combination with the mode of interaction (either unilateral action, hierarchical direction, decisions by majority vote or negotiated agreement) define the strategic power of substate governments.

Political influence

Bargaining is an essential part of intergovernmental disputes, competition and conflict-resolution (Weissert and Fahey 2018, 344) and depends on the political leverage or the means of governments to exert influence in negotiations – often used as a synonym for power. The decentralisation of authority, formal and informal institutions and practices, patterns of cooperation and conflict help us to comprehend the strategic choices of actors but their effectiveness may still vary (cf. Hunt and Minto 2017).[43] Influence differs also from formal authority, and "a valid measure of formal authority would not tell us how much power a regional government was able to exert", as Marks et al. (2008, 114) put it. Rather leverage is a subset or source of power within negotiations that allows one stakeholder to influence another stakeholder either by making threats or promises that would come with costs or benefits for the latter (Kirgis 2014, 103–105). Although knowing about the specific and general ability of the devolved governments to influence decisions of the UK Government is crucial to understanding the underlying conditions, existing studies have not yet systematically explained to what extent and under which conditions regional governments exert political influence in national decision-making beyond the formal institutions typically found in federations.

Measuring actual political influence beyond a legalistic analysis of political, legislative and fiscal authority is not an easy undertaking as it involves multiple actors with converging or diverging interests who deploy different strategies within varying contexts to achieve their goals. In order to ensure a systematic analysis of the devolved government's impact on the agenda-setting, policymaking and decision-taking of the UK Government, this study applies the so-called *EAR instrument*, introduced by Bas Arts and Piet Verschuren (1999). The EAR instrument provides a qualitative tool based on plausible and transparent criteria to assess complex, open-ended and multilevel decision-making processes by triangulating the perspectives of multiple stakeholders with different and opposing interests. Repeatedly observations of influence for various cases enables further conclusions on the general ability of actors to impact decisions, ergo on their power. Thereby, ego-perception (E) captures key player A's own perception of their level of influence; alter-perception (A) allows the comparison of A's perception with key players B-to-Z's perceptions of A's level of influence; and the researcher's analysis (R) validates these perceptions. In the context of this study, the ego-perception refers to the devolved governments (E) and the alter-perception to central government, the other devolved nations and to parliamentarians not represented in the government (A). The EAR instrument suggests that key topics and positive and negative examples of influence should be identified through ego- and alter-perceptions. This will inform the study's selection of examples along with theoretical considerations on the patterns of interaction.

According to the EAR instrument (op. cit., 412–414), actor A exerts influence when they modify the behaviour of decision-makers and consequently the outcome of a decision, either through their direct intervention or merely through the anticipation of their intervention by other actors. This assessment takes account of the *goal-achievement* of actors (GA), the extent to which goal-achievement can be *ascribed* to them (AS); and the *political relevance* of the policy outcome (PR). The political relevance depends on whether a decision is perceived as a key issue, the extent to which it is binding on stakeholders, and the level of controversy of the issue. If all of these appear to be 'strong', we can assume a 'high' political relevance, while trivial, non-binding or merely symbolic decisions will be considered of 'low' relevance. Only if all three conditions (GA, AS and PR) are met, can we attest influence, which is why the formula for *political influence* (PI) represents a multiplication instead of an addition: $PI = GA \times AS \times PR$. The EAR instrument uses four ordinal categories for each criterion: 0 means *no*; 1 means *some*; 2 means *substantial* and 3 means *great*. The results of the formula range from 0 to 27. If either GA, AS or PR scores 0, political influence will also be rated as 0. The nature of the multiplication prevents some scores, which means that the intervals between different outcomes are not exact. Instead, they are translated into verbal qualifications, whereby 0 means *no*; 1, 2 or 3 means *some*; 4, 6, 8, 9 or 12 means *substantial* and 18 or 27 means *great* political influence.

Qualitative case-study design

This study is based on a theoretically informed case-study design (cf. Muno 2009, 121–128). The theoretical concepts and approaches, as discussed in the previous sections, will guide the empirical analysis and allow an interpretation of the findings (cf. Eccleston et al. 2017b, 37). A case-based analysis will unravel how various factors relate to each other (Hague et al. 2016, 93) and to explain the 'causes-of-effects' rather than the 'effects-of-causes' (Vromen 2018, 243). Finding new patterns or unexpected results will subsequently support the building and advancement of theoretical explanations (Ridder 2016, 77–81) and inform existing research on federations and multilevel systems. As Bukve (2019, 115) put it:

> A case study needs to be focused; that is, it must be oriented towards a specific type of research purpose, and it must have a focus that is relevant for the purpose. Further, the collection of data must be structured in such a way that the collected information can be used for theoretical interpretation of the case or be relevant for the development or testing of theories.

The 'comparative merit' of case studies is based on their purpose to either generate or test theories, or in combining both elements by applying, testing and revising existing approaches (disciplined-configurative). While case studies can vary in their focus on many (large *n*), a few (small *n*) or only a single (one *n*) cases (as well as on the number of variables used), single-case studies also hold an important comparative value (Muno 2009, 113–121; Hopkin 2010, 285–286; Hague et al. 2016, 91).[44] According to Vromen (2018, 244): "But, even if it is classified as a single-site case study, the qualitative researcher is not only studying a single phenomenon as the case study generates many qualitative-interpretative, within case 'observation' that demonstrate patterns of interaction, practices, relationships, routines and actions [...]." The intensive field and analytical work required for this type of research allow only for a small-n case study. On the one hand, this study presents a single-case study with the UK presenting a 'critical case'[45] to confirm, challenge or extend the theoretical context provided by comparative federalism (cf. Ridder 2016, 115; Ryan 2018, 285; Bukve 2019, 122; 163). On the other hand, this research also works as a small-n study by comparing variations across Scotland and Wales within the UK. Either way, this research follows a comparative tradition by examining "a limited number of cases with the purpose of studying variation by use of non-statistical designs and methods." (Bukve 2019; 162)

In order to link macro-level explanations of institutional configurations to the micro-level analysis of specific examples of cooperation, conflict and influence, this study will further examine differences and commonalities in the operation of intergovernmental relations across various policy fields (cf. Bolleyer 2009, 16–17). Even though this study does not explicitly apply a process-tracing method, it still traces processes to understand the causalities behind certain outcomes (cf. Vromen 2018, 244), and thus enables a 'causal process observation' or a 'within-case analysis' based on intensive fieldwork interviews and documentary analysis (Ryan 2018, 286). Expert or elite interviews support this study in various ways by providing new, detailed information about relevant processes, events and the attitudes of key actors.[46] They help to confirm, clarify or falsify information from other sources, as documentary data often lack important evidence because they are not considered relevant or are too sensitive to the authors. Elite interviews should not of course be taken at face value without a careful reflection on the position and objectives of respondents and a comparison with other sources (Tansey 2009, 484–487). In order to ensure that the analysis has validity, this study triangulates data from different respondents, different sources and different perspectives (cf. Pickel and Pickel 2009, 518). Here, primary documents produced by political actors (e.g. executives, legislatures, judiciary and non-government organisations), including archival material, legal texts, protocols, meeting minutes, official records and statements, letters, press releases, party manifestos and reports, as well secondary literature will complement the findings from elite interviewing (Burnham et al. 2008, 232; Vromen 2018, 249).

The scope of this study and the access and availability of political and official experts make probability sampling unsuitable and impractical. Instead, respondents are chosen purposively through 'snowball' (also 'referral') sampling whereby respondents identified through initial research recommend further interviewees (Burnham et al. 2008, 231–233; Tansey 2009, 491–492; Bryman 2016, 415). The focus on informal dynamics and the EAR method essentially require insights from relevant policymakers, ministers and civil servants from the Scottish, Welsh and UK executives, which were chosen according to their expertise on intergovernmental relations and specific policy areas. These are complemented with perspectives from the devolved legislatures and the British-Irish Council. As the following list shows, civil servants clearly dominate the pool of interviewees. This was partly because they were more willing to respond but they were also better able to comment on detailed issues on which they had worked. While the major political positions are mostly publicly available, government officials offered insights that would otherwise not have been accessible. Importantly, since the early days of devolution, in intergovernmental relations civil servants have been central to solving disputes arising at a low level in order to avoid the politicisation of territorial issues (Bradbury 2021, 298). As this study will show, though open disagreements have become more common during the last decade, most interactions take place in the official space. Between March 2019 and December 2020, a total of 59 respondents contributed to this study: 19 face-to-face plus 1 written interviews were conducted with 16 special advisors and officials of the Scottish Government, 4 Members (including 1 former minister) and 1 Clerk of the Scottish Parliament; 11 special advisors and officials of the Welsh Government, 5 Members (including 3 former ministers) and 3 Clerks of the Welsh Assembly were interviewed in person (2 of them by telephone); a series of 10 interviews with 16 officials of the UK Government (3 interviews in person before the Covid-19 restrictions, 7 via video-call or telephone), 1 Member and 1 Clerk of the House of Commons; 1 official of the British-Irish Council was interviewed in person.

The questionnaire for this study was informed by theoretical considerations and based on the three research strands outlined above, and designed for the conduct of semi-structured interviews, which cover similar questions while providing a level of flexibility to adapt the question to the specific situation of an interviewee (Meuser and Nagel 2009, 476; see also Pickel and Pickel 2009, 446–447; Bryman 2016, 466 et seq.). All interviews were treated anonymously and confidentially after having obtained informed consent (cf. Ruane 2005, 19–26). Except for two interviewees, who refused to be recorded, audio recordings and complementary notes ensured the reliable reproduction of the respondents' answers. In order to secure that any information and quotes derived from interviews cannot be linked back to respondents, yet simultaneously making the different perspectives visible in the analytical chapters, references to interviews will be presented in the text as the following: Scottish Government: SG1, SG2, SG3 etc.; Scottish Parliament: SP1, SP2, SP3 etc.; Welsh Government: WG1, WG2, WG3 etc.; Welsh Parliament: WP1, WP2, WP3 etc.; UK Government: UKG1, UKG2, UKG3 etc.; UK Parliament: UKP1, UKP2, UKP3 etc.; British-Irish Council: BIC1.

The acquired qualitative data was transcribed and subsequently (cf. Bryman 2016, 584) analysed assisted by MAXQDA, a qualitative data analysis software. The coding of expert interviews was thematically guided, and respondents' statements were evaluated in relation to their respective institutional and organisational functions and roles, as well as to other interviews (Meuser and Nagel 2009, 476; cf. Pierce 2008, 243–254). First-level coding reflects groupings into powers (1); institutions (2); practices (3); patterns of interaction (4) and political influence (5). They were subsequently divided further into the second-level codes: dual and overlapping powers (1); formal and informal institutions (2); non-interaction, cooperation and conflict (4). The third level of codes contains specific examples of dual and overlapping powers (1); formal and informal institutions (2); practices (3); patterns of interaction (4) and political influence (5).

Table 2.1 Coding scheme

First level	Second level	Third level
Powers	Dual allocation of powers Overlapping powers	Area of competence
Institutions	Formal institutions Informal institutions	Arrangement
Practices	Actors' sphere	Arrangement
Patterns of interaction	Non-interaction Cooperation Conflict	Policy area/issue
Political influence		Policy area/decision

During the initial research phase and later in process of interviewing, it became clear that the period between 2010 and 2020 provides a reasonable time frame for this study. The 2010 General Election started a new era of intergovernmental relations with different parties in power across Westminster, Scotland, Wales and Northern Ireland. Most interviewees were not able to comment on earlier developments (and most could hardly comment on the first half of the investigated decade), since they did not work for the respective organisation at the time. Also, intergovernmental relations had no particular relevance until the devolution of new powers to Scotland and Wales from 2012 onwards, the 2014 Scottish independence referendum and the 2016 EU referendum. Northern Ireland was excluded for theoretical reasons, as its devolution settlement and power-sharing arrangements are very different to Scotland and Wales, "and it was only by chance that devolution arrived there at the same time as it came to Scotland and Wales at the end of the twentieth century." (Keating and Laforest 2018, 7) The Northern Ireland Assembly and Executive were not only suspended between January 2017 and January 2020, the initial plan to conduct fieldwork within Northern Ireland was made practically impossible due to the Covid-19 pandemic in 2020/2021.

Conclusion

Over the last two decades, more and more political, legislative and fiscal authority was devolved to the administrations in Scotland and Wales. Yet, as this chapter has discussed, territorial power is not merely a question of decentralisation but depends on the power relations with the central government. The next chapter provides a formal, legalistic analysis of territorial competences to understand the context in which intergovernmental relations take place. However, studies looking only at the competences regional governments can exert independently would be flawed. Accordingly, this research aims beyond capturing the self-rule capacities of each administration and focuses on the shared rule between levels of government. In the absence of formalised shared rule, intergovernmental relations are key to understanding questions of territorial power and autonomy, and among existing works there is still great potential for systematic investigations of the UK and other multilevel polities. To embed this in a wider theoretical perspective, which allows comparison with other political systems, comparative federalism provides the overall theoretical framework of this study. This will not only enable conclusions about the allocation and integration of competences, decision-making and conflict-resolution, but it will also contribute to our knowledge about multilevel systems. Due to the decentralised unitary nature of the UK's political system and its emphasis on informal rules, the UK presents a hybrid model and critical case providing new insights for a dynamic federal perspective. The focus on Scotland and Wales itself has an additional comparative merit being within an asymmetrical, multi-nation state.

Notes

1. For instance, decentralisation can also describe a horizontal transfer of power to markets and non-governmental organisation (Keuffer and Ladner 2021, 21).
2. Whereas power refers to the capacity to act, based on a complex relationship of influence shaped by force, persuasion, negotiation and loyalties, authority is the "acknowledged right to do so" (Hague et al. 2016, 9). In other words, authority refers to the codification of power by "explicit rules which govern the interaction between actors and reduce the gap between de jure and de facto authority." Power, in turn, can be exercised formally and informally by individuals who pursue their values, interests and objectives (Jensen et al. 2014, 1240).
3. Pasquier (2021, 58–59) calls this political regionalisation, which applies to Spain, Italy, Portugal and the UK; in contrast to regional decentralisation under strong constitutional hierarchies, as in France, the Czech Republic and Poland.
4. A fourth type, *economic decentralisation*, is related to deregulation, market liberalisation, privatisation of public services and the establishment of public-private partnerships.
5. Mueller (2011, 214 et seq.) argued that a comprehensive understanding of variations across subnational territories can only be gained if we consider the organisational freedom and the scope of local jurisdiction and autonomy (polity); local revenues, income and the nature of implementation (policy); and local actors (politics).
6. Authority migration refers to the movement of power within a political system, either upwards to higher levels or downwards to lower levels.
7. By regions, Marks et al. (2008, 113) mean clearly defined territories with legislative and executive institutions intermediate between national and local governments. Although the UK is a multinational union (cf. Martin 2021, 7–8), with different national identities prevailing across England, Scotland, Wales and Northern Ireland, this study will occasionally use the term regional government for the devolved executives and national government for the UK Government.
8. The *Local Autonomy Index* is another example of a recent study relying on multidimensional indicators (Keuffer and Ladner 2021, 20).
9. *Institutional depth* ranges from no administration (score of 0) to a general-purpose administration not subject to central government veto (score of 3).
10. *Policy scope* is divided into economic policy (regional development, public utilities, transport, environment and energy); cultural-educational policy (schools, universities, vocational training, libraries, sports and cultural centres); and welfare (health, hospitals, social welfare, pensions and social housing). The ranking reaches from having no competence in these areas (score of 0) to covering all three areas plus immigration, citizenship and right of domicile (score of 4).
11. No *fiscal autonomy* means, central governments set the base and rate of all regional taxes (score of 0), high fiscal autonomy allows regional governments to set the base and rate of at least one major tax (personal income, corporate, value-added or sales tax) (score of 4).
12. Ranging from no *borrowing autonomy* (score of 0) to borrowing unrestricted by central government (score of 3).
13. *Representation* refers to the capacity of regional actors to select regional office holders, ranging from not having a regional assembly and an executive appointed by central government (score of 0) to having elected assemblies and executives (score of 4).

40 *Theoretical and Methodological Perspectives*

14 Central decision-making is disaggregated across four areas: normal legislation, executive policy, taxation and constitutional reform.
15 Aggregated scores for different characteristics of *law making* range from 0 to 2.
16 *Executive control* reaches from no routine meetings (score of 0) to routine meetings with legally binding powers (score of 2).
17 In terms of *fiscal control*, regional governments may not be consulted on fiscal decisions (score of 0), be consulted (score of 1) or have a veto right (score of 2).
18 *Borrowing control* ranges from no consultation (score of 0) to veto-rights (score of 2).
19 *Constitutional reform* can vary from unilateral decision by central government (score of 0) to veto-right (score of 3).
20 According to Hueglin and Fenna (2010, 36): "In short, while federal systems are distinguished from unitary states by their constitutional division of powers, centralization and decentralization describe the character and dynamics of power allocation."
21 The 'federal philosophy' balances multiple territorial identities, may they be local, regional, national or transnational by acknowledging that humans belong to one or several communities with which they identify (Hueglin and Fenna 2010, 37).
22 Though federations are usually made up of more than two tiers, the local level is often subordinate and not privileged by the constitution.
23 In theory, federations can decide to alter their structure from a federal to a unitary one; however, in practice, it is unlikely that territorial units would agree to give up their sovereignty (Hueglin and Fenna 2010, 44–45). The requirement of super majorities in parliaments, and the approval from both legislative chambers for constitutional amendments, as well as rulings by impartial constitutional courts, ensure that the powers of the constituent entities are protected (Rodden 2004, 481, 489 et seq.; Burgess 2006, 157–158; Watts 2008, 18).
24 Hueglin and Fenna also describe these polities as legislative federalism.
25 *Cooperative federalism* is different form *integrated federalism*. Here, actors can in principle exit voluntary arrangements, but are likely to face substantial costs if they leave established paths. This produces de facto a *Politikverflechtung* or *Zwangsverhandlungssystem*, but individual jurisdictions are still able to act autonomously if they cannot reach an agreement (Kropp 2010, 12–13; 2011, 15–16; cf. Sturm 2020, 17–18).
26 Except for a small number of states (e.g. United Arab Emirates, Venezuela), constituent units in federations are represented through a second chamber in a *bicameral federal legislature* through which they can scrutinise legislation and promote their regional and minority preferences (Watts 2008, 153).
27 In Germany, for instance, 'allegiance to the federal government' *(Bundestreue)* ensures that both levels consider individual and collective interests.
28 Also, the Calman Commission in 2009 and House of Lords' Select Committee on the Constitution in 2016.
29 These include the degree of (de)centralisation; the exclusive competence over policy areas; structural asymmetries and the constellation of (overlapping) interests of actors.
30 A systematic investigation of different positions and preferences within administrations would exceed the scope of this study.
31 Although various studies and recent experiences of coalition and minority governments have to some degree challenged the majoritarian ideal of the Westminster model (cf. Strohmeier 2015; Russell 2016; Matthews 2018; Curtis 2020).

32 Instead of adhering to one particular strand of institutionalism (normative, rational choice of historical), neo-institutionalism is here seen as a "broad intellectual trajectory" covering a variety of dynamics (Lowndes 2018, 58–59; see also Hall and Taylor 1996, 957).
33 Informal institutions are based on established rules or guidelines, and therefore differ from ineffective formal institutions that are circumvented or ignored (Helmke and Levitsky 2004, 727).
34 Informal institutions and practices still meet Parker's criteria for intergovernmental arrangements as documents with shared meanings and norms that endure and transcend individual actors.
35 In order to reflect the different levels of intensity and escalation, the sequence of the patterns was altered.
36 These types resemble the forms of interaction used by Mitchell (2010, 62) in his analysis of the UK: non-interaction = uncooperative; cooperation = cooperative; conflict = adversarial.
37 The close interplay *(Arenenkopplung)* of party competition as a source of conflict, and functional integration, a source of cooperation, has been widely discussed in the context of Germany's *interlocked* federalism (cf. Lehmbruch 1976; 1998; Benz 2009b, 62–66; 2016, 34 et seq.; Kropp 2010; 61 et seq.).
38 Benz and Broschek (2013, 7) define territorial governments and political parties as the most relevant political actors.
39 Party congruency across governments is considered as a separate variable (IV3).
40 While Petersohn et al. (2015, 632) examine on unilateral, bilateral or multilateral negotiation modes, this study applies Scharpf's (1997, 46–49) modes of interaction as a more suitable perspective for this study. Alternatively, Benz and Broschek (2013, 7) use related modes: unilateralism, coordination, cooperation or highly interdependent forms of joint decision-making.
41 The comparison of competences, resources and performance can produce unintended coordinated effects.
42 *Weak trust* implies at least the *expectation that information communicated about Alter's own options and preferences will be truthful*, rather than purposefully misleading, and that *commitments explicitly entered will be honoured* as long as the circumstances under which they were entered do not change significantly; […] *strong trust* implies the *expectation that alter will avoid strategy options attractive to itself that would seriously hurt ego's interests* and that in case of need help can be counted on even if it entails considerable cost to the helper (Scharpf 1997, 137–138).
43 Strategic power and actual political influence are not the same.
44 In fact, many works that adopt a comparative approach focus on only one case, typically a state or country.
45 For the reasons outlined earlier, the UK is an unlikely case to fit the 'federal paradigm.'
46 See, for instance, Burnham et al. (2008), Meuser and Nagel (2009) and Pickel and Pickel (2009) for a detailed discussion of expert interviews.

Bibliography

Ackerman, Bruce (2018) *Why Britain Needs a Written Constitution – and Can't Wait for Parliament to Write One*. The Political Quarterly, Volume 89, Issue 4, pp. 548–590.

Agranoff, Robert (2004) *Autonomy, Devolution and Intergovernmental Relations*. Regional and Federal Studies, Volume 14, Issue 1, pp. 26–65.

Anderson, George and Gallagher, Jim (2018) *Intergovernmental Relations in Canada and the United Kingdom*. In: Keating, Michael and Laforest, Guy (eds.) *Constitutional Politics and the Territorial Question in Canada and the United Kingdom*. Cham: Palgrave Macmillan, pp. 19–46.

Andrews, Leighton (2021) *The Forward March of Devolution Halted – and the Limits of Progressive Unionism*. The Political Quarterly, Volume 92, Issue 3, pp. 512–521.

Arts, Bas and Verschuren, Piet (1999) *Assessing Political Influence in Complex Decision-Making: An Instrument Based on Triangulation*. International Political Science Review, Volume 20, Issue 4, pp. 411–424.

Behnke, Nathalie (2015) *Stand und Perspektiven der Föderalismusforschung*. Aus Politik und Zeitgeschichte, Volume 65, pp. 28–30.

Behnke, Nathalie (2018) *Federal, Devolved or Decentralized State: On the Territorial Architecture of Power*. In: Detterbeck, Klaus and Hepburn, Eve (eds.) *Handbook of Territorial Politics*. Cheltenham: Edward Elgar Publishing, pp. 30–44.

Behnke, Nathalie (2019) *How Bureaucratic Networks Make Intergovernmental Relations Work: A Mechanism Perspective*. In: Behnke, Nathalie, Broschek, Jörg and Sonnicksen, Jared (eds.) *Configurations, Dynamics and Mechanisms of Multilevel Governance*. Cham: Palgrave Macmillan, pp. 41–59.

Behnke, Nathalie and Mueller, Sean (2017) *The Purpose of Intergovernmental Councils: A Framework for Analysis and Comparison*. Regional and Federal Studies, Volume 27, Issue 5, pp. 507–527.

Benz, Arthur (2002) *Themen, Probleme Und Perspektiven Der Vergleichenden Föderalismusforschung*. In: Benz, Arthur and Lehmbruch, Gerhard (eds.) *Analysen in entwicklungsgeschichtlicher und vergleichender Pespektive*. Wiesbaden: Westdeutscher Verlag, pp. 9–50.

Benz, Arthur (2009a) *Intergovernmental Relations in German Federalism – joint decision-making and the dynamics of horizontal cooperation*. Paper at the Forum of Federations' Conference on Spanish Federalism, Zaragossa. 25–28 March.

Benz, Arthur (2009b) *Politik in Mehrebenensystemen*. Wiesbaden: Springer VS.

Benz, Arthur (2013) *Dimensions and Dynamics of Federal Regimes*. In: Benz, Arthur and Broschek, Jörg (eds.) *Federal Dynamics: Continuity, Change, and the Varieties of Federalism*. Oxford: Oxford University Press, pp. 70–90.

Benz, Arthur (2016) *Varianten und Dynamiken der Politikverflechtung im deutschen Bundesstaat*. Baden: Nomos.

Benz, Arthur and Broschek, Jörg (2013) *Federal Dynamics: Introduction*. In: Benz, Arthur and Broschek, Jörg (eds.) *Federal Dynamics: Continuity, Change, and the Varieties of Federalism*. Oxford: Oxford University Press, pp. 1–23.

Beyme, Klaus von (2010) *Vergleichende Politikwissenschaft*. Wiesbaden: Springer VS.

Birrell, Derek (2012a) *Comparing Devolved Governance*. Basingstoke: Palgrave Macmillan.

Birrell, Derek (2012b) *Intergovernmental Relations and Political Parties in Northern Ireland*. British Journal of Politics and International Relations, Volume 14, Issue 2, pp. 270–284.

Bogdanor, Vernon (2009) *The New British Constitution*. Oxford: Hart Publishing.

Bolleyer, Nicole (2009) *Intergovernmental Cooperation: Rational Choices in Federal Systems and Beyond*. Oxford: Oxford University Press.

Bolleyer, Nicole (2013) *Paradoxes of Self-Coordination in Federal Systems*. In: Benz, Arthur and Broschek, Jörg (eds.) *Federal Dynamics: Continuity, Change, and the Varieties of Federalism*. Oxford: Oxford University Press, pp. 321–342.

Bolleyer, Nicole (2018) *Challenges of Interdependence and Coordination in Federal Systems*. In: Detterbeck, Klaus and Hepburn, Eve (eds.) *Handbook of Territorial Politics*. Cheltenham: Edward Elgar Publishing, pp. 45–60.

Bolleyer, Nicole and Thorlakson, Lori (2012) *Beyond Decentralization – The Comparative Study of Interdependence in Federal Systems*. The Journal of Federalism, Volume 42, Issue 4, pp. 566–591.

Bradbury, Jonathan (2021) *Constitutional Policy and Territorial Politics in the UK. Volume 1: Union and Devolution 1997–2007*. Bristol: Bristol University Press.

Bröchler, Stephan and Lauth, Hans-Joachim (2014) *Die Lokalisierung von Schneisen im Dickicht – Konzeptionelle Grundlegungen und empirische Befunde informaler Governance*. Zeitschrift für Vergleichende Politikwissenschaft, Volume 8, Issue 1 (Supplement), pp. 1–33.

Broschek, Jörg (2011) *Conceptualizing and Theorizing Constitutional Change in Federal Systems: Insights from Historical Institutionalism*. Regional and Federal Studies, Volume 21, Issue 4–5, pp. 539–559.

Broschek, Jörg (2016) *Staatsstrukturen in der Vergleichenden Politikwissenschaft: Förderal- und Einheitsstaat*. In: Lauth, Hans-Joachim, Kneuer, Marianne and Pickel, Gert (eds.) *Handbuch Vergleichende Politikwissenschaft*. Wiesbaden: Springer VS, pp. 331–343.

Bryman, Alan (2016) *Social Research Methods*. 5th edition. Oxford: Oxford University Press.

Bukve, Oddbjorn (2019) *Designing Social Science Research*. Cham: Palgrave Macmillan.

Bulpitt, Jim (2008) *Territory and Power in the United Kingdom: An Interpretation*. Colchester: ECPR Press (first published in 1983).

Burgess, Michael (2006) *Comparative Federalism: Theory And Practice*. London: Routledge.

Burnham, Peter, Gilland Lutz, Karin, Grant, Wyn and Layton-Henry, Zig (2008) *Research Methods in Politics*. Basingstoke: Palgrave Macmillan.

Cairney, Paul (2012) *Intergovernmental Relations in Scotland: What Was the SNP Effect?* British Journal of Politics and International Relations, Volume 14, Issue 2, pp. 231–249.

Carrell, Severin (2021) *Keir Starmer Urged to Back Radical Constitutional Reform for UK*. 31 January. The Guardian. https://www.theguardian.com/politics/2021/jan/31/keir-starmer-urged-to-back-radical-constitutional-reform-for-uk

Cheema, G. Shabbir and Rondinelli, Dennis A. (2007) *Decentralizing Governance: Emerging Concepts and Practices*. Washington, DC: Brookings Institution Press.

Curtis, John (2020) *A Return to 'Normality' at Last? How the Electoral System Worked in 2019*. Parliamentary Affairs, Volume 73, Issue 1 (Supplement), pp. 29–47.

Dardanelli, Paolo and Kincaid, John (2016) *A New Union? Federalism and the UK*. Political Insight, Volume 7, Issue 3, pp. 12–15.

Deacon, Russell (2018) *Wales in Westminster and Europe*. In: Deacon, Russell, Denton, Alison and Southall, Robert (eds.) *The Government and Politics of Wales*. Edinburgh: Edinburgh University Press, pp. 45–71.

Dickovick, J. Tyler (2005) *The Measure and Mismeasure of Decentralisation: Subnational Autonomy in Senegal and South Africa*. The Journal of Modern African Studies, Volume 43, Issue 2, pp. 183–210.

Dickson, Brice (2019) *Writing the United Kingdom Constitution*. Manchester: Manchester University Press.

Eccleston, Richard, Hortle, Robert and Krever, Richard (2017a) *The Evolution of Intergovernmental Financial Relations in the 21st Century*. In: Eccleston, Richard and Krever, Richard (eds.) *The Future of Federalism – Intergovernmental Financial Relations in an Age of Austerity*. Cheltenham: Edward Elgar Publishing, pp. 1–12.

Eccleston, Richard, Krever, Robert and Smith, Helen (2017b) *Fiscal Federalism in the 21st Century*. In: Eccleston, Richard and Krever, Richard (eds.) *The Future of Federalism – Intergovernmental Financial Relations in an Age of Austerity*. Cheltenham: Edward Elgar Publishing, pp. 15–45.

Elazar, Daniel J. (1987) *Exploring Federalism*. Tuscaloosa, AL: University of Alabama Press.

Falleti, Tulia G. (2013) *Decentralization in Time: A Process-Tracing Approach to Federal Dynamics of Change*. In: Benz, Arthur and Broschek, Jörg (eds.) *Federal Dynamics: Continuity, Change, and the Varieties of Federalism*. Oxford: Oxford University Press, pp. 141–166.

Flinders, Matthew (2009) *Democratic Drift: Majoritarian Modification and Democratic Anomie in the United Kingdom*. Oxford: Oxford University Press.

Gallagher, Jim (2012) *Intergovernmental Relations in the UK: Co-operation, Competition and Constitutional Change*. British Journal of Politics and International Relations, Volume 14, Issue 2, pp. 198–213.

Gerber, Elisabeth R. and Kollman, Kenneth (2004) *Introduction – Authority Migration: Defining an Emerging Research Agenda*. Political Science and Politics, Volume 37, Issue 3, pp. 397–401.

Hague, Rod, Harrop, Martin and McCormick, John (2016) *Comparative Government and Politics*. 10th edition. Basingstoke: Palgrave Macmillan.

Hall, Peter and Taylor Rosemary (1996) *Political Science and the Three New Institutionalisms*. Political Studies, Volume 44, Issue 5, pp. 936–957.

Hamilton, David K. and Stenberg, Carl W. (2018) *Introduction: Intergovernmental Relations in Transition*. In: Stenberg, Carl W. and Hamilton, David K. (eds.) *Intergovernmental Relations in Transition*. New York, NY: Routledge, pp. 1–12.

Helmke, Gretchen and Levitsky, Steven (2004) *Informal Institutions and Comparative Politics: A Research Agenda*. Perspectives on Politics, Volume 2, Issue 4, pp. 725–740.

Hepburn, Eve and Detterbeck, Klaus (eds.) (2018) *Introduction to the Handbook of Territorial Politics*. Handbook of Territorial Politics. Cheltenham: Edward Elgar Publishing, pp. 1–14.

Hooghe, Liesbet, Marks, Gary and Schakel, Arjan H. (2008) *Operationalizing Regional Authority: A Coding Scheme for 42 Countries, 1950–2006*. Regional and Federal Studies, Volume 18, Issue 2–3, pp. 123–142.

Hooghe, Liesbet, Marks, Gary, Schakel, Arjan H., Chapman Osterkatz, Sandra, Niedzwiecki, Niedzwiecki, Sara and Shair-Rosenfield, Sarah (2016) *Measuring Regional Authority: A Postfunctionalist Theory of Governance*, Volume I. Oxford: Oxford University Press.

Hopkin, Jonathan (2010) *The Comparative Method*. In: Marsh, David and Stoker, Gerry (eds.) *Theory and Methods in Political Science*. Basingstoke: Palgrave Macmillan, pp. 285–307.

Hueglin, Thomas O. (2013) *Comparing Federalism: Variations or Distinct Models?* In: Benz, Arthur and Broschek, Jörg (eds.) *Federal Dynamics: Continuity, Change, and the Varieties of Federalism*. Oxford: Oxford University Press, pp. 27–47.

Hueglin, Thomas O. and Fenna, Alan (2010) *Comparative Federalism: A Systematic Inquiry*. Peterborough: Broadview Press.

Hunt, Jo (2021) *Subsidiarity, Competence, and the UK Territorial Constitution.* In: Doyle, Oran, McHarg, Aileen and Murkens, Jo (eds.) *The Brexit Challenge for Ireland and the United Kingdom: Constitutions under Pressure.* Cambridge: Cambridge University Press, pp. 21–42.

Hunt, Jo and Minto, Rachel (2017) *Between Intergovernmental Relations and Paradiplomacy: Wales and the Brexit of the Regions.* The British Journal of Politics and International Relations, Volume 19, Issue 4, pp. 647–662.

Hutchcroft, Paul D. (2001) *Centralization and Decentralization in Administration and Politics: Assessing Territorial Dimension of Authority and Power.* Governance, Volume 14, Issue 1, pp. 23–53.

Jensen, Mads Dagnis, Koop, Christel and Tatham, Michael (2014) *Coping with Power Dispersion? Autonomy, Co-ordination and Control in Multilevel Systems.* Journal of European Public Policy, Volume 21, Issue 9, pp. 1237–1254.

JMC Joint Secretariat (2018) *Report of the Joint Ministerial Committee: 2015–2018.* Policy paper. 14 March. UK Government. https://www.gov.uk/government/publications/joint-ministerial-committee-communique-14-march-2018

John, Peter (2008) *New Introduction: Territory and Power and the Study of Comparative Politics.* In: Bulpitt, Jim, *Territory and Power in the United Kingdom: An Interpretation.* Colchester: ECPR Press (first published in 1983), pp. 1–16.

John, Peter (2009) *Territory and Power: Jim Bulpitt and the Study of Comparative Politics.* European Political Science Volume 8, pp. 428–449.

John, Peter (2022) *British Politics: An Analytical Approach.* Oxford: Oxford University Press.

Keating, Michael (2012) *Intergovernmental Relations and Innovation: From Co-Operative to Competitive Welfare Federalism in the UK.* British Journal of Politics and International Relations, Volume 14, Issue 2, pp. 214–230.

Keating, Michael (2021) *State and Nation in the United Kingdom: The Fractured Union.* Oxford: Oxford University Press.

Keating, Michael and Laforest, Guy (eds.) (2018) *Federalism and Devolution: The UK and Canada. Constitutional Politics and the Territorial Question in Canada and the United Kingdom.* Cham: Palgrave Macmillan, pp. 1–18.

Keil, Soeren and Anderson, Paul (2018) *Decentralization as a Tool for Conflict Resolution.* In: Detterbeck, Klaus and Hepburn, Eve (eds.) *Handbook of Territorial Politics.* Cheltenham: Edward Elgar Publishing, pp. 89–103.

Kenny, Michael, Rycroft, Philip and Sheldon, Jack (2021) *Union at the Crossroads: Can the British State Handle the Challenges of Devolution.* Report by the Bennett Institute for Public Policy Cambridge. The Constitution Society.

Keuffer, Nicolas and Ladner, Andreas (2021) *Local and Regional Autonomy – Indexes and Trends.* In: Callanan, Mark and Loughlin, John (eds.) *A Research Agenda for Regional and Local Government.* Cheltenham: Edward Elgar Publishing, pp. 19–34.

King, Anthony (2001) *Does the United Kingdom Still Have a Constitution?* London: Sweet and Maxwell.

Kirgis, Paul F. (2014) *Bargaining with Consequences: Leverage and Coercion in Negotiation.* Harvard Negotiation Law Review, Volume 19, pp. 69–128.

Kjær, Anne Mette (2011) *Rhodes' Contribution to Governance Theory: Praise, Criticism and the Future Governance Debate.* Public Administration, Volume 89, Issue 1, pp. 101–113.

Kropp, Sabine (2010) *Kooperativer Föderalismus und Politikverflechtung.* Wiesbaden: Springer VS.

Kropp, Sabine (2011) *Politikverflechtung – und kein Ende? Zur Reformfähigkeit des deutschen Föderalismus*. In: Gagnon, Alain-G. and Sturm, Roland (eds.) *Föderalismus als Verfassungsrealität Deutschland und Kanada im Vergleich*. Baden-Baden: Nomos, pp. 15–37.

Lauth, Hans-Joachim (ed.) (2014) *Analytische Konzeption für den Vergleich politischer Systeme. Politische Systeme im Vergleich: Formale und informelle Institutionen im politischen Prozess*. Oldenbourg: De Gruyter, pp. 3–50.

Lauth, Hans-Joachim (2016) *Formale und informelle Institutionen in der vergleichenden Politikwissenschaft*. In: Lauth, Hans-Joachim, Kneuer, Marianne and Pickel, Gert (eds.) *Handbuch Vergleichende Politikwissenschaft*. Wiesbaden: Springer VS, pp. 181–195.

Lee, Simon (2017) *The Gathering Storm: Federalization and Constitutional Change in the United Kingdom*. In: Eccleston, Richard and Krever, Richard (eds.) *The Future of Federalism – Intergovernmental Financial Relations in an Age of Austerity*. Cheltenham: Edward Elgar Publishing, pp. 124–144.

Lehmbruch, Gerhard (1976) *Parteienwettbewerb im Bundesstaat*. Stuttgart: Verlag W. Kohlhammer.

Lehmbruch, Gerhard (1998) *Parteienwettbewerb im Bundesstaat: Regelsysteme und Spannungslagen im Institutionengefüge der Bundesrepublik Deutschland*. 2nd edition. Wiesbaden: Westdeutscher Verlag.

Lijphart, Arend (2012) *Patterns of Democracy*. New Haven, CT: Yale University Press.

Lowndes, Vivien (2018) *Institutionalism*. In: Lowndes, Vivien, Marsh, David and Stoker, Gerry (eds.) *Theory and Methods in Political Science*. 4th edition. London: Palgrave Macmillan, pp. 54–74.

Lowndes, Vivien and Roberts, Mark (2013) *Why Institutions Matter*. 4th edition. London: Palgrave Macmillan.

Marks, Gary, Hooghe, Liesbet and Schakel, Arjan H. (2008) *Measuring Regional Authority*. Regional and Federal Studies, Volume 18, Issue 2–3, pp. 111–121.

Marshall, Joe, Nice, Alex, Haddon, Catherine and Hogarth, Raphael (2020) *Coronavirus Act 2020*. Explainer. 26 March. Institute for Government. https://www.instituteforgovernment.org.uk/explainers/coronavirus-act

Martin, Ciaran (2021) *Resist, Reform or Re-Run? Short- and Long-Term Reflections on Scotland and Independence Referendums. Research and practitioners' Insight*. Oxford: Blavatnik School of Government Oxford.

Mason, Rowena (2020) *Keir Starmer: Only a Federal UK 'Can Repair Shattered Trust in Politics'*. 26 January. The Guardian. https://www.theguardian.com/politics/2020/jan/26/rebecca-long-bailey-calls-for-greater-powers-for-scotland-and-wales

Matthews, Felicity (2018) *Majoritarianism Reinterpreted: Effective Representation and the Quality of Westminster Democracy*. Parliamentary Affairs, Volume 71, Issue 1, pp. 50–72.

McEwen, Nicola (2017) *Still Better Together? Purpose and Power in Intergovernmental Councils in the UK*. Regional and Federal Studies, Volume 27, Issue 5, pp. 667–690.

McEwen, Nicola (2021) *Negotiating Brexit: Power Dynamics in British Intergovernmental Relations*. Regional Studies, Volume 55, Issue 9, pp. 1538–1549.

McEwen, Nicola and Petersohn, Bettina (2015) *Between Autonomy and Interdependence: The Challenges of Shared Rule after the Scottish Referendum*. The Political Quarterly, Volume 86, Issue 2, pp. 192–200.

McEwen, Nicola, Kenny, Michael, Sheldon, Jack and Brown Swan, Coree (2018) *Reforming Intergovernmental Relations in the United Kingdom*. Edinburgh: Centre on Constitutional Change and Cambridge: Bennett Institute for Public Policy.

McEwen, Nicola, Kenny, Michael, Sheldon, Jack and Brown Swan, Coree (2020) *Intergovernmental Relations in the UK: Time for a Radical Overhaul?* The Political Quarterly, Volume 91, Issue 3, pp. 632–640.

McEwen, Nicola, Petersohn, Bettina and Brown Swan, Coree (2015) *Intergovernmental Relations and Parliamentary Scrutiny: A Comparative Overview*. Edinburgh: Centre on Constitutional Change.

McEwen, Nicola, Swenden, Wilfried and Bolleyer, Nicole (2012a) *Introduction: Political Opposition in a Multi-Level Context*. British Journal of Politics and International Relations, Volume 14, Issue 2, pp. 187–197.

McEwen, Nicola, Swenden, Wilfried and Bolleyer, Nicole (2012b) *Intergovernmental Relations in the UK: Continuity in a Time of Change?* British Journal of Politics and International Relations, Volume 14, Issue 2, pp. 323–343.

Meuser, Micheal und Nagel, Ulrike (2009) *Das Experteninterview – konzeptionelle Grundlagen und methodische Anlage*. In: Pickel, Susanne, Pickel, Gert, Lauth, Hans-Joachim and Jahn, Detlef (eds.) *Methoden der vergleichenden Politik- und Sozialwissenschaft*. Wiesbaden: Springer VS, pp. 465–479.

Mitchell, James (2010) *Two Models of Devolution: A Framework for Analysis*. In: Stolz, Klaus (ed.) *Ten Years of Devolution in the United Kingdom: Snapshot at a Moving Target*. Augsburg: Wißner-Verlag, pp. 52–71.

Mueller, Sean (2011) *The Politics of Local Autonomy: Measuring Cantonal (De) Centralisation in Switzerland*. Space and Polity, Volume 15, Issue 3, pp. 213–239.

Muno, Wolfgang (2009) *Fallstudien und die vergleichende Methode*. In: Pickel, Susanne, Pickel, Gert, Lauth, Hans-Joachim and Jahn, Detlef (eds.) *Methoden der vergleichenden Politik- und Sozialwissenschaft*. Wiesbaden: Springer VS, pp. 113–131.

O'Neill, Michael (2004) *Devolution and British Politics*. London: Routledge.

Parker, Jeffrey (2015) *Comparative Federalism and Intergovernmental Agreements: Analyzing Australia, Canada, Germany, South Africa, Switzerland and the United States*. London. Routledge.

Parry, Richard (2012) *The Civil Service and Intergovernmental Relations in the Post-Devolution UK*. British Journal of Politics and International Relations, Volume 14, Issue 2, pp. 285–302.

Pasquier, Romain (2021) *Devolution, Functional Decentralisation or Recentralisation? Convergence and Divergence in the European Territorial Governance*. In: Callanan, Mark and Loughlin, John (eds.) *A Research Agenda for Regional and Local Government*. Cheltenham: Edward Elgar Publishing, pp. 49–62.

Petak, Zdravko (2004) *How to Measure Decentralization: the Case-Study from Central European Countries*. Workshop paper. WOW3: The Third Pentannual Workshop on the Workshop, Building Social Capital and Self-Governing Capabilities in Diverse Societies. Bloomington, 2–6 June.

Petersohn, Bettina, Behnke, Nathalie and Rhode, Eva Maria (2015) *Negotiating Territorial Change in Multinational States: Party Preferences, Negotiating Power and the Role of the Negotiation Mode*. Publius, Volume 45, Issue 4, pp. 626–652.

Pickel, Susanne and Pickel, Gert (2009) *Qualitative Interviews als Verfahren des Ländervergleichs*. In: Pickel, Susanne, Pickel, Gert, Lauth, Hans-Joachim and Jahn, Detlef (eds.) *Methoden der vergleichenden Politik- und Sozialwissenschaft*. Wiesbaden: Springer VS, pp. 441–464.

Pierce, Roger (2008) *Research Methods in Politics – a Practical Guide*. London: Sage.

Poirier, Johanne and Saunders, Cheryl (2015a) *Comparing Intergovernmental Relations in Federal Systems: An Introduction*. In: Poirier, Johanne, Saunders, Cheryl and Kincaid, John (eds.) *Intergovernmental Relations in Federal Systems*. Oxford: Oxford University Press, pp. 1–13.

Poirier, Johanne and Saunders, Cheryl (2015b) *Conclusion: Comparative Experience of Intergovernmental Relations in Federal Systems*. In: Poirier, Johanne, Saunders, Cheryl and Kincaid, John (eds.) *Intergovernmental Relations in Federal Systems*. Oxford: Oxford University Press, pp. 440–498.

Poirier, Johanne, Saunders, Cheryl and Kincaid, John (2015) *Intergovernmental Relations in Federal Systems*. Oxford: Oxford University Press.

Radical Federalism (2021) *We, the People: The Case for Radical Federalism*. 14 January. https://www.radicalfederalism.com/our-publications

Requejo, Ferran (2011) *Decentralisation and Federal and Regional Asymmetries in Comparative Politics*. In: Requejo, Ferran and Nagel, Hans-Jürgen (eds.) *Federalism Beyond Federations*. London: Routledge, pp. 1–12.

Ridder, Hans-Gerd (2016). *Case Study Research: Approaches, Methods, Contribution to Theory*. Augsburg: Rainer Hampp Verlag.

Rodden, Jonathan (2004) *Comparative Federalism and Decentralization – On Meaning and Measurement*. Comparative Politics, Volume 36, Issue 4, pp. 481–500.

Ruane, Janet M. (2005) *Essentials of Research Methods: A Guide to Social Research*. Oxford: Oxford University Press.

Russell, Meg (2016) *Parliament: A Significant Constraint on Government*. In: Heffernan, Richard, Hay, Collin, Russell, Meg and Cowley, Philip (eds.) *Developments in British Politics 10*. London: Palgrave Macmillan, pp. 99–121.

Ryan, Matt (2018) *The Comparative Method*. In: Lowndes, Vivien, Marsh, David and Stoker, Gerry (eds.) *Theory and Methods in Political Science*. 4th edition. London: Palgrave Macmillan, pp. 271–289.

Scharpf, Fritz (1997) *Games Real Actors Play – Actor-Centered Institutionalism in Policy Research*. Boulder: Westview Press.

Scharpf, Fritz (2000) *Interaktionsformen – Akteurzentrierter Institutionalismus in Der Politikforschung*. Wiesebaden: Springer VS.

Schimmelfennig, Frank, Leuffen, Dirk and Rittberger, Berthold (2015) *The European Union as a System of Differentiated Integration: Interdependence, Politicization and Differentiation*. Journal of European Public Policy, Volume 22, Issue 6, pp. 764–782.

Schneider, Aaron (2003) *Decentralization: Conceptualization and Measurement*. Studies in Comparative International Development, Volume 38, Issue 3, pp. 32–56.

Schütze, Robert (2018) *Introduction: British 'Federalism'?* In: Schütze, Robert and Tierney, Stephen (eds.) *The United Kingdom and the Federal Idea*. Oxford: Hart Publishing, pp. 1–26.

Schütze, Robert and Tierney, Stephen (2018) *The United Kingdom and the Federal Idea*. Oxford: Hart Publishing.

Strohmeier, Gerd (2015) *Does Westminster (Still) Represent the Westminster Model? An Analysis of the Changing Nature of the UK's Political System*. European View, Volume 14, Issue 2, pp. 303–315.

Sturm, Roland (2020) *Föderalismus*. Baden-Baden: Nomos.

Tansey, Oisin (2009) *Process Tracing and Elite Interviewing: A Case for Non-Probability Sampling.* In: Pickel, Susanne, Pickel, Gert, Lauth, Hans-Joachim and Jahn, Detlef (eds.) *Methoden der vergleichenden Politik- und Sozialwissenschaft.* Wiesbaden: Springer VS, pp. 481–496.

Tatham, Michael (2016) *With, Without, or Against the State? How European Regions Play the Brussels Game.* Oxford: Oxford University Press.

Tomkins, Adam (2018) *Shared Rule: What the UK Could Learn from Federalism.* In: Schütze, Robert and Tierney, Stephen (eds.) *The United Kingdom and the Federal Idea.* Oxford: Hart Publishing, pp. 73–99.

Trench, Alan (2012) *The Courts and Devolution in the UK.* British Journal of Politics and International Relations, Volume 14, Issue 2, pp. 303–322.

Vromen, Ariadne (2018) *Qualitative Methods.* In: Lowndes, Vivien, Marsh, David and Stoker, Gerry (eds.) *Theory and Methods in Political Science.* 4th edition. London: Palgrave Macmillan, pp. 237–253.

Watts, Ronald L. (2008). *Comparing Federal Systems.* Montreal and Kingston: McGill-Queen's University Press.

Weissert, Carol S. and Fahey, Kevin (2018) *Actor-Centered or Institutional Approaches in Europe and the US: Moving Towards Convergence.* In: Detterbeck, Klaus and Hepburn, Eve (eds.) *Handbook of Territorial Politics.* Cheltenham: Edward Elgar Publishing, pp. 341–353.

Wincott, Daniel, Murray, C. R. G. and Gregory Davies (2021) *The Anglo-British Imaginary and the Rebuilding of the UK's Territorial Constitution after Brexit: Unitary State or Union State?* Territory, Politics, Governance, Volume 10, Issue 5, pp. 696–713.

Wright, Deil S. (1988) *Understanding Intergovernmental Relations.* 3rd edition. Belmont, TN: Brooks/Cole Publishing.

Wyn Jones, Richard and Royles, Elin (2012) *Wales in the World: Intergovernmental Relations and Sub-State Diplomacy.* British Journal of Politics and International Relations, Volume 14, Issue 2, pp. 250–269.

3 Self-rule and the Devolution of Political, Legislative and Fiscal Authority

Over centuries the UK evolved into a union of integrated territories dominated since the 11th century by English interests and statecraft. Wales was annexed by England as early as 1283, and under Henry VIII become a full part of the Kingdom of England by the Acts of Union in 1536 and 1542. Though England imposed its laws and language onto Wales, the latter assimilated but preserved its national and cultural identity (Mitchell 2009, 8). Almost two centuries passed before the Kingdom of Scotland entered into a political union with England by the 1707 Act of Union. When England 'took over' its northern neighbour, Scottish elites could negotiate considerably more favourable terms than Wales and maintained separate legal, education, church and local government systems. Despite being ruled by a common monarch and the Westminster Parliament, Scotland retained its distinctive institutions with a reasonable degree of territorial self-determination and autonomy in regard to its church, education and legal systems. About a century later, the Act of Union 1800 abolished the Irish Parliament and created the United Kingdom of Britain and Ireland. Ireland did not integrate with the rest of the UK but kept a wide range of institutions akin to a colony under British sovereignty (O'Neill 2004, 21 et seq.; cf. Mitchell 2009, 10 et seq.; Sturm 2015, 314–315).[1] The demand for home rule in Ireland was substantially stronger than in Scotland, which drove British-Irish relations during the second half of the 19th century, following the Irish potato famine of 1845, a period of mass starvation, disease and emigration.[2] It took three attempts (after 1893 and 1912) until a Home Rule Bill was eventually passed in 1914, but due to the outbreak of World War I, the bill never took effect. The War of Independence between 1919 and 1921 resulted in the Ireland Act (1920) and the Anglo-Irish Treaty (1921) partitioning the island of Ireland into an independent Irish state with 26 counties in the south and six counties in the north belonging to the UK, both operating with separate parliaments. For a centralised unitary state such as the UK, Northern Ireland enjoyed an exceptional level of autonomy of financial and legislative powers, for instance in the fields of education and housing. The Catholic minority, however, was excluded from the debates and decisions regarding the newly formed Northern Irish polity, the borders of which had been

DOI: 10.4324/9781003349952-3

designed to ensure that Protestant unionists comprised the majority of the population (Mitchell 2009, 70). Despite systematic discrimination against the Catholic population, until the late 1960s, the situation in Northern Ireland remained relatively stable. Westminster retained the ultimate right to rule over Northern Ireland's affairs but, until 1969, did not use its powers to interfere (O'Neill 2004, 43), which is why O'Neill (ibid.) suggested: "To that extent, relations between Westminster and Stormont were more akin to a federal than to a merely devolved arrangement, but without the constitutional safeguards for the rights of minorities usually found in federal polities."

Between 1886 and 1997, the UK was one of the most centralised states in Western Europe, and, except for short periods, dispersed little political power across its territories. While the constituent parts maintained and cultivated their national identities, within Scotland, Ireland and to a lesser extent in Wales, the UK was perceived as a political union of multiple nations rather than as a unitary state (Keating 2004, 319–320).[3] And yet, to quote O'Neill (2004, 14) again: "The union state was, and it has remained, a project conferring much the greater advantage on its principal constituent. Political and material self-interest was discernible in the political culture of unionism."[4] The rise of nationalism during the 1960s marks the starting point of the modern devolution settlement (Deacon 2012, 5). Until then, Wales and Scotland had tolerated the strong dependency on England. However, due to economic and political disparities, national movements were growing, and the SNP and Plaid Cymru became increasingly electorally successful.[5] As Conservative MPs from Scotland and Wales started to lose their seats in Parliament, the question of adequate political representation for Scottish and Welsh interests became more and more pressing. For the administrations of Margaret Thatcher and John Major, decentralising legal authority was unpopular and seen as a step towards the break-up of the Union. Nevertheless, when New Labour came to power in 1997, it began to implement its campaign promises to decentralise political and legislative powers (Becker 2002, 63–64; Schieren 2010, 133–136; Deacon 2012, 5 et seq.).

Tony Blair's government adopted a pragmatic, "piecemeal" approach to devolution with little appetite for comprehensive reforms to integrate the Union (Jeffery 2009, 292). It was careful to avoid further battles with the opposition in Parliament and with the nationalist movements in Scotland and Wales. Opening up a discussion about the fundamental principles of Westminster and Whitehall would have presented a great electoral and organisational risk to the new Government and to the devolution project (Bradbury 2021, 275–278). Yet, the devolution process was revolutionary at the time and introduced a "multi-layered constitution," which subsequently added a great deal of complexity to the UK's unitary structures without settling calls for more territorial authority (Leyland 2011, 252). As Hazell (2015, 6) put it: "Devolution had got off to an easy start, lulling Whitehall into a sense of false security, which became complacency and neglect […]

with little regard for spillover effects or their impact on the UK as a whole." Although for many Westminster politicians Parliament has remained the ultimate source of legitimate authority which cannot be shared with or divided across different levels of government, devolution challenged "the mystique of the sovereign and all-powerful nation state and introduc[ed] a more pluralistic way of thinking about political authority" (Keating 2004, 326).[6] Explaining the self-rule dimension in relation to decentralisation and comparative federalism provides an essential basis for this study to comprehending the devolved administrations' relational autonomy (cf. Poirier and Saunders 2015, 445). This chapter will therefore examine in greater detail the allocation of political, legislative and fiscal authority across the different levels of government, including overlapping and concurrent legislative powers.

The devolution of political authority

By enabling substate legislatures and executives, and thereby citizens, to take decisions over a defined area of competences (Cheema and Rondinelli 2007, 6–7), political decentralisation changes the constitutional structures of a state (Pasquier 2021, 59). The Scotland Act, the Government of Wales Act and the Northern Ireland Act[7] of 1998 established in the following year legislatures in all three non-English parts of the UK. The different devolution settlements were not symmetrical but reflected the different ambitions and motives across the UK's territories. Only the Scottish Parliament and Northern Ireland Assembly were equipped with primary legislative powers, while Wales was more integrated with England and devolution enjoyed less popular support. In contrast to Scotland and Northern Ireland, where territorial autonomy enjoyed vast public support in the 1997 referendums (74.3 per cent in Scotland and 71.1 per cent in Northern Ireland), Welsh devolution was driven by the preservation of culture and language rather than self-determination (only 50.2 per cent voted for devolution). As a consequence, section 31 of the Government of Wales Act 1998 required the National Assembly for Wales to consult the Secretary of State about the Welsh executive's programme and it could only pass secondary legislation with the consent of Westminster (O'Neill 2004, 174–176). It was not before another referendum held in March 2011 that a clear majority of 63.5 per cent of Welsh voters opted for the conferral of full legislative powers to the Assembly (Leyland 2011, 261). All three devolved legislatures are elected for a four-year fixed term. The 60 members of the Senedd for Wales and the 129 members of the Scottish Parliament are elected through an additional-member-system combining representatives from majoritarian, single-member constituencies (40 in Wales and 73 in Scotland) and proportionally elected representatives from regional party lists (20 additional members from 5 regions in Wales and 56 additional members from 8 regions in Scotland). The Scottish Parliament building in Holyrood[8] in Edinburgh and the Senedd building a Cardiff Bay are modern buildings embracing open, transparent design with a semicircular seat order that reflects their working principles of deliberation, cooperation and dialogue rather than of adversarial competition. The First Ministers of Scotland and Wales are nominated by the members of their respective legislatures and subsequently appointed by the monarch.

The Scottish Parliament scrutinises the executive and can also initiate legislation. Notwithstanding its commitments to power sharing, accountability, transparency and equal opportunities, debates between Labour and SNP Members of the Scottish Parliament (MSPs) have at times been strongly adversarial, Scottish ministers have dominated the legislature and parliamentary committees have been less effective than envisaged (Cairney 2014, 160). In 1999 and 2003, Scottish Labour and the Liberal Democrats led the executive as a coalition based on partnership agreements. Although coalitions are more likely than for Westminster due to the additional member elections system, between 2007 and 2021 Scotland was run by a single-party government: 2007–2011 and since 2016 as a minority government; and since 2021 in coalition with the Scottish Greens. As part of the Scotland Act 2012, the Scottish Executive was renamed to the Scottish Government. The National Assembly for Wales was initially set up as an extensive administrative body to implement law but not to legislate itself. The head of the Welsh Executive carried the title First Secretary and only later became the First Minister (Sturm 2010, 113). The Welsh Executive and Assembly were not formally separated but rather the former was a committee of the latter without independent powers. Only the Government of Wales Act 2006 formally separated the executive, which called itself the National Assembly Government and after 2011 the Welsh Government,[9] from the National Assembly and provided the ministers with special executive powers (Deacon et al. 2018, 84–86).[10] The Assembly's committees have reviewing and scrutinising functions regarding legislation, policies and implementation (Deacon 2012, 142 et seq.). Since the establishment of the Welsh Assembly, the Labour Party has been in power either on their own or with a junior coalition partner.[11] In May 2020, the Assembly was officially renamed the Senedd Cymru (Welsh Parliament) to reflect its status as a national parliament, and Assembly Members (AMs) consequently became Members of the Senedd (MSs).

Although Scotland and Wales are the main focus of this study, for the purpose of completion and to clarify why they are difficult to compare with Northern Ireland, it seems useful to give the latter slightly more space here. The establishment of the Northern Ireland Assembly and Executive aimed at ending the cycle of violence and terror and stabilising the region by replacing direct rule from Westminster and allowing unionist Protestants and republican Catholics to participate in territorial decision-making. The devolved institutions in Northern Ireland partly resemble the Scottish model, but they are essentially designed to facilitate conflict mediation across the segregated communities and to deal with the question of Irish unification.

The organisation of the Assembly was informed by the idea of *consociationalism*, a response to intense divisions according to which power is shared across the different political and religious communities to prevent domination of the Protestant majority over the Catholic minority. According to Garry (2016, 1) "This involves recognizing the distinct community or identity groups that are in conflict, facilitating the sharing of power between the rival groups in a highly inclusive coalition government, and providing each competing identity group with veto powers to protect their group interests." The 1998 Good Friday and the 2006 St Andrews Agreements feature the four main elements of consociationalism: inclusive power-sharing, veto rights for minorities, proportionality and cultural autonomy (op. cit., 7). These principles are implemented in various ways. The Northern Ireland Executive is set up to produce inclusive, multiparty coalitions of 12 ministers who must commit to peaceful, democratic and non-discriminatory conduct. After their election, Members of the Legislative Assembly (MLA) need to register as either nationalist, unionist or other, and the appointment of the First and the Deputy First Ministers require cross-community support.[12] Instead of having an official opposition, the executive is a multiparty government in which the allocation of ministerial portfolios reflects the number of seats of each party in the Assembly.[13] Legislative decisions need either a parallel consent of the majority of the whole Assembly and of the majorities of both nationalist and unionist, or a weighted consent, whereby 60 per cent of all MLAs and at least 40 per cent of the representatives of each community have to vote in favour of a bill (O'Neill 2004, 199–200; Leyland 2011, 263–634; Garry 2016, 7–8).[14]

Until today, this system of power-sharing has been fragile and characterised by mutual distrust.[15] Between 1999 and 2007, the Assembly was suspended four times by the UK Government, including a lengthy suspension between October 2002 and May 2007, and relaunched after the St Andrews Agreement in 2006.[16] The Democratic Unionist Party (DUP) and Sinn Féin set up a fragile cooperative relationship. From 2013 onwards, disagreements within the executive over welfare reforms strained the work of the Assembly, and the relationship between DUP and Sinn Féin deteriorated. On 26 January 2017, the coalition between the DUP and Sinn Féin collapsed after First Minister Arlene Foster (DUP), who was accused of corruption and mishandling about £500 million through the Renewable Heating Incentive scheme, refused to step down from office. Subsequently, the late Deputy First Minister Martin McGuiness (Sinn Féin) resigned and his party withdrew from the government (cf. Birrell and Heenan 2017, 475–476). In the following elections on 2 March 2017, the unionists lost their majority in the Assembly for the first time since 1921, Sinn Féin was the biggest beneficiary of the new elections, and moderate parties, such as the Social Democratic and Labour Party (SDLP), the Alliance Party of Northern Ireland (APNI) and the Green Party, made some relative gains (considering that the number of MLAs shrunk from 108 to 90). The legacy of the Good Friday Agreement was put further at risk when Theresa May's minority government entered a supply and confidence agreement with the DUP after the General Election in June 2017. During the suspension of the Northern Ireland Assembly between 2017 and the beginning of 2020, only the DUP could thus effectively influence the Brexit negotiations at Westminster. In contrast to the referendum result and the will of most other parties in Northern Ireland, the DUP promoted their preferences for a hard Brexit and put strong pressure on Theresa May to negotiate a deal with the EU that would treat Northern Ireland differently from the rest of the UK (Heenan and Birrell 2018, 309). Their privileged position in the UK Parliament ended abruptly when Boris Johnson became Prime Minister with an absolute majority. In May 2022, Sinn Féin (27 MLAs; 29 per cent of votes) even overtook the DUP (25 MLAs; 21 per cent) as the largest party in the Assembly. Yet, at the time of writing this book the Northern Ireland Assembly remained suspended, as the DUP refused to support the appointment of the Assembly's speaker unless the Northern Ireland Protocol was altered according to their demands.

The devolution of legislative authority

In addition to political authority, devolution in the UK refers predominantly to the decentralisation of legislative and fiscal authority. A simple approach to the allocation of legislative powers to different governments in federal systems is to constitutionally assign a list of *enumerated powers* to one level and to provide the other level with *residual powers* that are not explicitly listed. Enumerated powers can be either *exhaustive* to narrow down the competences of governments or *indicative* which leaves flexibility over what governments can legislate on (Hueglin and Fenna 2010, 149–150). Watts (2008, 85 et seq.) distinguishes further between different types of legislative authority within federations: exclusive legislative authority, residual authority, concurrent legislative authority, shared authority and emergency overriding powers.[17] These are helpful to describe whether powers are shared or autonomously exercised. Federal governments typically have *exclusive legislative authority* over international affairs, defence, international trade, monetary and economic policies, major taxes, major infrastructure and pensions. *Residual authority* refers to powers that are not explicitly allocated to one level and are typically kept by the centre. Whereas this section is concerned with the allocation of exclusive (or enumerated) and residual legislative authority, the next section will focus on *concurrent legislative authority* which is not exclusively assigned to one level but rather is overlapping and complementarily exercised by different levels (either implicitly or explicitly). *Shared authority* is distinct from concurrent legislative authority and requires the consent of all levels, which have exclusive power over an area but no paramountcy. Some federations adopt *emergency overriding powers* to provide the federal government with the ability to interfere under exceptional circumstances in matters assigned to the constituents. Emergency overriding powers are not explicitly assigned to the UK Government, which is constitutionally speaking not superior to the devolved executives, but inherent in the sovereignty of Westminster. De jure, central government can act on every area of public policy and make laws for Scotland, Wales and Northern Ireland, if it has valid reasons to interfere. An act of Parliament can then allow the UK Government to overrule the devolved executives (SG4, WG8) (cf. Birrell 2012, 11). According to Section 58 of the Scotland Act 1998, the Secretary of State for Scotland can also prevent or require actions from the Scottish Government (Lazarowicz and McFadden 2018, 146–147). Furthermore, when the Northern Ireland Assembly is suspended, the UK Government exercises emergency overriding powers by secondary legislation (Order in Council). This was the case from 2002 to 2007 when direct rule was imposed by the UK Government, and between January 2017 and 2020, when Westminster and Whitehall also had to take certain decisions in transferred areas under careful consideration to respect the devolution settlement.

The initial transfer of legislative powers from the central government to the devolved administrations was a remarkably 'smooth' process (Gallagher 2012, 198). It was simply the responsibilities of the Scottish Office, the Welsh Office and the Northern Ireland Department that were handed over to the new legislatures. Even though the initial transfer of authority to the different parts followed three distinct approaches, over the last two decades they have adopted a similar model to envisage a dual allocation of power. This has created potent territorial legislatures with responsibility over residual powers that are not enumerated (explicitly reserved) to Westminster and Whitehall.[18] Similarly to federal polities, the Scotland Act 1998 established exclusive legislative authority over an extensive list of enumerated powers reserved to the UK Parliament. Reserved matters have covered the constitution;[19] political parties; public/civil service; defence and treason; as well as a long list of specific reservations for financial and economic matters;[20] home affairs;[21] trade and industry;[22] energy;[23] transport;[24] social security;[25] regulation of the professions; employment;[26] health and medicines; media and culture;[27] miscellaneous;[28] control of weapons; time; outer space (see Schedule 5). Neither can the Scottish Parliament modify law on reserved matters,[29] the European Communities Act 1972 nor the Human Rights Act 1998 (see Scotland Act 1998, Schedule 4). In contrast to federations where the federal government has residual authority over a set of not explicitly specified powers, the reserved powers model devolves anything to the Scottish Parliament that is not allocated to the UK Parliament: health and social work; education and training; local government and housing; justice and policing; agriculture, forestry and fisheries; the environment; tourism, sport and heritage; economic development and internal transport (Cabinet Office and Office of the Secretary of State for Scotland 2019). Various provisions of the Scotland Act allow for a further transfer of authority from the centre to Scotland.[30] Following the modest recommendations of the Calman

Commission,[31] the 2010 Coalition Government transferred further responsibilities to the Scottish Parliament (Birrell 2012, 23). Apart from changing the name of the Scottish Executive to the Scottish Government and transferring important fiscal competences, the new Scotland Act 2012 devolved legislative authority on matters relating to air weapons and executive powers on the misuse of drugs, drink-driving alcohol limits and the administration of the elections to the Scottish Parliament.

During the campaign of the Scottish independence referendum in 2014, former Prime Minister David Cameron promised a maximum devolution of powers to keep Scotland in the Union. After a majority of 55.3 per cent voted against secession, the Smith Commission was set up to recommend which new powers should be given to the Scottish Parliament. The Scotland Act 2016 then added to the list of enumerated powers substantial legislative authority on social security; employment support; equal opportunities; transport (road signs, speed limits, rail franchise); energy efficiency; onshore oil and gas extraction; consumer advocacy; the authority to manage the Crown Estate; Ofcom Scotland and railway policing; as well as new tax and borrowing powers. The new powers over social security "broke new ground" within the previously centralised welfare system and transferred competences from the Department for Work and Pensions to the new Scottish Social Security Administration. These include control over substantial benefits for disability living allowance, attendance allowance, carer's allowance, aspects of Universal Credit, winter fuel payments, funeral payments and the ability to top up reserved benefits of the UK Government and to create new benefits in areas not covered by existing UK-wide benefits. The Scottish Government can also change the conditions under which benefits are paid – for instance in regard to the frequency of payments. However, the new welfare powers did not come with additional resources but must be financed by reduction in spending in other areas (Bell and Vaillancourt 2018, 99).

Wales also inherited the main competences and functions of the Wales Office, including enumerated powers over secondary legislation and statutory instruments; the appointments of chairs and boards of public bodies; budget spending; the acquisition of land and the building of roads. Unlike in Scotland and Northern Ireland, in 1998, the National Assembly for Wales was not given full law-making powers but merely operated as a 'corporate body' or an 'advisory body' to Westminster. While the Assembly received executive and administrative powers to pass secondary legislation, it could only act by enabling legislation of the UK Parliament (Birrell 2012, 12; Bradbury 2021, 126–128). For Bradbury (2021, 130):

> It was not a legislature; instead its primary role was to bring accountability to executive government and in the sense that it did have a legislative role this was only to deliberate on statutory instruments placed before it by Welsh ministers to act under primary law still made at

Westminster. Nevertheless, within executive and secondary legislative powers lay significant capacity to shape key policy areas, notably economic development, health and education.

The Government of Wales Act 2006 marked a major step in enhancing the Assembly's constitutional status. It separated the legislature from the executive and provided the former with the power to pass its own laws, known as Measures, through Legislative Competence Orders within the scope of its competences. Because the Assembly's ability to pass Legislative Competence Orders was restricted by a lengthy and complex procedure that involved 11 stages and the approval of the UK Parliament, these were mainly used for non-controversial issues. The act also provided for a public referendum on the devolution of primary legislative authority. Subsequently, on 3 March 2011, 63.5 per cent of Welsh voters decided that the Senedd should receive full law-making powers in 20 conferred policy areas, which made the passage of Welsh legislation significantly easier and faster. The Welsh Assembly Government also simply became the Welsh Government (Birrell 2012, 18–20). In terms of legislative scope, Schedule 7 to the Government of Wales Act 2006 listed 20 broad enumerated areas within which the Assembly could exercise legislative competence: agriculture, forestry, animals, plants and rural development; ancient monuments and historic buildings; culture; economic development; education and training; environment; fire and rescue services and fire safety; food; health and health services; highways and transport; housing; local government; National Assembly for Wales; public administration; social welfare; sport and recreation; tourism; town and country planning; water and flood defence and Welsh language. While the Government of Wales Act 2006 brought Wales closer to the devolved models in Scotland and Northern Ireland, the conferred powers model for Wales was still different from the reserved powers model. Unlike the Scottish Parliament, which enjoyed residual powers over areas that were not under exclusive legislative authority of Westminster, the Welsh Assembly was provided with an exhaustive list of enumerated powers. Areas that were not explicitly listed in Schedule 7 remained under the residual authority of the UK Parliament. This required regular interaction between the different governments, particularly when the Welsh Government had to ask Whitehall to extend its legal competences. The UK Government could still make the transfer of powers dependent on how the Welsh Government intended to use them. According to an official of the Welsh Parliament: "The big friction or the big annoyance in Wales around conferred model, particularly from Welsh Government point of view, was always that if you went to the UK Government to ask for more power, they'd always ask you how you were going use it." (WP3)

Following the recommendations of the Silk Commission (officially the Commission on Devolution in Wales), the Wales Act 2014 sought to manifest the conferred powers model in Wales[32] and to establish a clear division of powers. In reality, however, it did not produce exclusive jurisdictions but implicitly assigned concurrent legislative authority to different legislatures. This became evident in occasional disputes over the need for the Assembly's legislative consent under the Sewel Convention when Westminster intended to pass legislation in conferred areas. On two remarkable occasions, the Supreme Court ruled in favour of the Senedd and allowed Welsh legislation to overrule UK acts when they touched upon a conferred matter.[33] The impact of the court's judgements potentially enabled the Welsh Assembly to legislate on a wide scope of 'silent' matters within UK legislation that represented not necessarily the primary focus of a bill but still were somehow related to the Assembly's competences. Realising the far-reaching impact that this could have on the UK Government's ability to govern for Wales, the allocation of legal responsibility was consequently altered. The Wales Act 2017 then abandoned the conferred powers model and introduced a reserved powers model for Wales from April 2019 on, which gave the Senedd similar powers to those in Scotland and Northern Ireland.[34] Schedule 7A, Part 1 of the Wales Act 2017 exclusive legislative authority over the following general areas to the UK Parliament: the constitution; public service; political parties; a single legal jurisdiction of England and Wales; tribunals; foreign affairs and defence. The act also re-reserved some competences to Westminster (Kellam 2018). Part 2 listed a range for specific reservations to the areas already devolved to Wales, and Schedule 7B set out certain restrictions on the powers of the Assembly, for instance, to prevent the modification of reserved legislation, private law, certain criminal offences and enactments of the Human Rights Act 1998 (Welsh Parliament 2021). As a senior Welsh Government official suggested, changing the principle of power allocation reduced the ambivalence of the previous model:

> When we had the conferred powers model, the ambiguities of that model was such that we did from time to time have disagreement about whether something was within the Assembly's competence or not. Since we've moved to the reserved powers model, it has been rather clearer as to what is within the competence or not.
>
> (WG8)

The Northern Ireland Assembly operates under a model similar but slightly different to the reserved powers model. The Northern Ireland Act 1998 provides exhaustive lists for excepted and reserved matters.[35] Schedule 3 of the Act establishes the reserved matters on which the Assembly can legislate with the consent of the UK Secretary of State for Northern Ireland (Burrows 2000, 66–67). These include firearms and explosives; financial services and pensions regulation; broadcasting; import and export controls; navigation and civil aviation; international trade and financial markets; telecommunications and postage; the foreshore and seabed; disqualification from Senedd membership; consumer safety and intellectual property.

60 *Devolution of Political, Legislative and Fiscal Authority*

The excepted matters under Schedule 2 are the Crown; the UK Parliament; international relations; the defence of the realm; control of nuclear, biological and chemical weapons and other weapons of mass destruction; dignities and titles of honour; treason; nationality immigration, citizenship; taxation (under any law applying to the UK as a whole, e.g. stamp duty); national insurance; political parties, elections and referendums; national security; nuclear energy and nuclear installations, regulation of sea fishing outside the Northern Ireland zone; regulation of activities in outer space. The Northern Ireland Assembly has full legislative competence over residual powers that are not explicitly reserved or excepted. These transferred matters include health and social services; education; employment and skills; agriculture; social security; pensions and child support; housing; economic development; local government; environmental issues, including planning; transport; culture and sport; the Northern Ireland Civil Service; equal opportunities and justice and policing (Cabinet Office and Northern Ireland Office 2019). Due to the absence of strong calls for new powers, the legislative competences of the Northern Ireland Assembly have not profoundly expanded over time; except for criminal justice and policing, which were transferred by the Northern Ireland Act 1998 (Devolution of Policing and Justice Functions) Order in 2010.[36] Table 3.1 provides a broad overview of the wide range of *residual powers* inexplicitly devolved to the Scottish Parliament, Welsh Parliament and Northern Ireland Assembly.

Overlapping and concurrent powers

The devolution settlement aimed at a clear separation of authority in order for the different administrations to operate largely independently within their jurisdictions. Entwistle et al. (2014) compared this to a 'layer cake' whereby a shift of authority from one to another level resembles a zero-sum transaction. However, as modern policy challenges are interconnected and spill over across different levels (McEwen and Petersohn 2015, 193–196), in reality, assigning authority over certain policies exclusively to one level often leads to overlapping responsibilities (Watts 2008, 83–87), Territorial autonomy is therefore not merely a question of decentralisation but depends on the degree to which interdependency interferes with and constrains the actions of governments (Bolleyer and Thorlakson 2012, 570; Bolleyer 2018, 47), which is why we need to look at the division of tasks in areas of shared and concurrent responsibility (Poirier and Saunders 2015, 445). First and foremost, legislative authority in the UK is not integrated or shared. The Sewel Convention may be seen as a weak form of shared authority, as it requires the consent of the devolved legislatures if Westminster seeks to pass a bill that affects their responsibilities. But the convention is neither legally binding nor a case of joint decision-making. Even though the Scotland Act 1998 gave the Scottish Parliament and Executive some say over subordinate legislation by the UK Parliament (Lazarowicz and McFadden

Table 3.1 Residual powers of the devolved legislatures

Matters devolved to the Scottish Parliament	Matters devolved to the Welsh Parliament	Matters transferred to the Northern Ireland Assembly
Health and social work	Agriculture, fisheries, forestry and rural development	Health and social services
Education and training		Education
Local government and housing	Ancient monuments and historic buildings	Employment and skills
Justice and policing		Agriculture
Agriculture, forestry and fisheries	Culture	Social security
	Economic development	Pensions and child support
Environment	Education and training	Housing
Tourism, sport and heritage	Environment	Economic development
	Fire and rescue services and promotion of fire safety	Local government
Economic development		Environmental issues, including planning
Internal transport	Food	Transport
	Health and health services	Culture and sport
	Highways and transport	Northern Ireland Civil Service
	Housing	Equal opportunities
	Local government	Justice and policing
	National Assembly for Wales	*Reserved matters which require consent*
	Public administration	Firearms and explosives
	Social welfare	Financial services and pensions regulation
	Sport and recreation	Broadcasting
	Tourism	Import and export controls
	Town and country planning	Navigation and civil aviation
	Water and flood defence	International trade and financial markets
	Welsh language	Telecommunications and postage
		Foreshore and seabed
		Disqualification from Assembly membership
		Consumer safety
		Intellectual property

Source: Cabinet Office, Office of the Secretary of State for Scotland, Northern Ireland Office and Office of the Secretary of State for Wales (2019).

2018, 113–114),[37] constitutionally speaking, joint powers do not exist in the UK (Birrell 2012, 14). The supremacy of Parliament presents a major obstacle to introducing a system of shared authority. Only Westminster holds any exclusive legislative authority, which theoretically and in practice puts the idea of a dual allocation of powers into question. The Memorandum of Understanding between the different governments acknowledges that the primary responsibilities of the devolved administrations limit Westminster's scope of action.[38] Although the centre is not supposed to directly interfere in devolved matters, decisions by the UK Government that concern England often have practical repercussions in the other territories (WP6). For instance, macroeconomic policy, which is a reserved matter, links strongly to responsibilities for economic development and other related areas within devolved competence (Bradbury 2021, 97). Hunt (2021, 30) therefore argued "[a] more constitutionally coherent conceptualisation of competence allocation might be to consider the sphere of devolved powers as concurrent, though with a strong presumption of devolved responsibility."[39] The devolution of more powers to Scotland after the 2014 independence referendum contributed strongly to overlapping competences (Jeffery 2015, 277). One Member of the Scottish Parliament suggested: "People would expect that with more devolution there is more separation but actually it is the opposite." (SP1). Powers that were clear-cut before the Scotland Act 2016, particularly in relation to taxation and social security,[40] can no longer be exercised without some cooperation between the different governments (SP2, UKG10). In particular, for Wales, the geographic proximity and a long-shared border have meant that political decisions in England have a profound impact in Wales, and vice versa:

> Our border with England is a lot more porous than the Scottish border with England. In Scotland everyone lives along the central belt. They're much more self-contained, and we're much more intertwined, which makes it much harder to separate everything out but also much harder for people to understand who they need to hold to account and that's not a healthy situation.
>
> (WP3)

Before the National Assembly for Wales received full law-making powers, primary legislative competence was explicitly made concurrent for Wales and could not be exercised without the UK Parliament. Even though the reserved powers model was introduced in Wales other concurrent powers were established in response to the rise of interconnected policy challenges (Hunt 2021, 26).

For about two decades, the devolution settlement has paid little attention to spill over effects of policies introduced in one territory on the other parts. Unlike federal, Whitehall is not used to setting common policy objectives or nationwide standards in the form of framework legislation on which the constituent parts can pass detailed laws to meet their specific circumstances. Even though the centre defines the distribution of resources and has the capacities to produce a greater share of the policy agenda, it did not provide a coherent set of rules and structures to which the devolved administrations could refer in order to prevent disruptive divergence across the UK (Keating 2012, 226). The implementation of EU legislation had been the area to which the idea of concurrent powers applied best (Gallagher 2012, 200), as the devolved competences around agriculture, fisheries and the environment automatically operated under EU law. Yet, by treating de facto concurrent powers as exclusive ones, questions of overlapping and shared responsibility could be ignored in the past (Hunt 2021, 36). Since the UK left the European Single Market, however, the potential for policy divergence has become a threat to its internal economic integrity and can impair the UK Government's ability to implement international agreements (SP2, WG11, UKG10). EU withdrawal has exposed the interdependencies that were previously regulated by the EU's regulatory regime and triggered the need for a stronger integration of jurisdictions. Under the reserved powers model, the devolved administration received the residual authority over retained EU legislation. As a consequence, Brexit-related legislation, such as the Environment Act 2021, introduced some concurrent powers that can be exercised by UK and devolved ministers, for instance in regard to waste and resource efficiency and producer responsibility, including electronic waste tracking. The implications of these dynamics on the integration of legislative authority under a new regime of concurrent powers will be discussed in the following chapters.

The devolution of fiscal authority

Fiscal authority is an essential source of power, legitimacy and stability, as well as of political conflict, and depends on the right to decide when, to what extent and for which purpose revenues are raised and how they are administered (Agranoff 2004, 43). Fiscal decentralisation then refers to the degree of autonomy governments have to decide over their revenues and expenditure (Schneider 2003, 36–37).[41] When central government controls spending priorities and can overrule local decisions, the availability of resources does not necessarily mean greater autonomy (Dickovick 2005, 186). In federations, the legislative responsibilities of each jurisdiction typically correlate with spending powers (Watts 2008, 100 et seq.), and fiscal relations are often used "to measure just how *federal* federations are" (Burgess 2006, 148–149).[42] The ability of governments to realise their policy objectives and their legislative and executive responsibilities depends on the allocation of financial resources across different levels of government. Devolving legislative authority without a transfer of adequate resources does not enhance territorial autonomy in practice (Cheema and Rondinelli 2007, 6–7). There are different ways to allocate fiscal resources across levels, either through formal revenue sharing, project-tied grants or general-purpose block grants. Under *coercive federalism*, for instance, central governments transfer money to the lower levels to promote their own policy agenda. And yet, systems of intergovernmental financial relations differ too widely to identify meaningful ideal types (Eccleston et al. 2017, 20).

The allocation of fiscal authority in the UK reflects the unitary nature of the system. The financial revolution in 17th-century England gave rise not only to the City of London's dominant global financial status but also led to a fiscal centralisation and empowered the Treasury. Following the 1976 financial crisis, under Margaret Thatcher, the Treasury's control over fiscal and macroeconomic decisions was further strengthened (Lee 2017, 125), as Lee (op. cit., 127–128) has suggested:

> [...] central prescription in the control of policy and the allocation of resources was driven by the institutional architecture of the 'new centre' – the Treasury, the Cabinet Office, and the Offices of the Prime Minister and Deputy Prime Minister. This framework allows little latitude for formal fiscal federalism at present because it is controlled from London by the Treasury.

Devolution has not fundamentally altered the system of public finance integrated at UK level (Bradbury 2021, 288). Instead of following a systematic (federal) approach to decentralising fiscal decisions, in "response to constitutional threats" (Bell 2016, 41), the UK Government only reluctantly and gradually handed down control over public revenues (O'Neill 2004, 193) through different bilateral ad hoc arrangements for the different parts (Bell and Vaillancourt 2018, 84). Nevertheless, according to the Regional Authority Index, within the last decade the Scottish, Welsh and Northern Ireland executives have all become fairly autonomous in regards to their fiscal capacities (score 3 out of 4) and their borrowing powers have increased for Scotland and Wales (score 2 out of 3) (Hooghe et al. 2016, 409 et seq.).[43] To get a better idea of the allocation of resources and the fiscal relations between the centre and the devolved administrations, the following will outline the four major sources of revenues and spending: block grants, ad hoc grants, tax powers and borrowing capacities.

Block grant

Central government grants provide about 90 per cent of the devolved revenues (Hooghe et al. 2016, 409).[44] Similar to fiscal federalism, resources are distributed horizontally between the different jurisdictions, whereby the transfer of resources is calculated on the basis of expenditure not on revenues or need (Birrell 2012, 26; Lee 2017, 129–131). Under the Barnett formula,[45] which dates back to 1978, the devolved administrations receive relatively generous block grants from the centre (Leyland 2011, 258). The Barnett formula is a non-statutory internal mechanism by the Treasury to apply spending changes in Whitehall to the rest of the UK.[46] While the grant is in theory meant to provide an objective calculus of territorial needs, populations and levels of social inclusion, in reality, rather than achieving an unbiased distribution of resources the level of financial transfer from the centre reflects the political influence and bargaining potential of each territory. Consequently, Scotland's share per capita is comparatively more favourable than the amount that Wales would receive under a straightforward

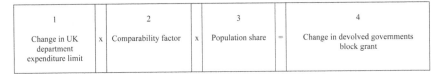

Figure 3.1 The Barnett formula

Source: HM Government and Welsh Government (2016). The agreement between the Welsh Government and the United Kingdom Government on the Welsh Government's fiscal framework. December. Welsh Government. https://gov.wales/sites/default/files/publications/2018-11/agreement-on-welsh-government-fiscal-framework.pdf

application of the formula (SG9) (O'Neill 2004, 194–198). The formula has also operated under the assumption that a 'Barnett squeeze' would gradually lead to convergence of spending per head across the UK, which was hardly achieved over the course of four decades (Bradbury 2021, 286; Keep 2021, 13–14). Because the block grant is unconditional, the devolved administrations enjoy wider spending powers than many regions in federal states (Gallagher 2016, 31–32). However, they have little influence over the amount they receive or other major fiscal decisions (Lee 2017, 126). These are up to the Treasury, which has the final say on fiscal matters for the whole of the UK and determines the annual amount of the block grant (HM Treasury 2015, 4; 2020a). Based on the annual Comprehensive Spending Review, the Treasury publishes the Statement of Funding Policy setting out the available resources for each departmental field. The changes to the assigned budget for a devolved administration are the Barnett consequentials of the ongoing budget decisions for England (Pidgeon 2012, 3). In Birrell's words (2012, 25), "when changes occur in the amount allocated in England the devolved administrations receive the amount allocated in the previous year, plus or minus a population share".

Under consideration of the planned spending of the UK Government departments (1); the extent to which services delivered by UK departments correspond to services delivered by the devolved administrations (2); and the relative populations (3) (see Table 3.2),[47] the devolved administrations receive their specific share of the UK overall budget, including reductions (4). The comparability factors for services range from 0 to 100 per cent, whereby 0 per cent indicates that a task (e.g. military defence) is not devolved, and 100 per cent means that a service (e.g. education) is fully devolved to an administration (see Table 3.3) (Keep 2021, 5–7; HM Treasury 2020a, 10). The block grant is calculated according to policy areas, but the devolved governments are not bound to use the resources for the same fields as the UK Government designates them for England (Cairney 2011, 209–210).

Though how the Barnett formula operates for each devolved administration may be controversial, the different governments avoid open disputes

Table 3.2 Population proportions applied on the 2020 spending review

Year of the spending review	1998	2000	2002	2004	2007	2010	2015	2019	2020
ONS mid-year population estimates (%) used	1996	1999	2001	2003	2006	2009	2014	2018	2019
Scotland's population as a proportion of the population of England	10.45	10.34	10.23	10.20	10.08	10.03	9.85	9.71	9.71
Scotland's population as a proportion of the population of England and Wales	9.86	9.77	9.66	9.63	9.52	9.48	9.31	9.20	9.19
Wales's population as a proportion of the population of England	5.95	5.93	5.89	5.89	5.84	5.79	5.69	5.61	5.60
Northern Ireland's population as a proportion of the population of England	3.39	3.41	3.40	3.42	3.43	3.45	3.39	3.36	3.36
Northern Ireland's population as a proportion of the population of England and Wales	3.20	3.22	3.21	3.23	3.24	3.26	3.21	3.18	3.19
Northern Ireland's population as a proportion of the population of Great Britain	2.91	2.93	2.92	2.95	2.96	2.98	2.93	2.91	2.92

Source: HM Treasury (2020a).

over its general principle as the block grant is a relatively straightforward way to allocate resources without telling the devolved administrations how to spend the money (Gallagher 2012, 207).[48] Depoliticising fiscal relations and keeping territorial finance integrated within the UK's unitary system of public expenditure has been also a way to hide the unilateral power of the Treasury, which retains control over spending decisions without having to engage in public negotiations or disputes (Bradbury 2021, 288–289). As stated in the 2020 Statement of Funding Policy: "linking funding for the devolved administrations to UK government spending and revenues largely removes the need to negotiate allocations directly." (HM Treasury 2020a, 7)

When Scotland received new tax powers as suggested by the Smith Commission after the 2014 independence referendum (see below), a block grant adjustment was negotiated between the UK and Scottish Governments to reflect an increase in tax revenues by reducing Barnett funding. The adjustment includes a 'comparability factor' accounting for the different tax capacities across the UK (ratio between mean income tax per taxpayer in Scotland and England) (Bell and Vaillancourt 2018, 86). Following new tax powers for Wales and the recommendations of the Holtham Commission, in

Table 3.3 Comparability factors applied in the 2020 spending review

Department	Scotland (%)	Wales (%)	Northern Ireland (%)
Business, Energy and Industrial Strategy	6.8	6.5	7.1
Business Rates	100.0	100.0	100.0
Cabinet Office	0.0	0.0	0.0
Ministry of Housing, Communities and Local Government: Communities	100.0	99.6	100.0
Ministry of Housing, Communities and Local Government: Local Government	100.0	100.0	100.0
Digital, Culture, Media and Sport	68.0	67.7	69.9
Environment, Food and Rural Affairs	96.9	96.9	96.9
Education	100.0	100.0	100.0
Transport	91.7	36.6	95.4
Health and Social Care	99.5	99.5	99.5
Work and Pensions	20.1	0.0	97.9
HM Revenue and Customs	4.0	4.0	3.4
HM Treasury	0.0	0.0	0.0
Home Office	74.1	1.7	74.1
Law Officers Departments	98.3	0.0	90.1
Justice	100.0	1.3	99.9

Source: HM Treasury (2020a).

the 2015 Spending Review, the UK and Welsh Governments also agreed to a block grant adjustment mechanism which added a need-based factor to the Barnett formula for Wales. As long as the funding per head remains above a funding floor of 115 per cent of equivalent funding per head in England, a transitional needs-based factor of 105 per cent was agreed. Considering that parts of England also suffer severe levels of deprivation, this was a remarkable concession to the Welsh Government (Lee 2017, 138). Figure 3.2 illustrates the Barnett formula for Wales.

Change in UK department expenditure limit	x	Comparability factor	x	Population share	x	**New needs-based factor**	=	Change in Welsh Government block grant

Figure 3.2 The Barnett formula for Wales

Source: HM Government and Welsh Government (2016). The agreement between the Welsh Government and the United Kingdom Government on the Welsh Government's fiscal framework. December. Welsh Government. https://gov.wales/sites/default/files/publications/2018-11/agreement-on-welsh-government-fiscal-framework.pdf

Table 3.4 Block grant allocation 2017–2021

£ billion	2017–2018	2018–2019	2019–2020	2020–2021
Scottish Government				
Before tax and welfare adjustments	30.3	31.1	33.2	38.9
Total block grant after adjustment	17.8	18.9	21.3	29.9
Welsh Government				
Before tax adjustments	15.1	15.6	16.7	19.6
Total block grant after adjustment	15.1	15.3	14.4	17.1
Northern Ireland Executive				
Total block grant after adjustment	11.2	11.8	12.7	14.8

Source: HM Treasury (2020b).

While the devolved administrations are free to decide how to use their grant, a major principle of the Statement of Funding Policy provides that financial impacts caused by actions of one government on another should be compensated (UKG4) (cf. Keep 2021, 16–17):

> [...] decisions taken by any of the devolved administrations or bodies under their jurisdiction have financial implications for departments or agencies of the UK government or, alternatively, decisions of UK government departments or agencies lead to additional costs for any of the devolved administrations, where other arrangements do not exist automatically to adjust for such extra costs, the body whose decision leads to the additional cost will meet that cost.
> (HM Treasury 2015, 4)

Table 3.4 presents how much funding the devolved administrations received from the block grant between 2017 and 2021. It also reflects the impact of the different tax powers and policies of each part, whereby the difference between the grant before and after tax and welfare adjustments are significantly higher in Scotland than in Wales (and do not matter in Northern Ireland). In addition, the Scottish Government received a total of £9.7 billion (Office of the Secretary of State for Scotland and HM Treasury 2021) and the Welsh Government £5.85 billion (Office of the Secretary of State for Wales and HM Treasury 2021) through the Barnett formula to support their health services and businesses in response to Covid-19 between spring 2020 and February 2021. For 2021–2022, an extra £8.7 billion per year on average for each of the devolved administrations added up to £43.2 billion for Scotland, £19.9 billion for Wales and £16.3 billion for the Northern Ireland (Department for Levelling Up, Housing and Communities 2022a, 17).

Ad hoc grants

Occasionally, the UK Government provides the devolved administrations with ad hoc grants outside of the Barnett formula which are subject to political circumstances and negotiations (Keep 2021, 3). These are given directly for specific, ring-fenced purposes to individual devolved administrations and cannot be spent on other issues. Examples hereof are additional resources for police and an allocation of £20 million for retiring part-time reserve police in Northern Ireland in 2010; or the UK Government's decision to provide the city of London with extra financial means for the 2020 Olympic Games (Birrell 2012, 28). As the empirical analysis will show, such transfers have at times caused major controversies between the different governments. The Statement of Funding Policy 2020 (HM Treasury 2020a, 16) set out the following funding for ring-fenced purposes beyond 2020: about £2.9 billion for 20 City and Growth Deals across Scotland, Wales and Northern Ireland; £1.1 billion for agriculture funding to support farmers and land managers in Scotland, Wales and Northern Ireland in 2021–2022; £28 million additional agriculture funding to Scotland and Wales in 2021–2022; about £20 million for fisheries funding to support the fisheries sector in Scotland, Wales and Northern Ireland in 2021–2022; £1 billion for the New Decade New Approach for reforms to deliver health, education and justice reforms in Northern Ireland; £200 million towards implementation costs (primarily in relation to Social Security Scotland) and £66 million per year towards administration costs as part of the Fiscal Framework Agreement.

While some of these grant allocations, for instance for agriculture and fisheries support, compensate for the loss of EU funding, the UK Government has also launched the Shared Prosperity Fund in April 2022 to replace the EU Structural Funds. Until March 2025, £2.6 billion of new funding will be available to local councils and mayoral authorities across England, Scotland, Wales and Northern Ireland to invest in "building pride in place, supporting high-quality skills training, supporting pay, employment and productivity growth and increasing life chances." The UK Government announced that it will oversee the funding in Northern Ireland, and work in partnership with the Scottish and Welsh Governments (Department for Levelling Up, Housing and Communities 2022b). The resources are allocated on the basis of a formula and match similar amounts to the European Structural Funds for equivalent purposes (Brien 2022). However, the new scheme does not grant the devolved administrations the same control as they had over the EU Structural Funds, and it allows the UK Government to work directly with local authorities. The Part 6 of the UK Internal Market Act 2020 further provided the UK Government with powers to bypass the devolved administrations and fund a wide range of purposes that are within devolved competence, including economic development, infrastructure and education. These grants are not given to the devolved governments and raised their vehement criticism (Welsh Government 2020).

Tax authority

As for legislative powers, the authority to raise revenue across different levels of government is usually constitutionally defined and can be either *exclusive, concurrent* or *shared*. Most federations allocate exclusive fiscal authority over customs and excise taxes and cooperate taxes at the federal level to ensure an effective internal market. There is also a clear tendency across federations to centralise other major taxes enabling the federal government to redistribute resources, avoid tax competition between the constituents and facilitate tax administration. The authority over personal income, sales and consumption taxes is in turn often shared (Watts 2008, 95–97). The significant legislative and spending powers of the early devolution settlement were not matched with equally extensive tax-raising powers. The UK Government maintained exclusive authority over reserved financial matters, including monetary policy and all major taxes (Paun and Cheung 2018). Scottish voters first had to agree to the transfer of some tax powers in the second question of the 1997 devolution referendum. Subsequently, the Scottish Parliament was given control over local council rates and business rates on property used for business purposes and could vary the basic income tax rate by up to three Pence in the Pound.[49] Effectively, still only local taxes that accounted for less than five per cent of tax revenues were devolved (Hazell 2015, 30). In the first decade of devolution until the financial crisis, this did not matter a great deal because UK public expenditure was generally high, changes were marginal and little attention was paid to public finances (Cairney 2011, 203–204). When, in 2010, the Coalition Government led by David Cameron introduced severe public budget cuts under its austerity agenda, the devolved administrations started to push for more fiscal powers. The resulting devolution of tax authority did not take place under a consistent framework to ensure fiscal equity and coordination. Instead, it incrementally followed political considerations, and became part of an increasingly complex system with asymmetrical tax powers for different governments (Bell 2016, 54).

To avoid tax competition between the different governments, Westminster has retained control over major taxes (corporation tax, VAT and income tax). Devolving property taxation, such as stamp duty land tax and landfill tax, has been fairly straightforward because these are attached to defined places and are difficult for taxpayers to circumvent by shifting assets. Scotland and Wales can make some adjustments to income tax, which gives them some control over a political instrument with high visibility (Paun and Cheung 2018). Each administration is also in charge of non-domestic business rates for private, public and third-sector organisations within its jurisdiction in order to pay for local council services (UKG6).[50] The Institute for Government (ibid.) estimated that in 2020/2021, the devolved and local governments controlled the following shares of tax revenue: 31 per cent in Scotland (including assigned VAT); 20 per cent in Wales; 9 per cent of tax revenue in Northern Ireland and 9 per cent in England (including council tax and business rates). Considering that the block grant guarantees the major share of funding, devolving taxes presents not only an opportunity but also a risk for the different governments. Depending on the state of their economies, the volatility of tax revenues leads to a great deal of uncertainty to the budgets of the devolved administrations. If Scotland for instance gained full fiscal autonomy, it would not only face severe financial challenges, including a high public deficit, but it would also no longer contribute to welfare spending in economically weaker parts of the UK, such as Wales and Northern Ireland (Gallagher 2016, 29–30). Bell (2016, 54) therefore argued that without horizontal fiscal redistribution across all nations "the postwar consensus around social insurance and risk pooling across the whole of the United Kingdom is disappearing rapidly". And yet, particularly in Scotland and Wales, there has been a strong desire to gain new tax powers during the last decade.

The Scotland Act 2012 extended the financial competences of the Scottish Parliament profoundly and enhanced the shared authority over income tax. The new arrangement increased the share of devolved tax revenues to about 30 per cent and enabled the Scottish Parliament to set a Scottish rate of income tax,[51] which is administered and collected by HM Revenue and Customs on behalf of the Scottish Government. The Scotland Act also devolved the exclusive authority over land and building transaction tax and landfill tax,[52] and conferred the competence to create and devolve new taxes (Hazell 2015, 14–15).[53] In 2015, Revenues Scotland was established as a non-ministerial department responsible for administering the devolved taxes in Scotland. After the 2014 independence referendum, Westminster followed the recommendations of the Smith Commission (though not entirely satisfactorily to the SNP), and substantially devolved fiscal competences. The Scotland Act 2016 gave the Scottish administration the authority to receive half of the value-added tax raised in Scotland, while the power to set VAT rates remained reserved to the UK Government. It also devolved the ability to replace the air passenger duty with an air departure tax, and to introduce an aggregates levy on the commercial exploitation of rock, gravel, sand and other minerals (Paun and Cheung 2018).[54] While the UK Government remained in control of tax-free personal allowances, income tax has implicitly turned into a shared tax: "We've gone from a one component system of just having a block grant to a three-component system, where you have a grant, which you reduce down and then increase it again with the tax revenues" (SG5). In reality, the Scottish Government is constrained in its ability to diverge its income tax from the rest of the UK, as an increase in the Scottish income tax rate would mean a reduction of the block grant (Bell 2016, 43). An official from the Scottish Government thus commented:

> We're not gaining much from those tax powers. But it gives us greater ability for making differential policy decisions between us and the UK

Government. [...] Through the block grant adjustment we're very closely tied to UK decisions on income tax. These decisions are not entirely independent as you would want them to be if you're looking for policy autonomy between the different parts of the UK.

(SG9)

Most importantly, the new power to set and retain income tax rates had been used to restructure the tax bands and increased the rates for higher earners by 1 Pence per Pound. The devolution of tax powers also required changes to the Barnett formula and a block grant adjustment mechanism was introduced to reflect the different tax rates. These were agreed by the UK and the Scottish Governments under the Fiscal Framework for Scotland in February 2019.

Initially, the National Assembly for Wales did not receive any taxation powers but responsibilities for revenues were incrementally handed over from Westminster to match its rise in legislative competences. In 2012, the Commission on Devolution in Wales (known as the Silk Commission) concluded:

We believe the block grant alone, or with assigned taxes, does not provide sufficient financial accountability and empowerment. Fuller fiscal autonomy would remove the fiscal transfer on which the successful Union is based. We have therefore concluded that a combination of block grant with some tax devolution would be best for Wales.

(Commission on Devolution in Wales 2012, 3)

The Wales Act 2014 then provided the Welsh Government with exclusive authority over land transaction tax (replacing stamp duty land tax), landfills disposal tax (replacing landfill tax) and business rates, and the possibility of holding a referendum on the devolution of an element of income tax (Keep 2021, 21). To implement the new powers, the Fiscal Framework for Wales was agreed in December 2016 (only 11 months after the Scottish one, yet with very different outputs). In order to compensate for an estimated loss of £2 billion of income tax to the UK Treasury (Poole et al. 2016, 3), the block grant adjustment was less generous than for Scotland, but a needs-based factor was added to the Barnett formula (HM Government and Welsh Government 2016). The Wales Act 2017 removed the requirement for a referendum to vary income tax by ten Pence in the Pound spent on Welsh services.[55] Unlike the Scottish administration, the Welsh Government cannot adjust the income tax bands and it did not make use of its power to set a Welsh rate diverging from the UK's income tax (Welsh Government 2021). Compared to Scotland, the Welsh income tax system is less comprehensive, yet also implicitly shared with the UK Government (Poole et al. 2016, 34). The Welsh Government has further explored the creation of new taxes such as social care levy, disposable plastic tax and tourism tax (Welsh

Government 2018).[56] Disagreements over the devolution of vacant land tax and air passenger duty will be examined in Chapter 5.

The Northern Ireland Assembly can levy any taxes that are not reserved to Westminster, which effectively means it can set the rates of minor taxes, such as the regional rate on property tax used for devolved services, and that it could abolish the long-haul air passenger duty in 2012 (Birrell and Heenan 2017, 474–475). The 2015 Corporation Tax (Northern Ireland) Act devolved the power to implement a 12.5 per cent rate of corporation tax in Northern Ireland by 2018 (Lee 2017, 128) to "reflect its unique economic position within the UK" (Hazell 2015, 16; 40). While corporation taxes are usually controlled by central government, devolving them to Northern Ireland aimed to counter tax competition with the Republic of Ireland (Paun and Cheung 2018). By 2020 the power over corporation tax had not been exercised due to the suspension of the Assembly in 2017.

Borrowing authority

Public borrowing makes up the last major source of fiscal autonomy examined here. The early devolution settlement did not provide significant borrowing capacities to Scotland and Wales. This aimed at preventing the new administrations from amassing excessive public debts, for which the UK Government would ultimately have to pay (Bradbury 2021, 288). The Scotland Act 1998, the Government of Wales Act 2006 and the Northern Ireland Act 1998 only enabled borrowing to manage short-term cash flows (Scholes 2014, 2–3). The Secretary of State for each part could distribute loans to cover temporary imbalances between revenues and spending, but more profound borrowing powers were only devolved at a later stage.[57] Whereas the Northern Ireland Executive was able to borrow to deal with infrastructure deficits of previous decades,[58] both the Scottish and Welsh Government also wanted additional borrowing powers as a means to fund capital investments (Birrell 2012, 41–42). These were eventually given by the Scotland Act 2012 and the Wales Act 2014.

The Scotland Act 2012 enabled the Scottish Government to borrow up to £2.2 billion from the National Loans Fund, from banks on commercial terms or through issuing their own bonds after approval by the UK Treasury. Scotland's capacities were further raised by the Scotland Act 2016 up to a total of £3 billion with an annual limit of 15 per cent of the capital borrowing cap of £450 million for infrastructure investments. To balance fluctuations in tax revenues and in-year excesses in expenditure over income, the Scottish Government can borrow a cumulative maximum of £1.75 billion (HM Treasury 2020a, 32). While the extra resources have been used to cover day-to-day spending and to compensate for forecast errors on tax revenues,[59] the Scottish Government has argued that the overall amount would be comparatively small for a country of that size and the borrowing limits would be too low to balance tax volatility (SG9).

The Wales Act 2014 provided the Welsh Government with a borrowing capacity up to a total of £500 million (£200 million per year) for short-term revenues to compensate mismatches between tax and spending. The Wales Act 2017 then increased its overall borrowing limit to £1 billion (and a 15 per cent annual limit of £150 million).[60] Like the Scottish Government, with the approval of the Treasury, Welsh ministers can borrow a maximum of £500 million (£125 million per year) to help smooth fluctuations in tax receipts and to provide a working balance between expenditure and income (HM Treasury 2020a, 36).[61]

The arrangement for the Northern Ireland Executive is slightly more complicated. The Northern Ireland (Loans) Act 1975 had already set an overall limit at £2 billion (which was extended to £3 billion by the Northern Ireland (Miscellaneous Provisions) Act 2006) (HM Treasury 2020a, 40).[62] Section 61 of the Northern Ireland Act 1998 granted another £250 million borrowing capacities subject to the consent of the Treasury. In addition, the Executive was enabled to borrow up to £200 million per year (with a total cap of £2 billion) under the 2002 Reinvestment and Reform Initiative from the National Loans Fund. This enabled the funding of capital investments in damaged and neglected infrastructure (Birrell 2012, 42; Public Finance Scrutiny Unit 2016, 6–7).

Conclusion

Examining the nature of the UK's multi-layered constitution and the allocation of political, legislative and fiscal authority across different levels provided the prerequisites to the following empirical analysis of intergovernmental relations. Devolution aimed at introducing a dual allocation of power providing the different governments with high levels of self-rule and exclusive jurisdictions over legislation, policymaking and implementation. While Northern Ireland has followed its own political logic, Scotland and Wales started from very different origins and over time the latter has converged towards the former by receiving full law-making powers under a reserved powers model, which did not require an advanced system of shared rule comparable to federal states (SG4, UKG10). In the words of a Member of the Senedd: "In Britain, there's not much idea of what federalism means, what are robust federal approaches, how to decentralise effectively. We've had quite uncontrolled decentralisation in many ways." (WP6) The reserved powers model uses a list of enumerated powers with exclusive legislative authority to the centre and residual powers that are not reserved to the devolved legislatures. Though this model does not foresee shared legislative powers, areas of concurrent legislative authority have unintendedly grown as more and more responsibilities were transferred, which has become all too obvious as the legal powers held at the EU level return to the UK.

The legislative authority of the devolved administrations is matched by their financial resources. The devolved administrations have hardly any say over the amount they receive but can autonomously decide how to spend it. The block grant system also sought to depoliticise fiscal decisions by integrating territorial finance within the UK's unitary system. In addition to the Barnett formula, the UK Government also gives out ad hoc grants directly for specific purposes, which have caused some controversies that will be analysed in the following chapters. To increase their fiscal authority, the Scottish and Welsh administrations received borrowing powers to fund public services and capital investments, as well as tax powers, for instance over land transaction tax and landfill tax. In practice, decisions over income tax are no longer exclusive to one jurisdiction, as both Scotland and Wales can modify their own rates (and in Scotland also the tax bands). However, their ability to diverge from the UK is constrained politically and would impact negatively on the amount of their block grant.

It may seem the expansion of devolved authority may have come to end, as has been argued by Andrews (2021, 1). However, legislative decentralisation has led to a complex and unanticipated overlap of competences and a departure from the reserved powers model. Even though the Westminster Parliament remains the supreme decision-maker, devolution has established an increasingly dispersed and pluralistic way to exercise power. Instead of being a zero-sum transaction, questions of territorial autonomy and devolution are then not merely about self-rule but about shared rule and the ability of the devolved administrations to influence decisions that are made at the centre.

Notes

1 As part of an administrative decentralisation, in 1885 the Scottish Office and the Secretary for Scotland were established. Since 1907 Scottish 'bills' were dealt with by a Standing Scottish Grand Committee of the Westminster Parliament. Considerably later, in 1951 the UK Minister for Welsh Affairs and in 1964 the Welsh Office were introduced to the UK Government.
2 About one million people died in Ireland and about three million emigrated to the rest of the UK, to the United States and elsewhere (Deacon 2012, 188).
3 Even though England, Wales, Scotland and Northern Ireland are not legally sovereign to sign treaties or other international obligations, they are internationally acknowledged as nations, for instance, when it comes sport (Deacon et al. 2018, 10). According to Sturm (2017, 45), the transformation from a unitary to a union state only began during the 1970s.
4 Mitchell (2009, 6) also thought of the UK as a 'state of union' rather than a union state to reflect the multiple unions that formed the UK.
5 However, on 1 March 1979 devolution was rejected in two separate referendums initiated by the Labour Government, which had to resign subsequently. In Wales only 20.3–79.7 per cent voted in favour, and although 51.6 per cent were in favour of devolution in Scotland (63.7 per cent turn out), the required threshold of 40 per cent of the overall electorate was not met.
6 Membership in the EU and the European Convention on Human Rights also integrated Scotland and Northern Ireland in an international legal and constitutional order (Keating 2004, 320).
7 Also known as the Belfast Agreement following the Good Friday Agreement.

8 Holyrood is often used as a synonym for the Scottish Parliament.
9 The change of name was formalised by the Wales Act 2014.
10 The act also laid down a maximum number of 12 ministers excluding the First Minister and the Counsel General, which means almost half of all Labour AMs are members of the government. Ministers who are heading a government department carry the title 'Cabinet Secretary', whilst the junior ministers are called 'Minister' and are not part of the Cabinet. In total, Welsh Cabinet includes a maximum of nine members, who are bound by collective responsibility for the decisions of the Cabinet.
11 The additional member system in Wales is less proportional than in Scotland and works in favour of the Labour Party's representation in the Assembly. Hence, in no other UK legislature has one party been so dominant since the late 1990s (Deacon et al. 2018, 73). Between 2003–2007 and 2011–2016 in Wales, Labour could rule on its own though it had no absolute majority. From 2007 to 2011, Labour entered a 'red-green coalition' with Plaid Cymru and despite their mutual animosity, they ran a stable government (Deacon 2012, 149). Between 2016 and 2021 Labour was supported only by one Liberal Democrat and one MS who became independent in 2017. After the Senedd elections in May 2021, Labour ruled again on its own as a minority government.
12 Both ministers have formally equal powers, whereby the First Minister comes from the largest and their deputy from the second largest party in the Assembly.
13 Based on the d'Hondt formula, the party with most seats gets the first choice of portfolio. Its seats are subsequently divided by two and the party that now holds most seats selects a portfolio. The procedure is repeated until all the portfolios are allocated to sizeable parties.
14 The Assembly holds 90 members (108 members before 2017) elected via a single transferable vote from 18 multimember constituencies.
15 The lack of collective responsibility allows members of government to pursue their individual or party agendas, and to act like they belong to the opposition. Thus, rather than living up to the ideas of collaborative, shared government as envisaged in the Good Friday Agreement, bloc voting has entrenched rather than loosened sectarian politics. Hence, the requirement of multi-party coalitions has frequently caused a deadlock in the political system of Stormont (cf. Deacon 2012, 209; Hazell 2015, 38–39).
16 Between February and May 2000, Secretary of State, Peter Mandelson, restored direct rule from Westminster after the leader of the Ulster Unionist Party (UUP), David Trimble, threatened to resign over the question of decommissioning the Irish Republican Army (IRA). Trimble stepped down between July and October 2001, resulting in a second phase of direct rule. Until October 2002, the Assembly operated fairly effectively. When Sinn Féin's Assembly offices were raided by the police after being accused of spying for the IRA, a lengthy period of suspension began that lasted until 2007, despite the Assembly elections in 2003. Only when in 2005 the IRA declared the end of its armed campaign was the way clear to negotiate a new agreement. By accepting the St Andrews Agreement, the Assembly was given more powers over justice and policing, Sinn Féin acknowledged the Northern Irish Police Service and the DUP made a commitment to share power with the nationalists (Deacon 2012, 211–216).
17 The sequence was altered by the author.
18 The Regional Authority Index assigns 3 out of 4 points for the *policy scope* of all devolved administrations, which is only restricted by Westminster's exclusive legislative authority over reserved and excepted matters (Hooghe et al. 2016, 407 et seq.).

19 Since constitutional matters are reserved, Westminster decides about a referendum on Scottish independence.
20 E.g. fiscal, economic and monetary policy, the currency, financial services and money laundering.
21 E.g. misuse of drugs, data protection, elections, firearms, immigration and nationality, and emergency powers.
22 E.g. insolvency, intellectual property, import and export control, consumer protection, product standards, safety and liability.
23 E.g. electricity, oil and gas, and nuclear energy.
24 E.g. road transport, rail transport, marine transport and air transport.
25 E.g. child support, occupational and personal pensions.
26 E.g. employment and industrial relations, health and safety, and job search and support.
27 E.g. broadcasting.
28 E.g. equal opportunities.
29 The presiding officer of the Scottish Parliament checks whether Scottish bills were within devolved competence, Scottish law officers could refer bills to judicial review, and the Secretary of State for Scotland could prevent a bill to be sent off for royal assent if it interfered with Westminster's powers (Bradbury 2021, 93).
30 Under Section 30(2), for instance, its powers can be further modified, as was done in 2002, when the Parliament was provided with new authority over the construction of railways within Scotland. According to Section 63, executive powers exercised by a UK Minister can also be transferred to Scottish Ministers (Deacon 2012, 76).
31 Officially called the Commission on Scottish Devolution.
32 The Wales Act 2014 also devolved some tax and borrowing powers, made changes to the election rules of the Assembly and prohibited dual mandates in the Welsh Assembly and the UK parliament (double jobbing).
33 The Enterprise and Regulatory Reform Bill 2012–2013 sought to abolish the Agricultural Wages Board for England and Wales. The Welsh Assembly then introduced the Agricultural Advisory Panel for Wales. The Trade Union (Wales) Act 2017 also disapplied provisions of Parliament's Trade Union Bill 2015–2016.
34 Again, the act also devolved further tax and borrowing powers (see below).
35 Entrenched matters present a third category and cover the European Communities Act 1972 and the Human Rights Act 1998 (see Section 7 1998 Northern Ireland Act).
36 The 2006 St Andrews Agreement also committed the Northern Ireland Executive and Assembly to new obligations concerning the Irish language and social inclusion. The Northern Ireland Act 2009 made some adjustments to the Act of 1998 and to the Justice Act 2002, and provided that certain policing and justice matters could become an executive function though not a legislative power (Birrell 2012, 16).
37 E.g. disqualifying public office-holders from becoming an MSP and payments to opposition parties requires approval from the Scottish Parliament. Both Westminster and Holyrood also need to agree to the modification of reserved matter on which the Scottish Parliament cannot legislate, a redistribution of functions between UK and Scottish ministers, and adding new devolved taxes. For a detailed overview of subordinate legislation subject to consent by the Scottish Parliament or Executive, see Lazarowicz and McFadden (2018, 113–114).
38 Memorandum of Understanding of October 2013 states: "15. The United Kingdom Parliament retains the absolute right to debate, enquire into or

make representations about devolved matters. It is ultimately for Parliament to decide what use to make of that power, but the UK Government will encourage the UK Parliament to bear in mind the primary responsibility of devolved legislatures and administrations in these fields and to recognise that it is a consequence of Parliament's decision to devolve certain matters that Parliament itself will in future be more restricted in its field of operation. 16. The devolved legislatures will be entitled to debate non-devolved matters, but the devolved executives will encourage each devolved legislature to bear in mind the responsibility of the UK Parliament in these matters."

39 The devolved legislatures can also override the UK Parliament and act on but not overrule Westminster statutes – and their laws have to comply with the European Convention on Human Rights and previously with EU legislation (Hunt 2021, 28–29).

40 E.g. disability living allowance, attendance allowance, carer's allowance, Universal Credit, housing costs, employment support programmes.

41 Whereas revenues refer to the amount of resources that pass through governments, including taxes, loans, credits and grants, expenditures are the cash outlays of governments. Viewing subnational expenditures as a percentage of total expenditures is an appropriate way to gauge fiscal decentralisation.

42 In some federations, such as Australia and India, the federal government dominates over revenues and expenditure, while states like Germany, Canada and Switzerland show a more balanced relationship (Burgess 2006, 148).

43 By 2010, Scotland was fairly *fiscally autonomous* and able to set "the rate of at least one major tax: personal income, corporate, value added, or sales tax" (score 3 out of 4); Northern Ireland could only set "the rate of minor taxes" (score 1 out of 4) and in Wales "the central government sets the base and rate of all regional taxes" (score 0 out of 4). *Borrowing autonomy* was for all the nations recorded as *"under prior authorization (ex ante) by the central government"* and restricted by various impositions (score 1 out of 3). Meanwhile, *fiscal autonomy* for Wales and for Northern Ireland has caught up with Scotland (score 3 out of 4) and the score for *borrowing autonomy* has risen in Scotland and Wales from 1 to 2, meaning that "regional government may borrow *without prior authorization (ex post)* under one or more of the same centrally imposed restrictions" (Hooghe et al. 2016, 409 et seq.).

44 England has no devolved budget but only measures to provide some additional spending and taxation powers to cities and local authorities (Bell 2016, 41).

45 Named after Joel Barnett, the Chief Secretary to the Treasury at the time, the formula was first applied in Scotland, and later in Northern Ireland (1979) and Wales (1980) (Keep 2020, 10).

46 While the Barnett formula is not explicitly manifested in statute, the Scotland Act 2016 put it on a firmer legal basis (Bell and Vaillancourt 2018, 100).

47 Percentages in relation to England based on mid-year estimates by the Office for National Statistics.

48 According to an official of the Welsh Government: "The system we have, the Barnet Formula, was invented in ad hoc way for a temporary solution that's lasted for 40 years because nobody can find a way of replacing it that doesn't cause huge arguments." (WG11)

49 Raising the income tax rate was a competence designed not to be used because it would mean burdening the electorate with tax raises and is an unpopular measure.

50 They set the level, determine the spending and can relieve specific sectors, which has been fairly similar across the different jurisdictions.

51 The UK Government was still in control over the structure of income tax and the personal allowance before income tax had to be paid.

52 However, with £4.7 billion in 2015–2016 the Scottish rate of income tax is significantly more important than land building and transaction tax (£0.4 billion) and landfill tax (£0.1 billion).
53 For more details on the new tax powers of the Scotland Act 2012, see HM Revenue and Customs (2015) and Seely (2015).
54 By the time this study was completed, neither the new VAT system nor the devolution of air departure tax and aggregates levy had been implemented yet.
55 The Wales Act 2017 also enabled the Welsh Assembly to create the Welsh Revenue Authority.
56 These had not been concluded by the end of this study.
57 £500 million for the Scottish Executive and the Welsh Assembly Government, and £250 million for the Northern Ireland Executive.
58 The total borrowing cap was £2 billion.
59 A set annual limit of £500 million for in-year cash management; of £300 million for forecast errors; and of £600 million for any observed or forecast shortfall in tax revenues or welfare spending pressure (HM Treasury 2020a, 32).
60 These can be borrowed from the National Loans Fund, from banks on commercial terms or through issuing their own bonds.
61 A set annual limit of £200 million for forecast errors; and of £500 million for in-year cash management (HM Treasury 2020a, 37).
62 The annual limit of £200 million for 2021–2022 was set by the Treasury.

Bibliography

Agranoff, Robert (2004) *Autonomy, Devolution and Intergovernmental Relations.* Regional and Federal Studies, Volume 14, Issue 1, pp. 26–65.

Andrews, Leighton (2021) *The Forward March of Devolution Halted – and the Limits of Progressive Unionism.* The Political Quarterly, Volume 92, Issue 3, pp. 512–521.

Becker, Bernd (2002) *Politik in Großbritannien: Einführung in das politische System und Bilanz der ersten Regierungsjahre Tony Blairs.* Paderborn: Ferdinand Schöningh.

Bell, David (2016) *The Aftermath of the Scottish Referendum: A New Fiscal Settlement for the United Kingdom?* In: Bailey, David and Budd, Leslie (eds.) *Devolution and the UK Economy.* London: Rowan and Littlefield, pp. 37–56.

Bell, David and Vaillancourt, Francois (2018) *Canadian and Scottish Fiscal Federal Arrangements: Taxation and Welfare Spending.* In: Keating, Michael and Laforest, Guy (eds.) *Constitutional Politics and the Territorial Question in Canada and the United Kingdom: Federalism and Devolution Compared.* Cham: Palgrave Macmillan, pp. 79–103.

Birrell, Derek (2012) *Comparing Devolved Governance.* Basingstoke: Palgrave Macmillan.

Birrell, Derek and Heenan, Deirdre (2017) *The Continuing Volatility of Devolution in Northern Ireland: The Shadow of Direct Rule.* The Political Quarterly, Volume 88, Issue 3, pp. 473–479.

Bolleyer, Nicole (2018) *Challenges of Interdependence and Coordination in Federal Systems.* In: Detterbeck, Klaus and Hepburn, Eve (eds.) *Handbook of Territorial Politics.* Cheltenham: Edward Elgar Publishing, pp. 45–60.

Bolleyer, Nicole and Thorlakson, Lori (2012) *Beyond Decentralization – The Comparative Study of Interdependence in Federal Systems.* The Journal of Federalism, Volume 42, Issue 4, pp. 566–591.

Bradbury, Jonathan (2021) *Constitutional Policy and Territorial Politics in the UK. Volume 1: Union and Devolution 1997–2007*. Bristol: Bristol University Press.

Brien, Philip (2022) *The UK Shared Prosperity Fund*. Briefing Paper Number 08527. 26 April. House of Commons. https://researchbriefings.files.parliament.uk/documents/CBP-8527/CBP-8527.pdf

Burgess, Michael (2006) *Comparative Federalism: Theory and Practice*. London: Routledge.

Burrows, Noreen (2000) *Devolution*. London: Sweet and Maxwell.

Cabinet Office and Northern Ireland Office (2019) *Devolution Settlement: Northern Ireland*. Guidance. 23 September. UK Government. https://www.gov.uk/guidance/devolution-settlement-northern-ireland

Cabinet Office and Office of the Secretary of State for Scotland (2019) *Devolution Settlement: Scotland*. Guidance. 11 September. UK Government. https://www.gov.uk/guidance/devolution-settlement-scotland

Cabinet Office, Office of the Secretary of State for Scotland, Northern Ireland Office and Office of the Secretary of State for Wales (2019) *Devolution of Powers to Scotland, Wales and Northern Ireland*. Guidance. 8 May. UK Government. https://www.gov.uk/guidance/devolution-of-powers-to-scotland-wales-and-northern-ireland

Cairney, Paul (2011) *The Scottish Political System Since Devolution: From New Politics to the New Scottish Government*. Exeter: Imprint Academic.

Cairney, Paul (2014) *A Crisis of the Union*. In: Richards, David, Smith, Martin John and Hay, Colin (eds.) *Institutional Crisis in 21st-Century Britain*. Basingstoke: Palgrave Macmillan.

Cheema, G. Shabbir and Rondinelli, Dennis A. (2007) *Decentralizing Governance: Emerging Concepts and Practices*. Washington, DC: Brookings Institution Press.

Cheung, Aron (2020) *Barnett Formula*. Explainer. 25 November. Institute for Government. https://www.instituteforgovernment.org.uk/explainers/barnett-formula

Commission on Devolution in Wales (2012) *Empowerment and Responsibility: Financial Powers to Strengthen Wales*. Part I and Executive Summary. 12 November. https://webarchive.nationalarchives.gov.uk/20140605075122/http://commissionondevolutioninwales.independent.gov.uk/

Deacon, Russell (2012) *Devolution in the United Kingdom*. Edinburgh: Edinburgh University Press.

Deacon, Russell, Denton, Alison and Southall, Robert (2018) *The Government and Politics of Wales*. Edinburgh: Edinburgh University Press.

Department for Levelling Up, Housing and Communities (2022a) *Intergovernmental Relations Annual Report—Reporting period 1 January–31 December 2021*. CP 655. March. UK Government.

Department for Levelling Up, Housing and Communities (2022b) *UK Shared Prosperity Fund: Prospectus*. Guidance. 19 July. UK Government. https://www.gov.uk/government/publications/uk-shared-prosperity-fund-prospectus/uk-shared-prosperity-fund-prospectus

Dickovick, J. Tyler (2005) *The Measure and Mismeasure of Decentralisation: Subnational Autonomy in Senegal and South Africa*. The Journal of Modern African Studies, Volume 43, Issue 2, pp. 183–210.

Eccleston, Richard, Krever, Robert and Smith, Helen (2017) *Fiscal Federalism in the 21st Century*. In: Eccleston, Richard and Krever, Richard (eds.) *The Future of Federalism – Intergovernmental Financial Relations in an Age of Austerity*. Cheltenham: Edward Elgar Publishing, pp. 15–45.

Entwistle, Tom, Downe, James, Guarneros-Meza, Valeria and Martin, Steve (2014) *The Multi-Level Governance of Wales: Layer Cake or Marble Cake?* British Journal of Politics and International Relations, Volume 16, Issue 2, pp. 310–325.

Gallagher, Jim (2012) *Intergovernmental Relations in the UK: Co-Operation, Competition and Constitutional Change.* British Journal of Politics and International Relations, Volume 14, Issue 2, pp. 198–213.

Gallagher, Jim (2016) *Where Next for Scotland and the United Kingdom?.* In: Bailey, David and Budd, Leslie (eds.) *Devolution and the UK Economy.* London: Rowan and Littlefield.

Garry, John (2016) *Consociation and Voting in Northern Ireland: Party Competition and Electoral Behaviour.* Philadelphia, PA: University of Pennsylvania Press.

Hazell, Robert (2015) *Devolution and the Future of the Union.* London: The Constitution Unit.

Heenan, Deirdre and Birrell, Derek (2018) *Between Devolution and Direct Rule: Implications of a Political Vacuum in Northern Ireland?* The Political Quarterly, Volume 89, Issue 2, pp. 306–312.

HM Government and Welsh Government (2016) The agreement between the Welsh Government and the United Kingdom Government on the Welsh Government's fiscal framework. December. Welsh Government. https://gov.wales/sites/default/files/publications/2018-11/agreement-on-welsh-government-fiscal-framework.pdf

HM Revenue and Customs (2015) *Scotland Act 2012.* Guidance. 26 August. UK Government. https://www.gov.uk/guidance/scotland-act-2012

HM Treasury (2015) *Statement of Funding Policy: Funding the Scottish Parliament, National Assembly for Wales and Northern Ireland Assembly.* November. 7th edition. UK Government. https://www.gov.uk/government/publications/spending-review-and-autumn-statement-2015-documents

HM Treasury (2020a) *Statement of Funding Policy: Funding the Scottish Parliament, National Assembly for Wales and Northern Ireland Assembly.* November. 8th edition. UK Government. https://assets.publishing.service.gov.uk/government/uploads/system/uploads/attachment_data/file/943689/Statement_of_Funding_Policy_2020.pdf

HM Treasury (2020b) *Block Grant Transparency: July 2020 publication.* July. UK Government. https://assets.publishing.service.gov.uk/government/uploads/system/uploads/attachment_data/file/904323/Block_Grant_Transparency_July_2020_explanatory_note_.pdf

Hooghe, Liesbet, Marks, Gary, Schakel, Arjan H., Chapman Osterkatz, Sandra, Niedzwiecki, Sara and Shair-Rosenfield, Sarah (2016) *Measuring Regional Authority: A Postfunctionalist Theory of Governance*, Volume I. Oxford: Oxford University Press.

Hueglin, Thomas O. and Fenna, Alan (2010) *Comparative Federalism: A Systematic Inquiry.* Peterborough: Broadview Press.

Hunt, Jo (2017) *The Supreme Court Judgement in Miller and Its Implication for the Devolved Nations.* Commentary, 1 February. UK in a Changing Europe. https://ukandeu.ac.uk/the-supreme-court-judgment-in-miller-and-its-implications-for-the-devolved-nations/

Hunt, Jo (2021) *Subsidiarity, Competence, and the UK Territorial Constitution.* In: Doyle, Oran, McHarg, Aileen and Murkens, Jo (eds.) *The Brexit Challenge for Ireland and the United Kingdom: Constitutions under Pressure.* Cambridge: Cambridge University Press, pp. 21–42.

Jeffery, Charlie (2009) *Devolution in the United Kingdom: Problems of a Piecemeal Approach to Constitutional Change.* Publius, Volume 39, Issue 2, pp. 289–313.

Jeffery, Charlie (2015) *Constitutional Change – Without End?* The Political Quarterly, Volume 86, Issue 2, pp. 275–278.

Keating, Michael (2004) *The United Kingdom as a Post-Sovereign Polity.* In: O'Neill, Michael (ed.) *Devolution and British Politics.* London: Routledge, pp. 319–332.

Keating, Michael (2012) *Intergovernmental Relations and Innovation: From Co-Operative to Competitive Welfare Federalism in the UK.* British Journal of Politics and International Relations, Volume 14, Issue 2, pp. 214–230.

Keep, Matthew (2021) *The Barnett Formula.* Briefing Paper Number 7386. 23 April. House of Commons. https://commonslibrary.parliament.uk/research-briefings/cbp-7386/

Kellam, Jack (2018) *The Wales Act: A New Dawn for Welsh Devolution?* Comment. 11 April. Institute for Government. https://www.instituteforgovernment.org.uk/blog/wales-act-new-dawn-welsh-devolution

Lazarowicz, Mark and McFadden, Jean (2018) *The Scottish Parliament – Law and Practice.* Edinburgh: Edinburgh University Press.

Lee, Simon (2017) *The Gathering Storm: Federalization and Constitutional Change in the United Kingdom.* In: Eccleston, Richard and Krever, Richard (eds.) *The Future of Federalism – Intergovernmental Financial Relations in an Age of Austerity.* Cheltenham: Edward Elgar Publishing, pp. 124–144.

Leyland, Peter (2011) *The Multifaceted Constitutional Dynamics of U.K. Devolution.* International Journal of Constitutional Law, Volume 9, Issue 1, pp. 251–273.

Marks, Gary, Hooghe, Liesbet and Schakel, Arjan H. (2008) *Measuring Regional Authority.* Regional and Federal Studies, Volume 18, Issue 2–3, pp. 111–121.

McEwen, Nicola and Petersohn, Bettina (2015) *Between Autonomy and Interdependence: The Challenges of Shared Rule after the Scottish Referendum.* The Political Quarterly, Volume 86, Issue 2, pp. 192–200.

Mitchell, James (2009) *Devolution in the UK.* Manchester: Manchester University Press.

O'Neill, Michael (2004) *Devolution and British Politics.* London: Routledge.

Office of the Secretary of State for Scotland and HM Treasury (2021) *Further £1.1 Billion Boost for Scotland's Response to COVID-19.* News story. 15 February. UK Government. https://www.gov.uk/government/news/further-11-billion-boost-for-scotlands-response-to-covid-19

Office of the Secretary of State for Wales and HM Treasury (2021) *Further £650 Million Funding Boost for Covid-19 Response in Wales.* Press release. 16 February. UK Government. https://www.gov.uk/government/news/further-650-million-funding-boost-for-covid-19-response-in-wales

Pasquier, Romain (2021) *Devolution, Functional Decentralisation or Recentralisation? Convergence and Divergence in the European Territorial Governance.* In: Callanan, Mark and Loughlin, John (eds.) *A Research Agenda for Regional and Local Government.* Cheltenham: Edward Elgar Publishing, pp. 49–62.

Paun, Akash and Cheung, Aron and Paun, Akash (2018) *Tax and Devolution.* Explainer. 3 April. Institute for Government. https://www.instituteforgovernment.org.uk/explainers/tax-and-devolution

Pidgeon, Colin (2012) *Barnett Consequentials.* Research and Information Service Briefing Paper 04/12. 16 January. Northern Ireland Assembly.

Poirier, Johanne and Saunders, Cheryl (2015) *Conclusion: Comparative Experience of Intergovernmental Relations in Federal Systems*. In: Poirier, Johanne, Saunders, Cheryl and Kincaid, John (eds.) *Intergovernmental Relations in Federal Systems*. Oxford: Oxford University Press, pp. 440–498.

Poole, Ed Gareth, Ifan, Guto and Phillips, David (2016) *For Wales Don't (Always) See Scotland: Adjusting the Welsh Block Grant after Tax Devolution*. First Report on the 2016-17 Fiscal Framework Negotiations for Wales. Wales Governance Centre at Cardiff University and Institute for Fiscal Studies.

Public Finance Scrutiny Unit (2016) *Forthcoming Executive Draft Budget2017-18: Assembly Consideration*. Research and Information Service Briefing Paper 74/16. 21 October. Northern Ireland Assembly.

Schieren, Stefan (2010) *Großbritannien*. Schwalbach: Wochenschau Verlag.

Schneider, Aaron (2003) *Decentralization: Conceptualization and Measurement*. Studies in Comparative International Development, Volume 38, Issue 3, pp. 32–56.

Scholes, Michael (2014) *European Investment Bank: Financial Assistance for UK Local Government*. Research and Information Service Briefing Paper 80/14. 20 June. Northern Ireland Assembly.

Seely, Antony (2015) *Devolution of Tax Powers to the Scottish Parliament: The Scotland Act 2012*. Research Briefing. 23 January. House of Commons. https://commonslibrary.parliament.uk/research-briefings/sn05984/

Sturm, Roland (2010) *Vereinigtes Königreich Von Großbritannien Und Nordirland – Devolution Und Parlamentssuprematie*. In: Dieringer, Jürgen and Sturm, Roland (eds.) *Regional Governance in EU-Staaten*. Opladen and Farmington Hills, MI: Verlad Barbara Budrich, pp. 107–126.

Sturm, Roland (2015) *Die britische Westminsterdemokratie – Parlament, Regierung Und Verfassungswandel*. Baden-Baden: Nomos.

Sturm, Roland (2017) *Das politische System Großbritanniens*. Wiesbaden: Springer VS.

Watts, Ronald L. (2008). *Comparing Federal Systems*. Montreal and Kingston: McGill-Queen's University Press.

Welsh Government (2018) *Developing New Welsh Taxes*. Policy and strategy. 28 June. https://gov.wales/developing-new-welsh-taxes

Welsh Government (2020) *Finance Ministers Express 'Real Concerns' over UK Internal Market Bill*. Press release. 17 September. https://gov.wales/finance-ministers-express-real-concerns-over-uk-internal-market-bill

Welsh Government (2021) *Welsh Rates of Income Tax*. Policy and strategy, 6 May. https://gov.wales/welsh-rates-income-tax

Welsh Parliament (2021) *Powers*. 22 January. https://senedd.wales/en/abthome/role-of-assembly-how-it-works/Pages/Powers.aspx

4 Formal and Informal Intergovernmental Institutions and Practices

When the devolved administrations were set up in the late 1990s and introduced quasi-federal arrangements at the periphery, Westminster and Whitehall did little to adapt to the new realities of having additional legislatures and executives operating next to them (Kenny et al. 2021, 10; Keating 2021, 75). Pressure for fundamental reforms, aiming for a more federal-like state architecture at the centre, was marginal, as Bradbury (2021, 292) notes: "The overall approach to the reform of the central state in the light of devolution was formed from a mixture of non-decisions, mild adaptations and developments from past conventions and practice". New Labour saw no need to formalise collaborative working but sought to maintain decision-making power depoliticised and bureaucratised at the centre (op. cit., 275–291). Because Labour was in government at UK level, in Wales and in Scotland, until 2007 it could rely on informal intra-party channels of communication to resolve any upcoming issues. Consequently, the ad hoc fashion of intergovernmental exchange failed to address long-term questions that have arisen as different political parties come to power at different levels and the gradual devolution of competences has diverged the politics and policies across the different jurisdictions. Instead of developing a robust intergovernmental framework, the different governments have had to rely on the formal institutions with intergovernmental relevance, informal institutions and practices that are discussed in detail throughout this chapter.

In January 2022, the UK Government finally released the review of intergovernmental relations, which was agreed in 2018 put postponed due to Brexit and the COVID-19 pandemic (UKG10).[1] The review is a statement of intent that does not "create new, or override existing, legal relations or obligations, or to be justiciable." (Cabinet Office and Department for Levelling Up, Housing and Communities 2022a). The suggested reforms build on existing principles and establish a new three-tier model to "provide a positive basis for productive relations, facilitating dialogue where views are aligned and resolution mechanisms where they are not. The review also introduces a new era for IGR with improved reporting on intergovernmental activity, providing greater transparency, accountability and scrutiny from each government's respective legislatures." The first tier refers to the

DOI: 10.4324/9781003349952-4

official and ministerial level and deals with specific policy issues, including multilateral Interministerial Groups (IMGs). The second tier is covered by two standing committees: the Interministerial Standing Committee and the Finance Interministerial Standing Committee. The Prime Minister and Heads of Devolved Governments Council make up the top tier to which the other two tiers are accountable. The different tiers are supported by a standing IGR Secretariat. The review also alters the existing procedure for avoiding, escalating and resolving disputes. These reforms were not in place while this study was conducted and are yet too young to allow for a meaningful assessment. Nevertheless, some prospects of the new mechanisms are incorporated into the various sections, where they have replaced previous arrangements.

Formal institutions with intergovernmental relevance

As discussed in Chapter 2, while non-binding *inter-institutional* set-ups allow governments to flexibly enter or exit any joint negotiations (Broschek 2011, 545; Hueglin 2013, 39), *intra-institutional* arrangements at the central level government integrate lower levels in central decision-making (Benz 2013, 82) and produce federal loyalties (Poirier and Saunders 2015a, 6–7; 2015b, 446). The UK has neither introduced intra-institutional modes of governance nor legally binding intergovernmental institutions. Although policymakers talk about the 'formal' procedures or machinery of intergovernmental relations, they are not *formal* according to the definitions used in this study. Yet, there are *formal institutions* with intergovernmental relevance at the centre, which will be examined in the following; including the Cabinet Office, the Scotland Office and the Wales Office, as well as the Supreme Court.

The Core Executive and the Cabinet

Prior to 2010, the responsibility for devolution changed across different UK Government departments. From 2003 on, devolution issues were allocated to the Department for Constitutional Affairs, which became the Ministry of Justice (MoJ) in 2007. Although the Secretaries of State for Scotland and Wales are not subordinate to the MoJ, the Scotland and the Wales Office were attached to the Ministry mostly for corporate service purposes.[2] Under the 2010 Coalition Government, devolution and intergovernmental matters were transferred to the Cabinet Office and the Deputy Prime Minister at the time, Nick Clegg, who also chaired the Cabinet's Devolution Committee (Birrell 2012a, 214; Deacon 2012, 10).[3] This role was subsequently taken on by the First Secretary of State and later by the Chancellor of the Duchy of Lancaster, who has a responsibility for constitutional affairs and managing relations with the Scottish Government, the Welsh Government and the Northern Ireland Executive (UKG1). Apart from these ministerial posts, in response to the Scottish independence referendum, the UK Governance Group was set up in 2015 as part of the Cabinet Office to lead on constitutional and devolution issues and to advise ministers and departments (UKG10). This allowed the Constitution Group of the Cabinet Office, the Scotland Office, the Office of the Advocate General for Scotland[4] and the Wales Office to work more collaboratively and to speak with a more collective voice (Cabinet Office 2021a, 16). It also provided the secretariat for the Joint Ministerial Committee (JMC) and hosts its successor the IGR Secretariat, and has been responsible for coordinating meetings with the devolved administrations, reviewing the intergovernmental architecture and ensuring that UK Government departments adopt capabilities to engage with the devolved administrations during policy development (UKG1). Despite their efforts to strengthen the UK Government's expertise in devolution issues, their success in increasing awareness among Whitehall politicians and officials has been slow, varied and insufficient to face the challenges of leaving the EU (Kenny et al. 2021, 22–23). The Dunlop Review (Cabinet Office 2021a, 14) found that responsibility for issues of the Union depends largely on the operation of individual departments and is not strongly coordinated within the core executive. The Cabinet lacks the longevity and authority required to achieve substantial changes within the practices of individual Whitehall departments, as a UK civil servant suggested: "The Cabinet Office is known for never really living up to its role as the centre of the civil service, the centre of the government. But it never seems to have that gravitas, that central force behind them." (UKG3). Another reason for the absence of coherent leadership on devolution and intergovernmental relations within the core executive lies in the lack of transparency and accountability.

To highlight the importance of sustaining the Union, in 2019 Prime Minister Boris Johnson added the title Minister for the Union to this portfolio (Keating 2021, 79), and a small Number 10 Union Unit was founded working next to the Union Directorate in the Cabinet Office led by the Chancellor of the Duchy of Lancaster.[5] In order to better manage the constitutional and devolution issues, the Dunlop Review (Cabinet Office 2021a, 16–19) recommended the introduction of a senior ministerial post, a new subcommittee to the Cabinet, as well as a permanent secretary head of the UK Governance Group. The Cabinet Office Minister, Michael Gove, responded to the review with a series of suggestions for new initiatives, including setting up a Union Strategy Committee and a Union Advisory Group (Gove 2021). However, according to Keating (2021, 79), such institutional initiatives to save the Union have only been short-lived in nature:

> At times of constitutional difficulty, the central apparatus has been strengthened and initiatives launched to sensitize departments to devolution. In 2019, the Prime Minister assumed the symbolic title of Minister for the Union. When matters have stabilized, the apparatus

has been run down again and predominantly English Whitehall departments allowed to forget about the devolved implications of their own polities.

Regular organisational changes, varying prioritisation and lack of assertiveness have limited the Cabinet Office and the Core Executive's role in providing effective leadership and coherent positioning in the engagement with the devolved administrations. And by all indications, this situation seems unlikely to change in the near future.

The Offices and Secretaries of State for Scotland and Wales

The territorial offices have a long history dating back to the 18th century to the Union of England and Scotland (Lazarowicz and McFadden 2018, 160). The Scottish Office was created in 1885, a Minister of Welsh Affairs in 1951 and the Welsh Office in 1964 (Sturm 2020, 178). Before 1998, the Secretaries of State for Scotland, Wales and Northern Ireland were the key democratically elected representatives of territorial interests to the UK Government and beyond. With the creation of the devolved administrations, however, the territorial offices and Secretaries of State lost the majority of their functions to the devolved administrations and their role and size diminished. During the first decade of devolution, the role of the territorial offices has varied and between 2003 and 2008 the Secretaries of State had only a shared portfolio.[6] Nowadays, the Wales Office is the smallest Whitehall department with less than 50 members of staff, followed by the Scotland Office with approximately 75 civil servants (UKG5, UKG7).[7] Even though the Scotland and Wales Offices did not become the main intergovernmental protagonists that one may have expected in the early days of devolution (Mitchell 2010, 59), the Secretaries of State liaised frequently with ministers from the devolved executives (Bradbury 2021, 283). While the political relations have changed since then, the three Offices still seek to operate as bridges between the different administrations and facilitate coordination between the UK Government and the devolved administrations. Their tasks involve briefing and advising other UK ministers and departments on legislation that affects devolved matters and to influence policy development. All three have corresponding offices in Edinburgh, Cardiff and Belfast to represent the UK Government in Scotland, Wales and Northern Ireland, and in turn, they feed the interests of stakeholders from the different parts of the UK into Whitehall. The respective Secretaries of State have Cabinet rank, which means they are directly linked to decisions by the core executive and have knowledge of relevant developments of individual departments.[8] Even though membership of the Scotland and Wales Offices in the UK Governance Group and their relationships to the Cabinet Office allows them to impact on decision-making (UKG5, UKG7), managing and mediating territorial interests effectively in Cabinet is not an easy task for comparatively small departments with few powers and a marginal role in Cabinet meetings (Deacon 2012, 174; cf. Gallagher 2012, 204; Lazarowicz and McFadden 2018, 160).[9] The Secretaries of State and the territorial Offices, particularly those for Scotland and Wales, therefore work closely together and coordinate their responses to policies of other departments, as an official from the Wales Offices put it: "We shamelessly unite together quite often against Whitehall departments. The same is true around the Cabinet table. There's been joint letters sometimes, where the Secretaries of State for Wales and Scotland write and say 'this won't work, this has been an English designed policy'. So we make common cause when we can." (UKG7). Officials from the Scotland Office also commented: "The Secretary of State [for Scotland] sits in Cabinet and quite a lot of the cross-Whitehall Committees, and that's the same for the Secretary of State for Wales. It's always a challenge, if you're small but hopefully we punch reasonably high above our weight." (UKG5).

While the first years of devolution were characterised by personal animosities and unwelcomed interventions by the Secretary of State into devolved affairs, over time the relationship between the Scotland Office and the Scottish Government improved (Cairney 2011, 105–106).[10] After the SNP gained the majority in the Scottish Parliament in 2007, the Scotland Office became more important as a mediator of conflict (McEwen and Petersohn 2015, 196). Particularly on major events, such as the Scottish independence referendum and the passage of the Scotland Acts of 2012 and 2016, the Scotland Office has been a central actor in formulating and implementing provisions within the UK Government (Scottish Affairs Committee 2019a, 36–38). Although the political relations between the UK and the Scottish Governments remain strained, the Scotland Office seeks to maintain good links to and cooperates with Scottish ministers and civil servants (UKG5). And yet, for the Scottish Government the Scotland Office is not an unbiased arbiter, and they prefer working directly with Whitehall departments and ministers and the Cabinet Office (UKG1):

> Scottish ministers will not see the Secretary of State for Scotland of sufficient seniority within Government for them to engage with. But that is partly the result of their underlying desire to be an independent country, and therefore they think Nicola Sturgeon as the Prime Minister of Scotland and therefore she should engage as an equal with the Prime Minister of the rest of the UK.
>
> (UKG1)

Furthermore, an official in the Scottish Government offered an alternative view for their preference to work with other departments:

> At times it feels like they're not completely involved in some of the most important conversation that we're having, where we will have

direct conversations with UK Government departments. [...] If there's a Cabinet process and a minister announced their plans, the Scotland Office sees that this has included direct input from Scottish ministers, there is a role for them there. Whether they are a) always doing that and b) to the right time, I have no reason to think that they aren't but after 20 years of devolution, individual departments in Whitehall should have a sense for how this should work. Most departments have a devolved a unit that helps them to considers those sorts of issues.

(SG2)

In particular, because of its relatively weak position among other Whitehall departments, the value and purpose of the Scotland Office has also frequently been put into question by the Scottish Government (SG6) (Scottish Affairs Committee 2019a, 37–38).

As with the Scotland Office, the relationship between the Welsh Government and the Wales Office improved over time. Since reserved matters increasingly touch on devolved matters, the Wales Office has sought to mediate policy preferences between the Welsh and the UK Governments (UKG7, WG4). This was particularly important when the National Assembly for Wales had no primary legislative competences and required the approval of the UK Parliament (Birrell 2012a, 214). The Wales Office can be a valuable vehicle to promote the Welsh Government's interests vis-à-vis the UK Government, and Welsh officials described their working relations as positive and useful (WG2):

I have a fantastic relationship in working with the Wales Office. We talk a lot, we talk very informally and confidentially about all sorts of things, and that helps smooth things over. And where they can, they do help unblock other things that are going on. For example, we have a problem with another department, then they are often part of the solution in terms of working through the issues and a lot of the time, they're on our side.

(WG10)

Notwithstanding such general appreciation, the need for the Wales Office has also been subject to ongoing contestation (cf. Deacon 2012, 174).[11] The Welsh Government is not always pleased with the Wales Office's involvement in negotiations and has increasingly developed its direct links with individual Whitehall departments to promote its preferences (WG2, WG10, WP5):

They are seeking to be an intermediator between us and other UK Government departments. But we don't start from that premise. We start from the premise that we represent the interests of Wales in devolved areas to UK Government departments directly, and that we don't need to go through the Wales Office. [...] There is still that tension in terms of where the Wales Office will want to represent Wales on reserved matters. From our point of view, we are seeing increasingly even reserved matters are so interconnected with our interests that we want to have a view. We want to express that directly to the people within the UK Government and the ministers who are decision-makers. We don't want that to be wrapped up in a Wales view presented by the Wales Office.

(WG10)

Overall, the extent to which the territorial officials maintain collaborative connections with the devolved administrations remains strongly dependent on personal relations and the minister in office.[12]

The Supreme Court

In federal polities, constitutional courts ensure the supremacy of the constitution on which the legitimacy of governmental authority at all levels is based. Their impartial interpretation of the constitution is essential to resolve intergovernmental conflicts (Burgess 2006, 158–159; Watts 2008, 158 et seq.; Adam 2021, 43). The fact that the UK did not have a constitutional court until 2009, and that the judiciary was not clearly separated from the legislature and the executive, reflects its unitary nature. When the Constitutional Reform Act 2005 created the new Supreme Court, it transferred the House of Lords' capacity to consider judicial appeals and the Judicial Committee of the Privy Council's responsibility for devolution (UK Parliament 2021). As the ultimate court of appeal, the Supreme Court takes an essential role in reviewing the division of power across the UK and devolved institutions and can decide whether primary legislation passed by the devolved legislatures is within their competence (Supreme Court 2021) – either before the enactment of a bill to prevent it from receiving Royal Assent or after its passage. Importantly, its rulings are only legally binding for the devolved institutions. The Supreme Court may not challenge the legality of statutes by the UK Parliament or decide whether Westminster acted within competence (Caird 2016, 3–4; Brouillet and Mullen 2018, 64).[13] This creates a strong judicial bias favouring the centre (McEwen et al. 2012, 337), as a UK official stated: "Ultimately the reference point for deciding on this is the UK Government itself. It cannot be anybody else in terms of intergovernmental dispute." (UKG10). The devolved administrations can only ask the court to clarify whether their parliaments are allowed to legislate in a specific area (Adam 2021, 48).

With the same party in power at central and devolved levels, there were no judicial disputes over the allocation of responsibilities between governments (Bradbury 2021, 297). Supreme Court cases that have concerned the legality of legislation by the Scottish Parliament were mostly not initiated by the UK Government but related to potential breach of personal rights[14] or other private parties.[15] The first judicial decision that an act of a devolved legislature was outside of their competence was *Salvesen v Riddell* (2013), which challenged provisions of the Agricultural Holdings (Scotland) Act 2003 to reform the regulation of the relationship between agricultural tenants and landlords (Caird 2016, 15–26; Brouillet and Mullen 2018, 65–68).[16] Although the impact of the Supreme Court on intergovernmental relations is comparatively weak (WP5), it was decisive in redefining the constitutional relations between the UK Parliament and the Welsh Assembly. Two cases highlighted the need for a clearer division of power between Westminster and the Senedd. First, the Local Government Byelaws (Wales) Bill 2012, which aimed at changing procedures for the making and enforcing of byelaws by local authorities, was reviewed by the Supreme Court after referral by the Attorney General for England and Wales (Caird 2016, 20–22). The Court ruled subsequently in favour of the Welsh Assembly and decided that the bill was within its legal competence (UKG7, WP5). Second, when Westminster passed the Enterprise and Regulatory Reform Act 2012–2013 abolishing the Agricultural Wages Board for England and Wales, the Welsh Government introduced the Agriculture Sector (Wales) Act 2014 to re-establish an Agricultural Advisory Panel for Wales. The Attorney General for England and Wales argued that the issue was a reserved matter of employment and industrial relations. When it referred the case for a review of competence, the Supreme Court decided that the Welsh legislation was also about agriculture and therefore within the Senedd's powers (WP5) (Caird 2016, 27; Cowie 2018a, 46). Both cases set a precedent which de facto enabled the Welsh Assembly to reverse any UK bill that touches on matters within its powers, and suddenly, the UK Government realised that Supreme Court judgements could have a far-reaching impact on intergovernmental relations. In order to clarify the allocation of legislative authority, the UK Government then introduced the Wales Act 2017 replacing the conferred with a reserved power model similar to that in Scotland (UKG7): "We had experience with this, we've lost two cases at the Supreme Court. We have got little doubt in our expert opinion that if you took this question to the Supreme Court, they would air on the side of the devolved because that's what they've done so far." (UKG7).

The third case where the Supreme Court decided over the Welsh Assembly's authority to pass a piece of legislation concerned the Medical Costs for Asbestos Diseases (Wales) Bill 2015. However, this time, it was not the UK Government but the Welsh Government's chief legal adviser, the Counsel General for Wales, who referred a private member bill to the Court. Although the Welsh Government thought the bill was within competence, it wanted a clarification of its lawfulness because they anticipated a legal challenge by private parties (Caird 2016, 29). The majority of judges decided that the Assembly did not have the fiscal powers to levy charges for health services, and if it had, the charge for employers and insurers was "not sufficiently related to the organisation of funding of the National Health Service" as it related to "compensators and insurers rather than patients and lack[ed] any direct or close connection with the provision of Welsh NHS services." (Supreme Court 2015). As the Senedd Member, who introduced the bill and was 'gutted' after the decision (BBC 2015), mentioned during an interview:

> We introduced legislation to recover the cost of the medical treatment for victims of asbestos with the view that that money would then be used to provide additional support for asbestos victims and families. The Supreme Court by a majority of 3 to 2 ruled that that was a tax raising matter and tax raising powers didn't exist then. At the time the issues was, if did we have competence to do it and to interpret whether it was a social measure, which was within our competence, or whether it was a tax raising measure. You can see the Supreme Court was quite split on it.
>
> (WP1)

Whereas the Medical Costs for Asbestos Diseases (Wales) Bill was not strictly speaking about an intergovernmental dispute but about a clarification of devolved competence, the Supreme Court took an important role in defining the extent to which the devolved administrations could engage in the process of the UK's withdrawal from the EU. Its judgement on *Miller v Secretary of State for Exiting the European Union* ruled against the appeal of the Scottish and Welsh Governments that primary Westminster legislation to trigger Article 50 TEU would require the consent of the devolved legislatures. The Supreme Court decided against the legal relevance of conventions, which would have only politically binding effects. When the Scottish Parliament refused to give legislative consent to the EU (Withdrawal) Bill, because it enabled Whitehall and Westminster to pass primary and secondary legislation in devolved areas, and instead passed its own UK Withdrawal from the European Union (Legal Continuity) (Scotland) Bill[17] on 18 March 2018, the UK Attorney General and the Advocate General for Scotland referred the bill to the Supreme Court. This was the first time that UK Law Officers challenged a Scottish bill before the Supreme Court. The latter disapplied the Scottish bill in December of the same year as the UK Parliament had already passed an act that superseded the Scottish legislation. Except for Section 17,[18] most of the bill was within competence (Boffey 2019; Adam 2021, 56–57).[19]

Overall, the Supreme Court does not have the same weight as constitutional courts in federations and "will naturally favour the Westminster Government" (WP4), in the words of a Senedd Member. This is partly due to the detailed nature of the devolution legislation, the specification of reserved and devolved matters, pre-enactment discussions between governments to avoid subsequent litigation, and perhaps most importantly, that the Supreme Court has also sought to avoid resolving political disputes in court. Its interpretations of bills and acts have been cautious and are text-bound rather than focused on the constitutional relevance of statutes (Brouillet and Mullen 2018, 63–74). And yet, as the different cases demonstrate, it has clearly become an established authority for devolution issues and intergovernmental disputes. As more powers are devolved to Scotland and Wales, the Court's role has grown and its decisions have had profound consequences on the devolution settlement, also in favour of the devolved institutions, particularly in Wales (WP1). Remarkably, the UK Government has adhered to the decisions of the Court even though its judgements cannot disapply Westminster legislation. If Whitehall did decide to ignore the Supreme Court's impartial rulings on such matters, it would raise serious constitutional conflicts and severely damage its role as an independent arbitrator (UKG7). Due to the increasing complexity of the devolution settlement post-Brexit, legal interpretations of the constitutional framework may become more important and the devolved administrations will seek more possibilities to access the Supreme Court (Adam 2021, 63); as it is the case with the Scottish Independence Referendum Bill, which the Scottish Government referred to the Supreme Court to clarify its lawfulness.

Informal intergovernmental institutions

Informal intergovernmental institutions are not legally codified but based on established rules or guidelines creating obligations that can be socially and politically sanctioned (cf. Helmke and Levitsky 2004, 727). In the UK, these are neither *competing with, accommodating* nor even *complementing* formal institutions but are *substantive* in the absence of any formal intergovernmental institutions.[20] The most important one is the Sewel Convention requiring the legislative consent of the devolved legislatures to Westminster bills that affect areas with their competences. The principles and operation of intergovernmental relations are set out in a network of non-legally binding agreements, memorandums of understanding, concordats and, recently, the UK Common Frameworks programme to establish new means for coordinating policies and dealing with divergence after leaving the EU's regulatory regime. At the peak of intergovernmental forums stood the JMC, which also included the Protocol on Dispute Resolution. Financial issues are covered by the Joint Exchequer Committee. The British-Irish Council completes the informal institutional arrangements between the different jurisdictions – although it is mainly an arena for information and best-practice exchange and does not feature in the following chapters.

The Sewel Convention

In 1998, the Sewel Convention[21] was introduced to protect territorial autonomy and to prevent Westminster from interfering arbitrarily in matters devolved to the Scottish Parliament. For Adam (2021, 49): "The Sewel Convention is the United Kingdom's own distinct model of incorporation or safeguarding of the federal principle in general terms". According to the convention, "it is recognised that the Parliament of the United Kingdom will not normally legislate with regard to devolved matters without the consent of the Scottish Parliament." It is at the discretion and in accordance with the Standing Orders of the devolved legislatures to decide whether an act of Westminster requires their legal consent. After the corresponding devolved executive forwards its views on a UK bill and either recommends giving consent or not in a legislative consent memorandum, the devolved legislature can then pass or deny a Legislative Consent Motion. This allows them to scrutinise and seek changes to primary legislation by the UK Parliament (Cowie 2018a, 4–8).[22] Nevertheless, to sustain the constitutional supremacy of Parliament the Sewel Convention cannot be legally enforced. Even after it was codified in the Scotland Act 2016 and officially extended to the Welsh Assembly by the Wales Act 2017, it remains an informal arrangement and there is no independent or judicial review deciding whether circumstances are 'normal' or not. In principle, the convention also applies to Northern Ireland where few Legislative Consent Motions have been passed. Between 1999 and 2020, the UK Parliament has passed over 200 laws that required the consent of either the Scottish Parliament (155),[23] the Senedd (61),[24] the Northern Ireland Assembly (65) or at least two of them (Paun and Shuttleworth 2020, 11).

For some Sewel is a constitutional guarantee and safeguard for territorial autonomy over the devolved powers. Others see it also a "political device" for negotiations across governments prior the formal introduction of bills (SG4, SP1) (cf. Keating 2021, 65):

> Legally it's not a strong guarantee but it had been observed until Brexit, including the 2012 and 2016 Scotland Acts in response to the demands from the Scottish Government and the Scottish Parliament. Deep down the Sewel convention is a guarantee about the constitutional position of the Scottish Parliament. Yes, it has been used to change Westminster legislation. It has been used to recognise the views of the Scottish Parliament and its competences.
>
> (SG4)

Prior to the 2016 EU referendum, Gallagher (2012, 205) suggested that Sewel seemed like "an example of remarkable intergovernmental cooperation". In the event that the UK Government acknowledges that it legislates in devolved areas, the Legislative Consent Motion has helped in enabling cooperation, influencing UK bills and in realising common policy goals through a UK-wide approach (Paun and Shuttleworth 2020, 11; Adam 2021, 52). As an official from the UK Government said:

> There are a lot of bills that go through that are actually quite technical. In a lot of cases, the UK Government and the Scottish Government have agreed that it makes sense to do a piece of legislation UK wide. [...] The Legislative Consent Motion is just a healthy way of keeping a little bit of that accountability in the system. We wouldn't generally put provisions in bill that legislate in devolved competence unless the Scottish Government were happy with it. There's incidents that are exceptional which make it difficult to find a common provision. But generally, it's a really positive tool of making the devolution settlement work well.
>
> (UKG5)

As Figure 4.1 demonstrates, passed Sewel motions vastly outnumber the occasions when one of the devolved legislature did not give its consent to a bill. By 2020, only 13 out of 350 times was consent withheld fully or partially, which demonstrates a remarkable lack of controversy on most issues due to their technical nature and the early engagement between governments before a bill is formally introduced (Paun, Sargeant, Nicholson and Rycroft S2018). Sewel motions are often used when they agree over the purpose of UK-wide legislation where the devolved legislatures could but do not necessarily want to bring their own laws on the way (SG4, UKG5, UKG7, WP5). In turn, some bills may fall under reserved competence, for instance in relation to immigration and asylum, but the UK Government relies on additional devolved legislation to implement its policies (Lazarowicz and McFadden 2018, 149–151).[25]

Until Brexit, there were a few occasions when the devolved legislatures had not given their consent, but the UK Government did not recognise their bill as interfering in devolved areas.[26] In February 2011, for the first time consent was denied by devolved administration and acknowledged as being necessary by the UK Government. Although the Senedd withheld consent to the Police Reform and Social Responsibility Bill, Westminster passed the bill with some changes[27] and Police and Crime Commissioners and Panels were established in Wales.[28] The UK Government also abandoned parts of the Local Audit and Accountability Bill 2013–2014 and Antisocial Behaviour, Crime and Policing Bill 2013–2014, after the Senedd had withheld legislative consent (Cowie 2018a, 48–50; Paun and Shuttleworth 2020, 12). In 2011, the Scottish Parliament refused to pass a consent motion on the Welfare Reform Bill, which proposed significant UK-wide measures that would have affected the powers of Scottish ministers in the areas of Universal Credit and Personal Independence Payment. The Welfare Reform Act 2012 was amended accordingly and in turn the Welfare Reform (Further Provision) (Scotland) Act 2012 was passed by the Scottish Parliament to provide Scottish ministers with the corresponding welfare powers. The Public Service Pensions Bill 2011–2012 presents another example where the Scottish Parliament threatened to deny consent and amendments were consequently made (Cowie 2018a, 45).[29]

96 Formal and Informal Intergovernmental Institutions

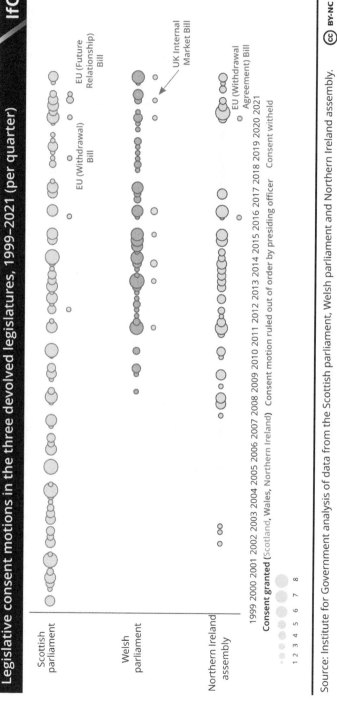

Figure 4.1 Timeline of Legislative Consent Motions, including refusal of consent

Source: Paun, Sargeant, Nicholson and Rycroft (2018) Sewel convention. Explainer. 8 December. Institute for Government. Used with permission.

Interestingly, the Senedd holds the record for rejecting most consent motions, which is due to the conferred powers model that was in place before the Wales Act 2017. The allocation of responsibility across the UK Parliament and the Welsh Assembly was ambiguous and the cause of occasional disagreement on whether legislative consent was required (Paun and Shuttleworth 2020, 11). The confusion became particularly evident when parts of the Enterprise and Regulatory Reform Bill 2012–2013 proposed to abolish the Agricultural Wages Board for England and Wales. In January 2013, the Welsh Assembly refused consent on the grounds that agriculture is a devolved area and it would circumvent the protections for cross-border public bodies under the Public Bodies Act 2011. Under the assumption that the bill was about employment and industrial relations and therefore reserved, the validity of the Welsh veto was not recognised. Consequently, the Welsh Assembly passed its own Agriculture Sector (Wales) Act, which replaced the Agricultural Wages Board with an Agricultural Advisory Panel for Wales only. The UK Government, represented by the Attorney General for England and Wales, brought the case to the Supreme Court, which confirmed the lawfulness of the Welsh Government's act. The UK Government abstained from introducing further bills that would override Welsh legislation. On a second occasion, in 2017, the Trade Union (Wales) Act disapplied provisions of the UK Trade Union Bill 2015–2016 and received Royal Assent. Based on their previous experience, the UK Government did not refer the Welsh bill to the Supreme Court (WP1) (Cowie 2018a, 46–51). Facing the far-reaching implications for Westminster's ability to pass UK-wide legislation, the UK Government sought to establish greater clarity on the allocation of powers through the Wales Act 2017 that introduced the reserved powers model in Wales. Since then, there have only been exceptional occasions where the Welsh Government insisted that a bill would impinge on devolved responsibilities but the UK Government treated it as a reserved matter (WG8).

The overall record of the Sewel Convention is mixed. For most of its existence, the convention was well-respected by all governments, even though, as an MS mentioned: "Sometimes I've said semi-humourlessly with the Legislative Consent Motion you have two choices: either vote for it or vote against it and be overruled." (WP4). Brexit has laid bare the vulnerability of an informal institution used to govern intergovernmental relations. When Theresa May's administration wanted to trigger Article 50 Treaty on European Union (TEU) and inform the European Council about the UK's intention to leave the EU, the Supreme Court ruled in its judgement on *Miller v Secretary of State for Exiting the European Union* on 24 January 2017 that this required primary legislation. Yet, the Court did not follow the appeal of the Scottish and Welsh Governments that the UK Government was legally bound by the Sewel Convention to secure the consent of the devolved legislatures. When the EU (Notification of Withdrawal) Act 2017 passed Westminster against the opposition of the two devolved administrations, which abstained from scheduling legislative consent memorandums, it deeply damaged their trust in UK's Governments respect for the devolved jurisdictions (Cowie 2018a, 26–27). Whereas the UK Government had not recognised the EU (Notification of Withdrawal) Act as relevant to Sewel, it acknowledged that the EU (Withdrawal) Bill, which was introduced in July 2017 to convert EU law into domestic law, would clearly affect devolved areas. The main area of contestation related to Clause 11 and Schedule 2, which the Scottish and Welsh Governments saw as a severe 'power grab' that would enable the UK Government and Parliament to pass primary and secondary legislations in repatriated policy areas without sufficient safeguards for the devolution settlement. The Welsh Assembly eventually gave its consent to the bill and the Scottish Parliament did not.[30] When, on 26 June 2018, the EU (Withdrawal) Act finally received Royal Assent, it was the first time that the need for consent was recognised by the UK Government yet the non-binding veto of a devolved legislature was ignored. The next serious blow to the Sewel Convention followed on 23 January 2020, when the EU (Withdrawal Agreement) Act was given Royal Assent despite rejected consent motions in all three devolved legislatures.[31] In light of the exceptional circumstances, the UK Government justified the passing of the bill without consent, which had not been done before, and rhetorically committed to Sewel:

> The circumstances of our departure from the EU, following the 2016 referendum, are not normal – they are unique. At every stage of the European Union (Withdrawal Agreement) Bill, the UK Government has demonstrated its enduring commitment and respect for the Sewel Convention and the principles that underpin our constitutional arrangements. The practices and procedures that have developed to deliver the Sewel Convention encourage the UK Government to consult with the devolved administrations on legislation at an early stage to ensure their views are taken into account.
>
> (UK Parliament 2020a)

The repeated disregard for the Sewel Convention left devolved administrations exposed not only to political frustration but also to constitutional uncertainty (SG11, WG8, WP1), as it was expressed by a civil servant in the Scottish Government:

> Until Brexit it has been a very powerful tool within our constitution. But it is not absolute. The Withdrawal Act, we saw its lack of definite bite and legal enforceability, which means that you're vulnerable in circumstanced where are acute disagreements, where you would hope that it would be at its strongest. [...] Conventions are supposed to be strong safeguards of the UK system, but they depend crucially on the actors in

the system believing that they are strong. The minute they say 'actually, we don't need to do this', they fall away because the courts won't step in, and we had the Miller case to test that.

(SG4)

The Welsh Government's view of the EU (Withdrawal Agreement) Act was slightly more optimistic accounting for the singularity of Brexit, and it proposed to formalise the convention and to specify the circumstances when devolved vetoes could be overridden by the UK Parliament (WG11) (Welsh Government 2019a, 8):

There were two important things which happened, which could help us get closer to where we want to be on Sewel. One of which was the UK Government started to explain, not in huge detail, why the situation was not normal. They used words like 'unique exceptional circumstances', which is more than we've had before, and second of all, those remarks were being made as part of proceedings in the UK Parliament.

(WG10)

As the saying goes: all good things come in threes. The UK Internal Market Act 2020, which was introduced by the UK Government on 9 September to ensure the integrity of the internal market for goods, services and professional qualifications post-Brexit, was the latest and highly controversial case where the Sewel Convention failed to ensure the interests of the Scottish and Welsh administrations. The Scottish Parliament denied its consent on 7 October 2020, and the Senedd followed on 8 December 2020 due to serious concerns about a re-centralisation of their powers. Once again, the UK Government ignored the veto of the devolved legislatures and the bill became statute on 17 December 2020. After three high-profile bills were legitimately refused by devolved legislatures but still enacted, some commentators have proclaimed the abandonment of Sewel (cf. Martin 2021, 8). At the same time, it seems fair to point out that during the same parliamentary sessions other bills continued to receive consent from the Scottish and Welsh Parliaments, including the Coronavirus Act 2020.[32] Throughout 2021, a combined number of 19 Legislative Consent Motions were recommended and passed in total (Department for Levelling Up, Housing and Communities 2022, 46). The Scottish Government (Constitution and Cabinet Directorate 2018) and the Welsh Government (2019a, 8) have forwarded proposals on how to strengthen and enforce the application of the convention within the UK Parliament. For the Legislative Consent Motion to become a formal safeguard of territorial autonomy, however, it would need to legally bind Parliament to the decisions of other legislatures, which currently does not seem like a realistic scenario.

The Memorandum of Understanding, intergovernmental agreements, concordats and UK Common Frameworks

In 1999, the UK Government, the Scottish ministers and the Cabinet of the National Assembly for Wales produced a Memorandum of Understanding (MoU) setting out guiding principles of intergovernmental communication, consultation, cooperation and the exchange of information. Since then, the MoU has frequently been redrafted (in 2000, 2001, 2010, 2012 and 2013) to adapt to the ongoing devolution of legislative and fiscal authority.[33] Paragraph 4 of the 2013 MoU states that:

> All four administrations are committed to the principle of good communication with each other, and especially where one administration's work may have some bearing upon the responsibilities of another administration. The primary aim is not to constrain the discretion of any administration but to allow administrations to make representations to each other in sufficient time for those representations to be fully considered.
>
> (Cabinet Office 2012)

The MoU is supplemented by four major intergovernmental agreements: (A) the Agreement on the Joint Ministerial Committee; (B) the Concordat on Co-ordination of European Union Policy Issues; (C) the Concordat on Financial Assistance to Industry and (D) the Concordat on International Relations; and by 15 Devolution Guidance Notes on the working relations for civil servants (Cabinet Office 2019c). As paragraph 2 of the 2013 MoU states, the MoU is only "a statement of political intent, and should not be interpreted as a binding agreement. It does not create legal obligations between the parties." (Cabinet Office 2012). This leaves room for different interpretations over principles, such as "good communication", and has therefore raised criticism of the Memorandum's usefulness by the devolved administrations (McEwen et al. 2018, 7).

The MoU is the most obvious intergovernmental agreement and sits at the top of a network of informal multilateral and bilateral compacts, concordats and protocols. Although these are not legally binding and hardly transparent to outsiders, they bear an important practical relevance for the joint working of the different administrations (Lazarowicz and McFadden 2018, 154). According to Leyland (2011, 255), "They have been referred to as 'a form of codification of the processes of government' that have not only contributed significantly to continuity and the smooth transition of policy but have also helped facilitate policy coordination between the many overlapping layers of modern governance." While it seems like an impossible task to gain a comprehensive overview of all relevant agreements (even the different governments themselves might struggle to achieve this, if they tried),[34] bilateral concordats between individual Whitehall and devolved departments set out principles, expectations and procedural guidance around consultation, communication and confidentiality (Horgan 2004, 116; Deacon 2012, 13). A UK official explained their political effect on different stakeholders:

> Inevitably there's always some reluctance to put something down formally in writing. When we managed to get ministers on both sides to agree on this, and something you can point to is very helpful in a number of reasons. [...] It's a very useful tool to us to say: this is the example of good practice that we should all be sticking to.
>
> (UKG4)

Intergovernmental agreements have become particularly important during the EU withdrawal process. New legislation and working arrangements have to ensure the functionality of many policy areas that were previously governed by EU-wide frameworks, as a Welsh civil servant elaborated:

> Brexit has produced a great many intergovernmental agreements covering all sorts of activity with different levels of intricacy. The Welsh Assembly and all legislatures in the UK are aware of them but how you input into them or coordinate them is very difficult. The UK is creating quite a substantial web of different types of agreement, this is a significant part of how devolution is working.
>
> (WG5)

Particularly interesting here is the UK Common Frameworks programme, which will be analysed as an example of cooperation and conflict. To coordinate the legislative powers returning from the EU to the UK, the different governments of the UK decided to introduce a joint approach to governance, decision-making and dispute resolution; the management of a UK-wide market; negotiations with the EU; the implementation of trade deals and international obligations and the position of Northern Ireland (Cabinet Office 2019a). For this purpose, on 16 October 2017, the JMC Europe agreed to the development of Common Frameworks:

> As the UK leaves the European Union, the Government of the United Kingdom and the devolved administrations agree to work together to establish common approaches in some areas that are currently governed by EU law, but that are otherwise within areas of competence of the devolved administrations or legislatures. A framework will set out a common UK, or GB, approach and how it will be operated and governed. This may consist of common goals, minimum or maximum standards, harmonisation, limits on action, or mutual recognition, depending on the policy area and the objectives being pursued. Frameworks may be implemented by legislation, by executive action, by memorandums of understanding, or by other means depending on the context in which the framework is intended to operate.
>
> (Cabinet Office 2021b)

The UK Common Framework programme set out as a new informal governance arrangement to integrate intergovernmental relations post-Brexit. According to the JMC Europe, this would "lead to a significant increase in decision-making powers for the devolved administrations" (ibid.).[35] The Scottish and the Welsh Governments expected that they would provide differentiated mechanisms to coordinate devolved and reserved powers, share information and to resolve disputes (SG4, WG9, WG11):

> It's not about detailed legal structures. It's about how you coordinate, how you resolved dispute and how you share information. [...] You make things work by working out the ways of operating, the way of sharing information, the ways resolving disputes. That non-legislative bit is the bit that makes the real difference, but you need the formal, legal framework as well.
>
> (WG9)

After two provisional assessments in 2018 and 2019, by the end of 2020, 154 policy areas were identified in which EU law intersected with devolved competence. Of these 115 required no further action because policy divergence was not expected or other arrangements already existed (category 1), 22 required non-legislative (category 2)[36] and 18 legislative (category 3) frameworks[37] (Cabinet Office 2020a). Due to Brexit and COVID-19 among other political challenges, the governments had finalised all stages of the UK Common Framework programme by the end of this study. During autumn 2020, three provisional Common Frameworks were published: Nutrition Labelling, Composition and Standards (Department of Health and Social Care 2020a); Hazardous Substance (Planning) (Ministry of Housing, Communities and Local Government 2020); Food and Feed Safety and Hygiene (Department of Health and Social Care 2020b). One year later, in October 2021, UK and devolved ministers approved 29 provisional Common Frameworks: Emissions Trading System; Radioactive Substances; Late Payment; Specified Quantities and Packaged Goods; Company Law; Agricultural Support; Agriculture – Fertiliser Regulations; Agriculture – Organic Production; Agriculture – Zootech; Animal Health and Welfare; Fisheries Management and Support; Plant Health; Plant Varieties and Seeds; Air Quality; Best Available Techniques; Ozone Depleting Substances and F-gases; Chemicals and Pesticides; Resources and Waste; Operator Licensing and Commercial Transport; Driver Licensing; Rail Technical Standards; Roads – Motor Insurance; Nutrition Labelling, Composition and Standards; Blood Safety and Quality; Organs, Tissues and Cells (apart from embryos and gametes); Public Health Protection and Health Security; Food Compositional Standards and Labelling; Public Procurement; and Food and Feed Safety and Hygiene Law. By the end of this study, most of these frameworks operated on an interim basis, while the Hazardous Substance (Planning) framework was the first to pass all four legislatures and published on 31 August 2021 (Department for Levelling Up, Housing and Communities and Cabinet Office 2021).

The nature of the Common Frameworks varies significantly in emphasis and level of detail depending on the needs of specific subject areas. Some adopted a common template or structure.[38] The frameworks are underpinned by a combination of primary legislation, and multilateral concordats or memorandums of understanding providing principles for collaborative working, decision-making and dispute resolution guidance from official to ministerial levels. For instance, the Common Framework on Public Health Protection and Health Security, which was provisionally finalised in October 2021, involves both legislative mechanisms (Health Security (EU Exit) Regulations 2021) and a non-legislative memorandum of understanding on public health protection and health security to coordinate public health protection and health security policies, responses to cross-border health threats, and to develop and implement a shared work programme (Department of Health and Social Care 2021). The Food Compositional Standards and Labelling Provisional Common Framework is supported by a concordat to set out governance arrangements around "commonality in approach and minimum standards." Similar concordats guiding the communication and cooperation between governments are part of the provisional Common Frameworks on Organs, Tissues and Cells (apart from embryos and gametes); Nutrition Related Labelling, Composition and Standards; Blood Safety and Quality; and Food and Feed Safety and Hygiene. The Common Framework programme has certainly expanded the web of informal intergovernmental agreements. However, by providing the UK Government with powers to overrule the devolved administrations in a wide range of policy areas, the passage of the UK Internal Market Bill has the potential to impose more central control and undermine the purpose of the UK Common Frameworks. It remains to be seen how these new institutional arrangements will facilitate intergovernmental working; and whether they will live up to the initial expectations of the Scottish and Welsh Governments by integrating policy development across different jurisdictions, or whether they will only be a means for operational coordination.

The Joint Ministerial Committee

The JMC was established by a supplementary agreement of the MoU "to consider non-devolved matters which impinge on devolved responsibilities, and devolved matters which impinge on non-devolved responsibilities" (Cabinet Office 2012, MoU A1.2). Meetings were supposed to take place at least once a year chaired by the Prime Minister and also attended by the First Ministers and one additional minister from Scotland and Wales, the First and deputy First Minister of Northern Ireland, and the Secretaries of State for Scotland, Wales and Northern Ireland. The JMC presented the highest intergovernmental forum to enable discussions on major constitutional and policy issues, which are too important or cannot be resolved at lower levels (WG9).[39] Although the JMC was set up as the "central pillar of the UK's intergovernmental machinery" (McEwen et al. 2018, 8), it was only *weakly* institutionalised as it lacked majority rule, legal status to produce binding agreements, or an autonomous intergovernmental body with statutory functions and its own resources and infrastructure (cf. Bolleyer 2009; 2013, 324–325; 2018, 48). The UK Governance Group within the Cabinet Office served as the primary contact point for the devolved administrations to request information (UKG1). The JMC is also supported by a secretariat, a virtual body led by the UK Cabinet Office and to which each administration dedicates staff to organise the meetings and draft the minutes (depending on in which jurisdiction they take place). Although the JMC Joint Secretariat was run by the Cabinet Office, in theory, it was supposed to be impartial:

> The lead role within the Secretariat will fall upon the UK Cabinet Office, including responsibility for servicing meetings and despatching documents as required. However, in accordance with the traditional role of the Cabinet Office, although it will retain a certain responsibility to the Prime Minister as chairman of the JMC, the Secretariat will be bound to provide an impartial service to all members of the JMC. It will remain possible for staff of the devolved administrations to be seconded to work in this as in other areas of the Cabinet Office.
> (Cabinet Office 2012, MoU A2.1)

The JMC was often criticised for its lack of transparency, as debates and agreements were not published in such detail and frequency as to allow political scrutiny, either by the public or by parliaments (JMC Joint Secretariat 2018, 11; McEwen et al. 2018, 11; Scottish Affairs Committee 2019a, 15). Instead, meetings were held in a private space with a high level of confidentially to "permit free and candid discussion" (Cabinet Office 2012, MoU A1.11), meaning that detailed protocols were not publicly available. Outside of meetings participants could publicly repeat their own statements but not quote other ministers (SG12, WG5).

The first JMC Plenary gathered in Edinburgh on 1 September 2000, followed by Cardiff on 30 October 2001 and London on 22 October 2002 (Horgan 2004, 116). Meetings did not then take place very frequently until they stopped in 2002 and were only revived in 2008 (Gallagher 2012, 201; McEwen and Petersohn 2015, 197). This was largely due to a lack of need for an official forum when the different Labour-led executives could rely largely on intra-party channels (Scottish Affairs Committee 2019a, 11). A member of the Welsh Government confirmed this: "For a quite a long time there were virtually no formal meetings of the JMC. That wasn't a sign that relations had broken down. It just wasn't really needed. We knew what we were doing, they knew what they were doing, and it sort of worked." (WG11). When the SNP took over the Scottish Government in 2007 and the Coalition Government formed in Westminster in 2010, intra-party channels were no longer available to resolve disputes (cf. Cairney 2011, 113). Until December 2018, when the Plenary met for the last time within the second decade of the new millennium, JMC sessions started therefore to take place on an annual basis (except between 2014 and 2016) (McEwen et al. 2012, 326). The Plenary was supported by subcommittees varying in importance and frequency according to policy area and prioritisation by UK Government.[40] As Figure 4.2 shows, the general meeting schedule remained sporadic with occasional disruptions. The only two subcommittees which met at regular intervals were the JMC Europe and subsequently the JMC European Negotiations (JMC EN).

Between 2001 and 2020, JMC Europe was the best working part of the intergovernmental machinery (JMC Joint Secretariat 2018, 4). Throughout its existence, it met on a regular basis, about four times per year and prior to summits of the European Council to coordinate policy, which allowed the devolved executives to feed in their priorities and expertise in areas, such as fisheries, agriculture and structural funds (WG5) (McEwen 2017, 676). An MS described the JMC Europe as "quite successful":

> One of the reasons is it was run by the Foreign Office and in an odd way it was by far the best department to understand devolution in the UK; which seems a bit odd that your Foreign Office gets the change and understands the culture more than the domestic departments, because the Foreign Office are used to dealing with other points of view and other government.
>
> (WP6)

Despite the praise for the JMC Europe, an effective intergovernmental exchange was partly constrained by the late circulation of papers, the brevity of meetings and the lack of follow-up feedback (McEwen et al. 2018, 9). After its last meeting, just before the UK officially exited the EU on 30 January 2020, the UK Government decided to cease the JMC Europe without prior consultation (Scottish Government 2020a). In October 2016, the JMC EN, chaired by the Secretary of State for Exiting the EU, had taken over the tasks of dealing with the EU withdrawal process. It was the only formation with terms of references set out in the communiqué of the JMC Plenary on 24 October 2016:

> Through the JMC(EN) the governments will work collaboratively to: discuss each government's requirements of the future relationship with the EU; seek to agree a UK approach to, and objectives for, Article 50 negotiations; and provide oversight of negotiations with the EU, to ensure, as far as possible, that outcomes agreed by all four governments are secured from these negotiations; and discuss issues stemming from the negotiation process which may impact upon or have consequences for the UK Government, the Scottish Government, the Welsh Government or the Northern Ireland Executive.
>
> (Cabinet Office 2021b)

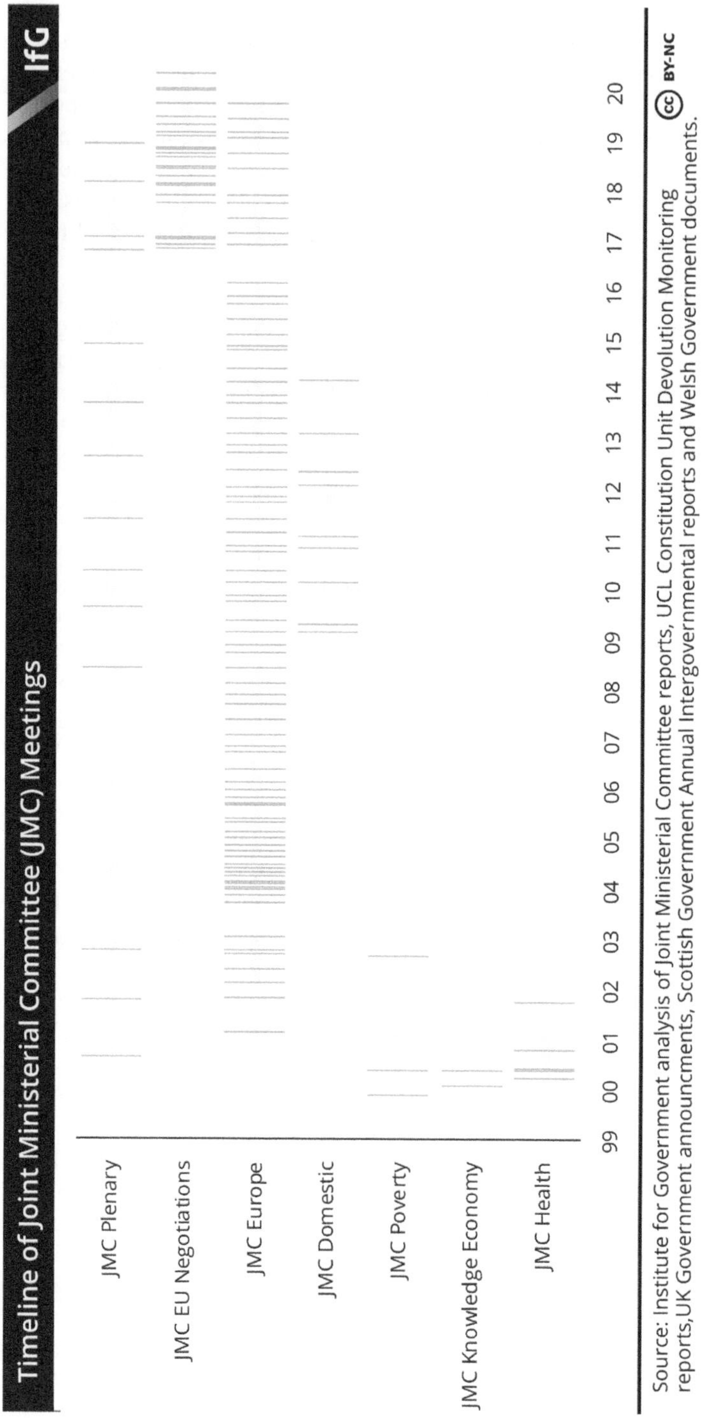

Figure 4.2 Timeline of JMC meetings

Source: Paun, Sargeant and Shuttleworth (2017). Devolution: Joint Ministerial Committee. Explainer. 11 December. Institute for Government. https://www.instituteforgovernment.org.uk/explainers/devolution-joint-ministerial-committee. Used with permission.

Though these terms were in principle favourable to the devolved administrations, in practice they did not meet the expectations of the Welsh and Scottish Governments. Instead, the lack of consultation and joint decision-making towards the UK's position on leaving the EU caused great frustration and was repeatedly criticised without effect (SG6, SG12, WG2, WG5, WG8). Officials from the Welsh and from the UK Governments recognised that the latter signed up to terms of references which would inevitably cause a deep misunderstanding (WG11):

> We've got this situation where it's terms of references are quite good, all the governments signed up, but it seems to me that the governments signed up to this and then went away with completely different views of how that was going work and what it meant. [...] That's why ministers after every JMC publicly express frustration about the fact that the level engagement that we have been expecting has just not come to pass, which we think poses serious risks to the UK as well as to Wales.
>
> (WG10)

> In hindsight, the way the terms of reference were constructed gave a false impression of how much consultation and influence was going to be possible. I mean that without criticism to those that were involved at the time. When you haven't done a negotiation like that, nobody has, we didn't know how those discussions were going to be sequenced, where the red lines on either side would be. [...] An upfront commitment that seemed very sensible and indeed deliverable from the outset in 2016 but then proofed very difficult to kind of make real in the way the devolved administration had understood.
>
> (UKG1)

Initially, the UK Government did not attach a high importance to the JMC EN, while its delegation clearly outnumbered the comparatively small teams from the devolved governments. Meetings lacked transparency and serious organisational and operational efforts, locations were announced and papers distributed only at very short notice. Far from fostering a meaningful exchange of information, positions and decision, the first four meetings between October 2016 and February 2017 were characterised as confrontational and antagonistic between the UK Government and the devolved administrations, and being used as opportunities for politicians to score points (BIC1, SG11, WG1, WG5) (cf. Hunt and Minto 2017, 651–652; McEwen 2017, 682; McEwen et al. 2018, 9).

> David Davies was in charge of Dexit [Department for Exiting the EU]. He was chair of the JMC EN for an extended period; this was a very fraud and difficult set of meetings. [...] This staggered on for about 18

months. A set of monthly, bi-monthly unsatisfactory meetings that didn't do anything to really establish confidence and trust, which is really the basis of what these meetings should be.

(WG5)

The JMC as it stands tends to operate and has done through the Brexit time, I caricature a bit but not a lot, as a way of UK Government formally telling the devolved governments what it's up to and the devolved governments complaining loudly to the UKG that they haven't been properly consulted or listened to.

(UKG10)

During the second year of the JMC EN, when legal disputes over the right of the devolved nations to give their Legislative Consent Motions to EU bills led to more dialogue, the situation slightly improved and domestic and technical issues were added to the agenda (SG11). But after a JMC EN meeting on 8 February 2017, tensions erupted again and meetings were put on hold. In October, the JMC EN started to reconvene in smaller groups which turned out to work more effectively on the basis of non-written updates (WG5) (JMC Joint Secretariat 2018; Scottish Government 2020b). In May 2018, the Ministerial Forum (European Negotiations) was introduced to complement the JMC EN and came together seven times until February 2019. Co-chaired by the Parliamentary Under Secretary of State for Exiting the European Union and the Minister for the Constitution, ministers discussed specific policy issues of the UK negotiation position with the EU (Cabinet Office 2019d; Scottish Government 2019a). Under Boris Johnson's premiership, the devolved administration JMC EN meetings were now held outside of London and frequently throughout 2020 in an effort to accommodate the devolved governments.[41] However, consultations and joint agreement on the UK's negotiation priorities did not substantialise (Welsh Government 2020b). In a written statement, Jeremy Miles (2020a), Counsel General and Brexit Minister of the Welsh Government, "regretted that papers shared ahead of JMC (EN) had not been proposed jointly and didn't address the outstanding issues comprehensively."

Insights from the various formations of the JMC reveal that it used to be a forum for communication and shared learning rather than for decision-making and conflict resolution. According to a UK official: "We should be completely upfront and recognise that the JMC is always going to have an element of politics involved, which will always make it difficult." (UKG1) (cf. Gallagher 2020, 572–573). The Scottish Affairs Committee (2019a, 12) concluded that "the conduct, outcome and frequency of JMC meetings is predominantly determined by the UK Government's interests and priorities, with little open-minded and meaningful engagement." The centre could pursue its own agenda, act unilaterally without the consent of the devolved administrations and hold the ultimate say (SG6, WP5, WP6).

Gatherings were often at best an opportunity for the devolved administrations to lobby for their interests or raise their discontent rather than for constructive debates (WP5).[42] As for the Sewel Convention, Brexit triggered new discussions to formalise the JMC, and the UK Government acknowledged the need for new modes of cooperation and decision-making:

> There is a recognition that, in the place of overarching arrangements provided for by EU membership, detailed technical arrangements will, in some areas, be supplemented by additional arrangements for policy cooperation and political engagement. The UK, Scottish and Welsh Governments and Northern Ireland Civil Service are working together to promote the establishment of such arrangements, as part of a broader review of intergovernmental relations commissioned by the Joint Ministerial Committee.
>
> (Cabinet Office 2019d, 11)

The JMC Joint Secretariat (2018, 21) and the Scottish Affairs Committee (2019a, 19–20) suggested the establishment of an independent secretary and to introduce legally binding requirements on a statutory basis. The Welsh Government also proposed a more robust, equal and independent institution (Welsh Government 2019a, 12):

> We would like a council of ministers which was a decision-making body that had an independent secretariat. This would be a huge leap forward from where we are now; but that requires a set of assumptions to be cast aside by Whitehall. Certainly, the way it appears to operate is that the UK Government likes to keep control of the agenda and timings of these things, and doesn't see, in particular with JMC P as a decision-making body, whereas we think that's at the apex of UK governance. They would see the apex of UK governance it would end with the UK cabinet, I guess.
>
> (WG10)

The 2022 review of intergovernmental relations marked the end of the JMC by introducing a new three-tier structure. The role of the JMC Plenary has now been taken by the Prime Minister and Heads of Devolved Governments Council, chaired by the former to consider "policy issues of strategic importance to the whole of the UK" by consensus and acting "as the final escalation stage of the dispute resolution process" (Cabinet Office and Department for Levelling Up, Housing and Communities 2022a). In addition to its annual meetings, the Council can gather more frequently and invite other ministers as needed. Below the most senior intergovernmental forum, two standing committees form the second tier. The Interministerial Standing Committee (IMSC) meets on a monthly basis, unless other schedules are agreed by consensus, to deal with cross-cutting, and in particular international policies that involve multiple portfolios, and to oversee the IMGs.[43] The chairing and hosting of meetings will rotate between governments, who can submit items for discussion in advance. For issues that required in-depth discussions they can also request for Interministerial Committees (ICs) to be set up temporarily.[44] As for the JMC, the committee members, who are relevant ministers from the different governments, must "not disclose information that breaches the confidential nature of such discussions." (ibid.) In addition, the Finance Interministerial Standing Committee (F:ISC) institutionalised the Finance Ministers Quadrilateral and is attended by all finance ministers plus other ministers, if appropriate, and is intended to meet four times a year. The forum is responsible for economic and financial matters and the resolution of financial disputes. The review further provides for a standing and impartial IGR Secretariat hosted and funded by the Cabinet Office and accountable to the Council, which provides a *medium* institutional depth to the new committee structure. While the JMC was deliberately set up as an informal arrangement that cannot legally bind the UK Parliament (UKG1), the same is true for the new Council. Nevertheless, the UK Government has committed to take decisions by consensus, and the standing secretariat includes official from all administrations – as it is the case for the British-Irish Council – which may increase their organisation and planning capacities (McEwen 2022).

The Protocol on Dispute Resolution

The MoU's Agreement on the Joint Ministerial Committee contains a protocol on dispute avoidance and resolution to guide ministers and senior officials through intergovernmental conflicts:

> There may be circumstances, particularly those arising from differences in political outlook, where the UK Government and one or more of the devolved administrations are unlikely to be able to agree. In these cases the parties to this agreement recognise that the JMC machinery is unlikely to offer any prospect of resolution. They also recognise, consistently with the principle that the JMC is not a decision-making body, that the basis on which the procedures will operate is the facilitation of agreement between the parties in dispute, not the imposition of any solution.
>
> (Cabinet Office 2012, MoU A3.4)

According to paragraph A3.6 of the Agreement on the Joint Ministerial Committee (Cabinet Office 2012, MoU), disputes should be avoided at an informal working level, and only if this fails, senior officials of the JMC Official, Domestic and Europe should become involved. If senior officials cannot reach an agreement, disputes will be escalated to ministers. After the *initial identification of disagreement*, ministers then have to approve raising the issue to the next *stage of disagreement* involving an official notification to the JMC Secretariat. They can raise the issue further to the *dispute stage*, where within one month ministers may agree a resolution, decide to not proceed any further or to bring the issue to the JMC Plenary to be processed within three months. This dispute resolution mechanism was described as "cumbersome, time-consuming, resource intensive", with uncertain outcomes and not suitable to solve political tensions (SG12). As stakeholders would usually seek to solve conflicts ad hoc at official levels, so far, the official resolution procedure has only been triggered five times (WG7). Previous disputes include a disagreement at official level over the allocation of the whiting fishing quota between the English and Scottish fleets, which was raised by the Scottish Government. Apart from this, all official disputes were about financial matters, raised by different devolved administrations and resolved at an early stage, not necessarily in agreement. After the 2017 General Election, Theresa May entered a supply and confidence agreement with the DUP in Westminster to support her minority government. In return, the UK Government directly allocated an extra £1 billion to Northern Ireland. For Scotland and Wales, this was grounds for the dispute resolution mechanism, but the UK Government did not recognise the validity of their claim and instead argued that the direct funding to Northern Ireland was not applicable to the Barnett consequentials for additional departmental spending (UKG1). This example demonstrates the UK Government's authority to accept an issue raised by the devolved administrations as an official dispute or not. The informality of the protocol and Whitehall's superiority essentially undermines the confidence of the devolved administrations in the resolution mechanism (WP6), as the former First Minister of Wales highlighted:

> Ridiculously there is a dispute resolution process that exists in the joint ministerial meeting. But if you're in dispute with the UK Government, the UK Government decides the dispute and they decide whether there is a dispute. So when ourselves and the Scots started the dispute resolution process because Northern Ireland had this money and we hadn't, we were told there isn't a dispute. If you're taking court action against somebody, and they're also the judge, you can see that would never work.
>
> (WP5)

The Scottish and Welsh Governments pushed for an independent mediation or judiciary reviewing process (SG9, WG2), and the Scottish Affairs Committee (2019a, 16–17) also supported reforms to prevent unilateral decisions by the UK Government. The review of intergovernmental relations has responded to such calls and has installed a new dispute resolution mechanism enabling all governments to refer disagreements to the IGR Secretariat: "This will include circumstances where governments disagree about the interpretation of, or actions taken in relation to, matters governed by intergovernmental agreements, rules or procedures". (Cabinet Office and Department for Levelling Up, Housing and Communities 2022a). Unlike the previous procedure, it will no longer be the UK Government but the impartial Secretariat, who decides on the basis of clear criteria whether the official dispute resolution applies to an issue and about the wider implications of the issue (Bosse 2022). For the Finance Interministerial Standing Committee, a separate mechanism was introduced that maintains the Treasury's authority over policy decisions on funding: "As outlined in the Statement of Funding Policy, funding disputes may only be raised where there is reason to believe a principle of the Statement of Funding Policy may have been breached." (Cabinet Office and Department for Levelling Up, Housing and Communities 2022a). As for the previous mechanism, official dispute resolution is only envisaged as a last resort when other attempts fail to provide agreement, and is designed to prevent an escalation through all stages (see Figure 4.3). Although this does not submit Westminster to a binding procedure, the UK Government cannot refuse to accept a dispute anymore and the involvement of third parties to advise and mediate, as well as the appointment of independent chairs put the devolved administrations on a more equal footing (McEwen 2022). For Sargeant (2022): "These arrangements are a solid basis for a fairer approach, more collaboration and joint working, but they are yet to be tested in practice."

The Joint Exchequer Committees

Next to the informal institutions structuring intergovernmental relations multilaterally, there are task-oriented arrangements in place dealing with the specifics of financial relations. Two bilateral groups, the Scottish and the Welsh Joint Exchequer Committees, were founded to ensure the implementation of tax, borrowing and social security powers devolved by the Scotland Acts of 2012 and 2016 and the Wales Acts of 2014 and 2017. The Joint Exchequer Committees are high-level discussion forums that comprise the Chief Secretary to the Treasury, the Exchequer Secretary and the Secretary of State for Scotland and Wales respectively, and from either the Scottish or the Welsh Governments the Cabinet Secretary for Finance, Employment and Sustainable Growth and the Cabinet Secretary for Parliamentary Business and Government Strategy (McEwen and Petersohn 2015, 199). Both Committees agreed the Fiscal Frameworks for Scotland and Wales, which themselves present non-statutory institutions governing the potential spill over effects of fiscal decisions by one government on the other and will be discussed in Chapter 5. Though the Treasury maintains its dominance in terms of constitutional authority and resources, the Scottish and Welsh Governments were still able to negotiate substantial concessions over the adjustment of their block grants and their fiscal autonomy (McEwen 2017, 678–680).

Formal and Informal Intergovernmental Institutions 113

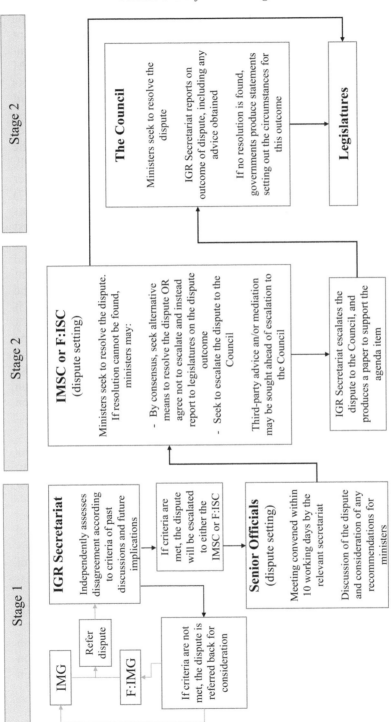

Figure 4.3 Dispute resolution mechanism under the 2022 intergovernmental review

Source: Cabinet Office and Department for Levelling Up, Housing and Communities (2022a). Review of intergovernmental relation. Policy paper.13 January. UK Government. https://www.gov.uk/government/publications/the-review-of-intergovernmental-relations

To ensure a successful transfer of fiscal powers, the Scottish and the UK Governments committed to a joint bespoke institution: "The Joint Exchequer Committee (JEC), operating by consensus, will govern the completion, implementation, operation and review of the fiscal framework." (HM Government and Scottish Government 2016, Section 97). Whereas the Scots saw themselves as equal partners in the negotiations, the UK Government only reluctantly acknowledged that it had to make concessions to get legislative consent for the Scotland Act 2016. Due to this early disagreement over the influence of the Scottish Government and the terms of references, the Committee did not meet between 2013 and 2015 (McEwen 2017, 679). Still, the UK Government relied on devolved capacities and expertise in order to successfully pass the Scotland Act 2016 (as well as the Wales Act 2017) (UKG10). The increasing overlap of fiscal competences across jurisdictions required the different governments to produce common agreements, first for Scotland in February 2016 and subsequently for Wales in December of the same year. Based on the conclusion of the Smith Commission, the Fiscal Framework for Scotland provided: "Specifically, where either government makes a policy decision that affects the tax receipts or expenditure of the other, the decision-making government will either reimburse the other if there is an additional cost, or receive a transfer from the other if there is a saving." (HM Government and Scottish Government 2016, Section 45). The Fiscal Frameworks allow the devolved governments to exercise their tax and borrowing powers within a wider framework for the whole of the UK, and introduced arrangements for operational cooperation and information sharing. Based on the MoU it also established separate dispute resolution mechanisms:

> These disputes will firstly be considered by officials, initially at working level and then by JEC (Wales) (Officials). Where officials are unable to reach an agreement this will be considered by Ministers at JEC (Wales). Discussions may be informed at any stage by seeking the view of independent bodies. If Ministers fail to reach agreement the dispute falls – there would be no specific outcome from the dispute and so no fiscal transfer between the governments. If either government wishes to pursue the dispute further, the processes outlined in the Memorandum of Understanding between the UK government and the devolved administrations provides that basis.
> (HM Government and Welsh Government 2016, Section 52)

Similar to the Protocol on Dispute Resolution, an official of the Scottish Government described the dispute resolution mechanism as dependent on the goodwill of the UK Government, leaving the devolved administration without effective means to raise their concerns.

> The resolution mechanism, however, essentially gives the Treasury the whip hand. It's up to Treasury to decide whether there's actually

dispute or not. We can say that there's a dispute but they may not agree that there is and if they don't agree, there's no dispute to be resolved. Ultimately Treasury takes the decision. [...] None of these arrangements would have the same constitutional protections that you would find in Germany. It's based on the UK Government's interest not to rock the boat but it could conceivably change the whole funding structure tomorrow if it were really inclined to do so. There's not a fundamental guarantee, but it would provoke a crisis.

(SG9)

The official dispute resolution was not triggered, as any relevant issues could be solved at lower levels (SG9). Once their core task was fulfilled, the Joint Exchequer Committees did not officially cease to exist but rather since 2016 to meet. While the Committees may meet again for periodic review of the Fiscal Framework,[45] fiscal relations have returned to the unilateral control of the Treasury and the informal meetings of the Finance Ministers' Quadrilateral. As the new Finance Interministerial Standing Committee also enables bilateral conversations, a revival of the Joint Exchequer Committees seems unlikely.

British-Irish Council

The British-Irish Council was established over two decades ago in 1999 by the Belfast Agreement to "promote the harmonious and mutually beneficial development of the totality of relationships among the peoples of these islands" (Northern Ireland Office 1998, Strand Three).[46] Since its creation, the British-Irish Council has taken an essential function as a mediator in the peace process in Northern Ireland, while also taking role a forum for intergovernmental cooperation (BIC1). Because the UK and the Irish Governments participate in meetings, both Unionists and Republicans in Northern Ireland have accepted the institution as a legitimate forum. In addition to the devolved administrations, the Isle of Man and the two Channel Islands Guernsey and Jersey also participate in the British-Irish Council.[47] The plenary summits are at the top of the hierarchy and take place twice a year[48] hosted by changing administrations which determine the overall policy theme of the individual summits. Below the plenary, ministerial level groups meet every two or three years to provide guidance for sector groups, and officials come together either physically or by call three to five times a year on an ad hoc basis to develop policy.[49] Possible areas for discussions are set out in the Belfast Agreement (Northern Ireland Office 1998, Strand Three, Article 5); including transport links, agricultural issues, environmental issues, cultural issues, health issues, education issues and approaches to EU issues. These are organised into 11 work sectors (see Figure 4.4).

The British-Irish Council is an autonomous intergovernmental body with statutory functions, its own resources, collectively financed staff and a

116 *Formal and Informal Intergovernmental Institutions*

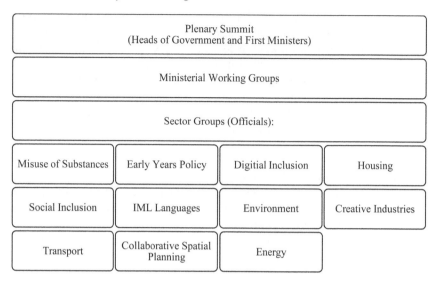

Figure 4.4 British-Irish Council organisational chart

standing secretariat that provides administers and organises frequent meetings. Hence, until the creation of the standing IGR Secretariat in 2022, it used to be the only institutionalised intergovernmental body for the UK with a *medium* institutional depth. All eight members (including Guernsey, Jersey and the Isle of Man) agree and contribute to a joint budget on an annual basis reflecting the size of each jurisdiction.[50] Before the establishment of a standing secretariat, the organisation of the Council was managed jointly by the Department of Foreign Affairs in Dublin and the Cabinet Office in London. The Scottish Government was particularly dissatisfied with the lack of a permanent reference point and pushed to have a standing secretariat staffed by seconded officials. It agreed to host the secretariat in Edinburgh, which was agreed in a secret vote. Since its opening on 4 January 2012, the secretariat has been led jointly by two officials from the UK and Irish Governments. The Scottish, Welsh and Northern Ireland administrations also each provide one member to the secretariat's staff. As a stand-alone body, the secretariat is accountable to the British-Irish Council and not the officials' home administrations, which allows it to operate as an independent arbitrator between governments (BIC1).[51]

The scope and purpose of the British-Irish Council is very different from those of the JMC. The different governments take non-legally binding decisions by consensus and unanimity, produce official statements and share examples of best-practice. According to a former secretariat's staff: "It was all voluntarily. There wasn't any repercussions if you said you would do something and then you didn't. There were no enforcement powers." (WP3). Even the comparatively small Channel Islands and the Isle of Man enjoy the same status and vote weight as two central governments, and the Scottish and the Welsh Governments recognise the added value of exchanging information and best-practice (SG12, UKG1, WG10):

> It's a forum that's not just about airing disagreements, which some intergovernmental things can be because it got work streams, there's a joint working and it includes all the Crown dependencies. The other thing we like about it, because we think it could be model for wider application. There's not hierarchy. The UK runs the show in relation to the JMC. So everybody on the British-Irish Council are equal partners. The summit moves around. Each country hosts it. The host country chairs the meetings. So it's all equal partners. So we value that highly.
> (WG2)

To ensure that all participants can contribute and implement joint programmes, the areas of cooperation fall within the jurisdictions of the devolved institutions. Environment (including different sub-working sectors on Climate Adaptation, Invasive and Non-native Species, Marine Environment and Marine Litter) and Misuse of Substances are two work sectors that allow for closer cooperation and have experienced a high level of engagement to promote evidence-based policies and best-practice exchange transferable across all members. Due the heterogeneity of its members' capacities – as well as to its historical origins as a post-conflict forum for reconciliation – the secretariat only monitors the progress of joint agreements, and the Council has no legal powers to enforce them. While politicians may exert pressure to ensure an implementation across all members, to avoid major disputes implementation issues are discussed prior to agreements and decision-making provides sufficient flexibility. There is a strong awareness not to exceed the capacities of the smaller islands, which in practice means that the least capable member's abilities usually determine the level of ambition (BIC1). A Welsh official therefore stated: "It creates that really sensible separation of duties in respect of advancing the interests of the council collectively, and also enabling the governments to have that space to engage on their own terms." (WG10).

In respect of the Belfast Agreement, the British-Irish Council is less politicised than the JMC and seeks to avoid conflict. Occasionally, governments disagree over who has jurisdiction in certain policy areas (BIC1), but officials take care to agree agendas and identify potential tension in advance of summits and meetings, as a member of the secretariat explained: "There's a high degree of choreography in advance. Avoiding a big argument is often more important than securing great outcome. There's a big effort from our side that you hold the high level of disagreement behind closed doors at official level." (BIC1). During the last decade the focus of meetings has slightly shifted from thematic discussion to more political sensitive and controversial debates (BIC1). EU withdrawal especially has contested, redefined and perhaps even strengthened the role of the British-Irish Council, as it offers a line of communication between the UK and Irish Governments, as well as for Scotland and Wales (BIC1, UKG1, WG10). Exemplary of this, on 22 July 2016, shortly after the referendum, the first and only extraordinary summit was held to discuss the implications of the decision to leave the EU. Yet, stakeholders were mindful not to undermine any official negotiations between the EU and the UK (BIC1). Notwithstanding the great value of this institution, as the empirical analysis in Chapter 5 will show, its relevance for the direct relations between the UK, Scottish and Welsh Government is only marginal.

Informal practices

The relations between the different governments rely heavily on a machinery of informal practices, which happen under the radar (Gallagher 2012, 200). When the same government was in power in Westminster, Holyrood and at Cardiff Bay, ministers could simply fall back onto their personal contacts (Jeffery 2009, 304) and meet regularly through intra-party channels (SP1, SP4, WG12, WP5). Until today the personal interests and relationships of individual ministers strongly affect how governments engage with each other (SG9, UKG1, UKG4, WG3, WG4, WP4): "Some are much more willing to engage the devolved administrations than others. Some are wary that it might overcomplicate it." (UKG8). As changes in ministerial and official portfolios can interrupt established links and therefore need to be constantly rebuilt (SG1, SG6, WG1),[52] this study seeks to focus beyond personal relations and ad hoc exchanges, and discusses intergovernmental practices as routines that, unlike informal institutions, cannot be sanctioned at all (cf. Bröchler and Lauth 2014, 3 et seq.; Lauth 2014, 20 et seq.). Given the limited access to relevant information and their fluidity, practices are difficult to examine and the following presents only a selection of the routine interaction between ministers, officials and parliaments.

Ministerial level relations

At ministerial level, intergovernmental business takes place in an opaque array of working groups, forums and quadrilateral meetings. Some of these have terms of reference and may even have politically binding effects. Yet, due to their flexible and constantly changing nature, they are considered as practices here. Before it was replaced by the Finance Interministerial Standing Committee, the Finance Ministers' Quadrilateral was the most prominent and established interministerial forum. According to the MoU of 2013:

> Before the JMC process set out in the Statement of Funding Policy is invoked for differences about financial issues including the interpretation

of the Statement of Funding Policy, these should generally be first discussed bilaterally between the Treasury and the relevant devolved administrations or if appropriate at a timely Finance Quadrilateral meeting bringing together Treasury ministers and finance ministers of the devolved administrations.

(Cabinet Office 2012, MoU A3.8)

Through the quadrilateral forum, the Chief Secretary to the Treasury, joined by the Secretaries of State for Scotland, Wales and Northern Ireland, informed the devolved Cabinet Secretaries and ministers about issues of general expenditure and announces the Statement of Funding Policy[53] and the application of the Barnett formula. Occasionally, the three devolved ministers could forward a joint issue but the meetings were hierarchically run and not intended as a space for negotiations (SG5) (Birrell 2012a, 212). Though the content of meetings was mostly not high profile, devolved ministers used them for political statements and to express their frustration (Gallagher 2020, 575), as a Scottish official said:

It is very much seen to be a talking shop from our side, where the Treasury tells us things. We tell the Treasury things as well, but whether they listen is another matter. The Finance Ministers Quadrilateral is really about the exchange of information. The fact that Treasury might not be listening reflects simply the power imbalance between the different ministers around the table.

(SG9)

Other quadrilateral meetings between ministers that took place between 2019 and 2021 include the Energy and Climate Change Quadrilateral, the Business and Industry Quadrilateral, the Higher Education Quadrilateral meeting (Welsh Government 2020a). By 2022, some of these had turned into IMGs with terms of reference (see below). On a bilateral basis, the Joint Ministerial Working Group on Welfare was founded by the UK and Scottish Governments in 2015 with its own terms of reference as a "forum for discussion and decision-making to ensure the implementation of welfare and employment-related aspects of the Scotland Act 2016" (Scottish Government 2020c).[54] The group has continued to meet on a biannual basis (Department for Levelling Up, Housing and Communities 2022, 41). According to a representative of the Scottish Government:

It has been used as a forum to talk about really difficult issues that exist between the governments, and for our government to raise areas of concern, and for the UK Government around, some of the policies their pursuing as well. Ministers come along with good intentions and where decisions are required, decisions are made and decisions are stuck to.

(SG10)

The UK's exit from the EU has led to the formation of new quadrilateral groups in other policy areas (WG5). In particular, the Welsh Government has pushed for the creation of interministerial working groups outside of the JMC architecture (UKG1),[55] and would like to establish a system of joint decision-making across different portfolios (WG8, WG10, WG11).[56] The Department for Environment, Food and Rural Affairs (DEFRA) and the devolved administrations were the first to introduce regular multilateral interministerial meetings in response to the EU-referendum. The Interministerial Group for Environment, Food and Rural Affairs (IMG EFRA) was then founded in 2016 and, in February 2019, terms of reference were agreed to set out the governance structure; including the conditions of engagement and methods of dispute resolution (WG9) (Welsh Government 2019b).[57] The IMG EFRA meets approximately every four to eight weeks and was initially chaired by the UK Secretary of State in London. Over time, the chair started to rotate between the ministers of all four governments and to take place in the other capitals or via video conference. Because of the long-standing engagement in areas that were regulated by EU legislation, such as agriculture, environment, fisheries and food standards, this forum was quickly set up and is widely considered a model of good intergovernmental practice (UKG2, WG7, WG9).[58] Following the 2022 review of intergovernmental relations, the format of IMGs provided more consistency across different portfolios by absorbing previous quadrilateral meetings and creating new groups. These include IMGs for Business and Industry; Education; Elections and Registration; Environment; Food and Rural Affairs; Housing, Communities and Local Government; Net Zero, Energy and Climate Change; Tourism; Trade; Transport Matters; as well as for UK-EU relations (Cabinet Office and Department for Levelling Up, Housing and Communities 2022b).

Official-level relations

From the outside, civil servants may not play an obvious role in managing intergovernmental relations, but their long-standing expertise, ideological neutrality and problem-solving capacities allow them to develop essential links and networks across different administrations (Behnke 2018). Unlike in Northern Ireland, where the civil service has been separate and under the control of the First Minister and the deputy First Minster since 1921,[59] responsibility for the civil service was not devolved to Scotland and Wales in 1999. Officials in Scotland and Wales are part of a unified UK-wide structure and employed by and accountable to the UK Government – although the 'dual alliance' of the civil service in Scotland and Wales has gradually shifted from London towards Edinburgh and Cardiff (cf. McMillan and Massey 2004, 237 et seq.), as it was mentioned by a Scottish Government official:

> The fact that we have now fewer people that have worked for a UK Government or vice versa means that we're beginning to lose some of that knowledge and understanding of how Whitehall works. Over time that might make it more difficult again. But we still have a fairly sizeable number of people who have experience of working in both.
>
> (SG2)

When Labour was leading all three administrations the civil service "provided an important bridge for the new system" (Kenny et al. 2021, 11), but the links between civil servants from both executives have loosened. Particularly, after the Coalition Government came to power in 2010, Whitehall officials have become more indifferent and insensitive towards devolved issues (SG1, UKG3, UKG10) (cf. Cairney 2012, 238–245; Keating 2012, 223):

> Pre-devolution, because all legislation had to be taken through Westminster there was a greater familiarity in Whitehall of the legislative requirements of the Scotland Office and the Wales Office. And their officials had to spend more time in London. So there was naturally more of a mingling of officials. That all faded away post devolution. [...] The number of officials who are grown up in both systems is now very, very small.
>
> (UKG10)

The expertise and capacities to deal with devolved issues vary strongly across UK Government departments (JMC Joint Secretariat 2018, 9; Scottish Affairs Committee 2019a, 27–34) with larger and 'devolution experienced' departments seeming to demonstrate a stronger awareness (SG12). To improve the engagement with devolved legislation and institutions, in July 2015, the Cabinet Office in collaboration with the Scottish and the Welsh Governments launched the 'Devolution and You' campaign to promote a better understanding of the governance of the whole of the UK through official devolution guidance, training events and staff exchanges for UK civil servants.[60] The campaign has been partly successful in deepening the understanding and engagement of Whitehall officials with the devolved administrations. Yet, frequent changes in positions set limits to institutional learning and the building of lasting expertise within departments as well as links to other administrations, which makes the devolved administrations' work with Whitehall departments volatile and less certain (SG5, SG8, UKG1, UKG3, UKG8, UKG10, WG10, WP2). Some departments therefore set up small devolution coordinating teams, which advise ministers and colleagues within the respective departments how to engage with the devolved administrations. They also work on strengthening the capability and skills within departments, engage with the devolved administrations and monitor the impact of devolved legislation on their department's policies (UKG3, UKG9).[61] In the aftermath of the 2016 EU referendum, these capacities have significantly increased across Whitehall to coordinate devolved and reserved issues. The teams' size across departments varies strongly depending on the overlap of devolved and reserved responsibilities within a department's portfolio.[62] The devolution coordinators have been effective in stimulating interactions with the devolved executives and can be a supportive access point within UK departments, if specific policy teams struggle to engage with each other (UKG8, UKG10), as a Welsh Government official stated:

> We would use the devolution teams firstly where we wouldn't really know who we need to speak to. That devolution team would be able to help, and secondly, you would go to them where there is a more general issue. We had two or three incidents of this happening, which probably ought not to have happened, and we might go to the devolution team in areas where it's the UK Government not following its own rules. [...] We wouldn't go to the devolution team, if we fundamentally disagreed with the UK Government's new policy on agriculture. That wouldn't be appropriate. But if they had said under these circumstances we'll consult you with this and that and they don't, and it happens more than once, that's when you would use the devolution team to sort that out for us.
>
> (WP2)

Despite existing challenges, official level relations continue to be at the heart of intergovernmental relations to ensure that all governments cooperate and resolve occurring issues at an early stage (UKG3) (Scottish Affairs Committee 2019a, 6). Personal contacts and ad hoc interactions are not a practice, but they are in fact so widely common that they make up the major part of exchanges between governments (SG11, SG15, UKG6, UKG8, WG12, WP3). Directors, deputy directors, policy teams and other officials within the devolved administrations have frequent catch-up meetings (weekly or monthly) with their Whitehall counterparts to exchange information, either in person or more commonly over the phone, conference calls or via email exchanges (SG4, SG5, SG8, SG13, UKG3, WG2, WG7):

> Our main strategy is going down to London as much as possible and make good relationships at official level because we know we can't rely on any judicial review or any kind of hard leverage over the UK Government. It requires their agreement as much as ours. We've got no hard tools in our arsenal. You need to try and sort out things at the lowest level possible with the least amount of discussion as possible, and accept at the same time that there are things which you can't agree on.
>
> (SG5)

There's a pretty regular ongoing dialogue at official level that takes place all the time and at all level and by employed by all medium and all contexts. That's happening all the time because ministers are not going to be able to do the detailed stuff in a meeting that lasts for an hour and a half and takes place at best once every four or five weeks. That's where real the detailed stuff ought to be getting done. [...] If you have a good relationship with a UK Government official who gets devolution and understands that it needs to be respected, that can make a huge difference as well.

(WG2)

Regardless of the political parties in power, the overall relationship between civil servants has widely been described as generally good, trusting and professional across different government (SG2, SG5, SG11, SG13, SP2, UKG2, UKG4, UKG8, WG10, WP3). Still, official level relations vary strongly across policy areas. DEFRA is commonly referred to as being the most successful and experienced in working with the devolved administrations (SG7, UKG1, WG7, WG9, WG10). The Department for Business, Energy and Industrial Strategy (BEIS), the Department for International Trade (DIT), the Department for Work and Pensions (DWP) and the Department for Transport (DfT)[63] were also seen as particularly cooperative (SG10, SG13, SG14, SG15, UKG5).[64]

Because of the asymmetrical devolution settlement, some practices have been bilateral involving only one devolved administration. HM Treasury has established close working relationships with each devolved administration, including a senior officials' group, to ensure the effective operation of the block grant and the implementation of devolved tax powers (SG9, UKG1). The DWP and the Scottish Government established the Joint Senior Officials' Group in 2016 supporting the Joint Ministerial Working Group on Welfare "to assure the successful implementation of the welfare benefits and employment support provisions of the Scotland Act 2016" (Office of the Secretary of State for Scotland 2016). As justice and policing is not devolved to Wales, the UK MoJ and the Welsh Government passed a concordant in 2018 to assess the impact of policies on the joint justice system.[65] Representatives of each government are invited to attend each other's internal meetings, to create integrated project teams, working groups and committees, such as the Justice in Wales Strategy Group[66] (UKG4).[67] Health services have also traditionally required a closer coordination across the English-Welsh border and therefore been subject to official working groups involving the Welsh Government, NHS England and occasionally the UK Department of Health and Social Care (WG12).

Brexit has clearly fostered the establishment of new practices in areas such as trade and investment (SG1, SG13, UKG8). The emergence of new officials working groups was again pioneered in the policy areas within DEFRA's remit. In October 2017, the Senior Officials Programme Board was set up to facilitate regular meetings between officials from the four governments on a monthly basis for the purposes of exchanging information and overseeing and steering the emerging working groups and subgroups working on operational issues in preparation for Brexit. Through the Senior Officials Programme Board, the devolved administration can participate in joint discussions, resolve issues and make recommendations. The board and specific working groups[68] also advise, report to or get instructions from IMG EFRA. Apart from officials from DEFRA and the devolved administrations, the Senior Officials Programme Board can be joined by representatives from the Cabinet Office, the Territorial Offices, DIT, HM Treasury and relevant agencies[69] (SG3, UKG2, WG7, WG9). In addition to the Senior Officials Programme Board, DIT and the devolved administrations also established senior official engagement and trade policy roundtables (Scottish Affairs Committee 2019b). The UK Common Frameworks programme further extended the range of senior official working groups as part of the individual framework structures, such as the Food Compositional Standards and Labelling Officials Group;[70] the Food and Feed Safety and Hygiene Frameworks Management Group and the Food and Feed Safety and Hygiene Four Nations Director Group;[71] the Nutrition Related Labelling, Composition and Standards Policy Group[72] and the UK Health Protection Committee and the Four Nations Health Protection Oversight Group, both of which require decisions to be made unanimously by a minimum of 75 per cent of its permanent membership and for a minimum of one representative from each nation to be present at meetings (Cabinet Office 2021c).[73]

The examples presented here only make up a share of an evolving web of practices.[74] Most official level arrangements are hidden away from the public and are constantly adapting to changing needs and circumstances. Although groups will effectively cease to meet after their task is completed, in recent years senior officials and working groups have become more common and without the EU's regulatory regime they will continue to manifest an essential intergovernmental practice: "It's quite fluid as well. We probably had lots of different groups that were already established before Brexit, more will have come on board, because changes come about all the time in regard to Brexit. It's not set in stone for particularly long." (WG7). Although officials are in principal neutral and their views should not be exposed to political dynamics, the willingness and priorities of ministers and permanent secretaries inform their outlooks. Frictions at the political level can trickle down and make cooperation difficult for civil servants (UKG8, UKG10) (cf. Wyn Jones and Royles 2012, 265–266):

> Scottish civil servants and their ministers will have different priorities and different political ambitions. As civil servants we have to respect that and find a way to work together but within those boundaries.
>
> (UKG3)

Civil servants in that departments will inevitably and quite rightful take to a degree their cue from the political noises that are coming down. So if they've got a minister who is inclined to be constructive and to engage, then inevitably they will be less inclined to do so as well, because that's the tone their ministry is setting and that they need to follow it.

(WG2)

Despite an increasingly difficult politically environment, without official relations the intergovernmental machinery would have long since broken down, as they are key to steering around tensions, resolving disputes and avoiding public fall outs, particularly over Brexit (SG1, SG5, SG12, SG13, UKG1, UKG4). The review of intergovernmental relations continues to build on the practices established among civil servants as part of the first tier (portfolio engagement) and the resolution of disputes:

Effective IGR must be underpinned by regular official-level engagement within a collaborative environment created and fostered by ministers. As a general principle, therefore, the majority of intergovernmental business should be conducted on an ongoing basis through normal official-level channels wherever possible.

(Cabinet Office and Department for Levelling Up, Housing and Communities 2022a)

In particular, the Senior Officials' Group is designated to take a central role in working with the new IGR Secretariat "to facilitate feedback between the ministerial and official levels of engagement" (ibid.).

Interparliamentary practices

Intergovernmental relations in federal and quasi-federal states are usually dominated by the executives and leave little room for parliamentary scrutiny (Hueglin and Fenna 2010, 216; McEwen et al. 2015).[75] Although parliamentary committees can enable legislatures to participate in some intergovernmental processes (Lhotta and Blumenthal 2015, 213; Poirier and Saunders 2015b, 453–454), they are usually not provided with meaningful access to the intergovernmental activities of the executives. In order to improve the accountability of the Scottish Government's interaction with the UK Government, the Scottish Parliament is provided with a written agreement to be consulted by its executive on issues discussed during JMC meetings. The agreement was signed in 2016 to support "the Scottish Parliament's capacity to scrutinise Scottish Government activity and to hold Scottish Ministers to account in the intergovernmental arena only." (Scottish Government 2016). In 2019, the Welsh Government and the Senedd also concluded an inter-institutional relations agreement, according to which the former will keep the latter updated and provide an annual report about the intergovernmental relations with the UK Government (Welsh Parliament 2021b). For each of the devolved territories, there are separate Select Committees within the House of Commons, and the House of Lords deals with overall questions of devolution in its Constitution Committee (Hazell 2015, 55). The Scottish Affairs Committee, Welsh Affairs Committee and Northern Ireland Affairs Committee scrutinise general matters reserved to the UK Parliament rather than specific bills, and they make recommendations to the UK Government on when to engage with the devolved administrations. They do neither represent a position of the devolved institutions nor do they scrutinise devolved bills (UKP2).[76] Specific provisions facilitate an engagement of the UK Government and Parliament with the devolved executives and legislatures. According to Standing Order 137A.1 of the House of Commons (2019):

> Any select committee or sub-committee with power to send for persons, papers and records shall have power to communicate its evidence to any other select committee or sub-committee of either House of Parliament or to the Scottish Parliament, the National Assembly for Wales or the Northern Ireland Assembly or to any of their committees; provided that evidence from the National Audit Office shall first have been agreed between that Office and the government department or departments concerned;

Devolution Guidance Note 12 also sets out that "any request for a Minister to attend a Committee of a devolved legislature should be treated with as much care and courtesy as an invitation to attend a Commons or Lords Select Committee." (Cabinet Office 2019b). The Speakers and Presiding Officers of the four UK legislatures, for instance, meet regularly on an informal basis dependent on goodwill, but the content and outcomes of their quadrilaterals are not transparent to the public (Evans 2019, 102; Public Administration and Constitutional Affairs Committee 2016, 26).[77] Despite these initiatives to enable cross-administrative scrutiny, the parliaments as a whole have lacked political incentives and the will to cooperate with each other through more systematic interparliamentary practices (Hazell 2015, 55–56; McEwen et al. 2015). The Public Administration and Constitutional Affairs Committee of the House Commons (2016, 26) found that "inter-parliamentary relations (IPR) in the UK is arguably the poorer and less well-developed relative of IGR. [...] As with IGR, IPR in the UK has largely relied upon informal, bilateral and ad-hoc arrangements." Still, there are some practices to enable interparliamentary cooperation and scrutiny – albeit their impact on intergovernmental relations is modest at best overall.

Due to the Senedd's lack of primary legislative powers during the days of the early devolution settlement, it has more experience in engaging with the Welsh Affairs Committee than the other devolved legislatures have with their corresponding Westminster committees. The former states that it "liaises closely with Welsh Parliament Committees and has established a way of working through consultation, visits and invitation to appear before each other's committees." (Welsh Affairs Committee 2022).[78] To reduce the duplication of scrutiny activities by both legislatures, particularly around health services, the Welsh Affairs Committee can conduct joint meetings with the Welsh Assembly, which took place for the first time in June 2004 (Evans 2019, 102–104). According to 137.A.3 of Common's Standing Order: "The Welsh Affairs Committee may invite members of any specified committee of the National Assembly for Wales to attend and participate in its proceedings (but not to vote)." (House of Commons 2019). In turn, Standing Order 17.54 of the Senedd provides that its "committees may meet concurrently any committee or joint committee of any legislature in the UK." (Welsh Parliament 2021c). Despite the possibility to hold joint sessions and inquiries, both institutions have only sporadically engaged in such interparliamentary practices (less than ten times), and the Silk Commission (Commission on Devolution in Wales Part II 2014, 161) recommended improving interparliamentary cooperation. Subsequently, in 2015, the Senedd's Constitutional and Legislative Affairs Committee and Westminster's Welsh Affairs Committee held a joint evidence session on the draft of the Wales Bill (Evans 2019, 104).

Unlike for Wales, there are no authorised interparliamentary channels of communication nor any provisions for joint sessions Standing Orders for Scotland and Northern Ireland.[79] Yet, the Scottish Affairs Committee can invite committees of the Scottish Parliament to give evidence (Birrell 2012a, 222–223). For instance, the Scottish Affairs and the Social Security Committee of the Scottish Parliament organised two joint meetings in Holyrood on 13 March and in Westminster on 20 March 2017 "to investigate inter-governmental co-operation on social security, in light of the new powers over social security which are being devolved to the Scottish Government following the Scotland Act 2016". (Scottish Affairs Committee 2017). This was formally not part of a joint inquiry and members of the visiting committee were only listed as witnesses, but practically, they were treated as equal members of a joint committee by the convener (Evans 2019, 105). Since then, dialogues across the Scottish Parliament and the UK's Scottish Affairs, Constitutional and European Committees have started to evolve on a fairly moderate scale, and parliamentarians from Westminster have been invited to give evidence before Scottish committees and vice versa (SP1, SP2). Westminster and Holyrood also held more joint evidence sessions on specific inquiries, where MSPs came to London.[80]

As for joint practices between the executives, Brexit has triggered ambitions to explore new opportunities for interparliamentary exchange. In October 2017, the Interparliamentary Forum on Brexit was established for Chairs and Conveners of relevant Committees in the Scottish and Welsh legislatures and both Houses of the UK Parliament (as well as observing officials from the Northern Ireland Assembly) to provide for a collective scrutiny of EU-related legislation and policies on an informal basis (Welsh

Parliament 2020). This was exercised through private meetings, which also involved ministers, and by the formulation of public statements and letters to the UK Government. Although the forum set out to provide the legislatures with a common voice (Sheldon and Phylip 2020), by September 2019, it had met seven times at rotating locations and then "appears to have lost momentum following the 2019 General Election and the subsequent outbreak of the coronavirus pandemic" (UK Parliament 2020b). Post-Brexit and in the light of the COVID-pandemic, new calls for an institutionalisation of interparliamentary cooperation have emerged (Evans 2019) and in September 2020, the House of Common's Procedure Committee launched an inquiry on how to improve joint working between committees of each of the UK's devolved legislatures and Westminster (UK Parliament 2020c). However, the review of intergovernmental relations only requires reports to their parliaments to increase transparency. As long as the majoritarian nature of Westminster continues to reinforce the executive's dominance over Parliament, initiatives that would give legislatures a greater role in intergovernmental relations seem unlikely to lead to substantial changes.

Conclusion

Intergovernmental relations in the UK are not built on a robust, formalised architecture, but they rest (or more accurately move) on a flexible web of informal institutions and practices. The Cabinet Office, the Scotland Office and the Wales Office can be described as formal institutions with intergovernmental relevance operating as bridges between the different administrations. Although they have generally maintained good relations with the Scottish and Welsh Governments, their usefulness has frequently been questioned, as the devolved administrations typically prefer working directly with other UK departments, which is further fostered by the review of intergovernmental relations. Meanwhile, bodies like the UK Governance Group within the Cabinet Office, or more recently the Number 10 Union Unit, were meant to strengthen the UK Government's awareness of devolution issues, but have lacked sufficiently strong authority to promote substantial changes across Whitehall departments. The nature of the devolution settlement and pre-enactment discussions between governments have helped to avoid litigation and the Supreme Court seeks to interpret cases based on the text of statutes rather than on their political and constitutional relevance. Legally, its judgements only bind the devolved administrations, but for political reasons the UK Government has followed the court's decisions. The Supreme Court's role in solving intergovernmental questions and disputes may not match the significance of constitutional courts in federations, but it has become increasingly important in reviewing whether governments act within competence.

Apart from these formal arrangements at the centre, the intergovernmental machinery relies entirely on informal institutions and practices that cannot be legally sanctioned. These are *substantive* and neither *competing* with, *accommodating* or *complementing* any formal institutions. The principles of intergovernmental communication, consultation and cooperation are set out across a range of multilateral and bilateral compacts, concordats and protocols with the MoU at the top. Such agreements depend on goodwill and mutual trust without legally binding effect. After the Brexit referendum, new informal institutions evolved to replace some of the arrangements that were provided by the EU, in particular the Common Frameworks as well as the Intergovernmental Agreement between the Welsh and the UK Governments. As Chapter 5 will show, informal institutions and practices have been most effective and reliable in governing operational issues at the official level rather than major political disputes. The Sewel Convention seeks to ensure that the devolved administrations can govern autonomously without having to fear interference from Westminster. Under normal circumstances, Legislative Consent Motions have been respected and a source of moderate political influence – given that the UK Government recognises that it acted on a devolved issue. Yet, despite the convention's codification, Parliament is not legally bound by vetoes from the devolved legislatures. On several occasions over the course of EU withdrawal, the trust in Sewel was severely damaged when Westminster passed bills without the consent of the devolved legislatures.

The JMC and its Protocol on Dispute Resolution were only *weakly* institutionalised without statutory functions and independent resources and infrastructure. In the JMC Plenary and its subcommittees, ministers came together, but merely for information exchange and at best consultation, not for joint decision-making or effective political scrutiny. Until 2020 JMC Europe was the best-working subcommittee. Its temporary successor JMC European Negotiations was based on a deep misunderstanding, as its terms of references led the devolved administrations to wrongly believe that they would have a meaningful say over the UK's future relationship with the EU. These expectations were bitterly disappointed and showed that the JMC's and the protocol's informality and the UK Government's unilateral dominance prevented effective intergovernmental engagements and conflict resolution. In contrast to the JMC, the meetings of the Scottish and the Welsh Joint Exchequer Committees were characterised by joint agreements and consensus-building due to functional necessities and common interests in implementing the devolution of tax, borrowing and social security powers by the Scotland Acts of 2012 and 2016 and the Wales Acts of 2014 and 2017. The British-Irish Council represented the only *medium* institutionalised intergovernmental body with statutory functions, its own resources, collectively financed staff and a standing secretariat. Based on consensus and unanimity it commits the different governments to joint actions and the sharing of best practices across different working groups and sectors. For patterns of interaction between the UK, Scottish and Welsh Governments, however, the British-Irish Council does not take a major role.

It seems hard to imagine how intergovernmental relations would work without the wide range of established practices, in particular at official level. These are not visible to the public and rely heavily on personal contacts and relations. The UK Government has taken initiatives to strengthen its devolution capabilities at official level with varying success, including the 'Devolution and You' campaign and the introduction of devolution coordination teams for individual departments. At ministerial level, multi- and bilateral working groups, forums and quadrilateral meetings have emerged over time to deal with common policy challenges. While political tensions have affected the extent to which government engage with each other, at official level, directors, deputy directors and policy teams work continuously together on pragmatic solutions before intergovernmental tensions escalate into the political sphere. Multilateral and bilateral senior official groups and other working groups were set up and abandoned as needed to deal with specific policies, like the devolution of fiscal or welfare competences, or justice and health cooperation in Wales. Official relationships have been widely described as trustful and professional whereby policy areas, such as agriculture and food, economy and trade, social security and transport, were highlighted as good examples. In contrast, interparliamentary practices are not strongly developed in the UK and are only officially authorised between the Senedd and Westminster. While occasionally the Scottish and Welsh Affairs Committees participate in joint sessions with the devolved legislatures, and the Speakers and Presiding Officers of the four legislatures meet on an informal basis, demands for interparliamentary exchanges have remained insufficiently strong to put them on a more systematic footing. The Interparliamentary Forum on Brexit seemed like a new opportunity to strengthen these links but it ceased to meet beyond 2019.

Summarising the state of intergovernmental institutions and practices over the last decade, they were characterised by similar dynamics whether at senior political, ministerial or official and interparliamentary levels. The light-weight intergovernmental architecture was dependent on goodwill and a mutual trust that neither centre nor periphery disrespects their boundaries by pushing their powers too far, but instead cooperate in the pursuit of common interests (McEwen and Petersohn 2015, 195–196; O'Neill 2004, 191). Informality renders the arrangements volatile and ultimately gives the centre the upper hand. The over-reliance on individual actors and personal relations prevents institutional learning at Whitehall and the building of stable links across administrations. Overlapping competences and EU withdrawal have further exposed the weaknesses and power asymmetries within the intergovernmental system and the need for a better understanding of the devolved jurisdictions in Whitehall. In recent years and due to Brexit, at political and official levels, new arrangements and groups have emerged to facilitate and intensify cooperation without fundamentally rethinking intergovernmental relations. Except for the Welsh Government, which has been a staunch advocate for institutional innovation, Westminster and Whitehall have been guided by short-term political and functional rationales neglecting the long-term implications of failing to build a coherent system of systematic intergovernmental relations. These findings are consistent with Bolleyer's (2009, 34–35) assessment that majoritarian, power-concentrating polities avoid a strong institutionalisation of intergovernmental relations and prefer to operate through more flexible arrangements. The political culture at the centre struggles to come to terms with the idea of sharing power on a formal and systematic basis (UKG1, UKG5). The JMC Joint Secretariat (2018, 10–17) concluded that the ad hoc, bilateral and non-transparent nature of intergovernmental relations works to the advantage of the UK Government, which sets the terms under which discussions take place and which stakeholders to involve. It also suggested that a formalisation of intergovernmental relations would be necessary to build continuous trust between governments beyond personal contacts.

The new three-tier system was introduced in 2022 as a statement of intent without legally binding assurances or provisions for joint decision-making by majority voting. It represents an overdue reform that adopts the existing principles and arrangements, albeit in a new disguise, and will have to stand the test of time. The review points to more frequent and substantive intergovernmental business in the future, for instance, to collaborate on economic recovery and climate change. Properly implemented, Whitehall has set out to share more control with its counterparts in Edinburgh, Cardiff and Belfast (Kenny and Sheldon 2022). According to Sargeant (2022): "These logistical considerations, which may seem minor, are crucial to allowing ministers to meet based on a parity of esteem – something that the devolved administrations argue have long been missing from their interactions with the UK government." Constitutionally speaking, this does not undermine the UK Government's dominance over the devolved governments, and the ongoing political disagreement between governments may obstruct the functioning of the new arrangements. While Scottish[81] and Welsh[82] politicians have already raised some criticism, on the day of publication, however, the Welsh First Minister, Mark Drakeford (2022), welcomed the review: "[...] we believe the new structures and process can enable more meaningful dialogue among governments across areas of mutual interest – including on finance, UK-EU relations, trade and international affairs – and underpinned by a clearer, fairer dispute avoidance and resolution mechanism." Considering the incoherent organisation of intergovernmental relations covered in this chapter, the new system seems almost revolutionary from the outset. By fostering greater consistency of departmental engagement across the different administrations and emphasising the need for consensus in taking decisions, the new committees, working groups, IGR Secretariat and dispute resolution may potentially lead to a deeper integration and federalisation of the UK's multilevel polity.

Notes

1. Meanwhile, under former Prime Minister Theresa May, the UK Government appointed Lord Dunlop to review the 'Union capability' of the UK Government, whose report was published in March 2021. The Dunlop Review (Cabinet Office 2021a) proposed a series of institutional reforms to improve territorial governance for the whole of the UK; including a Secretary of State for Intergovernmental and Constitutional Affairs, a dedicated Cabinet sub-committee, and an Intergovernmental Council.
2. The Secretaries of State for Scotland and Wales are not ministers of the Ministry of Justice.
3. However, according to the Dunlop Review (Cabinet Office 2021a, 15), the Devolution Committee lacked a clear purpose to support its effectiveness.
4. The Advocate General for Scotland is a Law Officer of the UK Governments and provides legal advice to departments regarding the devolution settlement. The Advocate General can also intervene in cases of potential unlawfulness of Scottish legislation and require the courts to scrutinise such acts (Lazarowicz and McFadden 2018, 162).
5. There is no government information publicly available on these units.
6. The Scottish Secretary was allocated responsibilities for Transport (2003–2007) and Defence (2007–2008); and the Welsh Secretary was sequentially also the Leader of the House of Commons (2003–2005), the Northern Ireland Secretary (2005–2007) and the Secretary of State for Work and Pensions (2007–2008).
7. Due to its wider range of functions, the Northern Ireland Office is comparatively better equipped.
8. In light of the frequent disruptions of the shared rule arrangements, the Secretary of State for Northern Ireland is particularly important to ensure the running of the constitutional settlement and "the effective working of the institutions set up under the Belfast Agreement" (Cabinet Office 2019c, Devolution Guidance Note 5). They also take responsibility for a wide range of excepted matters and needs to give consent to Bills of the Assembly affecting excepted matters, international obligations and national security (cf. Birrell 2012b, 275).
9. The Dunlop Review (Cabinet Office 2021a, 15) also suggests that the offices' policy teams are overstretched, which limits their capacity to impact on the UK Government's broader policy agenda.
10. As Cairney (2012, 239) notes, the first Secretary of State for Scotland John Reid "was prepared to intervene in Scottish politics in a way viewed by the Scottish Executive as interference [...], while Helen Liddell, the second Secretary of State, there was still a perception that it was a legitimate role to manage, if not the policy process, then at least the internal affairs of the Scottish cabinet". Lord Wallace, Deputy Minister for Scotland from 1999 to 2005, even suggested that the Scotland Office "added little value" because most exchange was channelled through specific departments (Scottish Affairs Committee 2019a, 37).
11. As an MS and Welsh former minister put it: "There's no role really anymore for a Secretary of State. It's a minor department that sits at the fringes of Whitehall. [...] They don't do very much. They have exceptionally few powers, which they hold on to." (WP5).
12. In a more recent interview with the Institute for Government (Paun and Nice 2021), for instance, former Welsh minister Alun Davies expressed his frustrations about the attitudes of the Secretary of State for Wales between 2019 and 2022: "[Simon Hart] says some ludicrous things about the Welsh government.

Not just attacking our decisions, or the Welsh government's decisions, but attacking the fact that we exist and attacking the fact that we have democracy in our country."
13 'Devolution cases' can be brought to the Supreme Court either by the Attorney General or other actors who can exercise relevant statutory powers; through an appeal from higher courts within the UK; or through a reference from appellate courts.
14 E.g. *Cadder v Her Majesty's Advocate* (2010) and *Fraser v Her Majesty's Advocate* (2011) concerned the legality of the treatment and conditions of individuals accused of criminal offences in Scotland under the European Convention on Human Rights. *Martin v Most* (2010) challenged the competence of the Scottish Parliament to pass the Criminal Proceedings etc. (Reform) (Scotland) Act 2007, which increased the sentencing powers of Scottish courts, in particular in relation to road traffic offences. The claim was rejected by the Supreme Court.
15 E.g. *AXA General Insurance v The Lord Advocate and others* (2011) on the legality of the Damages (Asbestos-related Conditions) (Scotland) Act 2009. *Scottish Whiskey Association v Lord Advocate* (2014) challenged the Alcohol (Minimum Pricing) (Scotland) Act 2012 for breaching the EU's freedom of goods. *Imperial Tobacco Limited v The Lord Advocate* (2012) contested the Scottish Parliament's competence to pass sections of the Tobacco and Primary Medical Services (Scotland) Act 2010. The Supreme Court rejected the challenge.
16 Decisions by the Scottish Supreme Court were reviewing the general competence and legality of the Scottish Parliament to pass certain acts, but not the division of powers between the UK and Scottish Parliaments.
17 Better known as the Continuity Bill.
18 Section 17 required UK Ministers to get the consent of Scottish Ministers when repealing a retained EU law that sits within the powers of the Scottish Parliament.
19 The Welsh Government had already introduced its own Law Derived from the European Union (Wales) Bill in February, which received Royal Assent on 6 June 2018 but was then referred to the Supreme Court by the Attorney General for England and Wales. Before it faced same fate as the Scottish Continuity Bill, the Senedd revoked its own continuity bill after the Welsh Government had reached an Intergovernmental Agreement with the UK Government to amend the UK EU (Withdrawal) Bill (George 2018).
20 *Complementing* informal institutions enhance the efficiency of effective formal institutions; *accommodating* informal institutions alter the effects of formal institutions; *competing* informal institutions violate formal institutions and *substantive* informal institutions achieve what ineffective formal institutions fail to do (Helmke and Levitsky 2004, 728–731).
21 The convention is named after Lord Sewel, who as the Scottish Office minister steered the Scotland Bill 1998 through the House of Lords.
22 This usually takes place at the last amending stage in the House of Parliament where the bill was introduced (Brand and Atherton 2020, 39).
23 For an overview of legislative consent memorandums see Scottish Parliament (2021a and 2021b).
24 For an overview of legislative consent memorandums see Welsh Parliament (2021a).
25 The UK and Scottish Governments have seen the need for a concerted approach, for instance, in regard to the Food Standards Agency set up by the Food Standards Act 1999; and on tackling terrorism and international crime (Anti-Terrorism, Crime and Security Act 2001, the International Criminal

Court Act 2001, Proceeds of Crime Act 2002, and the Terrorism, Prevention and Investigatory Measures Act 2011).
26 This was the case for the Enterprise and Regulatory Reform Bill 2012–2013 and the Housing and Planning Bill 2015–2016.
27 The panels were not directly appointed by the Home Secretary instead by local authorities, which would have been under a devolved competence.
28 The Welsh Government forwarded a memorandum to reject the Medical Innovations Bill 2014–2015 but the UK Parliament was prorogued before it had passed the bill.
29 The Scottish Government also submitted a legislative consent memorandum for the Trade Union Bill 2015–2016, which was rejected by the Presiding Officer of the Scottish Parliament who agreed with the UK Government that the bill was not ruling in areas of devolved responsibility. The only time the Northern Ireland Assembly withheld consent to a UK bill was the Enterprise Bill in October 2015, which sought to limit public sector exit payments at £95,000. The Northern Ireland Executive took the position that devolved ministers should be responsible for taking this decision. While the Scottish and Welsh legislatures gave their consent, the amended Enterprise Act 2016 exempts Northern Ireland from exit payment caps made by public authorities subject to the powers of the Northern Ireland Assembly (Cowie 2018a, 46).
30 The Northern Ireland Executive was suspended at the time.
31 Scottish Parliament on 9 January; Senedd on 21 January; Northern Ireland Assembly on 20 January.
32 For an overview of all consent motions, see Welsh Parliament (2021a) and Scottish Parliament (2021a).
33 In 2000 the Northern Ireland Executive Committee was included in the Memorandum and since 2010 refers to the Welsh ministers instead of the Welsh Assembly.
34 Here is a small selection of examples, of which some will be discussed in Chapter 5, to illustrate their general nature: The Memorandum of Understanding in Network Rail Reclassification was established in 2013 between the Department for Transport and Rail Network covering England, Scotland and Wales (Department for Transport 2013). The 2018 Cross Border Healthcare with Wales Statement of Values and Principles between England and Wales complements the National Health Service Act 2006 (NHS England and NHS Wales 2018). The 2018 Concordat between the Ministry of Justice and the Welsh Government provides non-statutory guidelines "for consultation and co-operation [...] covering exchanges of information, justice impacts, access to services, resolution of disputes and review of relations." (Ministry of Justice 2018). On more detailed justice issues, in 2019 both governments also agreed on Blueprints for Female Offending (Ministry of Justice and Welsh Government 2019a) and Youth Justice (Ministry of Justice and Welsh Government 2019b) that apply in Wales.
35 On 16 October 2017.
36 Of the 22 non-legislative frameworks, Transport covers 6 (e.g. rail technical standards, driver licensing, road-motor insurance); Business, Energy and Industrial Strategy 5 (e.g. company law, late payment, radioactive substances); Health and Social Care 4 (e.g. blood safety and quality, public health); Cabinet Office (public procurement, statistics), Environment, Food and Rural Affairs (e.g. air quality) and Housing, Communities and Local Government (e.g. hazardous substances planning) each 2 and the Government Equalities Office 1 (equal treatment legislation).

Formal and Informal Intergovernmental Institutions 135

37 Thirteen areas that require legislative frameworks are within the responsibility of the Department for Environment, Food and Rural Affairs, covering agriculture (support, marketing, fertiliser regulations, zootech, organic farming); animal health and welfare; chemicals and pesticides; fisheries management and support; food composition standards and labelling; ozone-depleting substances and F-gases; plant health, plant variety and seeds; and resources and waste. Three legislative framework areas fall under the responsibility of the Department for Business, Energy and Industrial Strategy: implementation of EU Emissions Trading System; mutual recognition of professional qualifications; service directive and mutual recognition of professional qualifications. Reciprocal and cross-border healthcare is subject to the Department of Health and Social Care, and the Food and Standards Agency is responsible for food safety and hygiene law.

38 The Nutrition Labelling Composition and Standards (NLCS) Provisional Common Framework provides, for instance, a gateway process that takes decision from officials and senior officials up to ministerial level. It also sets out the terms of reference for the NLCS Policy Group (including a dedicated Secretariat) to meet quarterly and arrangements for dispute resolution.

39 A UK Government official argued: "We're always going to have at the top of this pyramid a forum that is much more political and it is easier for departments to have technical discussions at official and ministerial level that are much more policy driven and much less political." (UKG1).

40 Senior officials from each administration play a strategic role in identifying the Committee's future agendas, producing discussion papers and preparing agreements. They meet in the Committee of Officials, which is chaired by the Cabinet Secretary (Cabinet Office 2012, MoU A1.12).

41 The 10 October 2019 meeting took place in Edinburgh, 9 January 200 in London and 28 January 2020 in Cardiff. Due to Coronavirus, meetings on 21 May, 3 September, 29 October, 3 December were held via video conference.

42 Leading ministers from the devolved administrations deem the JMC as "meaningless", "not jointly owned", "a forum for dispute declaration, if rarely for conflict resolution" (McEwen 2017, 673–675), or a "talking shop" without a clear purpose or outcome (McEwen et al. 2018, 9–10). But it was also mentioned during an interview that personal meetings between ministers prior to the official JMC meeting provide an opportunity to have some engagement with the UK Government (SG11).

43 The first meeting on 23 March 2022 was attended by the following ministers. From the UK Government: The Secretary of State for Levelling Up, Housing and Communities, Rt Hon Michael Gove MP; The Secretary of State for Scotland, Rt Hon Alister Jack MP; The Secretary of State for Wales, Rt Hon Simon Hart MP and the Minister of State for Northern Ireland, Rt Hon Conor Burns MP. From the Scottish Government: The First Minister of Scotland, Rt Hon Nicola Sturgeon MSP and the Deputy First Minister and Cabinet Secretary for Covid Recovery, John Swinney MSP. From the Welsh Government: The First Minister of Wales, Rt Hon Mark Drakeford MS and the Counsel General and Minister for the Constitution, Mick Antoniw MS. Northern Ireland Civil Service officials attended the meeting in an observational capacity (Cabinet Office and Department for Levelling Up, Housing and Communities 2022b).

44 "Any number of ICs can be created at any given time but must have a predetermined life-span, which can be extended by consensus. ICs, like the IMSC, will however only consider issues which cannot be considered by the relevant IMG."

45 The Fiscal Framework for Scotland agreed on an independent report by the end 2021.
46 The British-Irish Parliamentary Assembly is the equivalent for the legislatures. Founded in 1990 by the UK and Irish Parliaments as the British-Irish Parliamentary Body Assembly, it was renamed in 2008. Since 2001 both parliaments provide 20 members; the Scottish Parliament, the Welsh Assembly and the Northern Ireland Assembly send each five representatives; and Guernsey, Jersey and the Isle of Man have one each. The Assembly meets in biannual plenary sessions and in Committees on Sovereign, European Affairs, Economic and Environment and Social Affairs to work on non-legislative issues, and maintains a joint secretariat. Its main functions are information sharing, social exchange and symbolic representation in relation to British-Irish relations but not devolution (Evans 2019, 101; cf. Birrell 2012a, 224).
47 Northern Ireland is represented by two ministers. Between 2017 and 2020, officials from Northern Ireland participated as observers and were very limited in their engagement. In contrast to the Irish Taoiseach and the First Ministers of Scotland and Wales, who attended most summits, consecutive Prime Ministers have not shown the same commitment. Since 2009 when Gordon Brown was Prime Minister, the UK Government has sent the Deputy Prime Minister to the meetings (Birrell 2012a, 221).
48 Except for in 2017, when the Northern Ireland Executive was suspended, and 2020 during the COVID-19 pandemic. Extraordinary summits can be called; for instance, immediately following the 2016 EU referendum.
49 This usually involves eight to ten officials but some meetings were joined by over 60 participants.
50 The UK and Irish Governments provide about 60 per cent of the budget in equal shares; Scotland, Wales and Northern Ireland contribute equal shares; and Guernsey, Jersey and the Isle of Man also pay a more modest fee.
51 Each government also appoints a coordinator within their administration to prepare policies and events. For the UK Government, the Governance Group of the Cabinet Office responsible for coordinating the involvement.
52 Ministers of the Welsh and Scottish Governments are generally longer in office than their UK counterparts, where the reshuffling of the Cabinet has been particularly frequent since the 2016 EU Referendum (SP4).
53 "The purpose of this statement is to set out the policies and procedures which underpin the exercise of determining the UK government's funding of the devolved administrations, to set out the elements of that funding, and to explain the interactions with the resources it is within the devolved administrations' capacity to raise themselves. It is intended to inform those both inside and outside government how the funding process operates, particularly as the arrangements become less symmetric as the devolved administrations take responsibility for additional functions." (HM Treasury 2015, 1.3).
54 From the UK Government, the Secretary of State for Scotland (co-chair), the Secretary of State for Work and Pensions and the Minister for Employment, and from the Scottish Government, the Cabinet Secretary for Social Security and Older People (co-chair) and the Minister for Business, Fair Work and Skills, as well as a number of officials, meet two to three times a year.
55 These are outside the JMC and Protocol on Dispute Resolution but highly controversial and important issues could be escalated to informal institutions.
56 Though official documentation on this could not be accessed, interviewees also pointed towards the existence of a bilateral Trade Working Group, which was set up in 2018 for the DEFRA Secretary of State and the Scottish Cabinet Secretaries of State and junior ministers to meet on a monthly basis (SG3). The group is supported by an official working arrangement: "Because those

meetings that only last maybe one and half hours, it can be very high level and quite political, whereas the work than needs to be done at a lower level. So, we have some official level structure as well to support that and try to get the best out of that ministerial engagement." (SG3).

57 According to the IMG EFRA Communiqué from 24 June 2019, "Key areas of work include the preparations for the UK's exit from the EU, domestic policy and legislation, common frameworks and funding." For an overview of communiqués, see Department for Environment, Food and Rural Affairs et al. (2021).

58 Pre-EU Referendum, minister would also come together about every six months to coordinate policies for the EU Council of Ministers in advance.

59 The Civil Service Commission for Northern Ireland, however, is a reserved matter for the purpose of ensuring an independent supervision of fair practice and accountability.

60 The Guidance on Devolution for the civil service of the UK Government states: "When dealing with any policy, it's good to be clear at the outset where it takes effect. If you are working on a policy that will affect the devolved administrations, you should engage as early as possible, especially if you are developing legislation. Devolved administrations need time to consider the handling of issues, and gaining consent of devolved legislatures for Parliament to pass legislation in a devolved matter is rarely a quick process." (Cabinet Office et al. 2020)

61 UK officials also pointed towards a senior official group and a devolution network meeting, where officials from different government departments meet regularly to exchange their experience of engagement with the devolved administrations and try to establish some coordination across Whitehall (UKG3, UKG9).

62 By 2020, DEFRA's devolution team had grown from two part-time positions to a team of 16–17 officials; the Department for Business, Energy and Industrial Strategy employed six people, MoJ had three dedicated members of staff, and the Department for Digital, Culture, Media and Sports only two (UKG2, UKG3, UKG4).

63 There is a wide range of different interactions between officials from the UK DfT, Transport Scotland, as well as from Wales and Northern Ireland through forums and working groups, such as the Inclusive Travel Board, the UK Roads Board, the UK Bridges Board and Transport Focus (SG15).

64 In turn, the Department for Communities and Local Government was used as an example for little engagement with the devolved administrations, because responsibility for local government is devolved (UKG1).

65 The MoJ also works together with the Scottish Government and the Northern Ireland Executive on a smaller range of issues, like criminal injuries compensations, which was originally an England and Wales programme adopted by the Scottish Government, and sentencing implications of counter-terrorism. The MoJ intended to establish a four-nation criminal justice forum, but because of the essential differences in the justice system of Scotland and Northern Ireland most justice policies do not require routinely quadrilateral cooperation (UKG4).

66 The Justice in Wales Strategy Group was set up in 2018 and takes a central role as an interface between the two governments to develop a strategic approach to policy development and provide consistency for the application of Welsh and English legislation. It is chaired by the executive director HM Prison and Probation Service in Wales, and includes HM Courts and Tribunal Service, the All Wales Criminal Justice, and other agencies and authorities based in Wales (Welsh Government 2018).

67 For a comprehensive overview of the boards, forums and agencies related to UK-Welsh justice relations, see Commission on Justice in Wales (2019, 137).
68 For areas such as animal health, plant health, agriculture trade, fisheries and the future relationships with the EU.
69 The DEFRA devolution team provides a secretariat to manage the board's agenda.
70 Part of the Food Compositional Standards and Labelling Provisional Common Framework.
71 Both part of the Food and Feed Safety and Hygiene Common Framework.
72 Part of the Nutrition Related Labelling, Composition and Standards Provisional Common Framework.
73 Part of the Public Health Protection and Health Security Framework.
74 The Net Zero Nations Board is another recent example of a quadrilateral forum for senior officials to support the Net Zero, Energy and Climate Change IMG.
75 With the exception of Belgium, where parliaments have a statutory right to consent but not amend legislative and budgetary agreements between the different levels, in Canada, Germany, Spain, Switzerland and the US, intergovernmental relations are dominated by the executives with little influence for legislatures.
76 Typically, though not exclusively, committee members are recruited from constituencies in Scotland, Wales and Northern Ireland, respectively. In Scotland, 'double jobbing' was practically phased out after 2016 without a legal ban when in 2017 two MPs stepped down as MSPs. In Wales, dual mandates for the House of Commons stopped practically in 2011 and legally with the Wales Act 2014. For an overview of all dual mandates see Goldberg (2017). Until it was legally prohibited in 2016, dual mandates for the House of Commons or the Lords and a devolved legislature were most common in Northern Ireland (16 out of 18 MPs in 2010). As Sinn Féin has ever since refused to take their seats in Westminster, this has placed the DUP in an advantageous position and at times influenced intergovernmental bargaining – most obviously as the party is currently supporting the Conservative Government.
77 Some parliamentarians also have frequent exchanges, mostly when they belong to the same party (SP4, WP1, WP4). But this is not considered to be a frequent practice.
78 Interestingly, prior to 2022 the Welsh Affairs Committee stated that it "liaises closely" with the committees of the Senedd.
79 The Northern Ireland Affairs Committee has in the past asked the committees from the Northern Ireland Assembly to give evidence (Birrell 2012a, 224). Because Republicans in the Northern Ireland Assembly refuse to accept Westminster as legitimate legislature for Northern Ireland, the Northern Ireland Affairs Committee does not engage in joint sessions, as a member of the Committee pointed out: "It wouldn't have any engagement with the Northern Ireland Executive or Northern Ireland Assembly. They are autonomous in their own right. It's not there to hold them accountable. Whenever devolution was not in operation for the last two or three years, and Northern Ireland Executive's functions was taken on or supervising than the committee would have stepped into that space to a certain extent to fill a void. But with devolution functioning, it's not the role to intervene in that. That would be a serious breach of the boundaries between the different layers of government. It's here to scrutinise the functions of the Northern Ireland Office and what they are doing, and whole wider UK policy that interferes with Northern Ireland." (UKP1).

80 As happened on 4 June 2019 when two MSPs from the Scottish Health and Social Care Committee were guests at an evidence session of the Scottish Affairs Committee as part of the Problem Drug Use inquiry (Scottish Affairs Committee 2019b).
81 Former Cabinet Secretary for the Constitution, Europe and External Affairs, Michael Russell raised doubts about the commitment of Conservative Party to the intergovernmental review: "[...] no matter what is written down or agreed by the current government, they will not stick to it. If the notion of Westminster sovereignty continues as it is, then there is no long-term or even short-term solution to this, because whatever you do can be gainsaid. Whatever you do can be set aside." (Paun and Nice 2022).
82 The Welsh Minister for Economy, Vaughan Gething (2022c), stated: "I can report to Members that the first meeting of the UK-EU Relations Interministerial Group (IMG) took place on 17 February 2022. Following postponement of an earlier scheduled meeting that I was due to attend, this one was called at very short notice of around two hours and, as a result, I was not able to participate. This is not an acceptable way to conduct intergovernmental relations, and I expect to see much earlier and more meaningful engagement in relation to future meetings of this IMG."

Bibliography

Adam, Elisenda C. (2021) *Brexit and the Mechanisms for the Resolution of Conflicts in the Context of Devolution: Do We Need a New Model?* In: Doyle, Oran, McHarg, Aileen and Murkens, Jo (eds.) *The Brexit Challenge for Ireland and the United Kingdom: Constitutions under Pressure.* Cambridge: Cambridge University Press, pp. 43–63.

BBC (2015) *Asbestos NHS Costs Laws Overruled by Supreme Court.* News. 9 February. https://www.bbc.com/news/uk-wales-politics-31173309

Behnke, Nathalie (2018) *Federal, Devolved or Decentralized State: on the Territorial Architecture of Power.* In: Detterbeck, Klaus and Hepburn, Eve (eds.) Handbook of Territorial Politics. Cheltenham: Edward Elgar Publishing, pp. 30–44.

Benz, Arthur (2013) *Dimensions and Dynamics of Federal Regimes.* In: Benz, Arthur and Broschek, Jörg (eds.) *Federal Dynamics: Continuity, Change, and the Varieties of Federalism.* Oxford: Oxford University Press, pp. 70–90.

Birrell, Derek (2012a) *Comparing Devolved Governance.* Basingstoke: Palgrave Macmillan.

Birrell, Derek (2012b) *Intergovernmental Relations and Political Parties in Northern Ireland.* British Journal of Politics and International Relations, Volume 14, Issue 2, pp. 270–284.

Boffey, Emma (2019) *Case Comment: The UK Withdrawal from the European Union (Legal Continuity) (Scotland) Bill – A Reference by the Attorney General and the Advocate General for Scotland [2018] UKSC 64.* Blog, 11 January. UK Supreme Court. http://ukscblog.com/case-comment-the-uk-withdrawal-from-the-european-union-legal-continuity-scotland-bill-a-reference-by-the-attorney-general-and-the-advocate-general-for-scotland-2018-uksc-64/

Bolleyer, Nicole (2009) *Intergovernmental Cooperation: Rational Choices in Federal Systems and Beyond.* Oxford: Oxford University Press.

Bolleyer, Nicole (2013) *Paradoxes of Self-coordination in Federal Systems.* In: Benz, Arthur and Broschek, Jörg (eds.) *Federal Dynamics: Continuity, Change, and the Varieties of Federalism.* Oxford: Oxford University Press, pp. 321–342.

Bolleyer, Nicole (2018) *Challenges of Interdependence and Coordination in Federal Systems*. In: Detterbeck, Klaus and Hepburn, Eve (eds.) *Handbook of Territorial Politics*. Cheltenham: Edward Elgar Publishing, pp. 45–60.

Bosse, Annie (2022) *Intergovernmental Relations in the UK: New Structure, New Approach?* SPICe Spotlight. 18 January. Scottish Parliament. https://spice-spotlight.scot/2022/01/18/intergovernmental-relations-in-the-uk-new-structure-new-approach/

Bradbury, Jonathan (2021) *Constitutional Policy and Territorial Politics in the UK. Volume 1: Union and Devolution 1997–2007*. Bristol: Bristol University Press.

Brand, Anna and Atherton, Sarah (2020) *Revised UK Agriculture Bill 2020*. SPICe Briefing SB 20-28. 27 March. Scottish Parliament. https://sp-bpr-en-prod-cdnep.azureedge.net/published/2020/3/27/Revised-UK-Agriculture-Bill-2020/SB%2020-28.pdf

Bröchler, Stephan and Lauth, Hans-Joachim (2014) *Die Lokalisierung von Schneisen im Dickicht – Konzeptionelle Grundlegungen und empirische Befunde informaler Governance*. Zeitschrift für Vergleichende Politikwissenschaft, Volume 8, Issue 1 (Supplement), pp. 1–33.

Broschek, Jörg (2011) *Conceptualizing and Theorizing Constitutional Change in Federal Systems: Insights from Historical Institutionalism*. Regional and Federal Studies, Volume 21, Issue 4–5, pp. 539–559.

Brouillet, Eugénie and Mullen, Tom (2018) *Constitutional Jurisprudence on Federalism and Devolution in UK and Canada*. In: Keating, Michael and Laforest, Guy (eds.) *Constitutional Politics and the Territorial Question in Canada and the United Kingdom: Federalism and Devolution Compared*. Cham: Palgrave Macmillan, pp. 47–77.

Burgess, Michael (2006) *Comparative Federalism: Theory and Practice*. London: Routledge.

Cabinet Office (2012) *Devolution: Memorandum of Understanding and Supplementary Agreement*. Policy paper. 1 October. https://www.gov.uk/government/publications/devolution-memorandum-of-understanding-and-supplementary-agreement

Cabinet Office (2019a) *Common Frameworks Update*. Guidance. 3 July. UK Government. https://www.gov.uk/government/publications/common-frameworks-update

Cabinet Office (2019b) *Devolution Guidance Notes*. Guidance. 14 March. UK Government. https://www.gov.uk/government/publications/devolution-guidance-notes

Cabinet Office (2019c) *Letter from Chancellor of the Duchy of Lancaster to Scottish Affairs Committee*. 17 January. UK Government. https://www.parliament.uk/globalassets/documents/commons-committees/scottish-affairs/Correspondence/2017-2019/CDL2537-outgoing.pdf

Cabinet Office (2019d) *Revised Frameworks Analysis: Breakdown of Areas of EU Law That Intersect with Devolved Competence in Scotland*, Wales and Northern Ireland. April. UK Government. https://assets.publishing.service.gov.uk/government/uploads/system/uploads/attachment_data/file/792738/20190404-FrameworksAnalysis.pdf

Cabinet Office (2020a) *Frameworks Analysis 2020 Breakdown of Areas of EU Law That Intersect with Devolved Competence in Scotland*, Wales and Northern Ireland. UK Government. https://www.gov.uk/government/publications/frameworks-analysis

Cabinet Office (2021a) *Review of UK Government Union Capability*. Independent report. 24 March. UK Government. https://www.gov.uk/government/publications/the-dunlop-review-into-uk-government-union-capability

Cabinet Office (2021b) *Communiqués from the Joint Ministerial Committee (EU Negotiations)*. Collection. UK Government. https://www.gov.uk/government/collections/communiques-from-the-joint-ministerial-committee-eu-negotiations

Cabinet Office (2021c) *UK common frameworks*. Collection. 9 December. UK Government. https://www.gov.uk/government/collections/uk-common-frameworks

Cabinet Office and Department for Levelling Up, Housing and Communities (2022a) *Review of Intergovernmental Relation*. Policy paper.13 January. UK Government. https://www.gov.uk/government/publications/the-review-of-intergovernmental-relations

Cabinet Office and Department for Levelling Up, Housing and Communities (2022b) *Intergovernmental Relations*. Collection. 25 August. UK Government. https://www.gov.uk/government/collections/intergovernmental-relations#interministerial-group-for-trade

Cabinet Office, Office of the Secretary of State for Scotland, Office of the Secretary of State for Wales and Northern Ireland Office and (2020) *Guidance on Devolution*. Guidance. 28 September. https://www.gov.uk/guidance/guidance-on-devolution

Caird, Jack Simson (2016) *The Supreme Court on Devolution*. Briefing Paper Number 07670. 27 July. House of Commons. https://commonslibrary.parliament.uk/research-briefings/cbp-7670/

Cairney, Paul (2011) *The Scottish Political System Since Devolution: From New Politics to the New Scottish Government*. Exeter: Imprint Academic.

Cairney, Paul (2012) *Intergovernmental Relations in Scotland: What Was the SNP Effect?* British Journal of Politics and International Relations, Volume 14, Issue 2, pp. 231–249.

Commission on Justice in Wales (2019) *Justice in Wales for the People of Wales*. Report. October. https://gov.wales/sites/default/files/publications/2019-10/Justice%20Commission%20ENG%20DIGITAL_2.pdf

Constitution and Cabinet Directorate (2018) *Strengthening the Sewel Convention: Letter from Michael Russell to David Lidington*. Publication – Correspondence. 12 September. Scottish Government. https://www.gov.scot/publications/strengthening-the-sewel-convention-letter-from-michael-russell-to-david-lidington/

Cowie, Graeme (2018a) *Brexit: Devolution and Legislative Consent*. Briefing Paper Number 08274. 29 March. House of Commons. https://researchbriefings.files.parliament.uk/documents/CBP-8274/CBP-8274.pdf

Cowie, Graeme (2018b) *Last Chance for Compromise? Devolution and the EU (Withdrawal) Bill*. Insight. 11 June. UK Parliament. https://commonslibrary.parliament.uk/last-chance-for-compromise-devolution-and-the-eu-withdrawal-bill/

Deacon, Russell (2012) *Devolution in the United Kingdom*. Edinburgh: Edinburgh University Press.

Department for Environment, Food and Rural Affairs, Scottish Government, Welsh Government and Department of Agriculture, Environment and Rural Affairs (Northern Ireland) (2021) *Communiqués from the Inter Ministerial Group for Environment, Food and Rural Affairs*. Policy paper. 7 April. UK Government. https://www.gov.uk/government/publications/communique-from-the-inter-ministerial-group-for-environment-food-and-rural-affairs

Department for Levelling Up, Housing and Communities (2022) *Intergovernmental Relations Annual Report – Reporting period 1 January – 31 December 2021*. CP 655. March. UK Government.

Department for Levelling Up, Housing and Communities and Cabinet Office (2021) *The European Union (Withdrawal) Act and Common Frameworks: 26 June to 25 September 2021*. Policy paper. 9 December. UK Government. https://www.gov.uk/government/publications/the-european-union-withdrawal-act-and-common-frameworks-26-june-to-25-september-2021

Department for Transport (2013) *Network Rail Reclassification: Memorandum of Understanding*. Guidance. 17 September. UK Government. https://www.gov.uk/government/publications/network-rail-reclassification-memorandum-of-understanding

Department of Health and Social Care (2020a) *Nutrition Labelling Composition and Standards Provisional Common Framework Command Paper*. Policy paper. 9 October. UK Government. https://www.gov.uk/government/publications/nutrition-labelling-composition-and-standards-provisional-common-framework-command-paper

Department of Health and Social Care (2020b) *Food and Feed Safety and Hygiene: Provisional Common Framework*. Policy paper. 27 November. UK Government. https://www.gov.uk/government/publications/food-and-feed-safety-and-hygiene-provisional-common-framework

Department of Health and Social Care (2021) *Public Health Protection and Health Security: Provisional Common Framework*. Policy paper. 28 October. UK Government. https://www.gov.uk/government/publications/public-health-protection-and-health-security-provisional-common-framework

Drakeford, Mark (2022) *Written Statement: Review of Intergovernmental Relations*. Cabinet Statement. 13 January. Welsh Government. https://gov.wales/written-statement-review-intergovernmental-relations-0

Evans, Adam (2019) *Inter-parliamentary Relations in the United Kingdom: Devolution's Undiscovered Country?* Parliaments, Estates and Representation, Volume 39, Issue, 1, pp. 98–112.

Gallagher, Jim (2012) *Intergovernmental Relations in the UK: Co-operation, Competition and Constitutional Change*. British Journal of Politics and International Relations, Volume 14, Issue 2, pp. 198–213.

Gallagher, Jim (2020) *Intergovernmental Relations: Two Decades of Co-operation, Competition, and Constitutional Change*. Keating, Michael (ed.) The Oxford Handbook of Scottish Politics. Oxford: Oxford University Press, pp. 565–583.

George, Manon (2018) *Agreement Reached on Amendments to the EU (Withdrawal) Bill*. Senedd Research. 1 May. Welsh Parliament. https://research.senedd.wales/2018/05/01/agreement-reached-on-amendments-to-the-eu-withdrawal-bill/

Gething, Vaughan (2022) *Written Statement: Meeting of the UK-EU Relations Interministerial Group, 17 February 2022*. Cabinet statement. 10 March. https://gov.wales/written-statement-meeting-uk-eu-relations-interministerial-group-17-february-2022

Gove, Michael (2021) *Letter from the Chancellor of the Duchy of Lancaster to Lord*. 24 March. UK Government. https://assets.publishing.service.gov.uk/government/uploads/system/uploads/attachment_data/file/973001/L_Dunlop_Letter.pdf

Hazell, Robert (2015) *Devolution and the Future of the Union*. London: The Constitution Unit.

Helmke, Gretchen and Levitsky, Steven (2004) *Informal Institutions and Comparative Politics: A Research Agenda*. Perspectives on Politics, Volume 2, Issue 4, pp. 725–740.

HM Government and Scottish Government (2016) *The Agreement between the Scottish Government and the United Kingdom Government on the Scottish Government's Fiscal Framework*. Independent report. February. UK Government. https://www.gov.uk/government/publications/the-agreement-between-the-scottish-government-and-the-united-kingdom-government-on-the-scottish-governments-fiscal-framework

HM Government and Welsh Government (2016) *The Agreement between the Welsh Government and the United Kingdom Government on the Welsh Government's Fiscal Framework*. December. Welsh Government. https://gov.wales/sites/default/files/publications/2018-11/agreement-on-welsh-government-fiscal-framework.pdf

HM Treasury (2015) *Statement of Funding Policy: Funding the Scottish Parliament, National Assembly for Wales and Northern Ireland Assembly*. November. 7th edition. UK Government. https://www.gov.uk/government/publications/spending-review-and-autumn-statement-2015-documents

Horgan, Gerard W. (2004) *Inter-institutional Relations in the Devolved Great Britain: Quiet Diplomacy*. Regional and Federal Studies, Volume 14, Issue 1, pp. 113–135.

House of Commons (2019) *Standing Orders (Public Business 2019)*. HC 314. 5 November. https://www.parliament.uk/business/publications/commons/standing-orders-public11/

Hueglin, Thomas O. (2013) *Comparing Federalism: Variations or Distinct Models?* In: Benz, Arthur and Broschek, Jörg (eds.) *Federal Dynamics: Continuity, Change, and the Varieties of Federalism*. Oxford: Oxford University Press, pp. 27–47.

Hueglin, Thomas O. and Fenna, Alan (2010) *Comparative Federalism: A Systematic Inquiry*. Peterborough: Broadview Press.

Hunt, Jo and Minto, Rachel (2017) *Between Intergovernmental Relations and Paradiplomacy: Wales and the Brexit of the Regions*. The British Journal of Politics and International Relations, Volume 19, Issue 4, pp. 647–662.

Paun, Akash and Nice, Alex (2021) Alun Davies. Interview, Ministers Reflect. 12 October 2021. https://www.instituteforgovernment.org.uk/ministers-reflect/person/alun-davies/

Paun, Akash and Nice, Alex (2022) Michael Russell. Interview, Ministers Reflect. 26 January 2022. https://www.instituteforgovernment.org.uk/ministers-reflect/person/michael-russell/

Jeffery, Charlie (2009) *Devolution in the United Kingdom: Problems of a Piecemeal Approach to Constitutional Change*. Publius, Volume 39, Issue 2, pp. 289–313.

JMC Joint Secretariat (2018) *Report of the Joint Ministerial Committee: 2015–2018*. Policy paper. 14 March. UK Government. https://www.gov.uk/government/publications/joint-ministerial-committee-communique-14-march-2018

Keating, Michael (2012) *Intergovernmental Relations and Innovation: From Co-operative to Competitive Welfare Federalism in the UK*. British Journal of Politics and International Relations, Volume 14, Issue 2, pp. 214–230.

Keating, Michael (2021) *State and Nation in the United Kingdom: The Fractured Union*. Oxford: Oxford University Press.

Kenny, Michael and Sheldon, Jack (2022) *Green shoots for the Union? The Joint Review of Intergovernmental Relations*. The Constitution Unit Blog. 19 January. The Constitution Unit Blog. https://constitution-unit.com/2022/01/19/green-shoots-for-the-union-the-joint-review-of-intergovernmental-relations/

Kenny, Michael, Rycroft, Philip and Sheldon, Jack (2021) *Union at the Crossroads: Can the British State Handle the Challenges of Devolution*. Report by the Bennett Institute for Public Policy Cambridge. The Constitution Society.

Lauth, Hans-Joachim (2014) *Analytische Konzeption für den Vergleich politischer Systeme*. In: Lauth, Hans-Joachim (ed.) *Politische Systeme im Vergleich: Formale und informelle Institutionen im politischen Prozess*. Oldenbourg: De Gruyter, pp. 3–50.

Lazarowicz, Mark and McFadden, Jean (2018) *The Scottish Parliament – Law and Practice*. Edinburgh: Edinburgh University Press.

Leyland, Peter (2011) *The Multifaceted Constitutional Dynamics of U.K. Devolution*. International Journal of Constitutional Law, Volume 9, Issue 1, pp. 251–273.

Lhotta, Roland and Blumenthal, Julia von (2015) *Intergovernmental Relations in the Federal Republic of Germany: Complex Co-operation and Party Politics*. In: Poirier, Johanne, Saunders, Cheryl and Kincaid, John (eds.) *Intergovernmental Relations in Federal Systems*. Oxford: Oxford University Press, pp. 1–13.

Martin, Ciaran (2021) *Resist, Reform or Re-Run? Short- and Long-term Reflections on Scotland and Independence Referendums*. Research and practitioners' insight. Blavatnik School of Government Oxford.

McEwen, Nicola (2017) *Still Better Together? Purpose and Power in Intergovernmental Councils in the UK*. Regional and Federal Studies, Volume 27, Issue 5, pp. 667–690.

McEwen, Nicola (2022) *Intergovernmental Relations Review: Worth the Wait?* Commentary. 17 January. UK in a Changing Europe. https://ukandeu.ac.uk/intergovernmental-relations-review/

McEwen, Nicola and Petersohn, Bettina (2015) *Between Autonomy and Interdependence: The Challenges of Shared Rule after the Scottish Referendum*. The Political Quarterly, Volume 86, Issue 2, pp. 192–200.

McEwen, Nicola, Kenny, Michael, Sheldon, Jack and Brown Swan, Coree (2018) *Reforming Intergovernmental Relations in the United Kingdom. Centre on Constitutional Change and Cambridge*. Edinburgh: Bennett Institute for Public Policy.

McEwen, Nicola, Petersohn, Bettina and Brown Swan, Coree (2015) *Intergovernmental Relations and Parliamentary Scrutiny: A Comparative Overview*. Edinburgh: Centre on Constitutional Change.

McEwen, Nicola, Swenden, Wilfried and Bolleyer, Nicole (2012) *Intergovernmental Relations in the UK: Continuity in a Time of Change?* British Journal of Politics and International Relations, Volume 14, Issue 2, pp. 323–343.

McMillan, Janice and Massey, Andrew (2004) *Central Government and Devolution*. In: O'Neill, Michael (eds.) *Devolution and British Politics*. London: Routledge, pp. 231–250.

Miles, Jeremy (2020) *Written Statement: Joint Ministerial Committee (EU Negotiations)*. Cabinet statement. 6 February. Welsh Government. https://gov.wales/written-statement-joint-ministerial-committee-eu-negotiations-1

Ministry of Housing, Communities and Local Government (2020) *Hazardous Substances: Provisional Planning Framework*. Policy paper. 23 November. UK Government. https://www.gov.uk/government/publications/hazardous-substances-provisional-planning-framework

Ministry of Justice (2018) *Concordat between the Ministry of Justice and the Welsh Government*. Policy paper. 25 June. UK Government. https://www.gov.uk/government/publications/concordat-between-the-ministry-of-justice-and-the-welsh-government

Ministry of Justice and Welsh Government (2019a) *Female Offending Blueprint for Wales*. UK Government. https://gov.wales/sites/default/files/publications/2019-05/female-offending-blueprint_3.pdf

Ministry of Justice and Welsh Government (2019b) *Youth Justice Blueprint for Wales*. UK Government. https://gov.wales/sites/default/files/publications/2019-05/youth-justice-blueprint_0.pdf

Mitchell, James (2010) *Two Models of Devolution: A Framework for Analysis*. In: Stolz, Klaus (ed.) *Ten Years of Devolution in the United Kingdom: Snapshot at a Moving Target*. Augsburg: Wißner-Verlag, pp. 52–71.

NHS England and NHS Wales (2018) *England/Wales Cross-border Healthcare Services: Statement of Values and Principles*. Statement. 27 November. https://www.england.nhs.uk/publication/england-wales-crossborder-healthcare-services-statement-of-values-and-principles/

Northern Ireland Office (1998) *The Belfast Agreement*. Policy paper. 10 April. UK Government. https://www.gov.uk/government/publications/the-belfast-agreement

Office of the Secretary of State for Scotland (2016) *Joint Senior Officials Group Terms of Reference*. Corporate report. 15 December. UK Government. https://www.gov.uk/government/publications/joint-senior-officials-group-terms-of-reference

O'Neill, Michael (2004) *Devolution and British Politics*. London: Routledge.

Paun, Akash, Sargeant, Jess, Nicholson, Elspeth and Rycroft, Lucy (2022) *Sewel Convention*. Explainer. 8 December. Institute for Government. https://www.instituteforgovernment.org.uk/explainers/sewel-convention

Paun, Akash, Sargeant, Jess and Shuttleworth, Kelly (2020) *Devolution: Joint Ministerial Committee*. Explainer. 1 July. Institute for Government. https://www.instituteforgovernment.org.uk/explainers/devolution-joint-ministerial-committee

Paun, Akash and Shuttleworth, Kelly (2020) *Legislating by Consent: How to Revive the Sewel Convention*. IfG Insight. September. Institute for Government.

Paun, Akash, Sargeant, Jess, Shuttleworth, Kelly and Nice, Alex (2020) *Coronavirus and Devolution*. Explainer. 26 March. Institute for Government. https://www.instituteforgovernment.org.uk/explainers/coronavirus-and-devolution

Poirier, Johanne and Saunders, Cheryl (2015a) *Comparing Intergovernmental Relations in Federal Systems: An Introduction*. In: Poirier, Johanne, Saunders, Cheryl and Kincaid, John (eds.) *Intergovernmental Relations in Federal Systems*. Oxford: Oxford University Press, pp. 1–13.

Poirier, Johanne and Saunders, Cheryl (2015b) *Conclusion: Comparative Experience of Intergovernmental Relations in Federal Systems*. In: Poirier, Johanne, Saunders, Cheryl and Kincaid, John (eds.) *Intergovernmental Relations in Federal Systems*. Oxford: Oxford University Press, pp. 440–498.

Public Administration and Constitutional Affairs Committee (2016) *The Future of the Union, Part Two: Inter-institutional Relations in the UK*. Sixth Report of Session 2016–17. HC 839. 8 December. House of Commons.

Sargeant, Jess (2022) *New UK Intergovernmental Structures Can Work, But Only with Political Will*. Comment. 28 January. Institute for Government. https://www.instituteforgovernment.org.uk/blog/new-intergovernmental-structures-can-work-only-political-will

Scottish Affairs Committee (2017) *Oral Evidence: Inter-governmental Co-operation on Social Security*. HC 1095. 20 March. House of Commons. https://data.parliament.uk/writtenevidence/committeeevidence.svc/evidencedocument/scottish-affairs-committee/intergovernmental-cooperation-on-social-security/oral/49162.pdf

Scottish Affairs Committee (2019a) *The Relationship between the UK and Scottish Governments*. Eighth Report of Session 2017–19. HC 1586. 7 June. House of Commons. https://publications.parliament.uk/pa/cm201719/cmselect/cmscotaf/1586/1586.pdf

Scottish Affairs Committee (2019b) *Oral Evidence: Problem Drug Use in Scotland.* HC 1997. 4 June. House of Commons. https://data.parliament.uk/writtenevidence/committeeevidence.svc/evidencedocument/scottish-affairs-committee/problem-drug-use-in-scotland/oral/102845.html

Scottish Government (2016) *Inter-governmental Relations: Agreement between the Scottish Parliament and Scottish Government.* Publication agreement. 8 December. https://www.gov.scot/publications/igr-agr-scotparl-scotgov/

Scottish Government (2019a) *Ministerial Forum (EU Negotiations): Communiques.* Collection. https://www.gov.scot/collections/ministerial-forum/

Scottish Government (2019b) *Scottish Government Overview of 'No Deal' Preparations. Laid before the Scottish Parliament, October.* SG/2019/204. October. https://www.gov.scot/binaries/content/documents/govscot/publications/progress-report/2019/10/scottish-government-overview-no-deal-preparations/documents/scottish-government-overview-no-deal-preparations/scottish-government-overview-no-deal-preparations/govscot%3Adocument/scottish-government-overview-no-deal-preparations.pdf

Scottish Government (2020a) *Letter from Minister for Public Finance and Migration to the Convener Culture, Tourism, Europe and External Affairs Committee.* 5 March. https://archive2021.parliament.scot/S5_European/General%20Documents/20200305_MinisterPFMToConvener_JMC_E.pdf

Scottish Government (2020b) *Joint Ministerial Committee on EU Negotiations: communiques.* https://www.gov.scot/collections/joint-ministerial-committee-on-eu-negotiations-communiques/

Scottish Government (2020c) *Joint Ministerial Group on Welfare.* https://www.gov.scot/groups/joint-ministerial-group-welfare/

Scottish Parliament (2021a) *Legislative Consent Memorandums: 2005 – present.* Parliamentary Business. https://archive2021.parliament.scot/parliamentarybusiness/bills/31313.aspx

Scottish Parliament (2021b) *Legislative and Public Bodies Act Consent Memorandums and Motions statistics.* Parliamentary Business. https://archive2021.parliament.scot/parliamentarybusiness/bills/19023.aspx

Sheldon, Jack and Phylip Hedydd (2020) *Devolution Arrangements within the UK during the Next Phase of Brexit.* Commentary. 30 March. UK in a Changing Europe. https://ukandeu.ac.uk/brexit-and-intergovernmental-coordination-within-the-uk/#

Sturm, Roland (2020) *Föderalismus.* Baden-Baden: Nomos.

Supreme Court (2015) *Recovery of Medical Costs for Asbestos Diseases (Wales) Bill – Reference by the Counsel General for Wales.* Judgement. [2015] UKSC 3. 9 February. https://www.supremecourt.uk/cases/uksc-2014-0043.html

Supreme Court (2021) *Devolution Jurisdiction.* Practice Direction 10. https://www.supremecourt.uk/procedures/practice-direction-10.html

UK Parliament (2020a) *Update on the EU (Withdrawal Agreement) Bill.* Statement UIN HLWS55. 23 January. https://questions-statements.parliament.uk/written-statements/detail/2020-01-23/HLWS55

UK Parliament (2020b) *Written Evidence Submitted by Jack Sheldon, University of Cambridge and Hedydd Phylip, Cardiff University.* TTC 02. November. https://committees.parliament.uk/writtenevidence/14593/html/

UK Parliament (2020c) *Committee Launch New Major Inquiry on House of Commons Procedure and the Territorial Constitution.* News article. 24 September. https://committees.parliament.uk/committee/126/procedure-committee/news/119460/committee-launch-new-major-inquiry-on-house-of-commons-procedure-and-the-territorial-constitution/

UK Parliament (2021) *The Supreme Court 2009*. https://www.parliament.uk/about/living-heritage/evolutionofparliament/houseoflords/judicialrole/overview/supremecourt/

Watts, Ronald L. (2008) *Comparing Federal Systems*. Montreal and Kingston: McGill-Queen's University Press.

Welsh Affairs Committee (2022) *Role – Welsh Affairs Committee*. House of Commons. https://committees.parliament.uk/committee/162/welsh-affairs-committee/role/

Welsh Government (2018) *Concordat between the Welsh Government and the UK Ministry of Justice*. Policy and strategy. 25 June. https://gov.wales/concordat-between-ministry-justice-and-welsh-government-html

Welsh Government (2019a) *Reforming Our Union: Shared Governance in the UK*. Policy and strategy. 10 October. https://gov.wales/reforming-our-union-shared-governance-in-the-uk

Welsh Government (2019b) *Letter from the Minister for Environment, Energy and Rural Affairs to the Chair of Climate Change, Environment and Rural Affairs Committee*. 30 August. https://business.senedd.wales/documents/s93278/Letter%20from%20the%20Minister%20for%20Environment%20Energy%20and%20Rural%20Affairs.pdf

Welsh Government (2020a) *Providing Inter-governmental Information to the National Assembly: Annual Report 2019 to 2020*. Report. 26 October. https://gov.wales/providing-inter-governmental-information-national-assembly-annual-report-2019-2020

Welsh Government (2020b) *Letter from the Minister for Economy and Transport, the Minister for Environment, Energy and Rural Affairs, and the Minister for Education to the Chair of the Legislation, Justice and Constitution Committee*. 25 February. https://senedd.assembly.wales/documents/s99346/CLA5-08-20%20Paper%2015.pdf

Welsh Parliament (2020) *Interparliamentary Forum on Brexit*. Senedd Business. 9 July. https://business.senedd.wales/mgIssueHistoryHome.aspx?IId=22530

Welsh Parliament (2021a) *Legislative Consent*. Senedd Business. https://senedd.wales/senedd-business/legislative-consent/

Welsh Parliament (2021b) *Inter-Institutional Relations Agreement*. Senedd Business. 16 November. https://business.senedd.wales/mgIssueHistoryHome.aspx?IId=38300

Welsh Parliament (2021c) *Standing Orders of the Welsh Parliament*. Senedd Business. March. https://senedd.wales/NAfW%20Documents/Assembly%20Business%20section%20documents/Standing_Orders/Clean_SOs.eng.pdf

Wyn Jones, Richard and Royles, Elin (2012) *Wales in the World: Intergovernmental Relations and Sub-state Diplomacy*. British Journal of Politics and International Relations, Volume 14, Issue 2, pp. 250–269.

5 Patterns of Interaction and Political Influence

After over 20 years of devolution, when the empirical work for this study was conducted, the relationships between the Scottish and Welsh and the UK Government were at a dire state. In November 2020, during a virtual meeting of Conservative Members of Parliament (MPs) from the North of England, Prime Minister Boris Johnson was reported to have called devolution "a disaster north of the border" and Tony Blair's "biggest mistake" (BBC 2020a). Although Johnson claimed that his comment was directed at the performance of the SNP in handling devolution and not at "devolution as a concept" (Blackall 2020),[1] the damage in Scotland and Wales had already been done. In sharp words, the Welsh Minister for European Transition condemned Johnson's remarks: "The PM's comments are shocking but sadly not surprising. It has been clear for some time that this Conservative government is not remotely interested in respecting the devolution settlements across the UK. The prime minister is also minister for the union – but the conduct of his government is actually the biggest threat to the future of the union." (Morris and Brooks 2020). Whether the Prime Minister's comments aimed at the SNP or the devolution settlement itself, they supported the Scottish Government's secessionist reasoning. Scotland's First Minister Nicola Sturgeon (2020) capitalised on the moment and wrote on Twitter: "Worth bookmarking these PM comments for the next time Tories say they're not a threat to the powers of the Scottish Parliament - or, even more incredibly, that they support devolving more powers. The only way to protect & strengthen @ScotParl is with independence." Yet, regardless of the political tension between governments, their interactions are not only characterised by disputes but also by patterns of cooperation.

The previous chapter indicated how informal institutions and practices are supposed to provide a culture of good communication and cooperative working. Even though these are not politically binding, the different administrations communicate and coordinate their policies a lot more than is commonly implied. As outlined in Chapter 2, this study investigates the causal linkages between non-interaction (DV1),[2] conflict (DV3)[3] and cooperation (DV2),[4] and functional and political interdependence (IV1), preference intensity (IV2), party congruency (IV3) and strategic power (IV4) (cf. Tatham 2016, 16 et seq.).

DOI: 10.4324/9781003349952-5

It assumes that a dual allocation of authority, as envisaged by the reserved powers model, leads to non-interaction (DV1). Functional and political interdependence (IV1), however, have increasingly required intergovernmental coordination and bargaining. To prevent the negative impact of disruptive policies and decisions, governments either cooperate (DV2) if they share common interests, or engage in conflict (DV3) if the actions of one government have unwelcome consequences for the other jurisdiction. The pattern of interaction depends on the preference intensity (IV2) of the issues at stake. Particularly when preferences are high for both levels but diverge, conflict (DV3) is the likely outcome. Despite the fact that it only covers a time period when different parties were in power across the different governments, this study also accounts for the impact of party congruency (IV3) on the prevailing patterns of interaction. Lastly, strategic power (IV4) is introduced to this study as a variable focusing on the negotiations process within a given institutional setting.[5] This chapter then examines how *strategic preferences, negotiation power* (based on their electoral strength and public support) and the prevailing *mode of interaction* inform the strategic options and ability of governments to use cooperation (DV2) and conflict (DV3) to their advantage. The mode of interaction is distinguished here between *hierarchical direction, unilateral action* and *negotiated agreement*, which are possible either within *voluntary* or *compulsory negotiation systems* (Scharpf 1997, 46–49; 2000, 241–245).[6]

Strategic power (IV4) determines patterns of interaction but does not necessarily translate into impact. Knowing about the political influence of the devolved governments is key to this study and offers new conclusions about territorial power in the light of informal intergovernmental institutions and practices and patterns of cooperation (DV2) and conflict (DV3). Analysing the patterns of interaction and the political influence of the devolved administrations in two separate chapters would lead to substantial repetition. Hence, this chapter also assesses the political influence of the Scottish and Welsh Governments on the political, legislative and fiscal decisions of the UK Government. Looking beyond a legalistic analysis of authority as provided in Chapter 3, the *EAR instrument* provides a systematic qualitative triangulation tool;[7] according to which *political influence* then is the product of the devolved government's *goal-achievement* (GA), the extent to which the achievement can be *ascribed* to them (AS), and the *political relevance*[8] of the policy outcome (PR): PI = GA × AS × PR. The ordinal categories for each criterion are 0 means *no*; 1 means *some*; 2 means *substantial* and 3 means *great*, which are multiplied and translated into verbal qualifications: 0 means *no*; 1, 2 or 3 means *some*; 4, 6, 8, 9 or 12 means *substantial* and 18 or 27 means *great* political influence (Arts and Verschuren 1999).

This chapter covers a wide range of policy issues. Even though the sequence of the issues presented here is not strictly hierarchical in terms of their salience, it starts with broader topics and subsequently focuses on more policy-related examples. The analysis thus begins with the overall constitutional issues of the devolution settlement, which includes the question of independence from the Union. It then continues with the intergovernmental dynamics in the context of EU withdrawal, which, since the 2016 referendum, has been the most important issue with a wide and deep significance for the devolution settlement. Starting with this broader picture is essential to make sense of more specific policy areas: foreign affairs and international trade; immigration policy; fiscal policy; agriculture and food; environment, energy and climate change; economic policy and development; transport; public healthcare and safety and justice and policing. The selection of examples examined in the following is informed by the availability of data and the insights provided by the respondents of the different administrations. Fisheries, for instance, would have made an interesting intergovernmental matter for Scotland. But it was not possible to arrange an interview with the Marine Scotland Directorate. Social security and welfare may have also provided an interesting case of growing political and functional interdependence (IV1) where, in particular after the passage of the Scotland Act 2016,[9] civil servants have worked together on a frequent basis, for instance, through the Joint Ministerial Working Group on Welfare (Department for Levelling Up, Housing and Communities 2022a, 40–41). Yet, the analysis of this policy area could not be supported by sufficiently comprehensive data to be included here. Given the asymmetrical devolution of authority over policy areas, it is also important to note that the different sections vary in focus across the Scottish and Welsh Governments.

Constitution, powers and independence

Although the Scottish and the Welsh Governments have fundamentally different outlooks on their status within the UK, constitutional issues around the devolution settlement and the allocation of political and legislative authority naturally enjoy the highest preference intensity (IV2) and are at the top of both their political priorities (SG2, SP2). Whereas the Labour-led Welsh executive commits to the Union, shapes their respective engagement with the UK Government (WP4), the SNP's ultimate objective is for Scotland to become an independent state, which has certainly been a major source of tensions and mistrust (SG8). Nevertheless, the Scotland Act 2012, as well as the Edinburgh Agreement, which gave the Scottish Parliament temporary powers to hold a referendum on Scottish independence, were characterised by cooperation, competition and influence (Gallagher 2020, 577). Subsequently, the negotiations for the Scotland Act 2016 were also difficult but all stakeholders were determined to make the devolution of further powers a success. The Scottish Government wanted more competences, and similarly, the UK Government was eager to deliver its promise for a maximum level of devolution made over the course of the 2014 Scottish independence referendum. Between September and November 2014, the Smith Commission (chaired by Lord Smith of Kelvin) negotiated constitutional reforms for the devolution of new welfare and fiscal responsibilities, which were unanimously agreed

Patterns of Interaction and Political Influence 151

by all five main political parties from Scotland (HM Government 2015, 11; Scottish Affairs Committee 2015, 6). Civil servants who worked on the position of the Commission were vital in solving occurring frictions between the different parties and governments. Though not formally part of the Smith Commission, the UK Government profoundly shaped its outcomes, which, due to time pressures, reflected more the common concern to finding consensus than detailed solutions for contentious or complicated issues (Kenealy and Parry 2018, 492–499). The cooperation (DV2) on the Scotland Act 2016 can be explained by the functional and political interdependence (IV1), preference intensity (IV2) and strategic power (IV4) of the Scottish Government. Sewel Convention, the SNP's electoral strength, the threat of independence and the breakup of the Union provided significant leverage to commit the UK Government to a compulsory negotiation system through which an agreement could be reached. As a former senior UK official closely involved in the Smith Commission suggested: "It was a classic of an intergovernmental negotiation where, although the parties were very different in scale, there was a sort of an equality of need to get a deal done; and that's what really drove the deal at the end of the day." (UKG10)

In terms of political influence, David Cameron's administrations accommodated not all but enough Scottish demands for the Scottish Government to recommend the Scottish Parliament to consent to the bill on 16 March 2016 (UKG5, UKG9).[10] A detailed report of the Devolution (Further Powers) Committee (2015) of the Scottish Parliament came to the conclusion that the UK Government's proposal for the new Scotland Bill did not live up to the recommendations of the Smith Commission, for instance in regard to the permanency of the Scottish Parliament and Scottish Government.[11] Still, considering the strong input of the SNP in the Smith Commission and the Scottish Government during the implementation the Scotland Act 2016, a qualitative assessment through the EAR-instrument concludes the influence of the Scottish Government as *substantial*.

Scotland	
Goal-achievement	2 (substantial)
Ascription	2 (substantial)
Political relevance	3 (great)
Political influence ($GA \times AS \times PR$)	*12 (substantial)*

Following the Scotland Act 2016, the Welsh Government also asked for its competences to be expanded on a more modest scale. The Welsh Government's preference intensity (IV2) was slightly and its strategic power (IV4) significantly lower than those of the Scottish Government, which can explain why the intergovernmental engagement towards the Wales Act 2017 was easier. As a UK official put it: "It was never going to be as difficult with Wales because there isn't the appetite for independence in Wales that there is in Scotland." (UKG9). Nevertheless having suffered two defeats before the Supreme Court, the UK Government was eager to cooperate (DV2) with the Welsh Government in a compulsory negotiation system to change the conferred into a transferred powers model and to fulfil its commitment made in the St David's Day Agreement to devolve legislative and fiscal authority (UKG10) (Cameron 2015). The Senedd was not happy to give consent to the initial bill, which was too complicated and bureaucratic to provide a lasting settlement, and it worried about the possibility of rolling back its powers instead of expanding them sufficiently (Constitutional and Legislative Affairs Committee 2016). Looking at the track record of written exchanges between the Welsh Assembly and Government and UK ministers (Welsh Parliament 2020b), the former were able to push for amendments to the Wales Bill, which received the Assemblies legislative consent on 17 January 2017. Similar to the Scotland Act 2016, the Wales Act 2017 presents an example of *substantial* political influence for the Welsh Government.

Wales	
Goal-achievement	2 (substantial)
Ascription	2 (substantial)
Political relevance	3 (great)
Political influence ($GA \times AS \times PR$)	12 (substantial)

In Wales, the boundaries between reserved and devolved powers have been subject to ongoing disputes, but until Brexit disagreements were mostly over policy rather than constitutional issues (WG11). While the next section will comprehensively address the political tensions that have been awakened by the EU withdrawal, the UK Government's intention to centralise some of the powers that returned to the devolved administrations has triggered new concerns about the status of Wales in the Union[12] (WG1, WP1, WP4): "There are real constitutional concerns about giving such massive, far ranging powers to the ministers, that effectively bypass parliamentary democracy." (WP1). Meanwhile, the support for Wales's secession has significantly increased, and since 2019 independence marches have become more common in Wales. This has forced the Welsh Labour Party to articulate a new political narrative about the worthiness of the Union for Wales and demand constitutional reforms (WP5) (Chappell 2020). In autumn 2020, the Welsh First Minister Mark Drakeford (2020) made an exemplary statement:

> Unfortunately, relations with the UK Government are not as we would wish them to be. Sometimes carelessly, and sometimes deliberately, in its desire to centralise power and remove obstacles in all branches of government to exercising that power, the UK Government is undermining devolution. The constitutional settlement that has been supported by the people of Wales in two referendums is under serious threat.

Despite high levels of functional and political interdependence (IV1) and preference intensity (IV2), the Welsh Government's low strategic power

(IV4) within a strongly hierarchical system means, however, that it needs to be cooperative to get any concessions from the UK Government. When it issued the policy paper Reforming Our Union in 2019, the Welsh Government (2019a) aimed to "stimulate new thinking in this area" and "constructive engagement" for a more systematic intergovernmental framework:[13]

> Whatever its historical origins, the United Kingdom is best seen now as a voluntary association of nations taking the form of a multinational state, whose members share and redistribute resources and risks amongst themselves to advance their common interests. Wales is committed to this association, which must be based on the recognition of popular sovereignty in each part of the UK; Parliamentary sovereignty as traditionally understood no longer provides a sound foundation for this evolving constitution.
>
> (op. cit., 4)

By highlighting the voluntary nature of the Union, the paper proposed a substantial adjustment of the devolution settlement, replacing Parliamentary sovereignty, introducing co-decision-making and constitutional guarantees, and allowing for public referendums about the future of the devolved institutions. The Scottish Government also made proposals to strengthen and enforce the Sewel Convention, the Joint Ministerial Committee (JMC) and dispute resolution, but these were less comprehensive and seemed to have little impact (SG6) (Constitution and Cabinet Directorate 2018). And yet, the 2022 review of intergovernmental relations (Cabinet Office and Department for Levelling Up, Housing and Communities 2022) reflects a range of reforms that were suggested by the Scottish Government, and in particular by the Welsh Government (2019a, 12–13); including a decision-making UK Council of Ministers to replace the JMC structure, interministerial forums, an independent secretariat based on the one of the British-Irish Council, dispute resolution by independent third-party arbitration and mediation, participation in the formulation of the UK's policy position in international negotiations, and greater transparency of intergovernmental relations (see sections 4.2.3 and 4.2.4). Kenny and Sheldon (2022) argued that "[t]he direction of travel reflects some of the constitutional thinking that has been developing in the Welsh government in Cardiff." Mark Drakeford (2022) further highlighted the impact of the devolved governments on the intergovernmental reforms:

> Following years of intensive work by Ministers and officials during the joint Review of Intergovernmental Relations, the Welsh Government, along with the UK government, the Scottish Government, and the Northern Ireland Executive, have agreed to use the package of reforms which has emerged from the Review as the basis for the conduct of intergovernmental relations. The package makes important progress in advancing the objectives the Welsh Government set out in 'Brexit and Devolution' and 'Reforming our Union', and as such is a welcome

154 *Patterns of Interaction and Political Influence*

development which can bring benefits for all 4 governments and the 4 nations. The final package of reforms builds on the draft set of proposals that was published on 24 March last year. Further progress has been made since then to strengthen the package, focusing on the concerns we expressed with the earlier proposals.

Notwithstanding such a positive reception, there remain limits to any constitutional reforms that would constrain the UK Government or Parliament by any form of binding co-decision-making, as a UK official argued, as a UK official reflected:

> In the UK it is Parliament that is sovereign and it is only Parliament that can make a decision that affects the whole of the UK, not the UK Government. So I always struggled to understand how the co-decision model that the Welsh Government put forward would work in practice. Politically it is very clever because they are the one other solely unionist government and therefore they would often be the 'go-to-co-decision' so it would greatly empower their influence [...] The other factor, the way the devolution settlement was set up means there is particularly now with the reserved powers model, there is clarity about who has responsibility for respective powers; and therefore there shouldn't need to be areas of co-decision. There needs to be areas of consultation and dialogue, and that's what intergovernmental relations is there to support. And then it is clear who is the ultimate decision-maker.
>
> (UKG1)

The intergovernmental review does not revise the constitutional structures or set the Council of Ministers on a statutory footing with binding provisions for co-decision-making. Considering that the goal-achievement of the Welsh and Scottish Governments was partially successful, but the practical application of the new system was not fully clear, and the ascription of the outcome involved other important actors,[14] their political influence for the time being was rated *substantial*.

Scotland	
Goal-achievement	2 (substantial)
Ascription	1 (Some)
Political relevance	3 (great)
Political influence (GA × AS × PR)	6 *(substantial)*
Wales	
Goal-achievement	2 (substantial)
Ascription	2 (substantial)
Political relevance	3 (great)
Political influence (GA × AS × PR)	12 *(substantial)*

EU withdrawal

Before the EU referendum in 2016, intergovernmental relations within the UK did not enjoy a great deal of attention (SP2). And yet, the implementation of EU legislation and policies has caused high political and functional interdependencies, which required coordination across European, national and regional levels (Gallagher 2012, 200; Keating 2012, 225–226; McEwen and Petersohn 2015, 195; Tatham 2016, 156 et seq.). As EU law reached deep into the devolved competences (SG3, SP2), ministers from the different governments discussed the UK's positions before the UK Government represented these during meetings of the European Council and the Council of Ministers. According to Alun Davies, the former Welsh Minister for Natural Resources and Food:

> We would agree a UK position, and I tried to push the idea of a single UK voice speaking in different accents. So, for example, if we were talking about sheep farming, for argument's sake, then it would clearly be something that the Welsh government would want to take a lead on because it's more relevant in Wales than elsewhere. But if we're talking about the cod recovery plan, then clearly that's more relevant to Scotland than it is to Wales or England.
>
> (Paun and Nice 2021)

Scottish and Welsh ministers and officials could participate in EU meetings on behalf of the UK and have occasionally done so, but typically the UK Government preferred to send their own delegates (SG3), who were not bound to accommodate the priorities of the devolved administrations. A Scottish official remembers: "Sometimes we had to be quite vocal with UK Government if we saw them about to take a position that was out of line with our interests. Sometimes we couldn't stop them entirely but we could at least maybe take the rougher edges off of what they were presenting." (SG3). Taking away the EU's regulatory framework, in which the devolution settlement was embedded, has reshaped the UK's constitution (SP2), put the whole system under stress (SG8), and exposed the weaknesses of the UK's light-weight intergovernmental architecture. The UK's withdrawal from the EU has been a lengthy and tedious process involving internal and external dynamics and, although these are interlinked, this section seeks to disentangle the different stages of cooperation (DV2) and conflict (DV3). The first stage focuses therefore on the tensions around the repatriation of legislative powers from the EU and the EU Withdrawal Act 2018. The second stage concerns negotiations over the UK's Withdrawal Agreement and the future relationship with the EU, for which the UK and the devolved governments' ambitions were hardly compatible. The third stage then examines the notable cooperation (DV2) during the development of the UK Common Frameworks programme, which was subsequently overshadowed by the conflict (DV3) around the Internal Market Act and the Shared Prosperity Fund.[15]

The European Union (Withdrawal) Act 2018

When it became clear that legislative authority would return from the EU to the UK, the UK Government acted under the assumption that retained EU law would continue to apply and could subsequently be altered by secondary legislation by UK ministers. It argued that these powers were never really controlled by the devolved administrations and therefore should return to Westminster and Whitehall. The Scottish and Welsh Governments insisted that the repatriated powers were not reserved by statute but rather were devolved, and therefore fiercely resisted this de facto centralisation of powers (SG4, SG6, SG7, WP1) (Keating 2021, 98): "The original position of the UK Government was that all powers would come to them, and they would decide when and if those powers would be repatriated to us, even in areas that were devolved. Obviously, that was wholly unacceptable." (WP5). Without prior consultation, the UK Government introduced the EU (Withdrawal) Bill 2018 (previously named the Great Repeal Bill) on 13 July to repeal the European Communities Act 1972 and ensure a temporary continuity of laws after leaving the EU by converting EU law into UK law. Only a fortnight before its introduction was the bill presented to the Scottish and the Welsh Governments (Public Administration and Constitutional Affairs Committee 2018a, para. 35). The Withdrawal Bill restricted the devolved competences on specific subjects to ensure that the UK would not breach its international obligations during the transition period (Cowie et al. 2020, 73). The original Section 11 of the bill intended to 'freeze' devolved powers for retained EU law. Accordingly, the devolved executives and legislatures would not have been able to modify retained EU laws unless the UK Government enabled them to do so. On the same day, the First Ministers of Scotland and Wales published a joint statement stating that they would not recommend giving consent to the bill:

> We have repeatedly tried to engage with the UK government on these matters, and have put forward constructive proposals about how we can deliver an outcome which will protect the interests of all the nations in the UK, safeguard our economies and respect devolution. Regrettably, the bill does not do this. Instead, it is a naked power-grab, an attack on the founding principles of devolution and could destabilise our economies.
>
> (Welsh Government 2017a)

The Scottish and Welsh Governments wanted to retain all powers coming back from the EU to the UK and had already made the necessary provisions to transpose them into devolved legislation through statutory instruments (WG11). Their position was that any restrictions by the Withdrawal

Bill should be narrowly defined in terms of scope and time and require the consent of the devolved legislatures (Cowie 2018b):[16]

> The approach that UK Government had first published in the Withdrawal Bill wasn't practical in terms of the legal provision they had put in was so difficult to operate and so unpredictable in its effect, so difficult for us to comprehend what powers we would be left with and the interaction between EU law that had been transferred into domestic law EU law that had been frozen and competence to change.
>
> (SG4)

That the bill was debated for over 272 hours by the Commons and the Lords and increased in length by 63 per cent before it received Royal Assent on 26 June 2018 (Jack 2017) speaks to the wider struggles within the UK Parliament, Government and with the devolved administrations. Between September 2017 and April 2018 (Cowie 2018b), ministers from the UK, Scotland and Wales held tricky conversations in the JMC European Negotiations (EN) and beyond (Public Administration and Constitutional Affairs Committee 2018a, para. 46). UK civil servants worked hard to ensure that the bill would respect the devolution settlement (UKG5). The Scottish and Welsh Governments set up a concerted campaign to exert pressure on Whitehall that included representatives from various sectors, including business organisations, trade unions and academia, and they held awareness sessions in London and lobbied members of the Commons and Lords from various parties to amend the bill (SG6, WG11). When David Lidington became Chancellor of the Duchess of Lancashire in January 2018, he was determined to find a solution that acknowledged the position of the devolved administrations (SG11, WG2) (Public Administration and Constitutional Affairs Committee 2018b). In closed negotiations, senior officials from all three governments met off the record to find compromises that all governments would agree to (WG2). After a session of the JMC EN on 22 February 2018, however, the Scottish and Welsh Governments took measures "escalating their conflict with the UK Government over the EU Withdrawal Bill – and edging intergovernmental relations closer to a constitutional crisis." (Kellam 2018). Insisting that the EU Withdrawal Bill would not apply to the responsibilities of the Scottish and Welsh legislatures, the Scottish and Welsh Governments each introduced their own continuity bills, which were similar in scope to the UK bill and sought to ensure the continuation and modification of retained EU law – as well as a dynamic alignment with EU rules. Their bills were as much based on a political as a legal rationale to provide certainty while seeking to increase the strategic pressure on Westminster (McHarg 2018; Adam 2021, 56). As the former Council General who worked on the Welsh bill stated:

> If the whole Withdrawal Bill failed and we ended up leaving the EU without any legislative framework, where would that leave Wales and

Scotland. We would have no legislative continuity. It was a relatively simple principle but it also provided a setting within which to give leverage in terms of the UK legislation itself.

(WP1)

Both governments announced that they would withdraw or repeal their bills, if the UK Government would consider their concerns in the EU Withdrawal Bill. Tabled as emergency bills, they hurried the passage of their legislation in order to out speed the EU Withdrawal Bill, which amended the existing devolution statutes to prevent the devolved legislatures from modifying the UK bill (McHarg 2018). It took only three weeks from introduction to the passage of the UK Withdrawal from the European Union (Legal Continuity) (Scotland) Bill on 18 March 2018, and even less time to pass the Law Derived from the European Union (Wales) Bill on 21 March 2018 (Welsh Parliament 2020d). From the onset, it was controversial whether the bills were within the devolved legislatures remits. To prevent the Scottish Continuity Bill from receiving Royal Assent, on April 2018 the UK Government's Law Officers, the Attorney General and the Advocate General for Scotland referred both bills to the Supreme Court to decide whether this legislation was within devolved legislative powers (Attorney General's Office 2018).

The House of Lords was central to changing the EU Withdrawal Bill. Though the Welsh Government could rely on Labour and LibDem peers to amplify its argument, the UK Government would not have agreed to amendments supported merely by opposition parties. After a coalition of Conservative, Labour, LibDem and Crossbench peers signed the proposed amendments, the UK Government introduced the amendments to the bill (WG2, WG11). The final legislation was a remarkable achievement and a significant improvement for the devolved administrations. The UK Government reversed the initial approach to centralise all repatriated powers by default under Section 11. Under the new Section 12 of the bill, most competences went to the devolved levels and would not be altered by any government until further agreements were reached (Public Administration and Constitutional Affairs Committee 2018a, para. 48–50). Even though the Scottish and Welsh Governments did not achieve a legally binding veto on the UK Government powers to alter retained EU laws that are within devolved jurisdictions (Cowie 2018b), under Section 12, UK ministers need to specify if any laws cannot be modified by the devolved administrations. Devolved powers could now only be frozen or amended during a two-year period after leaving the EU and for a maximum of five years. For the Welsh Government, collaborating with the UK Government seemed to be the best way to ensure their interests and prevent the freezing of their powers (WG8). Jeremy Miles, the Welsh Counsel General and Brexit Minister, was pleased with the outcome:

But, working with the Scottish Government, we secured major concessions, significantly extending the powers exercisable by the devolved institutions and building in controls for us over how the powers in all parts of the UK might be frozen, including the requirement for both Houses of Parliament to resolve separately if they are to override the objections of the devolved administrations. Those powers have not actually been used of course, and the UK Government has confirmed in its two published reports to date that it has no reason to use them.

(Welsh Government 2019b)

Despite being remarkably successful, the Scottish Government did not feel that their devolved competences were sufficiently respected by the EU Withdrawal Bill and therefore did not recommend legislative consent (SG2, SG4):[17]

The UK Government did modify the bill. Still as far as we're concerned, nowhere near good enough because in effect they bound the Scottish Parliament. They froze the devolved powers without our consent. Is it better than the initial drafting? Probably. Still the principle has still been breached that they shouldn't be legislating over the heads of the Scottish Parliament but the bill was modified after considerable pressure from the Scottish Government.

(SG6)

Feeling that it had made sufficient amendments to meet the concerns of the devolved governments, the UK Government was not prepared to regard the Sewel Convention as an ultimate veto over its decisions, and for the first time ignored the Sewel Convention on a statute that it had recognised as relating to devolved matters (Public Administration and Constitutional Affairs Committee 2018a, para. 52). After they had worked intensively together, the Scottish Government's rejection of the bill also came as a disappointing surprise to the Welsh Government (WG11, WP1). The UK Government, however, could at least rely on the support of one devolved legislature, as a UK civil servant argued:

It was important that we got the Welsh on board, to get their legislative consent motion. That was important, not just optically to have at least one of the devolved administrations coming on board. It was also important for the passage of the bill in the House of Lords, because that allowed the government to say: 'well, this isn't about the substance because the Welsh Government is on the side. It's about politics, that's why the SNP are upholding their legislative consent.'

(UKG10)

To accommodate the Welsh priorities, on 24 April 2018 the UK and the Welsh Governments passed a non-binding Intergovernmental Agreement on the EU (Withdrawal) Bill and the Establishment of Common

Frameworks, which complements the Withdrawal Bill. In the event that the UK Government considers taking powers unilaterally without the agreement of the devolved administrations, "UK Ministers will be required to make an explanatory written statement to the UK Parliament if a decision is taken to proceed." (Cabinet Office 2018a). Ultimately, this cannot legally prevent the UK Parliament from exercising powers that are devolved but it did prevent an automatic repatriation of powers to the UK level (WG11). David Lidington, the Chancellor of the Duchy of Lancaster at the time, welcomed the agreement:

> I am very pleased that the many months of detailed negotiation have got us to a point where we have now reached an agreement with the Welsh Government on changes to the Bill. This is a significant achievement that will provide legal certainty, increase the powers of the devolved governments and also respect the devolution settlements. The UK Government has made considerable changes to the EU Withdrawal Bill to address issues that have been raised in Parliament and by the devolved administrations. It is disappointing that the Scottish Government have not yet felt able to add their agreement to the new amendments that Ministers and officials on all sides have been working on very hard over recent weeks.
>
> (Cabinet Office 2018b)

After its passage through Parliament, the EU (Withdrawal) Act 2018 received Royal Assent on 26 June. Next to the negotiation towards the bill, intense behind-the-scenes intergovernmental cooperation (DV2) took place to manage the challenges of a looming no-deal Brexit (SG6, SG10, SG14). The UK Government improved its flow of information and engaged "unseen, and largely unreported" with the Scottish and Welsh Governments. Whitehall shared over 100 technical notes and invited devolved ministers and officials to meetings of the European Exit and Trade (Domestic Preparedness, Legislation and Devolution) Cabinet sub-committee and working groups (Kenny et al. 2021, 28). According to a UK official (UKG1): "What we did at official level, was trying to supplement the political challenges by trying to make sure that the official dialogue was as enriched as it could possibly be." All governments worked closely together at ministerial, official and parliamentary levels without major disputes to close potential legislative loopholes.[18] The Scottish Parliament introduced almost 50 and the Welsh Assembly 43 Statutory Instruments. Both legislatures also gave consent to around 150 statutory instruments by the UK Parliament (Scottish Government 2019a; Welsh Government 2019c).[19]

The actual judgement on the Scottish Continuity Bill was made in December 2018 long after the passage of the Withdrawal Bill. Although the Supreme Court rejected the UK Attorney General's claim that the bill was outside Holyrood's competences, it concluded that the Scottish Parliament cannot legislate on the same objective as the UK Parliament and thereby constrain Westminster's future actions. Only Section 17 of the Scottish bill was outside of competence, as it required UK ministers to get the consent of Scottish ministers when repealing a retained EU law that sits within the powers of the Scottish Parliament (Supreme Court 2018; Boffey 2019; Cowie et al. 2020, 73).[20] Despite the unlawfulness of the bill, the judgement was still perceived as useful to the devolved administrations, as it implied their entitlement to legislate on the implementation of international obligations (WP1) (Miles 2018). Although the UK's Attorney General had also referred the European Union (Wales) Bill to the Supreme Court in April 2018, he later withdrew his reference after the UK and Welsh Governments reached their intergovernmental agreement (Welsh Parliament 2020d). The Welsh Act received Royal Assent on 6 June 2018 and would have faced the same fate as the Scottish Continuity Bill (Miles 2018). But as part of their deal the Welsh Government repealed its own act in November 2018 (WG2, WP1).

By 31 January 2022, when Section 12 expired, the UK Government had not used the EU (Withdrawal) Act to freeze devolved legislation (Department for Levelling Up, Housing and Communities and Cabinet Office 2021). Considering the high functional political interdependence (IV1) and preference intensity (IV2) of the matter at hand, the preparations for leaving the EU presented a mix of cooperation (DV2) and conflict (DV3). Due to the missing intra-party links to the UK Government (IV3) the Scottish and Welsh Governments had to skilfully operate through the House of Lords and other stakeholders. The devolved administrations expressed their strong concerns in public and they passed their own continuity bills, but their strategic power (IV4) was low. The negotiation mode was set by the hierarchical direction of the UK Government, which felt only slightly restricted by the given strategic constellations. Nevertheless, the Withdrawal Bill changed significantly due to the efforts of the Scottish and the Welsh Governments, and their political influence was at least *substantial*. Because the former was slightly less satisfied with the outcome of the negotiations, and the latter was more committed to bringing them to an end and concluding an intergovernmental agreement with the UK Government, the ascription of influence is rated higher for Wales resulting in *great* political influence.

Scotland	
Goal-achievement	2 (substantial)
Ascription	2 (substantial)
Political relevance	3 (great)
Political influence (GA × AS × PR)	*12 (substantial)*

Wales	
Goal-achievement	2 (substantial)
Ascription	3 (great)
Political relevance	3 (great)
Political influence (GA × AS × PR)	*18 (great)*

The European Union (Withdrawal Agreement) Act 2020

Whereas the Scottish and Welsh Governments could impact on the domestic issue of the repatriated powers, their role in the external negotiations with the EU was very different due to their different political outlooks. Scotland voted largely to remain in the EU and the Scottish Government has aimed to re-join as an independent state; in Wales, a majority favoured leaving and the Welsh Government is led by the unionist Labour Party. However, as foreign affairs and signing international treaties are reserved matters, the UK Government did not recognise that the devolved administrations would have a legitimate role in the withdrawal process (SG6). Though the Supreme Court acknowledged that Brexit affects devolved competences, in its judgement on the Miller case, it also clarified that the Sewel Convention does not legally bind the UK Parliament to rely on the legislative consent of the devolved legislatures (Hunt, 2017).[21] This confirmed the UK Government's legitimacy to act unilaterally on the withdrawal process and not to consult the devolved administrations prior to triggering Article 50 TEU. The political tensions between the different governments stemmed in part from the weak position of Theresa May's premiership and the internal divisions over the terms of leaving the EU within the Conservative Party. Without a majority in Parliament, Whitehall was generally cautious to share information outside of a small circle, which constrained its intergovernmental engagement (SG4, SG11, WG11). As the centre struggled to adopt a unified position which they could reliably present to the Scottish and the Welsh Governments, the latter published various policy papers to present their priorities for a future relationship with the EU.[22] These were to stay economically and politically closely aligned with the EU, to maintain EU standards in areas such as the environment, manufacturing, chemicals, and consumer and worker rights, to allow for the free movement of goods, services and also people, and to participate in EU programmes, such as Erasmus+, Horizon Europe and INTERREG (SG1, SG2, SG6, SG14, WG11).

Neither the Scottish nor the Welsh Governments could effectively participate in the policymaking at UK level or have a meaningful impact on the UK Government's positions towards the EU (SG4, WG2, WG5). A Scottish official reported: "We have thought to influence but those attempts have either been ignored or dismissed. It has felt like there were potential some little bits where we had influence on but for such a significant issue to have been sidelined in that process is hugely frustrating." (SG2). Scottish and Welsh ministers frequently expressed their discontent about the lack of timely consultation during the quadrilateral meetings and the JMC EN (SG6, SG8, WG6, WG10). Particularly, when David Davies was Secretary of State for Exiting the EU and chaired the meetings, the devolved administrations criticised the JMC EN for its chaotic preparations and poor quality of discussions. The atmosphere was described as antagonistic and their outcomes "deeply unsatisfactory". After a six-month suspension from early

2017 on, the meetings became slightly more fruitful and the sharing of information improved (WG5). However, the UK Government had never intended to give the devolved administrations an equal say in its policy-development (UKG1). At no point did the JMC EN live up to its terms of reference as a forum to achieve a joint position on the UK's negotiation strategy with the EU (WG11). Preference intensity (IV2) and the referendum result in Scotland can explain the outspoken disagreement with the UK Government's lack of engagement, but the Scottish and Welsh Governments had hardly any credible political leverage to make conflict (DV3) a fruitful option to pursue their objectives. The Welsh Government has been generally thought of as lacking strategic power (IV4) and more inclined to cooperate (DV2) with the UK Government over Brexit (Hunt and Minto 2017, 653 et seq.; Rawlings 2017, 22). The Scottish Government was also aware that it relied on the goodwill of Westminster and Whitehall and therefore shifted from its initial confrontational to a more cooperative approach (SG2, SG11):

> All ministers are absolutely clear that they believe it is better for Scotland and the UK as a whole to be in the EU. However, we were the first administration in the UK to say: we recognise the reality of the vote, here is our compromise which was let's stay in the single market's customs union. That was a very practical step and a compromise on our part in order to get the best of what we consider a really bad situation.
> (SG2)

The ongoing differences between administrations and also within the UK Government meant that Theresa May continued to take a unilateral approach. Without any prior intergovernmental consultation, the Department for Exiting the European Union (2018) published the policy paper. The Future Relationship between the United Kingdom and the European Union, better known as the Chequers Plan, to set out the UK Government's negotiation priorities (SG6).

When May concluded the first Withdrawal Agreement with the EU in 2018, she could not rely on full support within her party and failed three times to push her deal through Parliament, which eventually led to her resignation on 24 May 2019. With Boris Johnson taking over as Prime Minister in July 2019, the position of the UK Government diverged even further from those of the Scottish and Welsh Governments towards a minimal economic trade agreement that ended the free movement of people (SG4, SG6). By 17 October 2019, Johnson had renegotiated the previous Withdrawal Agreement with the EU. Among the main provisions were citizens' rights, existing financial commitments and the transition towards a new trade agreement by 31 December 2020. In fact, only two articles differed from the previous version, and the Political Declaration on the future relationship and the Northern Ireland Protocol provided the most important changes. The 'backstop' model, which would have kept the whole of the UK within a customs territory with the EU, was replaced by checks and controls on goods between Northern Ireland and the rest of the UK (Curtis et al. 2019). After Johnson had won an outright majority in the General Election on 12 December 2019, he enjoyed a clear mandate for his policy position and could confidently introduce the EU (Withdrawal Agreement) Bill to the House of Commons on 19 December 2019. The UK Government had kept the devolved administrations largely in the dark about its negotiation priorities, and no opportunity was given to effectively feed into either the EU Withdrawal Agreement or the EU Withdrawal Agreement Bill, which was passed within a month (WG2) (Scottish Government 2019a, 3; Scottish Parliament 2020f). A UK official involved in the negotiations with the EU suggested that:

> The handling of Brexit has been very, very driven from the heart of the UK administration, and that was almost bound to happen once the choice was made to leave the single market and the customs union because this meant that the Scottish and Welsh Government have taken antithetical positions to the UK Government. To some extent you could excuse the UK Government and say: 'there weren't much point in having these conversations because there was never any prospect of meeting of minds'. That said, the UK Government got better at sharing documents in advance and letting the devolved administrations know what's going on. But it's not really consultation in a meaningful sense. It's more showing and telling, because of the starkness of the differences of views about Brexit, maybe the best you can achieve.
>
> (UKG10)

In their Legislative Consent Memorandum to the Scottish Parliament, the Scottish Government stated that Brexit had no democratic mandate in Scotland, would have damaging effects and provided UK ministers with powers to make regulations on devolved matters without the consent of the Scottish Government and Parliament. The memorandum also argued that Clause 38 of the EU (Withdrawal Agreement) Bill, which "recognised that the Parliament of the United Kingdom is sovereign", would "represent[s] a contested conception of the constitution, and fails to respect the different constitutional traditions that apply in and between the nations of the United Kingdom." (Scottish Parliament 2020f, 10). The Welsh Government also objected to the 'Henry VIII powers' in the Withdrawal Agreement Bill, as they allowed the UK Government to unilaterally change legislation underpinning the devolution settlement (WG11):[23]

> Some of the amendment give enormous powers to UK Government, unregulated powers, powers to change the devolved legislation by act of ministers. What is being proposed is doesn't fit within any normal democratic process. There are real constitutional concerns about giving

such massive, far ranging powers to the ministers, that effectively bypass parliamentary democracy.

(WP1)

Drawing on a successful collaboration with the House of Lords on the EU (Withdrawal) Act 2018, the Welsh Government asked the House again to table amendments that would limit the Henry VIII powers and provide for greater parliamentary scrutiny and a consultative role for the devolved administrations within the future agreements with the EU (Welsh Parliament 2020e). This time the UK Government was not willing to give in to the concerns of the Welsh Government or the Lords that would delay it in its commitment to delivering Brexit, which also challenged the value of previous intergovernmental agreements between the UK and the Welsh Governments. The Welsh Government did not really believe they could change the bill, but they were yet hoping for a commitment by UK ministers to not use certain powers without devolved consent, which then could be used as arguments before court (WG11).[24] Historically unprecedented, on 23 January 2020 Westminster passed the EU Withdrawal Agreement Bill against the veto of all three devolved legislatures.[25] While the event undermined the constitutional principle of the Sewel Convention, the UK Government for the first time provided an explanation for ignoring the devolved vetoes. Hence, the Welsh Government was reluctantly optimistic about the future of the convention (WG8, WG11):

> We have just seen the unprecedented situation where the three other legislatures withheld consent for the Withdrawal Agreement Act, and UK Parliament proceeded anyway. Now that could have sparked a constitutional crisis with everyone up in arms about the fact the Sewel convention is no longer operating. We saw it slightly differently that it was very disappointing outcome from the Welsh Government's point of view but we felt that it was contained as an event. There were special circumstances that applied and we didn't see that as necessarily needing to provoke a constitutional crisis.
>
> (WG10)

On the day the EU (Withdrawal Agreement) Act 2020 came into force, the Welsh Government published its negotiation priorities for the future relationship between the UK and the EU. It aimed for a closer alignment with the EU than set out in the Political Declaration between the UK and the EU, and for a strong role for the devolved governments in the negotiations and the oversight of the agreement with the EU (Welsh Government 2020b). One month later, the Welsh Counsel General and Brexit Minister, Jeremy Miles (2020c), aired his frustration that the UK Government had disregarded their concerns about trade frictions with the EU: "The UK government's approach is based on ideology, putting the narrative of 'taking back control' ahead of people's livelihoods. We do not accept their underlying principles for the most important and detailed negotiations for a generation."[26] The Scottish Government also continued to promote its position, and in June 2020 introduced a new UK Withdrawal from the European Union (Continuity) (Scotland) Bill to stay aligned with EU law after the end of the transition period on 31 December 2020 and to ensure a smooth admission to the EU in case of Scottish Independence (Keating 2020a). On 31 January 2021, the bill was enacted and enables Scottish ministers to use secondary legislation to adjust Scottish law to EU legislation (primarily in relation to the environment) (Scottish Parliament 2020a).

Considering that from the start the priorities of the different government were not reconcilable and even diverged over time, it seems unsurprising that the UK Government did not engage with the devolved administrations in a fashion that would give them some influence over the terms of leaving the EU. Neither open disputes nor cooperative engagements could prevent the centre from taking unilateral action and hierarchical direction when negotiating the EU Withdrawal Agreement with the EU and subsequently passing the EU Withdrawal Agreement Bill. Not only did the UK Government struggle to get a withdrawal deal with the EU over the line in time, but the Trade and Cooperation Agreement, which regulates the post-Brexit relationship between the EU and the UK,[27] was a last-minute deal made on 30 December 2020 with many vague provisions left to be solved at a later stage. While the negotiations between the UK and the EU are the subject of other studies, the respective political influence of the Scottish and Welsh Governments on the UK's withdrawal, in particular on the EU Withdrawal Agreement Bill, and on the future relations with the EU was null.

Scotland	
Goal-achievement	0 (no)
Ascription	0 (no)
Political relevance	3 (great)
Political influence ($GA \times AS \times PR$)	0 (no)
Wales	
Goal-achievement	0 (no)
Ascription	0 (no)
Political relevance	3 (great)
Political influence ($GA \times AS \times PR$)	0 (no)

The UK Common Frameworks programme

Without the EU's regulatory frameworks, the different governments in the UK would have been able to pass diverging laws within their areas of competence and thereby negatively affect the production, buying and selling goods and services across the different jurisdictions (UKG10, WG7). As explained earlier, the initial approach of the UK Government to centralise all retained competences to stop policy divergence would have undermined the devolution settlement and was strongly contested. Yet, the need for joint governance arrangements, rules and standards to coordinate and implement internal and external trade arrangements was commonly recognised and triggered cooperation (DV2) across all administrations (SG2, WG2, WG8, WG9, WP1). As a civil servant from the Welsh Government pointed out: "The prospect of Brexit has completely transformed the need to think about the in which we interact, where policy responsibility has to be shared." (WG11). Functional and political interdependence (IV1) and preference intensity (IV2) were high, and so was the strategic power (IV4) of the Scottish and Welsh Government (SG6, SG7). Because the UK Government relied on their support (SG7, SP3, WP4, WP6), it agreed to establish the UK Common Frameworks programme. On 16 October 2017, the JMC EN set out the principles that govern a Common Framework to "enable the functioning of the UK internal market, while acknowledging policy divergence; ensure compliance with international obligations; ensure the UK can negotiate, enter into and implement new trade agreements and international treaties; enable the management of common resources; administer and provide access to justice in cases with a cross-border element; and safeguard the security of the UK." These principles provide "to respect the devolution settlements and the democratic accountability of the devolved legislatures" (Cabinet Office 2021b). Notwithstanding the political tensions between the different governments over EU withdrawal and the repatriation of powers, as long as the Scottish and Welsh Governments felt that their competences were not restricted but respected by the Common Frameworks, they were willing to cooperate (DV2) and sought to avoid conflict (DV3) (SG7, SG12). To ensure that all administrations agree to the different frameworks, they engaged intensively in consensual discussions, either multi- or bilaterally (SG2, SG4, SG7, SG11, UKG1, UKG5, WG7, WG11), over five phases: agreement of principles and proof of concept (phase 1), policy development (phase 2), review and consultation (phase 3), preparation and implementation (phase 4), and post-implementation (Cabinet Office 2020b).

During the first phase in the first half of 2018, civil servants from all administrations engaged in deep-dive discussions to identify priorities and ensure the consistency of the Common Frameworks for different policy areas (UKG5). These sessions took place across the different territories during over 30 one-day workshops which followed a structured approach and were often chaired by a facilitator. To reinforce their multilateral nature, meetings were held across the different territories (SG7). A provisional assessment by the UK Government published on 9 March 2018 found that across 153 different policy areas, in which EU law intersected with devolved competence, in 49 areas no further action was required (category 1), 82 areas needed non-legislative frameworks based on memorandums of understanding and concordats (category 2), and 24 priority areas required common legislative frameworks (category 3) (Cabinet Office 2019b; Welsh Parliament 2020f). During the second phase, which began in April 2018, policies were developed during regular meetings of dedicated teams. Although they did not always adopt the same positions, they managed to find solutions to reconcile their different outlooks (SG7, UKG10). A Scottish official described these negotiations as a process of mutual learning and recognition:

> You need to see the difference in policies because our public institutions are not the same, environmental enforcement bodies are not the same. Then you get into a much more cooperative position. It didn't happen straightaway. It took a long time and a lot of recognition for it to dawn in Whitehall that we had a very positive contribution to make to this exercise.
>
> (SG4)

The Frameworks Project Team held weekly meetings at official level to ensure a joint development of the different frameworks (Department for Levelling Up, Housing and Communities and Cabinet Office 2021). Not all Whitehall teams were equally collaborative. The extent to which the UK officials cooperated (DV2) with their devolved counterparts depended in particular on whether they had a track record of working together on specific issues, with DEFRA being especially experienced and covering most legislative Frameworks (SG7, UKG10, WG2, WG7).[28]

In April 2019, the revised framework analysis increased the number of intersecting policy areas to 160:[29] in 63 areas no further action was thought to be needed (category 1), the number of areas which required non-legislative arrangements was reduced to 78 (category 2), and the number of legislative frameworks was also limited to 21 (category 3) (Cabinet Office 2019b). The third framework analysis in September 2020 decreased the number of intersecting policy areas down to 154. Governments agreed that 55 policy areas be moved from category 2 to category 1, because divergence between the administrations was either not expected or arrangements were already in place. This raised the areas requiring no further actions up to 115 and decreased the non-legislative frameworks down to 22. Under category 3, only 18 legislative frameworks were now needed of which 13 lay within DEFRA's responsibility (Cabinet Office 2020a).[30] Due to internal struggles within the UK Government and the no-deal contingency planning in 2019, as well as the Corona pandemic in 2020, the third phase (review and consultation) progressed slowly, which caused some frustration among the Scottish and Welsh Governments (SG3, SP3, WG7, WG11). Although it was agreed to finish their implementation by the end of 2020, only some provisional frameworks were agreed and no framework had reached phase four (preparation and implementation and ministerial agreement) by then (Paun, Klemperer and Sargeant 2017). In October 2020, the Nutrition Labelling Composition and Standards Provisional

Common Framework[31] was the first of its kind to be published, followed by the Hazardous Substance (Planning)[32] and the Food and Feed Safety and Hygiene[33] Provisional Frameworks in November 2020.

Since the end of the UK's transition period on 31 December 2020, during which the UK remained subject to the rules of the European Single Market, most UK Common Frameworks have been in operation on an interim basis at official level. By the end of 2021, 29 Common Frameworks were provisionally approved by the UK and devolved ministers (Department for Levelling Up, Housing and Communities and Cabinet Office 2022). Although a number of frameworks seem to aim at a coordination of operational issues rather than multilateral policy development, all of them set out principles for collaborative working, decision-making and dispute resolution guidance from official to ministerial levels, often based on multilateral concordats and official working groups (see sections 4.2.2 and 4.3.2). A broad-brush analysis, which does not account for variations across individual frameworks, suggests that the political influence of the Scottish and Welsh Governments was rated as *substantial*. The Welsh Government was more proactive in shaping the outcome of some frameworks (WG7, WG9), but it worked closely together with the Scottish Government, which rejected the notion of the 'UK Internal Market' from early on (SG2, UKG8), to ensure that the UK Government did not impose decisions onto them. Since both devolved administrations would have liked to gain more binding assurances and arrangements for decision-making and conflict resolution (SG7), rating the political influence as *great* seems to be overly optimistic, especially as Johnson's commitment to the UK Common Frameworks programme was described as 'luke warm at best' by the Welsh Minister for Brexit in early 2021 (Cardiff University 2021). As the next section will show, the achievements of the Common Frameworks were at the same time seriously undermined by the UK Internal Market Bill (Paun, Sargent and Klemper 2020), which enabled the UK Government to exercise more control over some of the related policy areas (Wincott et al. 2021, 708. Concerns have remained about whether powers may be recentralised and the devolved governments overruled by the centre when issues are more controversial (SG7, SG11). In acknowledgement of the success of the Common Frameworks Programme, the UK Government did not use the powers under Section 12 of the EU (Withdrawal) Act 2018 to interfere on devolved matters, but announced the repeal of the provision, which ended after 31 January 2022 (Department for Levelling Up, Housing and Communities and Cabinet Office 2022). It was too soon for the scope of this analysis to examine how the Common Frameworks operated in practice, and a subsequent assessment may come to a very different result. Nevertheless, due to the commitment of all governments, the UK Common Frameworks programme was a remarkable example of intergovernmental cooperation with the potential to integrate the different jurisdictions under a new web of informal institutions.

Scotland	
Goal-achievement	2 (substantial)
Ascription	2 (substantial)
Political relevance	3 (great)
Political influence ($GA \times AS \times PR$)	12 (substantial)

Wales	
Goal-achievement	2 (substantial)
Ascription	2 (substantial)
Political relevance	3 (great)
Political influence ($GA \times AS \times PR$)	12 (substantial)

The United Kingdom Internal Market Act 2020

Under Theresa May's administration, the negotiations over the EU (Withdrawal) Act 2018 and the UK Common Frameworks programme had offered some reassurance that the UK Government was not interested in interfering with the business of the devolved legislatures unless absolutely necessary. For Whitehall, a main principle of the UK Common Frameworks was to support the functioning of UK-wide market policies. Yet, after Boris Johnson became Prime Minister, his administration argued that sector-specific frameworks would not be sufficient to guarantee the integrity of an internal market (Cabinet Office 2020b).[34] On 16 July 2020, the Department for Business, Energy and Industrial Strategy (2020) therefore published a White Paper on the UK Internal Market proposing to legally enshrine the principles of mutual recognition and of non-discrimination. The development of the Internal Market Bill lacked any form of joint working and was imposed upon the devolved administrations by the UK Government (Dougan et al. 2020, 11), which was prepared to push its will through Parliament without paying attention to concerns from other stakeholders. The Scottish Government criticised the lack of engagement and did not share the UK Government's view of the necessity of statutory provisions beyond the UK Common Frameworks programme. They argued that the suggested provisions would defy the devolution settlement and existing mechanisms of cooperation (Constitution and Cabinet Directorate 2020).[35] Just before the UK Government made its plans public, the Scottish Cabinet Secretary for the Constitution, Europe and External Affairs (2020a) wrote in a letter to the Chancellor of the Duchy of Lancaster: "I want to make it crystal clear at the earliest possible moment, that the Scottish Government could not, and would not, accept any such plans. Nor would we co-operate with them." Against such fundamental opposition, on 9 September, the UK Government introduced, the UK Internal Market Bill.[36] In its original form, the bill was not only at odds with the devolution settlement but would have also breached the Withdrawal Agreement with the EU. Clauses 42–45 of Part 5 would have allowed ministers to make regulations for customs procedures and state aid that were out of line with the Northern Ireland Protocol.[37] It would have also undermined the rule of law and constrained parliamentary scrutiny and any judicial review by domestic courts (Hogarth 2020; Mandal 2020).

The UK Government's ongoing row over the Northern Ireland Protocol has drawn much attention away from the bill's impact on the devolved jurisdictions, which allowed other governments to undermine production standards and policy objectives developed within other jurisdictions. Whereas the UK Common Frameworks programme has aimed at establishing joint working arrangements with the possibility for policy divergence, the UK Internal Market Act enabled the UK Government to impose the application of regulations and practices in England onto the jurisdictions of Scotland and Wales without any requirements for prior consultation. Under the mutual recognition and non-discrimination principles for goods and services, no administration can restrict the sale of goods and services coming from or imported into other parts of the UK, even if they introduced higher product and service standards for their own business. These provisions would lead to a crucial competitive disadvantage for Scottish or Welsh manufacturers and service providers, if they were subject to costlier requirements (Paun, Klemperer and Sargeant 2017; Wincott et al. 2021, 708–709). For the Scottish and Welsh Governments, this was an outrageous manoeuvre culminating in an even more serious dispute than that over the Withdrawal Act (Andrews 2021, 3). Scotland First Minister Nicola Sturgeon claimed that: "The Tories' proposed bill for a so-called UK internal market is an abomination. It is a naked power grab which would cripple devolution." (BBC 2020c). In a similar vein, Welsh Brexit Minister Jeremy Miles said: "This bill is an attack on democracy and an affront to the people of Wales, Scotland and Northern Ireland." (BBC 2020d). Even among the Conservative Party, the UK Government's plan was highly controversial. Senior law officers, including the Advocate General for Scotland, resigned over the issue, and David Melding stepped down from the Conservative Shadow Cabinet of the Senedd (BBC 2020e). Although the UK Government did not seek consent for its bill from the devolved legislatures, the Scottish Parliament pre-emptively denied its consent on 7 October 2020 after the Scottish Government rejected the bill. The Senedd also announced in November that it would withhold consent since the bill was to reduce its powers and "to impose the UK Government's will on Wales, in a way that disproportionately favours the interests of England." (External Affairs and Additional Legislation Committee 2020).

The House of Lords was seriously concerned with the threat that the bill posed to the devolution settlement and the state of the Union – as well as with the breaching of international law (Torrance et al. 2020, 4). The Select Committee on the Constitution (2020) of the House of Lords reported that the UK Government had failed to explain sufficiently why the bill was needed to complement the UK Common Frameworks, which were not referred to in the bill. The Welsh Government tried to soften the bill's implications for the devolution settlement and forwarded a set of model amendments to the Lords. It asked for consultation rights on the usage of delegated powers by UK ministers, and wanted provisions to be removed which gave UK ministers powers to fund initiatives and make rules on state aid in devolved areas and which made the bill a 'protected enactment' that cannot be altered by the devolved legislatures (Miles 2020b). By December 2020, the UK Government suffered a series of defeats in the House of Lords (Welsh Parliament 2020g).[38] However, despite what Jeremy Miles (Cardiff University 2021) called a 'heroic effort' of the House of Lords, the final act remained far from being acceptable to the devolved administrations. The Lords were unsuccessful in removing powers for UK ministers to provide financial assistance to a wide range of purposes under devolved responsibility. Neither did the UK Government accept amendments that would have given the devolved administrations strong consultation rights,[39] nor did it refuse to exclude the UK Common Frameworks programme from the principle of mutual recognition and non-discrimination (Torrance et al. 2020). Upon recommendation by the Welsh Government, the Welsh Parliament eventually refused its legislative consent to the UK Internal Market Bill on 8 December 2020 (Welsh Parliament 2020g). On 16 December, the day before the bill received Royal Assent, Jeremy Miles (2020b) announced that the Welsh Government was considering taking legal action. His Scottish counterpart, Michael Russell (Cabinet Secretary for the Constitution, Europe and External Affairs 2020b), agreed that changes made by the Lords were appreciated but not sufficient to "mitigate the damage the Bill will do to devolution [...] We stand firmly alongside the Welsh government with a shared determination to continue to challenge the bill. Consequently we can confirm that when the UK government replies to the legal letter from the Welsh government we will work with Wales to consider next legal and constitutional steps." In April 2021, the Welsh Government's legal challenge was rejected by the High Court, which ruled it was 'premature' and that the UK Internal Market Act 2020 did not alter the Senedd's powers, but granted the right of appeal on 23 June 2021 (Andrews 2021, 3).

Since the act became law on 17 December 2020, the devolved administrations can continue to set standards for goods and services produced within their territory, but their rules do not apply to goods and services coming from other jurisdictions. They also must accept products imported into one part of the UK. This undermines their legislative autonomy and renders certain policies ineffective in practice. A ban on single-use plastic bags or cutlery, for instance, would not prevent the sale of such items from England (Dougan et al. 2020, 7). As a protected enactment the devolved legislatures cannot amend or modify this statute. For the Scottish and Welsh Governments, the act has therefore not only been an immense power grab but also created a 'race to the bottom' obstructing innovative policies. The provisions of the act also allow UK ministers to intervene in the devolved jurisdictions through financial assistance on a wide range of issues, such as a UK-wide scheme to control state aid, and direct payments to economic development, infrastructure, public services, transport facilities, health, education and training, culture and sports activities, courts, prisons and housing (Sargeant and Stojanovic 2021). For the Welsh Government (2021b):

> It is wholly unacceptable that the UK government is using the financial assistance powers in the Internal Market Act to create new UK-wide programmes in devolved areas of responsibility, bypassing the Barnett formula, and reducing the money available to the devolved governments and their respective Parliaments. Far from strengthening the Union this approach only serves to increase divisions and inequalities. It risks duplicating efforts, impeding value for money and blurring accountability resulting in an incoherent delivery landscape for programmes and services.

Overall, the UK Internal Market Act has essentially challenged the autonomy of the devolved jurisdictions. Despite the high functional and political interdependence (IV1) and preference intensity (IV2) of the issue, the actor constellation and mode of interaction left the Scottish and Welsh Governments with hardly any strategic power (IV4). They had little or no ability to counter the hierarchical direction of the UK Government. Conflict (DV3) was here not a deliberate strategy to affect the UK Government but a way to gather support for the devolution settlement and Scottish independence by appealing to their respective electorates. In the end, neither the Scottish nor the Welsh Government was able to exercise any meaningful political influence on the UK Government.

Scotland	
Goal-achievement	0 (no)
Ascription	0 (no)
Political relevance	3 (great)
Political influence ($GA \times AS \times PR$)	*0 (no)*
Wales	
Goal-achievement	0 (no)
Ascription	2 (substantial)
Political relevance	3 (great)
Political influence ($GA \times AS \times PR$)	*0 (no)*

The Shared Prosperity Fund

Through the passage of the Internal Market Act, the UK Government exercised its new powers to provide financial assistance across the UK; for instance, to replace the EU's Erasmus+ programme with the Turing scheme (Department for Education 2020). More controversially, the UK Government introduced the idea of a Shared Prosperity Fund to replace the EU's Cohesion Policy and to reduce inequalities between communities across the UK. The 2017 Conservative and Unionist Party Manifesto announced they would "consult widely on the design of the fund, including with the devolved administrations, local authorities, businesses and public bodies." Under EU membership, the devolved governments operated as the managing authorities for the major EU's Structural Funds and were in control over the allocation of funding for designated policy priorities in agreement with and oversight by the EU (Brien 2022).[40] In order to remain in control of spending targets, the Scottish and the Welsh Governments wanted to become involved in the development of the scheme and to receive the new funding directly from the UK Government (SG9, WG11). In July 2020, the Scottish Cabinet Secretary for the Constitution, Europe and External Affairs (2020a) wrote to the Chancellor of the Duchy of Lancaster:

> I am concerned at the near absence of detailed information from UK Ministers about how the Shared Prosperity Fund –as the proposed successor to EU Structural Funds (ESF) programmes across the UK –will operate and that there may be an intention to erode devolved responsibilities in that area too. I must again stress to you that unless these funds are to be available for the Scottish Government and our partners to spend at our discretion in the same areas as ESF and as the scheme currently operates, we will have no option but to see that decision as a further example of an attempt by UK Ministers to 'grab powers', constraining, for purely political reasons, the authority of Scottish Ministers and Scottish Parliament; and very significantly damaging all those areas of national life which have been helped by EU programmes for many years.

Despite such calls, the UK Government acted unilaterally without engaging or even mentioning the devolved administrations in this context. In the Spending Review of November 2020, it announced that it will use its new powers given by the UK Internal Market Bill to match the annual average of £1.5 billion of EU funding with a focus on ex-industrial areas, deprived towns and rural and coastal communities (HM Treasury 2020b, 37). In response, the Welsh Minister for Finance, Rebecca Evans (2020a), suggested that the Wales would receive significantly less money than it had under the EU's programmes:

> It is now completely clear that the UK Government want to bypass the Welsh Government in allocating funding from the Shared Prosperity Fund if they can persuade Parliament to give them the new spending powers they want. The UK Government appears to be prepared to trample over the many years of hard work we have undertaken with

stakeholders to provide a greater role for our regions in decision-making on how funds are spent through our regional investment framework. Moreover the funding they are putting on the table is derisory – only £220 million across the whole of the UK in the next financial year, whereas Wales alone would have had a legitimate expectation of an additional £375 million, which we currently receive each year through the European Structural and Investment Programmes.

Neither the Welsh Minister for Economy (Gething 2022a) nor the Scottish Minister for Business, Trade, Tourism and Enterprise (2020) felt adequately consulted and proposed their own Scottish Shared Prosperity Fund. In its policy paper After Brexit: The UK Internal Market Act and Devolution (Constitution and Cabinet Directorate 2021) the Scottish Government stated:

> In January 2021, the UK Government announced it would use the power to bypass the devolved administrations to replace European Structural Funds with a centrally controlled fund: the Shared Prosperity Fund. For Scotland, this means more than £100 million a year could be spent in areas that are normally devolved to the Scottish Parliament – with no say for Scotland's elected representatives in the Scottish Parliament.

In April 2022, the UK Government launched the Shared Prosperity Fund and announced £2.6 billion of new funding for local councils and mayoral authorities across England, Scotland, Wales and Northern Ireland until March 2025 (Department for Levelling Up, Housing and Communities 2022b):

> The Fund will operate UK-wide and use the financial assistance powers in the UK Internal Market Act 2020 to deliver funding to places across the UK. In addition to the devolved administrations' existing powers, this allows the UK government to complement and strengthen the support given to local people, businesses and communities in Scotland, Northern Ireland and Wales, as well as England. We have worked with each of the devolved administrations to develop interventions that follow the fund's principles of local autonomy while recognising the different policy and funding landscapes of each nation.

Though an issue of high preference intensity (IV2), where the Scottish and Welsh Governments did not hold strong strategic power (IV4) and would therefore have been prepared to cooperate (DV2) with the UK Government. Both have held valid concerns that the UK Government would bypass them to realise projects that might by contrary to their policy objectives (WG6, WP3). Despite Whitehall's stated intent to work in partnership with the devolved governments, it maintained control over the programme to engage directly with local authorities.[41] The Welsh Minister for Economy, Vaughan Gething (2022b), claimed that Wales would need more than an additional £1 billion to adequately replace the lost EU funds by 2025 and stated: "The proposed role of the Welsh Government also falls short of a genuine co-decision making function essential to maximising investment and respecting devolution in Wales." Similarly, the Scottish Minister for Just Transition, Employment and Fair Work, Richard Lochhead, said in the Scottish Parliament (2022): "By using the 2020 act to start spending in devolved areas directly with local government, the UK Government is sidelining the Scottish Government and the wider ecosystem that we have in Scotland of all our agencies and regional players." In addition, the Scottish Government (2022) claimed that £32 million allocated to Scotland for 2022–2023 would be only a tiny share of the £183 million that were estimated to provide an appropriate compensation for EU Structural Funds. Overall, both administrations had *no* political influence over the new funding regime.

Scotland	
Goal-achievement	0 (no)
Ascription	0 (no)
Political relevance	3 (great)
Political influence ($GA \times AS \times PR$)	*0 (no)*
Wales	
Goal-achievement	0 (no)
Ascription	0 (no)
Political relevance	3 (great)
Political influence ($GA \times AS \times PR$)	*0 (no)*

Foreign affairs and international trade

Beyond relations with the EU, foreign and trade policies are a fairly new field of ambition and activity for the devolved administrations, which has emerged after the 2016 referendum due to the different outlooks of the governments. The Concordat on International Relations of the 2013 MoU states that "[t]he FCO, or as appropriate another lead UK Department, will consult the devolved administrations about the formulation of the UK's position for international negotiations, to the extent that the negotiations touch on devolved matters". Despite this commitment, the centre has treated international relations as its exclusive responsibility without effectively engaging the devolved governments in its policy development (cf. Hunt 2021, 41). Giving Scotland and Wales a greater say in international negotiations has not been viewed as an opportunity but rather as a constraint to its own position vis-à-vis other countries (SG2). The UK Government has only reluctantly granted them a strong engagement outside of the UK's borders and supported their external activities as long as they do not affect its own international engagement (SG2). Both the Scottish Government[42] (see e.g., A Trading Nation[43] and Scotland's International Framework[44]) and the Welsh Government[45] (see e.g., International Trade Strategy for Wales[46] and International Action Plans[47]) have developed their own international affairs and trade agendas.[48] Whereas the UK Government generally supports their activities, the political disagreements over leaving the EU presents a fundamental challenge to joint engagements.

> We normally have really good relationships on the ground with UK Government foreign officials help us pick together programmes. That works really well. Of course, there's always a bit of sensitivity, particularly if some of our messaging publicly will be in a different way to the UK Government. But my general experience is that the FCO always wanting to help and recognise that we come at this from a slightly different political space. Brexit is making all of that more difficult.
> (SG2)

The predominant source of tensions is the making of new trade deals to replace the EU's agreements with other states. As many international obligations would fall into the remit of devolved under responsibility, for instance in areas such as agriculture, fisheries and the environment, and need to be implemented by the Scottish and Welsh Governments, the functional and political interdependence (IV1) of trade agreements is high. Due to the potential impact on the economies and competences of the devolved jurisdictions, both governments see themselves as legitimate stakeholders on these issues and show strong preference intensity (IV2). Their strategic power (IV4) in the interaction with the UK Government has been mixed. Despite regular intergovernmental engagement, tensions over future trade deals have not disappeared (WG1, WG9). Two examples were often used to highlight the differing priorities: Scottish and Welsh ministers have been strongly opposed to allowing private companies from the US to deliver more NHS services, as well as having to allow the import and sale of chlorinated chicken and hormone-injected beef (SG1, SG2, WG8, WP1, WP4).[49] As Members of the Welsh Parliament and Government reported:

> So you would have the devolved government potentially refusing to implement something on the basis that legislation gives responsibility to Wales. You then end up with a full conflict in the trade agreements between what has been agreed and what could actually be delivered; that might then require UK Government to either override the devolved governments via legislation that than creates an ever further constitutional conundrum or crisis.
> (WP1)

> We can't force ourselves into those conversations. All we can do is just keep saying: 'you really, really need to talk to us because even though there are lot of things that you are negotiating might well be reserved, but you may well be coming to the Welsh Government or to the Welsh Assembly saying: we've agreed this new deal with X or Y and therefore you need to legislate to bring it into effect.' So our view would be, we have to be in the discussion because you're going to expect us in the future at some point to implement, at least several aspects, of any deal that you come up with in the future.
>
> (WG2)

A Scottish Government official also stated:

> The UK Government says that anything that has any international angle is de facto reserved. The Scottish Government position is that actually if you're signing in international agreement on education or on health or agriculture. All of those matters are completely devolved, therefore, we need to be involved and agree to things because you cannot deliver anything you promised without us. That's not a generally accepted view in Whitehall.
>
> (SG12)

Reliance on the implementation of trade deals through the devolved governments did not resonate as convincingly with the UK Government, as ultimately the former would have to implement the international agreements made by the latter (SG1). In particular, the Internal Market Act has allowed the centre to override devolved legislation when making new trade deals, which to the Scottish Government "undermines the benefits of devolved nations' expertise, collaboration and trust in international negotiations." (Constitution and Cabinet Directorate 2021, para. 125). Because economic arguments have been the most effective way to get Whitehall engaged, the Scottish and Welsh Governments have tried to cooperate (DV2) and forward their concerns and assessments during intensive and frequent discussions with Whitehall (SG1, SG2, SG3, SG7, SG12, WG1) (Welsh Government 2021a). The UK Government started slowly to engage with the devolved governments in regular interactions with DIT and DEFRA, for instance in the Ministerial Forum for Trade. These provided useful opportunities to comment on trade negotiations and the UK Government selectively listened to the views of the Scottish and Welsh executives (SG1, SG2, SG3, SG4, WG1, WG2, WG10, WP1) (Welsh Affairs Committee 2020a, 2020b; Welsh Government 2020a). The UK Government suggested that it was "committed to working closely with" and "listened carefully to the views" of the devolved administrations (Department for International Trade 2019, 5), and an official from DEFRA said:

> Initially DEFRA felt 'oh, international trade is reserved, so we don't need to talk to the DAs.' But we quickly arranged meetings with them

because we said 'although it's a UK Government decision, it's important that the DAs' views are taken into account because international trade affects them as much as it affects us.' So they were a little slow initially to engage but we worked with them and the devolved and quickly got them engaged. Now there is a discussion on trade just to make sure that everyone's views are taken into account.

(UKG2)

By the end of 2021, the UK had signed 36 trade agreements (excluding the Trade and Cooperation Agreement with the EU), most of which copy the EU's agreements with third states.[50] Meanwhile, the devolved administrations have continued to push for a more a systematic involvement in development of trade deals with trade negotiations with Japan, the US, Australia and New Zealand. Whereas, according to the Scottish Government, their impact remained "limited and patchy" (Constitution and Cabinet Directorate 2021, para. 129), the Welsh Government (2021b) stated that their engagement with DIT was constructive but expected improvements around the sharing of information and consultation on specific matters.

On 29 April 2021, Westminster enacted the Trade Act 2021, which was introduced on 19 March 2020 and has given UK and devolved ministers powers to make subordinate legislation for the implementation of trade agreements by removing non-tariff barriers (e.g., labelling or product specifications) (Clause 2).[51] The UK Government had already introduced a Trade Bill on 7 November 2017 but by March 2019 had failed to bring it through Parliament. The Welsh Government believed in the necessity of the bill for future trade relations but wanted similar powers to UK ministers and binding consultation rights if UK ministers were to legislate on devolved matters or extend the temporary five-year limitation on the new powers (Thomas and Thomas 2019). As a response, the UK Government made amendments and non-legislative commitments to "not normally use concurrent powers to legislate in devolved areas without the consent of the devolved governments, and never without consulting them." Sufficiently pleased with the engagement and commitments by the UK Government, the Welsh Government recommended consenting to the bill on 14 February 2019 (Welsh Parliament 2020h). The Scottish Government was opposed to the first Trade Bill's initial constraints to its powers and wanted more robust veto rights and guaranteed involvement in the development, agreement and implementation of future trade deals (Scottish Parliament 2018a). The UK Government insisted that making international agreements was its prerogative power and pointed towards its non-binding commitment to ask the devolved legislatures for their consent if their jurisdictions are affected (Thom 2020). Although not all of the Scottish Government's proposed amendments were successful (Constitution and Cabinet Directorate 2021, para. 132), it recommended giving legislative consent to the new Trade Bill on 18 August because its "primary objection to recommending legislative consent to the previous Trade Bill concerned the restrictions it placed on the Scottish Ministers' ability to amend retained EU legislation when exercising the powers of implementation. This constraint has been removed from the current Trade Bill." The Scottish Parliament on 12 October 2020 and the Senedd on 12 January 2021 consequently agreed to the new Trade Bill (Scottish Parliament 2020c).

Considering Whitehall's prerogative to deal with foreign affairs and international agreement, the Scottish and the Welsh Governments have only been modestly successful in influencing the latter's trade positions (SG1, WG2). Among those of other stakeholders, their preferences fed into the consultation procedures of the UK Government, and ministers and officials have worked together on various items. While the devolved governments have continued to criticise the lack of influence on international obligations and control over the impact of trade agreements on their own powers (SG4, SG6, WG11, WP1), under consideration of their achievements during the passage of Trade Act 2021, they had *some* political influence on foreign policy and trade decisions.

Scotland	
Goal-achievement	1 (some)
Ascription	1 (some)
Political relevance	3 (great)
Political influence ($GA \times AS \times PR$)	3 (some)
Wales	
Goal-achievement	1 (some)
Ascription	1 (some)
Political relevance	3 (great)
Political influence ($GA \times AS \times PR$)	3 (some)

Immigration

Immigration was at the heart of the leave campaign during the EU referendum, and the UK Government committed itself to ending the free movement of people and introducing a more restrictive immigration policy. In December 2018, the May administration published its plans for a skill-based immigration system without concessions to the devolved administrations (Home Office 2018). Although a reserved matter, immigration has become a highly salient issue for the devolved administrations, as their jurisdictions suffer from a decline in population, which until recently could be compensated for by immigration from the EU (SG2, SP2). The Scottish Government (2018) therefore announced:

> We need to ensure that come what may from the Brexit negotiations, Scotland is able to continue to benefit from free movement from Europe; and, in addition, to ensure that Scotland is able to manage international

migration in a way that addresses our specific needs. [...] UK government policy is not meeting those needs. The case for new powers for the Scottish Parliament on migration is clear.

The Welsh Government (2017b, 6) also prioritised maintaining a free movement of people but linked this closer to employment:

We oppose the UK Government's aim of reducing migration numbers to an arbitrary target, as this risks the sustainability of our key economic sectors and delivery of our public services. In the longer term, we would like to discuss with the UK Government a reform of wider UK migration policy which would recognise that the distinct needs of Wales and indeed other nations and regions within the UK cannot easily be met through the blunt and resource-intensive UK-wide approach currently in place.

Considering that their preference intensity (IV2) was high but their strategic power (IV4) low, both the Scottish and the Welsh Governments sought to cooperate (DV2) constructively with the UK Government and presented evidence and used statistical modelling in order to shape UK migration policy and gain regional exemptions to meet their migration needs (SG2, SG6) (Miles 2019). Yet, the lack of engagement was described as "shocking" by the Scottish Government (SG11), and calls from the Scottish Migration Minister to establish regular interactions between ministers and officials had no effect. Exchanges between ministers ended with the last ministerial round table on immigration in July 2019 shortly before Johnson became Prime Minister (Scottish Government 2019c; External Affairs Directorate 2020a). The Scottish Government continued to propose tailored policies for Scotland that would reintroduce the post-study work visa, end the net migration target and the immigration skills charge, allow for shortage occupation lists, and extend and protect rights in family migration. In the foreword to the policy paper Migration: Helping Scotland Prosper (External Affairs Directorate 2020b) Scotland's First Minister Nicola Sturgeon wrote:

Yet the proposals from the UK Government to end freedom of movement and put in place inappropriate salary and skills requirements for all migrants would be disastrous for our economy and society and would risk acute labour shortages. This approach by the UK Government ignores the wider issue of social value and the importance of jobs in sectors like social and health care or in rural and island communities. It ignores the contribution that people who have moved to Scotland make to our cultural life and to our communities. Migration is an issue which is crucial for our future economic and social wellbeing. We need a solution that meets Scotland's needs and allows our communities and our economy to flourish.

Table 5.1 UK points-based immigration system

Characteristics	Tradeable	Points
Offer of job by approved sponsor	No	20
Job at appropriate skill level	No	20
Speaks English at required level	No	10
Salary of £20,480 (minimum) – £23,039	Yes	0
Salary of £23,040 – £25,599	Yes	10
Salary of £25,600 or above	Yes	20
Job in a shortage occupation	Yes	20
Education qualification: PhD in subject relevant to the job	Yes	10
Education qualification: PhD in a STEM subject relevant to the job	Yes	20

Source: Home Office (2020).

Regardless of the Scottish position, on 19 February 2020, Johnson's government published a new policy paper introducing a point-based immigration regime applicable to EU citizens after the transition phase in January 2021 (Home Office 2020), which Sturgeon called the new system "devastating for Scotland" (BBC 2020f). Depending on the educational qualification, the nature of jobs (based on skills and need), salary and English language abilities, applicants must acquire 70 points for a visa (see Table 5.1). In March 2020, the UK Government introduced the Immigration and Social Security Co-ordination (EU Withdrawal) Bill to realise its new immigration regime.[52]

The Welsh Government (2020f) argued that the system would not work for Wales and wanted to reward migrants who wish to move to Wales by lowering the financial thresholds when they apply for a work visa for work inside Wales to an annual salary of 20,000 for a full-time employee (compared to the UK threshold of £25,600) (Welsh Government 2020g). Regardless of their positions, on 11 November, after a series of amendments by the House of Lords, the Immigration and Social Security Co-ordination (EU Withdrawal) Act 2020 received Royal Assent to end the free movement of people on 31 January 2021.[53] Overall, immigration is a clear example where the UK Government did not cooperate (DV2) with the Scottish and Welsh Governments and acted unilaterally without considering their interests. The latter had *no* political influence on the former's decisions.

Scotland	
Goal-achievement	0 (no)
Ascription	0 (no)
Political relevance	2 (substantial)
Political influence (GA × AS × PR)	*0 (no)*
Wales	
Goal-achievement	0 (no)
Ascription	0 (no)
Political relevance	2 (substantial)
Political influence (GA × AS × PR)	*0 (no)*

Fiscal policy

Fiscal policy presents a likely conflict area in multilevel systems because it has a high salience to governments bargaining for financial resources and attracts a strong interest among voters (Bolleyer 2009, 51; Gallagher 2012, 206). The same is true for the UK, where some of the most important disputes have revolved around money (SP2, UKG1, WG2), especially concerning the block grant provided to the devolved administrations and the devolution of tax and borrowing authority.

Spending decisions and block grant allocation

According to the Statement of Funding Policy, inter-administration financial relations are based on consent and the devolved administrations can propose changes to the UK Government's spending plans (HM Treasury 2020a, 3–6). In reality, however, the devolved administrations have few means to impact on the amount they receive through the Barnett formula and can only negotiate to some extent the application of funding (UKG6). Meetings of the Finance Ministers Quadrilaterals provide less of an occasion for cooperation (DV2) than opportunities for the UK Government to announce its economic and fiscal policies and the application of the Statement of Funding Policy, as a Scottish official argues:

> Treasury doesn't have to listen if it doesn't want to. It depends on the person and the UK minister's attitude towards devolution, whether they want to help or not. Nothing's to be gained from being actively obstructive but there's also not much gained to be giving any concessions to the devolved nations.
>
> (SG9)

During the first decade of devolution the different administrations could rely on considerable funding. Public spending was on the rise across all jurisdictions and peaked in 2009/10 at 47 per cent of the UK's GDP (Cairney 2011, 203–204). In the aftermath of the 2008 financial crisis, like many federal and multilevel systems, the UK faced ongoing conflict (DV3) over the allocation of financial resources (Eccleston et al. 2017, 3). By 2012/13, the Coalition Government had cut public spending down to 44.8 per cent without substantially reducing the budget deficit (Lee 2017, 133). This significantly constrained the ability of the devolved executives and legislatures to use their evolving powers effectively (Andrews 2021, 2), and was therefore strongly opposed by the Scottish and Welsh Governments, who sought to tackle the crisis with public investments (SG5, SG9, WG2, WG11, WP3, WP5). In August 2015, the finance ministers of all three devolved administrations issued a jointly written statement against the extent and speed of the budget cuts without their prior notification and consideration and calling for a fair application of the Barnett formula (Hutt 2015). As an official from the Welsh Government put it:

> They had a policy of cutting back public investment, policy of austerity. We made a different argument as a Labour Party. Never mind the differences in devolved governments and UK Government. Yes, we've gone through a crash but our argument as a government was: 'yes, it is an economically difficult situation but the way you get out of a recession, at the time, is by investing in infrastructure, skills.' You make the investments that grow the economy and then you can grow yourself out of a recession. A sort of New Deal, Keynesian tradition. Conservative Government had a different view: the economy runs like a household economy, when you're in difficult times, you've got to cut back. That drove the institutional dynamic between the two governments because we started having less money to spend on public services, infrastructure.
>
> (WG6)

As spending decisions for England have a 'knock-on effect' on the resources available to Scotland and Wales (WG11, WP6), the functional and political interdependence (IV1) and preference intensity (IV2) are both high for the Scottish and the Welsh Governments. Yet, because the hierarchical direction by the centre provides the Scottish and Welsh Governments with little strategic power (IV4), they have avoided open conflict (DV3) over the general funding allocation. Rather both have adopted cooperative (DV2) approaches in their negotiations with the UK Government over fiscal matters, and their officials work closely together with the Treasury:

> Our main strategy is going down to London as much as possible and make good relationships at official level because we know we can't rely on any judicial review or any kind of hard leverage over the UK Government. It requires their agreement as much as ours. We've got no hard tools in our arsenal.
>
> (SG5)

Even though there seems to be little to be gained from open conflict (DV3), they have at times raised their discontent with the centre's policies – either to their own electorates or directly with Whitehall to get concessions. On the rare occasions when the formal dispute resolution mechanism was triggered the issue of contestation was about financial disagreements – except for a disagreement over the allocation of the whiting fishing quota between English and Scottish fleets.[54] In 2010, the Northern Ireland Executive challenged whether the UK Government's public budget cuts and reduction in capital spending breached the investment commitment for reconstruction works. The issue was resolved at official level. In the same year, a dispute raised by the Welsh Government over capital funding for affordable housing and the application of the Barnett consequentials was also dealt with at official level and led to a change of wording in the Statement of Funding Policy. The only dispute that progressed through all stages up to the JMC Plenary concerned the funding of regeneration and public transport in East London during the 2012 Olympics. Together with the other devolved administrations, the Scottish Government argued that additional funding in England should be made part of the Barnett consequentials and would require financial compensation. The issue was resolved in 2011 at *dispute stage* and the Scottish and Welsh Governments could exert some influence (SG5). Agreeing on the "importance of learning lessons from all disputes in order to make them less likely to arise in the future", the UK Government changed the Statement of Funding Policy and provided the devolved administrations with an additional "one-off sum equivalent to the Barnett formula consequentials". Altogether, they only received about a tenth of the initial claim of £330 million: Scotland £16 million, Wales £8.9 million and Northern Ireland £5.4 million (Cabinet Office 2011).

Despite some successes for the devolved administrations, the dispute resolution process depends on the willingness of the UK Government. This became most evident when after the 2017 General Election Theresa May's minority government had to strike a deal with the parliamentary party of the DUP. In return for a total of £1 billion to Northern Ireland allocated outside of the Barnett formula, DUP MPs agreed to supply confidence on the Government's key policies and fiscal matters. The Scottish and the Welsh Governments demanded a more transparent and equal application of the Treasury's Statement of Funding Policy and the Barnett consequentials. But when they wanted to trigger the official dispute resolution protocol in the JMC Plenary, the UK Government did neither recognise the issue as a dispute nor did it publicly respond to the matter (WG2, SG5, SG9, SG12) (Scottish Affairs Committee 2019a, 17). Instead, it was argued that money was given directly to Northern Ireland for specific purposes and therefore neither the Barnett consequentials for departmental spending nor the dispute resolution mechanism would apply (SG5, UKG1, UKG10).[55] The Scottish and Welsh Governments were frustrated by the lack of cooperation (DV2) and the ineffectiveness of the existing provision to solve intergovernmental arguments (WP5):

> We were aggrieved of what had been done. But we were probably even more aggrieved about the fact that there's a dispute resolution procedure for things like this and it wasn't that we went through it and we didn't get the result we wanted, because we weren't even allowed to go through it. It was vetoed. The UK Government was saying: we're not treating this as a dispute.
>
> (WG2)

When in 2019 another £140 million was directly allocated to Northern Ireland, the Scottish Cabinet Secretary for Finance, Economy and Fair

Work wrote to the Chancellor of the Exchequer (Scottish Government 2019c):

> [...] the Scottish Government fundamentally disagreed with the way in which additional funding was provided for Northern Ireland as part of the deal reached with the DUP. Following the well-established arrangement set out in the Statement of Funding Policy would have resulted in Scotland receiving almost £3 billion of additional funding. As this issue is yet to be resolved, I was surprised and disappointed by the UK Government's announcement that Northern Ireland has received an additional £140 million for its 2019–2020 Budget on top of the £1 billion already allocated.

To prevent the UK Government from being able "arbitrarily to allocate additional funding to any particular part of the UK outside these arrangements", the Welsh Government (2019a, 16–17) asked for a multilateral, needs-based funding regime "underpinned by the principles of parity of participation, collaborative working, and shared responsibility". Despite the new dispute resolution mechanism for the Finance Interministerial Standing Committee, which was introduced by the 2022 intergovernmental review (Cabinet Office and Department for Levelling Up, Housing and Communities 2022), there are no indications that the Treasury would commit to any such compulsory negotiation system.

This is not to suggest that the devolved administrations have no political influence at all, as the UK Government seeks to avoid frictions with the former. Although the Barnet Formula was meant to be an objective block grant on the basis of territorial needs, size of populations and levels of social inclusion, Scotland's greater political influence shows in the share per capita, which is higher than for Wales than a neutral application of the formula would provide for (SG9) (O'Neill 2004, 194–198). In particular, the threat of Scottish independence has been a source of leverage over budget decisions. As a result, Scotland enjoys about 25 per cent higher level of expenditure for equivalent spending than in England (Gallagher 2020, 574–575). A Member of the Senedd claimed:

> There isn't a needs assessment for central government grant. It's a historic grant with some ad hoc modification. It's not reviewed on a needs basis. This is probably because if Scotland then would get a lower grant this is ought to be quite damaging for the UK's coherence. It would increase national resentment in Scotland. Wales has probably lost out about two or three per cent on the central government grant. We'd have a couple of per cent more, if there was needs based system, and that's quite extensive and a lot of money over the years.
>
> (WP6)

Patterns of Interaction and Political Influence

On an ad hoc basis, the devolved governments can realise their claims and the different levels of capital funding suggest that the devolved administrations have had some relational influence over the UK Government's spending decisions (UKG6). According to the Institute for Government, spending per head was 125 per cent higher in Northern Ireland, 121 per cent higher in Scotland and 115 per cent higher in Wales than in England in 2018/2019. Although costs for public services and socio-economic needs in Scotland, Wales and Northern Ireland are also higher than the UK average (see Figure 5.1) (Cheung 2020; HM Treasury 2020a, 8) the block grant is generous and its usage not controlled by the centre (Gallagher 2012, 207; Bradbury 2021, 288–289).[56]

COVID-19 triggered further frequent engagement between finance ministers to coordinate their fiscal responses (Welsh Government 2020b, 3), through which the Scottish and Welsh Governments could affect the provision of additional funding (UKG6). Between spring 2020 and February 2021, an extra total of £9.7 billion for Scotland (Office of the Secretary of State for Scotland and HM Treasury 2021) and £5.85 billion for Wales (Office of the Secretary of State for Wales and HM Treasury 2021) were allocated through the Barnett formula. Hence, the overall assessment here is that the Scottish Government has *substantial* and the Welsh Government at least *some* political influence on the UK's Government's allocation of public funding.

Scotland	
Goal-achievement	2 (substantial)
Ascription	1 (some)
Political relevance	3 (great)
Political influence ($GA \times AS \times PR$)	*6 (substantial)*
Wales	
Goal-achievement	1 (some)
Ascription	1 (some)
Political relevance	3 (great)
Political influence ($GA \times AS \times PR$)	*3 (some)*

The devolution of tax and borrowing authority

During the first one and a half decades of devolution, the devolved administrations themselves did not have significant fiscal powers. When the Scotland Acts 2012 and 2016 and the Wales Acts 2014 and 2017 provided them with new tax and borrowing authority, the functional and political interdependence (IV1) of fiscal relations grew. Unlike the block grant funding, the implementation of the new fiscal powers has required the cooperation (DV2) of different levels and was based on a joint bilateral negotiated

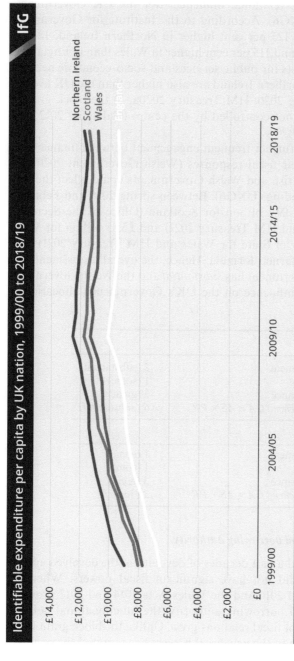

Figure 5.1 Expenditure per capita across the UK

Source: Cheung, Aron (2020) Barnett formula. Explainer. 25 November. Institute for Government. https://www.instituteforgovernment.org.uk/charts/identifiable-expenditure-uk Used with permission.

agreement (SG5, UKG6). In order to keep Scotland in the Union over the course of the 2014 independence referendum, the UK Government promised greater fiscal responsibilities to the Scottish Parliament (SG5, SG9). Subsequently, the Scotland Act 2016 needed to be complemented by the Fiscal Framework Agreement, which was of high preference intensity (IV2) to the Scottish as well as to the UK Government (SP2). However, due to deep-reaching disagreements on the amounts and governance of the new fiscal model, the passage of the whole Scotland Bill 2016 was at stake (Eiser and Roy 2019, 3). The first phase of negotiations failed to deliver, as the Scottish Government rejected the terms of references and wanted a greater say in the negotiations. Between 2013 and 2015, it refused to meet in the Joint Exchequer Committees, and only reluctantly the UK Government came to accept the Scottish Government as an equal partner in these negotiations (McEwen 2017, 679). Eventually, the governments began to cooperate (DV2) closely and were able to find joint solutions (SG5, UKG6) (Bell et al. 2016). According to a Scottish civil servant, the Scottish Government held considerable strategic power (IV4) based on a strong political mandate:

> In terms of how the tax powers can be devolved, nothing can be agreed unless both parties have agreed to it, which has been a quite helpful principle on our part. This moved the relationship into a new phase [...] In that case it is a quite particular circumstance because we had to give consent to the Scottish Bill to be passed in Westminster Parliament. In that case we had quite hard leverage in a way that we were holding consent until in the framework was agreed what we thought was appropriate and met the Smith Commissions principles since then we don't have the legislative leverage.
>
> (SG5)

While the centre did not want to appear to favour Scotland over the other territories and was constrained by its own austerity agenda, it relied on the Scottish Government's consent and had to engage in a compulsory negotiation system (Lee 2017, 136). The following discussions were long and intense, and in particular the method to calculate block grant adjustment was controversial. While the UK Government pushed for a method similar to the existing Barnett formula, the Scottish Government wanted a better protection against demographic risks. Both governments reached a compromise in favour of the Scottish positions under the condition that the Fiscal Framework would be reviewed by the end of 2021. The Scottish Government gained not only greater flexibility to manage its annual budget but it could also secure £90 million more per year (for 2019/2020) than under the UK Government's initial proposal (Eiser and Roy 2019, 2–3). In return, the Scottish Government agreed to lower borrowing limits than it had pushed for (SG5, SG9).[57] The Fiscal Framework was published on 25 February 2016 and enabled the Scottish Government to exercise its new fiscal powers within a wider framework for the whole of the UK (HM Government and Scottish Government 2016). As for the Scotland Act 2016, which was almost simultaneously agreed, the political influence of the Scottish Government in the Fiscal Framework negotiations was *substantial* and partly based on the involvement of other political actors and the Smith Commission, as well as on the need to obtain legislative consent from the Scottish Parliament (Gallagher 2020, 568; 575). The Scottish Cabinet Secretary for Finance and the Constitution (2016) thus announced:

> We believe that the Fiscal Framework represents a fair financial settlement to underpin the powers set out in the Scotland Act 2016. [...] We did not achieve our desired position on some elements of the framework, but the deal recognises the central importance of the Barnett formula in determining changes to the Block Grant, and of the principle of no detriment which Lord Smith's report emphasised.

Scotland	
Goal-achievement	3 (great)
Ascription	2 (substantial)
Political relevance	3 (great)
Political influence ($GA \times AS \times PR$)	18 (great)

After the Fiscal Framework was agreed and the political and functional interdependence (IV1) became less relevant again, the Joint Exchequer Committee ceased to meet regularly and officials continued to cooperate (DV2) ad hoc on more low-level issues. Both (HM Government and Scottish Government 2016) agreed to an independent review of the Fiscal Framework due at the end of 2021, on which they have worked closely together (UKG6). By the end of this research in late 2022, the review was not concluded yet, and it remained to be seen whether the review of the Fiscal Framework features another round of tough negotiations on the general nature of fiscal devolution or whether it only adjusts minor technicalities (Eiser and Roy 2019, 1–2). At the same time, the Scottish Government (2021b) has continued to ask for a higher borrowing limit to deal with potential forecast errors,[58] but the UK Government argued that it devolved sufficient financial levers (UKG6). Calls for greater fiscal autonomy in Scotland continue to remain part of intergovernmental politics, and the Scottish Government, not least for political reasons, publicly communicates their discontent with unfavourable budget decisions by the Treasury (SG5) (Gallagher 2016, 30).

The Fiscal Framework for Wales was published in December 2016, shortly after the Scottish agreement and a period of difficult, yet cooperative negotiations (HM Government and Welsh Government 2016). The Welsh Government was "able to make some productive progress with the Treasury, which is traditionally quite a difficult entity" (WG2), and could secure an outcome with which they were very pleased (see sections 3.5.1 and

3.5.2) (WG11, WP2). Like the Scottish Government, the Welsh Government has repeatedly tried to get the UK Government to agree to higher borrowing limits without success (Tipples 2021). The disputes that followed the Fiscal Framework have been predominantly about the devolution of further taxation powers. While the Wales Act 2014 provided control over stamp duty land tax, landfill tax and business rates to the Welsh Assembly,[59] in March 2020, the Welsh Minister made a formal request to gain competence over a vacant land tax. The tax devolution mechanism provided by the Wales Act 2014, however, requires the approval of the Treasury, which rejected and delayed the request due to the lack of sufficient information. The Welsh Government argued that the Treasury's decision was based on their different views towards policy and the usage of vacant land tax (WP2), and in a letter to the Financial Secretary to the Treasury, the Welsh Minister for Finance Rebecca Evans (2020b) expressed her discontent:

> Our formal request for tax competence is the first time we have tested the mechanism and the request follows over two years of work by Welsh Government to ensure HM Treasury had sufficient information to assess Welsh Government proposals. The experience of moving through the process has been protracted and challenging, with HM Treasury continually requesting detail related to the specific operation of the proposed tax – a matter for Wales – rather than information related to devolving competence for legislation in a new area of taxation. It has become clear the agreed process for devolution of further tax competence to Wales is not fit for purpose, and in practice bears a striking similarity to the previous process of Legislative Competence Orders. This is compounded by the fact HM Treasury are able to move the goalposts as to what information is required at any point.

The Welsh Government has continuously asked for control over air passenger duty to set and receive the tax rate for Welsh airports, as it is the case in Scotland and for long-haul flights in Northern Ireland.[60] The UK Government has refused transferring the power to Wales arguing that it would distort the competition to other UK airports, if the Welsh Government would reduce or abolish the air passenger duty. In particular, this concerns the close proximity between the Bristol and Cardiff airports, but also the airports in Birmingham and Manchester (Welsh Affairs Committee 2019a).[61] Consequently, the Welsh Government has accused the UK Government of misusing its control over fiscal policies in Wales to represent an English rather than a UK-wide interest instead of devolving powers on the basis of a constitutional principle (WG1, WG10). Shortly after the Welsh Affairs Committee (2019a) recommended the devolution of air passenger duty to Wales so it could adopt its own policy, the Welsh Assembly unanimously passed a joint motion calling for a devolution of the tax (Evans 2019). Nevertheless, the Treasury reasserted its decision to the Welsh Affairs

192 *Patterns of Interaction and Political Influence*

Committee.[62] Though the Welsh Government restated its ambition to "continue to press the UK government to review its untenable position" (ibid.), its attempt remained unsuccessful and was put on hold during the travel restrictions of the 2020 pandemic.

The fiscal devolution mechanism demonstrates the functional and political interdependence (IV1) of the UK and the Welsh Governments, and in particular the dependency of the latter on the former. Whereas the Welsh Government enjoyed considerable strategic power (IV4) during the development of the Fiscal Framework, subsequently the negotiated agreement has worked strongly in favour of the UK Government. The fact that the contested tax powers are not of the highest preference intensity (IV2) may be an additional factor why the level of conflict (DV3) has not escalated. Still, the Welsh Government's political influence over the devolution of tax and borrowing authority has overall been *substantial*.

Wales	
Goal-achievement	2 (substantial)
Ascription	2 (substantial)
Political relevance	3 (great)
Political influence ($GA \times AS \times PR$)	12 *(substantial)*

Agriculture and food

Agriculture and food are among the most important devolved matters, make up a great share of the Scottish and Welsh economies, and have therefore been highly salient issues (WG1, WG2). The preference intensity (IV2) has even grown in light of Brexit, which has been a real game changer. Until not too long ago the agriculture and food policies of all administrations were developed under the EU's regulatory regime and the Common Agriculture Policy (CAP), which has caused a high level of functional and political interdependence (IV1) and harmonisation across the UK. Hence, the different governments share a long history of cooperation (DV2), joint policymaking and agreement on common positions for Brussels negotiations, and the relationships between DEFRA and the devolved governments were widely described as the most developed inter-administrative interactions (SG3, SG7, UKG1, UKG2, UKG5, UKG10, WG2, WG3, WG9).[63] Next to the day-to-day collaboration and consultation on operational issues at official level, ministers dealt with major issues in the JMC Europe (SG3, WG9). And yet, before the EU referendum the mutual engagement was significantly lower and mostly about preparing joint positions for the meetings of the Council of the EU. During the EU withdrawal process, functional and political interdependence (IV1) suddenly had to be dealt with predominantly in the domestic sphere. As the responsibility for agriculture and food returned to the UK, the overlap of reserved and devolved powers has presented new challenges, for instance in regard to agricultural subsidies to farmers, competition regulation, common production standards and, of course, international trade agreements. While the Interministerial Group for Environment, Food and Rural Affairs (IMG EFRA) operated as a regular forum for exchanges between ministers (Welsh Government 2020b, 4), at official level, DEFRA increased its devolution capacities significantly: "We realised that we couldn't just not engage with them. Most of the policy areas are devolved, environment, farming, but it's been ruled by EU law. Now that the EU law doesn't look after that anymore, you have to do a lot more engagement and working together." (UKG3). In early 2018, the Department for Environment, Food and Rural Affairs (2018, 30) published the document Health and Harmony: the Future for Food, Farming and the Environment in a Green Brexit, which introduced reforms for a new agriculture policy across all parts of the UK: "We will [...] continue to work closely with the devolved administrations to agree where a common approach is required across the UK. Where commonality is essential we expect to need UK wide legislative frameworks." Since then, the Scottish and the Welsh Governments worked closely with DEFRA to put statutory instruments for a potential no-deal in place and develop Common Frameworks (SG3, SG7, WG9). The following presents a number of examples demonstrating the range of intergovernmental interaction and the extent to which the Scottish and Welsh Governments could shape policy outcomes: geographical indications for food, drinks and agriculture products; CAP; and especially the Agriculture Bills 2017–2019 and 2019–2021.

Geographical indications for food, drinks and agriculture products were previously regulated by the European Union Protected Food Name (EUPFN). While intellectual property is a reserved matter, geographical indications are partly within devolved responsibilities and salient to Scotland, Wales and Northern Ireland. The Scottish Government wanted a statutory role in the UK's new Geographical Indication Scheme (UKGI),[64] but the UK Government only settled for a working-level arrangement between all four administrations under the management of Department for Environment, Food and Rural Affairs (2021). In November 2018, Michael Gove, the Secretary of State for Environment, Food and Rural Affairs (2018), wrote to Fergus Ewing, the Scottish Secretary for the Rural Economy: "A Memorandum of Understanding setting out the governance structure of the new UK schemes is being co-developed with devolved administrations. The MoU outlines how all four of the UK's administrations will work together to administer various aspects of the new UK GI schemes." Subsequently, the GIs Joint Administration Panel was founded to review applications for geographical indications, whereby the DEFRA Secretary of State officially approves successful applications and has the final say in the event that the review process does not come to a decision (UKG2).

Under CAP, Member States receive substantial subsidies for their agriculture sectors, which in the UK was allocated from the centre to the devolved

Table 5.2 CAP payments and the total income from farming across the UK in 2018

Country	Total direct CAP payments (£ million)	Total income from farming (£ million)	% of total income from CAP payments
England	2,177	3,358	65
Wales	298	308	97
Scotland	549	672	82
Northern Ireland	307	360	85
UK total	*3,331*	*4,697*	*71*

Source: Coe and Finlay (2020).

jurisdictions. As Table 5.2 shows, this provided an essential source of income for farmers, particularly in Wales, Scotland and Northern Ireland. Due to the low payment rate per hectare in so-called less favoured areas in Scotland, where growing conditions are difficult, the UK qualified for an additional £190 million from the convergence mechanism of the 2014–2020 CAP programme. The UK Government allocated the extra money across the whole of the UK of which Scotland only received £30 million since 2014. After a lengthy yet successful campaign of correspondence and engagement by the Scottish Government, in September 2019, the UK Government eventually agreed to transfer £160 million of funding to Scotland (SG3, SP4) (Kenyon 2019; Coe and Finlay 2020, 13).

The Agriculture Bill 2017–2019 was a particularly important issue for the devolved administrations and reflected the difference in agriculture sectors across the UK. To provide a legal framework for the UK after leaving CAP, the UK Government introduced the bill on 12 September 2018. While it sought to establish a new system based on 'public money for public goods' in England (Brand and Atherton 2020, 10), Scotland (and Northern Ireland) planned a system similar to the existing EU scheme and insisted on receiving direct subsidies from the centre to implement their own policies (SG9). The Agriculture Bill mainly applied to England, but some clauses affected the devolved parts and therefore required their legislative consent. The UK Government also offered to include executive powers for the Scottish and Welsh ministers to ensure the continuation of payments to farmers after 2020. Before the Bill was stopped by the dissolution of Parliament in October 2019, it included provisions on financial assistance and support to replace CAP; the collection and sharing of data; interventions in agricultural markets; marketing standards and carcass classification; fairness in the supply chain; World Trade Organisation (WTO) obligations and on the Red Meat Levy. Whereas the Welsh Government happily accepted the bill because they would not have had the capacities themselves to develop their own statute in time (WG8) (Griffiths 2020), cooperation (DV2) between the Scottish Government and UK Government turned out to be more difficult (UKG3, WG9). The Scottish Government criticised the lack of early engagement from the UK Government and rejected provisions that would give the Secretary of State unilateral powers despite agriculture being a devolved responsibility (Ewing 2018a):

> Before the bill was introduced there was no dialogue between the DEFRA and the devolved administrations. They didn't share their instructions for the bill. When you're creating a bill like this, the process is you develop the policy instruction which sets out what policy you're trying to achieve that then gets turned into the draft text. We didn't see any of that policy instructions, so we didn't have the opportunity to influence at that stage. The first that we saw was when DEFRA would say here's some draft clauses for the bill and we would have to comment on those, at which time it was probably already too late for our view to be really taken into account.
>
> (SG3)

After the Agriculture Bill was introduced to the House of Commons, the Scottish Government proposed a series of amendments and laid out the conditions under which it would recommend giving legislative consent to the bill (Scottish Parliament 2018b). The levy on the production and processing of red meat was an important area of contestation, and subsequently altered to the satisfaction of the Scottish Government (SG3).[65] The Scottish Government claimed that Scottish rural businesses would lose up to £2 million per year and had been trying for a decade to ensure that the levy would benefit the Scottish meat production sector (Ewing 2018b). At the end of a series of exchanges, Michael Gove (Secretary of State for Environment, Food and Rural Affairs 2018) responded to Fergus Ewing: "I've asked my officials to work with yours to ensure there is nothing in the text of the proposed amendment that would prevent you recommending legislative consent." The Scottish Government also disagreed with the WTO obligations, which would have transferred powers from the Scottish Parliament to the UK Secretary of State (SG3). Fergus Ewing claimed that the Bill "completely fails to meet the key tests of delivering on promises made to Scotland, respecting the devolved settlements and righting longstanding issues". He insisted that farm support, food security and supply chains were devolved responsibilities, and particularly that the bill's requirement to meet WTO obligations "could create sweeping unilateral powers". The Scottish Government threatened not to recommend legislative consent to the bill, even though the UK Government did not believe provisions concerning international obligations needed approval of the Scottish Parliament. Before a Legislative Consent Motion was initiated, the resolution of the House of Commons in October 2019 stopped the Agriculture Bill (Coe and Finlay 2020, 15–16). In November 2019, the Scottish Government then initiated its own Agriculture (Retained EU Law and Data) (Scotland) Bill to continue CAP payments beyond 2024, which was passed by the Scottish Parliament in August 2020 (Scottish Government 2020a).

In contrast to the Scottish Government, the Welsh Government suggested that it was "fully integrated into the DEFRA bill team" and cooperated (DV2) extensively on the development of the Agriculture Bill (WG9). According to Lesley Griffith (2018), the Welsh Minister for Environment, Energy and Rural Affairs, the bill was "the first test of the principles [...] of collaboration, cooperation and respect for devolution" set out in the Intergovernmental Agreement on the European Union (Withdrawal) Bill and "demonstrates the considerable engagement and collaboration that is taking place to establish a UK common framework for agriculture support." She also shared the Scottish concerns over compliance with WTO obligations. On 26 March 2019, Lesley Griffith presented a second supplementary Legislative Consent Memorandum with respect to the Agriculture Bill to the Welsh Assembly, in which she stated that outstanding concerns relating to the WTO obligations and the Red Meat Levy had been resolved and that the Bill was amended in the House of Commons (Welsh Parliament 2020i). The agreement included a Bilateral Agreement on WTO provisions within the Agriculture Bill (21 March 2019), which committed the UK Government to consultations with the devolved administrations before bringing forward regulations under this power (Department for Environment, Food and Rural Affairs and Welsh Government 2019). The Senedd's Constitutional and Legislative Affairs Committee, as well as the Climate Change, Environment and Rural Affairs Committee were not yet prepared to give consent since the bill would have transferred some of its primary legislative powers to UK and Welsh ministers.[66] In July 2019, Lesley Griffith wrote to the Welsh Assembly that further discussion with the UK Government and the other devolved administrations had taken place to enhance their consultation rights (Welsh Parliament 2020i). As a civil servant of the Welsh Government put it: "We at the last minute asked for some quite substantial changes which DEFRA fully accommodated. [...] DEFRA ministers have given a very clear commitment, if we need to make amendments because they're not quite legally, they're more than happy to do that." (WG9). Since the bill stopped before it passed all stages in the UK Parliament, these agreements did not come into effect.

The newly elected UK Government started a second attempt to ensure the payment of farmers in line with the existing CAP regime until the end of 2020 and introduced the Agriculture Bill 2019–2021 on 16 January 2020. The new bill built on the previous Agriculture Bill and made provisions for direct payments and financial support to farmers; data management; processing of agricultural products; and marketing, classification and certification standards. It also included additional measures on food security; agricultural tenancies; fertiliser regulation; identification and traceability of animals and the Red Meat Levy. While the bill mainly applies to England, Schedule 5 of the bill provides Wales and Schedule 6 Northern Ireland with executive powers to ensure continuity after leaving the EU. No Schedule refers explicitly to Scotland (Coe and Finlay 2020, 6–7). The

WTO obligations remained a controversial matter because it enabled the UK Government to set limits for farm subsidies (op. cit., 72–74).[67] The cooperation (DV2) had intensified significantly since the development of the first Agriculture Bill and this time all devolved administrations got more involved in the discussions at the centre. As a Whitehall civil servant commented: "Generally with the Agriculture Bill, the engagement with the DAs has been quite good. Scotland, they probably did want more warning but because there was so much to do in such short space of time it wasn't always possible to have as much engagement as they wanted. I think that's improved." (UKG2). IMG EFRA and the Senior Officials Programme Board provided high-level communication channels to resolve any issues that could not be solved by the policy teams. Controversial issues, including those clauses of the first bill that would have enabled the UK Government to exercise powers that are devolved, were either removed or amended.[68] After the Scottish Government had been able to reshape the bill according to its preferences, the Scottish Parliament gave its consent to the bill in September 2020.[69] While the Bilateral Agreement on WTO provisions within the Agriculture Bill 2017–2019 did not formally make it into the new bill (Orford and Henderson 2020, 24), the UK Government agreed to develop a multilateral concordat between all four governments to complement the bill. The UK Government also accommodated other demands of the Welsh Government and amended the respective clauses in the bill (UKG2). On 11 September, Lesley Griffith informed the Senedd's Legislation, Justice and Constitution Committee: "I am pleased to inform the Committee that following many weeks of close working between officials from all four administrations [...] government amendments were tabled and agreed at Committee Stage (Lords)."[70] (Welsh Parliament 2020j). Consequently, the Welsh Government recommended consent to the bill, which was given on 29 September 2020 by the Senedd. On 11 November, after a long period of extensive exchanges across the different administrations, the Agriculture Act 2020 was passed by the UK Parliament.[71]

The engagement around the Agriculture Bill was clearly shaped by the different political outlooks, but due to the functional and political interdependence (IV1) and preference intensity (IV2), the governments were willing to work together. Pragmatism drove the different levels to overcome initial disputes and cooperate (DV2). Considering the great relevance of agriculture to the Scottish and Welsh economies, strategic power (IV4) of the devolved governments was fairly strong, and the Sewel Convention allowed them to exercise some pressure on DEFRA. The UK Government wanted to make the new legislation work for all parts of the UK despite the fact that it could have acted unilaterally, as it did on other statutes. The Scottish and Welsh Governments were not initiating the bill, but their political influence was *substantial*, as they could shape it according to their preferences and the UK Government adopted the bulk of their requests (UKG2).

Scotland	
Goal-achievement	2 (substantial)
Ascription	2 (substantial)
Political relevance	2 (substantial)
Political influence (GA × AS × PR)	*8 (substantial)*

Wales	
Goal-achievement	2 (substantial)
Ascription	2 (substantial)
Political relevance	2 (substantial)
Political influence (GA × AS × PR)	*8 (substantial)*

Environment, climate change and energy

Environmental, climate change and energy policy are "so intermingled and it's not possible for either one government to deliver its objectives without working with the other", as an interviewee put it (SG12). Environmental policy is devolved, but many important energy policy levers related to environmental issues are reserved to the UK Government.[72] Whereas functional and political interdependence (IV1) has so far been a reliable predictor for interaction between governments, environmental issues have not triggered a great deal of cooperation (DV2) but are largely dealt with on a unilateral basis (SP3). The different targets to reduce greenhouse gas emissions are an obvious example of non-interaction. While the Climate Change (Emissions Reduction Targets) (Scotland) Act 2019 sets 2045 as a target date for net-zero emissions (Energy and Climate Change Directorate 2020), the UK Government amended its Climate Change Act 2008 by the (2050 Target Amendment) Order 2019 and announced the aim of net-zero emissions by 2050. Cairney et al. (2019, 463) suggested that energy policy has rarely been discussed as a high-profile issue in the UK's intergovernmental relations (except in preparation for meetings in the Council of Ministers), and highlighted that "[t]he UK government has largely acquiesced in the Scottish Government's carving out of a larger policy role in relation to renewable energy than its legal capacity would indicate because this has been helpful to it in fulfilling its own (demanding) obligations to increase UK renewable energy consumption." Cooperation (DV2) has mostly taken place at official level and in relation to funding for renewable energies and green infrastructure, and conflict (DV3) has occurred when the Scottish Government lacked the competence and means to realise its own energy priorities. Without prior consultation with the Scottish Government (Brooks 2015), the UK Government stopped subsidising renewable energy plants in April 2016 because of a strong opposition to land wind turbines in England (UKG8). The Scottish Government "fought various battles" (SG8) to ensure the continuation of future investments in onshore wind farming (SP3) without success. Although the UK Government reversed its decision in March 2020 and lifted its ban on subsidies for wind turbines on land (Ambrose 2020), this was not to accommodate the Scottish Government but to meet its net zero targets by 2050 (SP3; UKG8).

As for agriculture, protection was regulated through EU Directives and Regulations. Anthony (2021) pointed out: "Leaving the EU has created significant gaps in the UK's legal and institutional framework for the environment. One of the most significant is the absence of UK-wide cooperation on the environment. [...] UK environmental governance is fragmenting." In a policy paper on the draft Environment (Principles and Governance) Bill 2018, the Department for Environment, Food and Rural Affairs (2019) acknowledged the interplay of devolved and reserved powers in this policy area:

> Environment is a devolved matter, subject to a small number of areas that are reserved. In consequence, this Bill applies to England and to the UK for reserved matters. Overall, we recognise that protecting the environment is inherently an issue that cuts across boundaries, and we continue to welcome the opportunity to co-design with the Devolved Administrations, should they wish to join any proposals, to safeguard our shared natural environment.

While Brexit required replacing European with new UK-wide standards (SG3), the Welsh Assembly had already passed the Environment (Wales) Act 2016 and the Scottish Parliament had also approved the Climate Change (Emissions Reduction Targets) (Scotland) Act 2019 dealing with some of the issues raised by the UK Government. Before Whitehall announced the initial Environment Bill 2019 on 15 October, there was little cooperation (DV2) or consultation with the devolved governments (SG8). After the first attempt at a bill ended after its second reading with the dissolution of Parliament in autumn 2019 (Smith 2021, 2), the newly elected Government re-launched the Environment Bill 2019–2021 on 30 January 2020 to establish a new domestic framework for environmental governance and to make provisions in relation to environmental protection; waste and resource efficiency; air quality; water; nature; biodiversity; and chemicals and environmental standards of products. Because environmental protection is a reserved matter, large parts of the bill only apply to England. The bill still introduced a range of concurrent powers held by UK and devolved ministers in regard to waste and resource efficiency and producer responsibility, including electronic waste tracking, as well as on cross-border river basin districts and the regulation of chemicals. Devolved ministers would also be enabled to make subordinate legislation, and their consent was needed when the UK Secretary of State exercised powers within the devolved jurisdictions (Environment, Climate Change and Land Reform Committee 2020; Welsh Parliament 2020k). Many clauses required the legislative consent of the devolved legislatures, and

Clause 146 sets out how the bill extends to Scotland, Wales[73] and Northern Ireland.[74] Whereas the Scottish Parliament raised concerns about its role in scrutinising secondary legislation, the Scottish Government was content with the provisions of the bill to adopt a single UK-wide approach for some areas and recommended giving consent. A policy paper by the Department for Environment, Food and Rural Affairs (2020) highlighted that "extensive and continued collaboration has been undertaken with the Scottish and Welsh Governments",[75] and the Scottish Government testified that provisions that affect Scotland "were prepared and subsequently amended in a manner that adequately respected the legislative competence of the Scottish Parliament" (Scottish Parliament 2021). The Legislative Consent Motion was approved by the Scottish Parliament on 12 November 2020 (Scottish Parliament 2020e).[76]

In 2021, the UK Government made two controversial amendments to the bill, which sparked a legal dispute over constitutional rather than policy issues. Whereas most amendments made after the Scottish Parliament had passed legislative consent did not significantly affect its competence, Clause 116 allows the UK Government to regulate on products, which are at high risk to be illegally deforested,[77] and Clause 19(4–6) applies the UK Government's guiding principles on the environment to decisions that affect Scotland.[78] In contrast to the UK Government, the Scottish Government refused to consider this a reserved matter and wanted stronger involvement in recognition of devolved competences (Net Zero, Energy and Transport Committee 2021). In October, Michael Matheson, the Cabinet Secretary for Net Zero, Energy and Transport, claimed that contrary to what had been agreed with the UK Government, this would undermine the powers of the Scottish Parliament and apply "the UK environmental principles when making policy affecting Scotland in reserved areas." (Scottish Parliament 2021). Despite their regular engagement, the Scottish Government was unable to change the new amendments and achieve "a proper recognition of devolved competence", as UK Government did not recognise them as requiring legislative consent but only informally committed to consult the Scottish Government when its policies would impact on Scotland (Net Zero, Energy and Transport Committee 2021).

The Welsh Government also supported a coordinated environmental approach across all administrations but sought to ensure that the Environment Bill would not interfere with the Senedd's powers without consent and that it could exercise some of the powers in the bill (WG9). In February 2020 and again in June, September and October 2021, it recommended legislative consent following successful requests on specific provisions, such as conferring powers for Welsh ministers to charge for single-use plastic items (James 2021), which were included in Clause 56 and Schedule 9 of the Environment Bill. On 28 September 2021, the Welsh Minister for Climate Change Julie James explained to the Senedd's Climate Change, Environment and Infrastructure Committee why the Welsh Parliament should accept a non-binding informal agreement to resolve the dispute with the UK Government over legislative competence in relation to forest risk commodities. As with the Scottish concern, DEFRA did not recognise the need for legislative consent, but the Welsh Government had received written confirmation that it would be involved in the development of policies and subordinate legislation. For this purpose, Welsh Government officials have been in regular exchange with DEFRA to set up a consultation procedure. Whereas for a long time, the Senedd withheld its consent due to concerns over the transfer of its primary legislative powers to the UK and Welsh executives (Welsh Parliament 2020l), on 28 September and on 2 November 2021 it approved the Legislative Consent Motion in favour of the bill.

By 9 November, when the Environment Act 2021 passed, the Scottish and Welsh Governments had exercised *substantial* political influence, though on the lower end of the scale. The ascription to their engagement and the political relevance of the bill was *substantial*. But the overall goal-achievement has been comparatively low as both governments have aimed to stay closely aligned to the EU's environmental regulations, an objective which they have pursued through their own legislation (UKG8) (Scottish Government 2020b).[79] Although the UK bill serves functional policy needs, because governments follow different agendas it has not been a project driven by joint political aspirations. Rather, non-interaction (DV1) has been the general pattern in the field of environmental, energy and climate change, despite their obvious interdependence. Moreover, constitutional tensions about policy responsibility, future trade agreements and the Internal Market Act, which Michael Matheson referred to as "a particular concern in relation to our ability to make environmental policy in the future" (Scottish Parliament 2021), have caused worries that the devolved jurisdictions have to accept lower environmental regulations and will not introduce innovative policies that could disadvantage local producers.

Scotland	
Goal-achievement	1 (some)
Ascription	2 (substantial)
Political relevance	2 (substantial)
Political influence ($GA \times AS \times PR$)	*4 (substantial)*
Wales	
Goal-achievement	1 (some)
Ascription	2 (substantial)
Political relevance	2 (substantial)
Political influence ($GA \times AS \times PR$)	*4 (substantial)*

Economic policy and development

Responsibilities for economic policy and development are separated according to macro-areas of activity that are reserved (e.g., corporation and income tax, trade policy and research and developments, industrial regulations, financial services, and monetary and currency issues) and micro-areas that are devolved (e.g., vocational education and skills training, investing in infrastructure and communication, business support, business rates and manufacturing). Though the allocation of economic responsibilities aims at a clear separation of powers, they are still functionally and politically interdependent (IV1) and require some coordination to be effective and avoid counterproductive measures (SG14, WG6, WP3).[80] Despite the interplay of different competences, the UK and the devolved governments follow different approaches and have exercised their powers at a political level largely unilaterally (SG14, WG6). In 2017, the Department for Business, Energy and Industrial Strategy (2017, 26) launched the UK Industrial Strategy stating that "[t]he UK government and the devolved administrations can each learn from each other in areas of common interest." According to the Welsh Government (2020a, 3), however, "intergovernmental relations and joint working with BEIS were not well established", quadrilateral ministerial meetings were not effective and reliable, and there was a lack of involvement in the development of joint economic resilience and support. Relations were better at official level. Scottish officials maintained good working relationships at an operational level and shared information and knowledge around inward capital investment and export strategies (SG13). Events like economic recessions (cf. Birrell 2012, 217) and Brexit (SG14) have increased the preference intensity (IV2) for government and triggered more cooperation (DV2) to support economic development. During the COVID-19 pandemic, for instance, the different administrations worked together to help businesses (UKG8). There was daily coordination and joint measures to ensure the distribution of food supplies in supermarkets during the lockdown in early spring 2020 (UKG2), and through the Barnett formula, the UK Government announced an additional £780 million to Scotland, £475 million to Wales and £260 million to Northern Ireland (Paun, Sargeant, Shuttleworth and Nice 2020). The need for more economic cooperation (DV2) is also reflected in the new Finance Interministerial Standing Committee, which is not only responsible for financial but also for macroeconomic and ad hoc matters to deal with "longer-term challenges that affect all administrations" (Cabinet Office and Department for Levelling Up, Housing and Communities 2022).

The city and growth deals in Scotland and Wales, as well as in Northern Ireland,[81] are a rare example where the different levels of governance use their respective powers to invest in a defined area and fund projects developed in cooperation with local authorities. The Localism Act 2011 and the document Unlocking Growth in Cities, in which the UK Government outlined its plans for creating jobs and increasing economic prosperity at a city-regional level, laid the foundation of the city deals (Deputy Prime Minister's Office et al., 2011). From 2012 on, English city regions outside of London, such as Greater Manchester, Bristol and Sheffield, were the first to receive extra funding through the UK Government's city deals. Subsequently, the growth deals have enabled the centre to get involved in local policymaking networks, gain visibility in the devolved territories (Keating 2021, 80) and to (re-)stablish itself as an investor outside of England (Welsh Affairs Committee 2019c). A UK Government official stated:

> When we had the independence referendum in 2014, there was desire there that the UK Government, London, needs to be seen adding something to the devolved administrations and doing something for Scotland and Wales. These deals were seen as a way of which the UK Government could be funding economic development directly in the devolved administrations.
>
> (UKG8)

Though this kind of economic support is a devolved responsibility, the projects that are funded through this measure are developed bottom-up by local authorities and stakeholders in cooperation with the UK Government and the devolved governments (WG6). The Parliamentary Under Secretary of State in the Scotland Office reported to the Local Government and Communities Committee (2017):

> [...] the deals should be a means by which our Governments can co-operate and collaborate; after all, we are governing the same people and both Governments have the same objective at heart, which is to deliver better lives for the people who live in those areas. [...] It is important to stress that projects still must grow organically from the local level. It is not the job of either the Scottish Government or the UK Government to impose projects or to determine what projects are included.

To gain more control over regional policy within the devolved parts, resources were not allocated through the Barnett formula but directly designated for each deal, which was perceived as a politically motivated intrusion in Scotland and Wales (SP1, WG6). Strikingly, the first growth deal outside of England was not made in consultation with the Scottish Government. Only shortly before the 2014 referendum on Scottish independence, the UK Government unilaterally announced the City Deal Glasgow and the Clyde Valley financed with £1.2 billion over 20 years to which the Scottish Government contributes £520 million investment for improved infrastructure, as the main priority; growth in life sciences; supporting business innovation and tackling unemployment (Minister for Just Transition, Employment and Fair Work 2021). At first, the local authorities were uncertain how to use the unexpected resources, as an MSP suggested:

> Glasgow didn't have any idea what they were going do with it. It was the sketchiest of bids I have ever seen, and my local authorities involved along with them, because its Glasgow in the west of Scotland; and contrast that with Stirling, which is one of the more recent ones, which

204 *Patterns of Interaction and Political Influence*

were so detailed they had implementation plans that were ready to go the next day. But it was so powerful, the UK government here with that big money and the Scottish Government were left scrambling around trying to match it, making promises they didn't know how they were going to fund.

(SP1)

The governments reluctantly worked together to the benefit of those local areas in a strategic way (SP1), and their discussions were described as quite administrative and technical with only occasional disagreement about which government was responsible for a specific matter (SG14). The Scottish Government committed to matching the UK Government's funds and on some occasions increased their share to get more money from the centre, and vice versa (SG14, SP1). Keith Brown, Scottish Cabinet Secretary for Economy, Jobs and Fair Work, said before the Scottish Local Government and Communities Committee (2018) that except for the Glasgow City Region City Deal, the areas of funding were allocated according to devolved and reserved matters – although in practice this was not strictly followed through. He further described how the two governments competed over the amount of funding:

The Stirling and Clackmannanshire deal is the most interesting one in this regard. We had early indications from the UK Government that it was willing to spend £50 million, then what I can only describe as a fiasco developed towards the end of the deal. We had something like 10 different figures from the UK Government in the last two weeks and four different figures in the last two days. On, I think, the night before the deal was announced, we were told that the UK Government had suddenly changed its funding commitment from 10 years to 15 years. That has a huge impact on the quantum.

The second deal was the Aberdeen and Aberdeenshire City Region Deal in 2016 with the aim to encourage investment in innovation, internationalisation, digital connectivity and infrastructure across the region. In the same year, the Inverness and Highland City Region Deal was set up to support improvements to the region's digital connectivity, digital healthcare, skills, innovation and infrastructure. In 2017, both governments committed to the Edinburgh and South East Scotland City Region Deal for housing, innovation, transport, skills and culture; and in 2018, Stirling and Clackmannanshire City Region Deal and the Tay Cities Region Deal were agreed. Four more smaller growth deals followed in 2019: the Ayrshire Growth Deal, Borderlands Inclusive Growth Deal, Moray Growth Deal and Argyll and Bute Growth Deal. Finally, the Falkirk Growth Deal and the Islands Growth Deal were announced in 2020 (Minister for Just Transition, Employment and Fair Work 2021).[82]

Table 5.3 Overview of city and growth deals in Scotland

	City and growth deal	Total funding (in million/period)	Funding Scottish Government (in million)	Funding UK Government (in million)
2014	Glasgow and the Clyde Valley	£1,200/20 years	£520	£500
2016	Aberdeen and Aberdeenshire	£826/10 years	£125	£125
2016	Inverness and Highlands	£315/10 years	£135	£53
2017	Edinburgh and South East Scotland	£1,300/15 years	£300	£300
2018	Stirling and Clackmannanshire	£214/15 years	£45.1	£45.1
2018	Tay Cities	£350/10–15 years	£200	£150
2019	Ayrshire	£251.5/15 years	£103	£103
2019	Borderlands Inclusive	£350/10–15 years	£85	£65
2019	Moray	£100/10–15 years	£32.5	£32.5
2019	Argyll and Bute	£70/10–15 years	£25	£25
2020	Falkirk	£90/10 years	£50	£40
2020	Islands	£335/10 years	£50	£50

Source: Minister for Just Transition, Employment and Fair Work (2021).

The Welsh Government found itself in a similar situation as the Scots when the UK Government announced the first city and growth deals for Wales without prior engagement:

> There was no consultation, no prior discussion. There was just a public announcement: 'here's a block of money, if you don't work with us, there's a risk that W might not get any of this funding at all.' We were hostaged a little bit. Even though we didn't like the system, and would have liked to design something better, had we simply said 'no, we're not taking part', either Wales would not have received any money or they may still have gone ahead and Welsh Government would have had no influence how that money is spent. So even if we don't like it, better to be at table and then try to influence it from the insights than just simply stand apart.
>
> (WG6)

The negotiations towards the different deals took place behind closed doors, which some local stakeholders described as difficult and challenging as the policy priorities and the funding had to be agreed by two different governments (WP3, WP7).[83] As with the Scottish growth deals, the UK and the Welsh Governments competed with each other over their respective contributions, and the latter committed to matching the former's funding to not lose out on the additional resources. Nevertheless, the Welsh and

Table 5.4 Overview of city and growth deals in Wales

Year	City and growth deal	Total funding (£ million/ period)	Funding Welsh Government (£ million)	Funding UK Government (£ million)
2016	Cardiff Capital Region	1,200/20 years	500	500
2017	Swansea Bay	1,300/15 years	125.4	115.6
2019	North Wales	240/15 years	120	120
2020	Mid Wales	110/15 years	55	55

Source: Welsh Affairs Committee (2019c); Office of the Secretary of State for Wales (2020).

the UK Governments closely collaborated on the delivery of the growth deals (UKG7, WG6, WP3). Because of the rurally dominated structure in large parts of Wales, there are four very different types of growth deals for Wales. The Cardiff Capital Region City Deal was agreed in March 2016 and included ten local authorities.[84] One year later in March, the Swansea Bay City Deal targeted the internet of economic acceleration; skills and talent initiatives; the internet of energy; and smart manufacturing.[85] In November 2019, both governments together with the North Wales Economic Ambition Board[86] agreed on the heads of terms of the North Wales Growth Deal, which was finalised in December 2020. The deal has been funded with £240 million to deliver seven programmes,[87] which is not only a significantly smaller amount than the Cardiff and Swansea deals but also sparked some controversy about the UK Government's decision to reduce its financial commitment down to £120 million. In contrast to the Welsh Government, they saw the proposed action not as sufficiently ambitious to justify the original total investment of £340 million (Welsh Affairs Committee 2019c). This caused frustration within North Wales, and the Welsh Affairs Committee (ibid.) expressed their concern "at the manner in which the UK Government announced that less funding than was anticipated was to be provided and recommend[ed] that, in future, the UK Government should communicate more clearly with Growth Deal bodies." Due to the COVID-19 pandemic, the Mid Wales Growth Deal was delayed until it was agreed in December 2020 (Office of the Secretary of State for Wales 2020).

Although the UK Government did not intend for the city and growth deals for Scotland and Wales to become a joint political endeavour, fairly high interdependence (IV1) and preference intensity (IV2) turned them quickly into a voluntary negotiation system between the HM Treasury, the devolved administrations and local authority partners. At first, their strategic power (IV4) was limited as they did not want to miss the extra funding and the opportunity to shape the outcome of the deals, and therefore could only react to Whitehall's call but not develop their own ideas for a coherent economic development agenda. The following engagement towards the growth deals was based on preliminary political debates and political bargaining towards negotiated agreements. After signing the heads of terms for each deal at the political level, officials have worked together on the delivery and monitoring of each project (SG14, UKG8). While it was not possible to fully examine the contributions and impact of the different stakeholders for each deal, the political influence of both devolved administrations was nevertheless *substantial*.

Scotland	
Goal-achievement	2 (substantial)
Ascription	2 (substantial)
Political relevance	2 (substantial)
Political influence (GA × AS × PR)	*8 (substantial)*

Wales	
Goal-achievement	2 (substantial)
Ascription	2 (substantial)
Political relevance	2 (substantial)
Political influence (GA × AS × PR)	*8 (substantial)*

Transport

Like economic policy, the central and the devolved levels hold different responsibilities for transport: UK-wide strategic road and rail planning, air and maritime transport are reserved to the UK Government,[88] and local transport services, walking and cycling are devolved (Butcher 2017, 3). The Government of Wales Act 2006 and the Railways Act 2005 enabled the devolution of executive authority over rail strategy, infrastructure and transport services to Scotland and Wales.[89] Under the Scotland Act 2016, local responsibilities for transport, such as rail passenger services and rolling stock, buses, speed limits, road signs, cycling and parking, and many operational issues followed; and the Railway Policing Scotland Act 2017 removed the functions of the British Transport Police in Scotland and merged them with Police Scotland (Strickland and Pepin 2018).[90] The Wales Act 2017 also transferred similar powers over speed limits, pedestrian crossings and traffic signs, bus services, taxi licensing, and harbour regulations (Butcher 2017, 5–14). Because transport is a cross-border issue, functional and political interdependence (IV1) are high, and in particular the geographical centrality of England means that decisions by the UK Government have strong implications for transport considerations in Scotland,[91] and even more so in Wales. As this requires a close coordination of work across the different jurisdictions (UKG10, WP3), officials from the different governments have regular meetings to cooperate (DV2) discuss the planning and construction of road infrastructure stretching across borders (UKG9).[92]

The preference intensity (IV2) among the Scottish and the Welsh Governments is particularly high for the railway franchise (SG15). While neither the Scottish Parliament nor the Senedd has legislative powers over the rail infrastructure and framework under which rail operates, both governments were given executive powers over the operation of railway services within their borders. After the Scottish independence referendum in 2014, the strategic power (IV4) of the Scottish Government was high due to David Cameron's commitment to and the public support for more territorial autonomy. Based on the recommendations of the Smith Commission to permit public providers to operate the Scottish rail franchise, the Scotland Act 2016 (amending the Railway Act 1993) transferred competences to directly procure and manage the rail service, either through private or public sector organisations (Butcher 2017, 5; Corbyn 2021). The following negotiated agreement between the Scottish and the UK Governments was a fairly straightforward issue.

The same powers over the rail franchise were only reluctantly 'lent' to the Welsh Government. Since the early days of devolution, the Welsh Government had shown an interest in the provision of rail services in Wales and had built up pressure and increased its strategic power (IV4). Eventually, in 2016, its arguments resonated in Whitehall, and the UK Government entered the negotiations. The following engagement was not a partnership of equals but as much characterised by consensus as by hierarchical direction. As in Scotland, the Welsh Government wanted the option to allow public sector operators to run the rail franchise. Yet, the UK Government insisted that under the Railway Act 1993, which bars public sector operators from competing, the Welsh franchise would have to be contracted to private providers. Further disputes concerned the funding of rail services in Wales, which the Welsh Government claimed to be insufficient to deliver the new railway system. The Wales Office and the Secretary of State for Wales mediated between both governments to solve their political tensions and disagreements. After an initial broad negotiated agreement between ministers on how to transfer executive responsibilities for the train franchise, officials worked out the details over the course of two years, which were signed off by ministers.[93] In 2018, the UK Government's Welsh Ministers (Transfer of Functions) (Railways) Order gave the Welsh Government new executive powers to design the rail franchise for 15 years. The order is supplemented by a series of arrangements on the funding, services specification and management of the Wales and Borders Rail Franchise; including the Cooperation and Collaboration Agreement between the Secretary of State for Transport and the Welsh Ministers, of which Article 11.2 states: "The Parties agree to co-operate fully with each other for the purposes of communication, publicity and liaison matters, including Ministerial correspondence, which relate to the Parties' interests in the Welsh services or the wider activities, roles, responsibilities or obligations of the Parties under this Agreement." (Department for Transport 2018).[94] Although the Welsh Government has expressed an ongoing disappointment over a lack of rail infrastructure investments and hopes in the long term to gain full control over infrastructure, the selection of franchise models (including public operators) and rolling stocks (Welsh Government 2019d; Corbyn 2021), it has subsequently cooperated (DV2) intensively with the UK Government to make the new rail environment work in Wales (UKG7, UKG9, WG6).

Despite the UK Government's resistance to allowing public train operators to run franchises in Wales, due to the low number of passengers during the COVID pandemic, Wales was the first nation to renationalise its railway services in February 2021. According to the Welsh Minister for Economy, Transport and North Wales, the collapse of English rail franchises required Wales to put the publicly owned company Transport for Wales Rail Limited in control as a last resort to stabilise the Wales and Borders network (Welsh Government 2020h). The Scottish Government subsequently announced that it will also take over the Scottish franchise in 2022 as the operator of last resort under the COVID-19 emergency measures (Transport Scotland 2021). Even though the Scottish Government was initially more successful in achieving its priorities for the rail franchise, due to the slightly different ascriptions of the outcomes, its influence is only evaluated as substantial whereas the Welsh Government had *great* political influence over the UK Government's transport decisions.

Scotland	
Goal-achievement	3 (great)
Ascription	2 (substantial)
Political relevance	2 (substantial)
Political influence (GA × AS × PR)	*12 (substantial)*
Wales	
Goal-achievement	3 (great)
Ascription	3 (great)
Political relevance	2 (substantial)
Political influence (GA × AS × PR)	*18 (great)*

It is worthwhile to briefly look into an ongoing and highly contentious conflict (DV3) between the Welsh and the UK Governments, which was often raised by interviewees: the building of a relief road for the M4 motorway. When the UK Government abolished the tolls for the Prince of Wales Bridge over the River Severn into South Wales in December 2018, this increased the traffic on the M4 around Newport significantly (BBC 2018). In the words of one Senedd clerk:

> The M4, when it gets to Wales, is three lanes on both sides for most of Wales. But there are parts where it goes down to two lanes, and one of those parts is just before it gets to Newport, and it goes through a tunnel. A very large amount of people commute along the M4 from South Wales into England across to Bristol. So in the morning they all get stuck filing into those two lanes, and in the evening they all get going the other way; and you be stuck in congestion for one and half hours.
> (WP3)

In discussion with the UK Government, the Welsh Government was initially planning a major road infrastructure project to solve constant traffic congestion in the area of Newport and the Brynglas tunnels in South Wales by building a new relief road. Since 2013, assessments and consultations were conducted to build this new section of the M4 (the so-called black route) (Howorth 2021). While the outcome of a thorough inquiry by the Welsh Planning Inspector between 2017 and 2018 was in favour of building the relief road, in April 2019, Welsh Government decided that for financial[95] and environmental[96] reasons the project was to be replaced by other potential solutions involving public transport services.[97] Though the Welsh Government has responsibility for the road network in Wales, the UK Government has continuously expressed its commitment to realising the relief road (UKG9, WG6, WP3). The Conservative Party's 2019 election manifesto stated: "A Welsh Conservative Government would deliver the M4 relief road which has been mothballed by the Labour administration. We gave financial support to the Welsh Government to build the relief road, yet the Labour administration decided to abandon those plans out of timidity." Believing that the infrastructure project would enjoy wide public and business support, the UK Government has sought to seize this opportunity to gain a stronger foothold in Wales (UKG7, UKG9). As a Whitehall official commented: "The reason we are probably so public about it is we just want businesses and others in Wales to know that the reason that M4 relief road is not happening, it's got nothing to do with the UK Government because we believe it should be done." (UKG7). In October 2019, the Secretary of State for Wales, Simon Hart even indicated that the UK Government may bypass the Welsh Assembly and use the Shared Prosperity Fund to this end (BBC 2020h). The Welsh Government has condemned this as a party-political stunt: "The UK Government have spotted an opportunity here to win the political argument, and the Conservatives have spotted an opportunity to win more votes in Wales to say: 'we would have done the M4'." (WG6). After Labour's victory in the election to the Senedd in May 2021, the Welsh Government cancelled any plans to build a new motorway section. In the light of the high preference intensity (IV2), the Welsh Government's electoral support and its legislative competences on the matter gave it strong strategic power (IV4) to take a firm stance and to not cooperate with the UK Government on this issue. At the same time, party (in)congruence (IV3) played a more obvious role than for other examples presented in this chapter. Any unilateral action by the centre undermining the Senedd's legislative authority would increase the political salience of the issue and escalate the conflict (DV3).

Public healthcare and safety

Scotland, Wales and Northern Ireland all have their separate health systems and can legislate on healthcare. At official and, sometimes, at ministerial levels, governments coordinate payment rates and conditions or cross-border treatment (Gallagher 2020, 570). Also, the Health and Safety

Executive (HSE) coordinates the different health services at an operational level on behalf of the devolved governments in Scotland and Wales (WG8), and is guided by the centre (SG7).[98] Nevertheless, because political interdependence (IV1) is generally low, there is little interaction (DV1) to adopt common approaches for the development of policies (WG8). Unless there is an outbreak of a global pandemic, the Scottish Government and the UK Government hardly work together on healthcare issues. During the first months of the COVID-19 pandemic cooperation (DV2) between ministers and officials was exemplary, as the preference intensity (IV2) was pressing and due to the cross-border implications of the virus (UKG1, UKG5, UKG7, UKG8, UKP2). Between January and June 2020, the Civil Contingencies Committee (COBR) included the Prime Minister and the First Ministers (and Deputy First Minister for Northern Ireland), met over 20 times, and five ministerial implementation groups (MIGs) covered more specific matters (health, public services, the economy and international engagement) – though the Welsh Government (2021b) reported they had "a mixed experience in terms of meaningful engagement across these groups".

On 3 March, all four executives produced a joint Coronavirus Action Plan (Department of Health and Social Care 2020c) and agreed on lockdown measures for the whole of the UK from 23 March on (Kenny et al. 2021, 31–32). The Coronavirus Act 2020, which was fast-tracked through the UK Parliament, followed close consultations and quickly received the legislative consent of all three devolved legislatures on 25 March 2020.[99] Among other issues, the act aimed at stabilising the healthcare sectors across the UK.[100] In contrast to the severe tensions over Brexit, all governments were in fair agreement over the overall policy objective, shared information and coordinated their measures. Yet, the previous lack of engagement and trust soon led to the return of non-interaction (DV1). When in May 2020 the lockdown restrictions were eased the four governments returned acting largely unilaterally. The announcement by the UK Government to reopen schools and parts of the economy happened without prior consultation with the Scottish and Welsh Governments, which opted for a more cautious approach. Subsequently, the intergovernmental engagement between ministers turned from a cooperative (DV2) to a competitive and conflictual (DV3) pattern. COBR meetings stopped due to a lack of coordination in June, and the UK Cabinet's new committees working on COVID-19 did not involve devolved ministers (Andrews 2021, 4; Kenny et al. 2021, 31–33).

The different geographical alignments with England have a strong impact on the engagement of Scotland and Wales with the UK Government. Unlike for Scotland, the Welsh-English border area is populated by a large number of people who often access the healthcare of the other jurisdiction. Hence, their policies mutually affect NHS England and NHS Wales, and the UK and Welsh Governments have to coordinate issues such as the onward referral of patients. These are typically dealt with through cross-border protocols concerning access to and costs of medical services and the treatment of patients (WG2, WG12). Under the constitution of NHS England, patients are free to choose where they want to be treated.[101] The UK Government therefore had asked the Welsh Government to ensure that English patients could access the healthcare services they wanted after being referred onward by a Welsh general practitioner. Both governments then needed to sort out the new financial implications for when patients who are initially treated in Wales go back into the English system, which used to be financed through a standard annual payment from England to Wales based on anticipated numbers of English patients once they entered the Welsh healthcare services. Yet, when the UK Government changed the tariff system for healthcare services in England, it also increased the costs for the Welsh health boards when accessing services in England. This sparked serious tensions, as the Welsh Government was not consulted in time and refused to accept the new system. Because the Welsh Government stopped compensatory payments, in April 2019 the Countess of Chester hospital in England temporarily refused the treatment of patients referred from Wales (WG12) (Committee for the Scrutiny of the First Minister 2019). In May, both governments reached an agreement over the funding of services and the hospital started to accept referrals from Wales again.[102] The strategic power (IV4) to pursue conflict (DV3) on this matter rested on the centre's dependency on the Welsh Government to provide healthcare for English patients. As a Welsh Government official argued:

> You need us to implement. You need us to instruct or GPs, to go out and encourage GPs to behave in certain ways. They couldn't tell GPs in Wales to behave in any certain way and to refer patients back in. They wouldn't be able to set up a referral mechanism for moving patients from Wales into England without the full cooperation really being delivered by the Welsh Government and by the health boards in Wales.

EU withdrawal has triggered serious concerns that new trade deals with other states undermine the devolution settlement and lead to a further privatisation of healthcare services (SG2). When the UK Government introduced the Healthcare (International Arrangement) Bill 2017–2019 in the House of Commons on 26 October 2018, it had not engaged effectively with the devolved administrations in advance (WG12) (Scottish Parliament 2018b). The bill, which became the Healthcare (European Economic Area and Switzerland Arrangements) Act 2019, enabled the UK Government to reciprocally fund and implement healthcare schemes outside of the UK and to share data with EU Member States and other countries after leaving the EU (Powell 2019). The UK Government acknowledged that Clauses 1 (powers to make welfare payments), 2 (healthcare agreements) and 4 (data processing) of the initial bill required the consent of all devolved legislatures (Constitutional and Legislative Affairs Committee 2019a).[103] The Delegated Powers and Regulatory Reform Committee (2018, para. 10) of the House of Lords had reported that the scope of Clause 2 was "breath-taking", "could hardly be wider", and its powers went much wider than the essential matters: "We are concerned that the Brexit process has given rise to a series of Bills, of which this is the latest, containing unprecedented powers for Ministers to make law by statutory instrument." (Delegated Powers and Regulatory Reform Committee 2019, para. 3). Clause 5(3) on regulations directives was particularly controversial as it would have potentially enabled the UK Government to amend, repeal or revoke a measure or act of the devolved legislatures (Health, Social Care and Sport Committee 2019). Although the Welsh Government believed in the necessity of the bill, it felt that it was not consulted early enough (Constitutional and Legislative Affairs Committee 2019b, positions 8–11) and concerned about the burden of costs. As it wanted to be involved in the development of international agreements,[104] the Welsh Government threatened to not recommend legislative consent unless the bill included the requirement to give notice, consult or get consent from the devolved ministers on regulations made by international agreements on healthcare (WG12) (Welsh Parliament 2020m).[105] In October 2018, the Welsh Cabinet Secretary for Health and Social Services wrote to the Parliamentary Under Secretary of State for Health:

> Provision of health services is a devolved matter, and I am therefore surprised and disappointed to only be informed this week that you are looking to introduce this Bill. There has been limited engagement on the content of any legislative fixes, and no engagement on the wording of a healthcare specific piece of legislation. As I am sure you will be aware I will be unable to agree to any legislation which has implications for the powers devolved to the Welsh Ministers, without thorough engagement leading to legislative reassurance. The proposed legislation is therefore unacceptable in its current form.
>
> (ibid.)

The UK Government subsequently started to cooperate (DV2) with the Welsh Government, and the Parliamentary Under Secretary of State for Health replied to the Welsh Cabinet Secretary for Health and Social Services:

> As we take the Bill and regulations forward it will be important we do so in a way that is collaborative and respects the devolution settlement and conventions for working together. The UK Government is committed to working closely with the devolved administrations to deliver an approach that works for the whole of the UK.
>
> (ibid.)

After the Scottish Government had already recommended consent to the bill in November 2018, which the Scottish Parliament gave on 16 January 2019 (Scottish Parliament 2019), the Welsh Government took the lead in the negotiations with the UK Department of Health and Social Care and the Cabinet

Office. The Scottish Government supported the multilateral approach pursued by its Welsh counterpart. Following a series of written correspondence and telephone calls between the UK Parliamentary Under Secretary of State for Health and the Welsh Cabinet Secretary for Health and Social Services, policy teams and working groups of both governments worked on a day-to-day basis to amend the bill. In February 2019, the different governments agreed on the final wording of the memorandum of understanding and the amendments to the bill, which were then made at the Report Stage in the House of Lords (WG12). Apart from refining the scope of the bill to the European Economic Area and Switzerland, the duration of the bill was limited to five years after EU exit day (Clause 2(7)), the requirement for consultation with devolved authorities was added (Clause 5), and its regulations can no longer amend, repeal or revoke primary legislation of devolved legislatures (Clause 7(3)).[106] All four executives signed the Memorandum of Understanding for Consultation under Section 5 of the Healthcare (International Arrangements) Bill. The multilateral, non-binding agreement committed the UK Government (in particular the Department of Health and Social Care) to meaningful consultation, consensual and regular engagement with the devolved administrations on development of international healthcare agreements. The Welsh Government recommended the Senedd to give legislative consent, which it did on 12 March 2019 (Welsh Parliament 2020m).[107] The Healthcare (European Economic Area and Switzerland Arrangements) Act passed the UK Parliament on 26 March 2019.

Given the high interdependence (IV1) and the political support of the Lords, the devolved administrations enjoyed sufficient strategic power (IV4) to push the UK Government into a cooperative engagement (DV2) towards a negotiated agreement. Overall, the political influence of the Welsh and Scottish Governments was *substantial*. The goal-achievement on this matter can be ascribed *substantially* to the former, and the political relevance and the constitutional implications of the act were equally *substantial*. While the Welsh Government could not obtain legally binding guarantees, together with the Scottish Government, they were still able to alter the UK Government's legislation and set up a consultation procedure for the development of international healthcare agreements.

Scotland	
Goal-achievement	2 (substantial)
Ascription	1 (some)
Political relevance	2 (substantial)
Political influence (GA × AS × PR)	*4 (substantial)*

Wales	
Goal-achievement	2 (substantial)
Ascription	2 (substantial)
Political relevance	2 (substantial)
Political influence (GA × AS × PR)	*8 (substantial)*

Justice and policing

The allocation of powers over justice and policing is strongly asymmetrical across Scotland and Wales, which determines the different patterns of interaction. Even before 1998, Scotland had its own legal system autonomous to the rest of the UK, which is why the UK Government treats justice as an entirely devolved matter in Scotland. Due to the limited political and functional interdependence (IV1) around justice and policing, non-interaction (DV1) between the Scottish and the UK Governments is the general pattern of engagement.[108] Still, the working relations across the administrations have been described as fairly cooperative (DV2) (UKG4). When reserved legislation affects people in Scotland, for instance in regard to national security, counter-terrorism or the Human Rights Act 1998, governments have coordinated their implementation (UKG4). A rare example of conflict (DV3) has been the prevention of drug use and misuse, an issue of high preference intensity (IV2) in Scotland, which "is in the midst of a drug death crisis" (Scottish Affairs Committee 2019c, 4).[109] Both administrations have powers in regard to drug-related crime but adopted different approaches in dealing with these issues.[110] Whereas the UK Government deals with drug use as a criminal justice matter and followed "a more assertive approach", for the Scottish Government it is a public health issue linked to access to social and care services (UKP2).[111] In 2018, the latter asked the UK Government to allow the introduction of a pilot scheme with safe injection facilities and services by the Glasgow City Council (Scottish Parliament 2018c) without success (BBC 2020i). The Scottish Affairs Committee (2019b, 55) supported the Scottish position and recommended both governments work together on "an integrated, cross-departmental, and cross-government approach to drugs, which fully utilises the potential impact of joined-up policing, justice, employment, welfare, housing, physical and mental health policies and services." In response, the UK Government committed itself to work with the other administrations and held a UK Drug Summit in Glasgow on 27 February 2020, which was however announced without prior consultation with the Scottish Government (Holyrood 2020). Following the Summit, the UK Government set up a UK Drugs Ministerial Meeting "to enable the UK Government and devolved administrations to discuss the actions we can take individually and collectively across the UK." (Scottish Affairs Committee 2020). Hosted by the UK Crime and Policing Minister and Public Health Minister, the meeting took place on 17 September 2020 and discussed approaches to reducing drug deaths, treatment and recovery (Home Office et al. 2020). Despite some engagement between governments, the Scottish Government – with the support of the Scottish Affairs Committee (2019b) – was not successful in its ambition to devolve criminal justice sanctions for drugs and other drug-related laws (SG13), or remove legal barriers to measures, such as safe injection facilities, by changing reserved legislation, namely the Misuse of Drugs Act 1971. The political influence on decisions of the UK Government has therefore been none.

Scotland	
Goal-achievement	0 (no)
Ascription	1 (some)
Political relevance	1 (some)
Political influence (GA × AS × PR)	*0 (no)*

Compared to Scotland, the political and functional interdependence (IV1) in Wales reaches profoundly deeper, as here justice and policing have remained reserved to the centre (UKG4). During the passage of the Wales Bill 2017, the UK Government committed to an Independent Expert Advisory Committee for Ongoing Review of the Operation of Justice in Wales, including members of the UK and the Welsh Governments, to advise the Ministry of Justice (MoJ) on the effective delivery of justice in Wales when policies diverge.[112] The Wales Act 2017 further requires the Welsh Government to publish justice impact assessments to improve the transparency over the financial impact of Welsh legislation on the justice system. Accordingly, policy teams from both governments discuss the potential implications of legal measures on each other, as well as compensation payments for the financial consequences caused by actions of one administration (HM Treasury 2015, 4; 2020a, 7). Interestingly, arguing that justice is not devolved to Wales, so far the Welsh Government has refused to make such payments for the costs of Welsh legislation to the MoJ (UKG4, WG10). The devolution of other interconnected responsibilities has increasingly added complexity to the joint legal system and led to ongoing cooperation (DV2) between governments (WG10), as a UK official highlighted: "Everything we do will affect Wales and similarly a lot of the things that the Welsh Government does will affect justice in some ways as well. So, the vast majority of our day to day business relates to Wales."[113] While the Senedd passed its own legislation on matters, such as health, education, social care, and in regard to child welfare, and the Welsh Government finances the Children and Family Courts Advisory and Support Service (CAFCASS), legal aid support and family law (including divorce and civil partnerships) are reserved justice matters (Commission on Justice in Wales 2019, 293). The Welsh Assembly also created new offences, such as the Children (Abolition of Defence of Reasonable Punishment) (Wales) Act 2020 penalising the corporal punishment of children in Wales (but not in England), which need to be imposed by a unified court, justice and prison system. The Independent Expert Advisory Committee for Ongoing Review of the Operation of Justice in Wales (2019, 5), which was set up by the MoJ to coordinate the increasing legal divergence, highlighted the mutual impact of policies and legislation on both administrations:[114]

> It is vital, therefore, under the current devolution settlement, that in order for justice to be delivered effectively in England and Wales, there is a close and collaborative relationship between devolved and reserved

authorities. There must be clear mechanisms in place to ensure that the interface, in terms of justice, between reserved and devolved matters is identified and managed appropriately by MoJ and the Welsh Government.

At operational level, the Welsh Government maintains good relations to the MoJ and the Home Office for the delivery of police services (UKG4, WG2, WG10). Yet, in case of political disagreement, the UK Government can in principle direct hierarchically leaving the Welsh Government with little strategic power (IV4) to engage in severe conflicts (DV3). In February 2011, for instance, the Police Reform and Social Responsibility Bill introduced Police and Crime Commissioners and advisory committees (Police and Crime Panels) in local authorities across England and Wales. The Welsh Government opposed the new system and argued that the bill's requirement for local authorities to set up the advisory committees was a devolved responsibility. For the first time, the Welsh Assembly withhold consent to a UK bill. The bill was subsequently amended to reflect the formal allocation of powers, which would suggest some formal influence of the Welsh Government (WG8). In practice, the UK Government still established Police and Crime Commissioners and Panels (UKG7, WP4), only now the panel members were appointed by the UK Home Secretary and not by local authorities (Cowie 2018a, 47). When the UK Government enforced public budget cuts as part of its austerity agenda, the funding and eligibility for legal aid support was another controversial matter. The Welsh Government was against the reduction of legal aid and the replacement of physical access to courts located within Wales through online services:

> The legal aid legislation imposed a wide range of cuts and reduced not only the funding available but the eligibility and all of that. We've argued that there are particular challenges in Wales around rural areas. For instance, legal aid is reduced, various legal practices across Wales have become less viable, there are fewer services being offered by solicitors in rural areas, and this is a particular issue for Wales because of its rural nature.
>
> (WG10)

Whereas the Commission on Justice in Wales (2019, 10) also concluded that cuts to legal aid "have hit Wales hard" and access to justice is not sufficiently provided in rural areas, the UK Government argued that it is a spending decision that did not affect Wales differently than England (UKG4).

Turning to criminal justice and prison services, policy divergence across England and Wales has caused increasing complications in intergovernmental relations. The five prisons located in Wales are run by the UK Government.[115] Because Wales lacks certain prison facilities, such as high security or female-only prisons, the prisoner population cannot be strictly separated between Welsh and English inhabitants, many offenders from England are imprisoned in Wales and vice versa (Welsh Affairs Committee 2019d, 5–6). With Wales having one of the highest prison population per head in Western Europe, the Welsh Government seeks to spend more money on crime reduction than on prison services (Commission on Justice in Wales 2019, 11) and designed its education, social and health services, and health and drug prevention policies to reduce criminal activities and enable the rehabilitation of prisoners. But the Senedd has no power over the overall imprisonment strategy nor over infrastructure planning and maintenance. Policing, prison and probation services, as well as the overall rehabilitation measures are controlled by the MoJ (WG2) (op. cit., 55). Although the Welsh Government has strongly disagreed with the UK Government over the need and usefulness of new prisons in Wales (UKG4, WG10), the UK and the Welsh Governments needed to closely coordinate the building of HM Prison Berwyn in North Wales – not least to identify a suitable location in Wales – which was opened in 2017 to become the largest prison in the UK. A Welsh official described the different views as the following:

> We've been very clear that the Welsh Government's policy on prison is that there should not be any new prisons in Wales. [...] But the UK Government has made it very clear quite recently that they are still actively wanting a new prison in Wales. [...] Those fundamental big decisions are very difficult and that's where you get a lot of contention because the UK Government is it within its rights to decide where a prison should be and if it can work its way through and if it can work its way through the system to get that prison built, then that's it. But in the Welsh Government's view the sighting is something in Wales, assuming that you get through planning policies which are set in Wales, has not only enormous impact not only in terms of our policy on prison population generally, but also in terms of the impact on that location, wherever it is.
>
> (WG10)

To ensure that both governments consider each other's interests and responsibilities when designing and exercising their respective policies related to justice, prison and related services, in June 2018 the Ministry of Justice (2018) together with the Welsh Government published a concordat providing working-level guidance for intergovernmental consultation and cooperation. The concordat sets out that representatives of each government attend each other's internal meetings, and set up integrated project teams, working groups, committees or meetings, such as the Justice in Wales Strategy Group.[116] Through the joint negotiated agreement, the UK Government has committed itself to closer cooperation (DV2) on the basis of mutual consent, as a UK official suggested:

The concordat was a very significant turning point because fundamentally, the desire behind it, the need to work more closely together, engage early, all the principals in the concordat, everyone knows that that was a good idea. Inevitably there's always some reluctance to put something down formally in writing, when we managed to get ministers on both sides to agree on this, and something you can't point to know, is very helpful in a number of reasons. One of them is very helpful to us, as a devolution team. We can point to it and say, whenever there's late engagement, or they haven't really thought through the devolution implications, we can use that document and say: 'MoJ has signed up to this and this says: you should engage early'.

(UKG4)

The change in working relations to coordinate diverging policy approaches on criminal justice issues is reflected in the Blueprints for delivery of Female Offending and Youth Justice services. Before Boris Johnson became Prime Minister in July 2019, the MoJ aimed at reducing short-term sentences for minor offences to under six months, which was supported by the Welsh Government. The ministers and officials from the Welsh Government and the UK Government, together with HM Prison and Probation Service and policing in Wales, were "very keen" to agree on the aims of the two blueprints (UKG4). While the Female Offending Blueprint for Wales sets out the "gender-specific needs of women, promotes positive wellbeing and supports successful long-term outcomes to reduce reoffending" (Ministry of Justice and Welsh Government 2019a), the Youth Justice Blueprint for Wales "aims to improve criminal and social outcomes for children in contact with the youth justice system and to support them to develop resilience and to fulfil their potential" (Ministry of Justice and Welsh Government 2019b).[117]

Despite such initiatives, the Welsh Affairs Committee (2019d, 9–15) concluded that the different political positions and limited understanding of Welsh policies within the MoJ remain an ongoing challenge that required "a new framework for closer cooperation and integration in the provision of prison services, with clear points of contact". The Commission on Justice in Wales (2019, 10), also known as the Thomas Commission,[118] also criticised the lack of a coherent arrangement to coordinate the actions of the UK and the Welsh Governments,[119] and even suggested a legislative devolution of justice (Commission on Justice in Wales 2019, 25). This has been a strong preference for the Welsh Government. Though acquiring control over justice and policing would enable the integration of different relevant services in Wales, the UK Government has argued that the policies were not sufficiently diverging to justify a transfer of competence, and that crime in particular was a cross-border issue which requires a coherent approach. Instead, the MoJ has provided advice on the implications of new Welsh legislation and the consistency of sentencing for offences across England and Wales

(UKG4, UKG7). Due to their limited strategic power (IV4) on such constitutional matters, and despite their differences and the risk of undermining its claim for the devolution of justice, the Welsh Government continues to cooperate (DV2) closely with and seeks to learn from the MoJ to increase its own capability. Whereas the Welsh Government could not impact the UK Government's decisions about Police and Crime Commissioners and Panels, the support for legal aid services and the devolution of justice and policing, overall, when it comes to criminal justice and related areas it has opportunities to exercise *substantial* political influence on outcomes that affect Wales (WG2, WG10).

Wales	
Goal-achievement	1 (some)
Ascription	2 (substantial)
Political relevance	2 (substantial)
Political influence ($GA \times AS \times PR$)	4 (substantial)

Conclusion

This chapter has covered a wide range of intergovernmental dynamics, including major constitutional issues and the multilevel dynamics of leaving the EU; as well as foreign relations and international trade; immigration; spending, taxation and borrowing decisions; agriculture and food; environment, energy and climate change; economic development; transport, public health; and justice and policing. As more powers were devolved to Scotland and Wales, and Brexit required new UK-wide coordination of many policy areas previously governed by the EU's regulatory regime, intergovernmental relations have evolved substantially over the last decade. While the relations between the centre and the devolved governments have been severely strained, the different examples also demonstrated that the administrations cooperate (DV2) on many issues. Whether they interacted with each other was dependent foremost on their functional and political interdependence (IV1), as well as on their preference intensity (IV2). Since the investigated period was characterised by party incongruency (IV3) across the different levels, the strategic power (IV4) of the Scottish and Welsh Governments played a significant role in their willingness and need to cooperate (DV2) with the UK Government. In turn, the latter was interested in avoiding conflict (DV3) when it relied on the former to realise its policies or was concerned about the political consequences of not appealing to the electorate in Scotland and Wales. When policy priorities are too divergent and the UK Government is vested in a particular political cause, Whitehall can and will ultimately act unilaterally or direct hierarchically regardless of vetoes from the devolved legislatures. On issues, such as the EU (Withdrawal Agreement) Act 2020, the Internal Market Bill and immigration policy, the Scottish and

Welsh Governments had *no* impact despite being profoundly affected by the outcome of the centre's actions. And yet, this chapter also found that the devolved administrations have often exercised *substantial* (though rarely *great*) political influence on decisions by the UK Government.

Notes

1. Downing Street also responded that "the PM has always supported devolution, but Tony Blair failed to foresee the rise of separatists in Scotland" (BBC 2020b).
2. A state where levels of government do not attempt to coordinate their policies or are indifferent about policymaking at the other level.
3. When governments stand in competition with each other and pursue diverging outcomes contrary to the other's interests.
4. Here, governments work together to achieve common goals by exchanging information, pooling resources or by coordinating their legislation and implementation of policies.
5. Based on the research of negotiations about territorial change by Petersohn et al. (2015), and building on Scharpf's (1997) actor-centred institutionalism.
6. As Chapter 4 has demonstrated, the existing intergovernmental institutions do not provide for *decisions by majority vote* but for *unilateral actions* by governments and *hierarchical direction* by the centre.
7. Ego-perception (E) refers to player A's own perception of their level of influence (here the Scottish and Welsh Governments), and is compared with alter-perception (A) of player B-to-Z (the UK Government, other devolved governments, opposition parties and other stakeholders), as well as with the researcher's analysis (R).
8. If a decision is perceived as a key issue, binding on stakeholders, and bears a high level of controversy, the political relevance is considered to be high.
9. Prior to the 2016 Scotland Act the Scottish Parliament only had some minor competences around social security allocated to local authorities; including the housing benefits and the Scottish Welfare Fund. Under the 2016 Act, the powers of the Scottish Parliament in the area of social security and care have increased substantially. It can create new benefits for specific elements in regard to carers' allowance and disability benefits, but also for winter fuel payments and funeral support payments. The social security benefits covered by new competences add up to around £3 billion. Major welfare benefits, such as Universal Credit, pensions, child benefits, job seeker allowance and employment benefits, remain reserved but can be raised by the Scottish Government (UKG5).
10. How the devolution of new fiscal powers played out will be examined at a later stage.
11. For a detailed comparison between the recommendations of the Smith Commission and the initial proposals by the UK Government see the full report.
12. A position that has been much clearer for the Scottish Government since 2007.
13. Rather than being a blueprint for the future development of the UK, Reforming Our Union was sought to stimulate public debate based on 20 propositions (WG6).
14. These include reports by the Public Administration and Constitutional Affairs Committee (2018a), the Scottish Affairs Committee (2019a), the JMC Joint Secretariat (2018), the Dunlop Review (Cabinet Office 2021a) and the Centre on Constitutional Change together with the Bennett Institute (McEwen et al. 2018). For instance, the JMC Joint Secretariat (2018, 21) and the

222 *Patterns of Interaction and Political Influence*

      Scottish Affairs Committee (2019a, 19–20) proposed an independent secretary and legally binding requirements for the Joint Ministerial Committee, and the Dunlop Review (Cabinet Office 2021a) suggested an Intergovernmental Council.

15 Other acts that deal with the implications of EU withdrawal, including the Trade Act 2021, Agriculture Act, the Immigration and Social Security Co-ordination (EU Withdrawal) Act 2020, the Environmental Act and the Healthcare (European Economic Area and Switzerland Arrangements) Act 2019, are discussed in greater detail as examples for the different policy areas.

16 See also the Legislative Consent Memorandum of the Welsh Government (Welsh Parliament 2020c).

17 A final proposal by SNP and Plaid Cymru MPs, reflecting the Scottish Government's position, to remove any provisions that would allow the UK Government to control retained EU law was not adopted in the bill (Cowie 2018b).

18 Even though many of these did not require substantial changes (SG8, SP1, SP4, SP3), the implementation of statutory instruments was still a burdensome exercise and created a vast array of new functions to the devolved administrations was more than simply a box-ticking exercise (WG7, WP1). As the Welsh Government (2019c, 4) reported: "This has placed an unprecedented demand on both the Welsh Government and the National Assembly to draft, consider, consent to, scrutinise and pass legislation within extremely tight timescales."

19 Subsequently, some non-critical amendments to the existing statutory instruments were made before the end of the extended transition period on 31 October 2019.

20 According to the Supreme Court: "The UK Parliament has the power to authorise Ministers to make subordinate legislation, but the effect of section 17 would be to make the legal effect of such subordinate legislation conditional upon the consent of the Scottish Ministers. The imposition of this condition would be inconsistent with the recognition in section 28(7) of the Scotland Act that the UK Parliament has unqualified legislative power in Scotland. It would therefore have to be treated as impliedly amending (and thus modifying) section 28(7) of the Scotland Act."

21 *R (Miller) v Secretary of State for Exiting the European Union* [2017], para. 151: "In reaching this conclusion we do not underestimate the importance of constitutional conventions, some of which play a fundamental role in the operation of our constitution. The Sewel Convention has an important role in facilitating harmonious relationships between the UK Parliament and the devolved legislatures. But the policing of its scope and the manner of its operation does not lie within the constitutional remit of the judiciary, which is to protect the rule of law." The Supreme Court (para. 86) also ruled that leaving the EU was not to be treated as royal prerogative exercised by the UK Government, but "inextricably linked with domestic law" and therefore needed approval by an Act of the UK Parliament.

22 Examples hereof are The Future UK/EU Relationship: Negotiating Priorities for Wales (Welsh Government 2020d) and the Scotland's Place in Europe series covering different thematic areas (Scottish Government 2021a).

23 Clause 22 of the EU (Withdrawal Agreement) Bill amended the EU (Withdrawal) Act 2018 and provided the devolved administrations powers either unilaterally or together with UK ministers, to enact the Northern Ireland Protocol with secondary legislations regulations (Torrance 2019).

24 While the changed circumstances have made it more likely that the former would freeze competences of the latter, the UK Government did not impose any restriction on retained EU law on the devolved legislatures (Department for Levelling Up, Housing and Communities and Cabinet Office 2021).

25 The Scottish Parliament withheld its consent to the bill on 8 January and the Senedd on 21 January 2020. The Northern Ireland Assembly and Executive had just been restored when the bill went through the House of Commons in January 2020 and did not give its consent either (Cowie et al. 2020, 75).
26 Concerns were in particular about the negative effect on the Welsh agri-food, aerospace, automotive and service sectors, as well as about the continuing participation in EU policy programmes.
27 In areas such as trade in goods and in services, digital trade, intellectual property, public procurement, aviation and road transport, energy, fisheries, social security coordination, law enforcement and judicial cooperation in criminal matters, thematic cooperation and participation in Union programmes.
28 The Frameworks Project Teams continued to support the development of the various Common Frameworks at operational level, while UK Government-Devolved Administrations Framework Project Board brought senior officials together to monitor the progress of the frameworks. DEFRA, for instance, set up working groups for Animal Health and Welfare, Plant Health, Waste, Chemicals and Pesticides, and Fisheries held regular meetings (Cabinet Office 2020b).
29 The EU (Withdrawal) Act 2018 required the UK Government to publish quarterly reports on the frameworks' progress.
30 Three under BEIS, one under the Department of Health and Social Care, and one under the Food Standards Agency.
31 See Department of Health and Social Care (2020a).
32 See Ministry of Housing, Communities and Local Government (2020).
33 See Department of Health and Social Care (2020b).
34 As Michael Russell, the Scottish Cabinet Secretary for Government Business and Constitutional Relations at the time, described the change of attitudes in the UK Government: "Once that [Boris] Johnson gang had taken over, it made no difference at all. And I think the difference between the May and Johnson administration[s] is that there was a recognition under May, no matter how limited and grudging, of the legitimate interests of the devolved governments and their rights, whereas there was nothing but contempt for devolution from the Johnson government, expressed at every level even by the territorial secretaries of state." (Paun and Nice 2022).
35 In its Legislative Consent Memorandum to the Internal Market Bill, the Scottish Government states: "30. The Scottish Government withdrew from the BEIS-led internal market project in March 2019. It did so because it was obvious at that point that the UK Government was not prepared to take into account the arguments the Scottish Government had presented, based on legal, economic and academic evidence, that the mechanisms agreed in individual framework areas – as well as existing provision in the devolution statutes – are sufficient to address any internal market issues that might emerge on EU exit. It became clear that the UK Government approach to work on the UK internal market presented a clear risk to the devolution settlement." (Scottish Parliament 2020b)
36 Parts 1-3 of the bill deal with market access for goods and services, and the recognition of professional qualifications. Part 4 establishes the Competition and Markets Authority (CMA) to advise and monitor the UK Internal Market. Part 5 deals with the access of goods from Northern Ireland to the rest of the UK. Controversially, the bill aimed at giving UK ministers powers to prevent the application or disapply parts of the Northern Ireland Protocol relating to trade and state aid. Part 6 enabled the UK Government to directly fund a wide range of purposes in all four nations of the UK. Lastly, Part 7 provided the UK Parliament with the exclusive right to legislate on distorting or harmful subsidies (Torrance et al. 2020, 7).

37 In the event that provisions are made that impinge on the Withdrawal Agreement, the European Commission would be able to take the UK before the Court of Justice of the EU.
38 Following concerns over the teaching standards in Wales, school teaching was removed from the *automatic recognition of professional qualifications principle* (Part 3, Section 27). The Lords' amendments limited the Secretary of State's powers to change the scope and application of the bill through secondary legislation subject to adding reporting duties on Part 1 and 2 and requiring the devolved legislatures' consent within a period of one month after announcement. Part 4 of the bill now provided a consultative role for the devolved administrations in relation to the functions and working of the newly created Competition and Markets Authority responsible for monitoring the internal market, and for the appointment of the Office for the Internal Market (OIM). Because the UK Government had reached an agreement with the EU over the implementation of the Withdrawal Agreement, controversial provisions in Part 5 of the bill that allowed UK ministers to override the Northern Ireland Protocol were also removed (Owen and Valsamidis 2020).
39 BEIS only committed itself to annual ministerial meetings with the devolved administrations to discuss the UK Internal Market system.
40 As West Wales qualified as a 'less developed' region (below 75 per cent of the average EU per capita GDP) in the EU, Wales received by far the most assistance from EU Structural Funds, followed by Scotland (Nice 2018).
41 In the absence of the Northern Ireland Assembly, funding for this part will be overseen by the UK Government.
42 An essential part of its international activities are the offices in Beijing, Berlin, Brussels, Dublin, London, Ottawa, Paris and Washington DC which seek to raise Scotland's international profile and foster investments and business relations in the EU and beyond (External Affairs Directorate 2019).
43 International Trade and Investment Directorate (2019).
44 Economic Development Directorate (2017).
45 Its international offices are located in New York, Washington DC, Atlanta, Chicago, San Francisco, Montreal, Dublin, Paris, Brussels, Dusseldorf, Berlin and London, Chongqing, Beijing and Shanghai, New Delhi, Mumbai and Bangalore, Tokyo, Dubai and Doha (Welsh Government 2020e).
46 Welsh Government (2020c).
47 Welsh Government (2020d).
48 The international relations of substate governments take many forms, depending on the aspirations and allocation of powers across different levels of government, and can be subsumed under the term 'paradiplomacy'. Central and decentralised government can act cooperatively, integrated, parallel in harmony or in disharmony. For a detailed discussion, see Schiavon (2019, 5 et seq.).
49 In their 2019 election manifesto, the SNP announced: "The trade deal the Tories plan with Donald Trump also risks opening the NHS up to US multinational companies. It risks opening our markets to chlorinated chicken and hormone injected beef." In March 2020, the Welsh Government stated: "We now need to be fully involved in negotiations to ensure Welsh interests are protected and promises made about our NHS, food standards and other areas are honoured." (Morgan 2020).
50 For a list of all agreements, see Department for International Trade (2021).
51 The Trade Act also conferred powers to implement the Agreement on Government Procurement (GPA) between the UK and other states providing mutual access to public procurement markets (Clause 1) and established the Trade Remedies Authority (TRA) to assist the UK Government in relation to international trade policy and disputes (Clauses 9 and 10).

52 In light of the Corona pandemic, the Scottish Migration Minister asked the UK Home Secretary again for a different approach: "[...] the COVID-19 pandemic and resulting economic shock should provide an important opportunity to reconsider the UK Government's overall aim of reducing levels of inward migration into the UK, which even before the COVID-19 pandemic was projected to have a deeply damaging impact on Scotland. [...] It is abundantly clear that reducing migrant numbers will detrimentally impact on many sectors and industries that are particularly key to Scotland and the other Devolved Governments, including social care, agriculture, food processing, manufacturing, construction and tourism." (External Affairs Directorate 2020a).

53 Only the consent of the Northern Ireland Assembly was required and given on 28 September 2020.

54 The protocol on dispute avoidance and resolution of the MoU guides ministers and senior officials through intergovernmental conflicts. According to the Statement of Funding Policy (HM Treasury 2020a, 8): "If there is a disagreement between HM Treasury and the devolved administrations about the application of the Statement, the relevant devolved administration can pursue the matter with HM Treasury. This is the normal procedure for resolving disputes on all financial issues and mirrors the arrangements between HM Treasury and United Kingdom departments."

55 The funding was ring-fended for infrastructure development (£200 million for 2 years); health service transformation (£100 million for 2 years); broadband development (£75 million for 2 years); immediate pressures in health and education (£50 million for 2 years); pockets of severe deprivation (£75 million for 5 years) and mental health (£100 million for 5 years); and could only be spent on these purposes (Muthumala and Keep 2018).

56 According to an official of the Welsh Government: "The system we have, the Barnet Formula, was invented in ad hoc way for a temporary solution that's lasted for 40 years because nobody can find a way of replacing it that doesn't cause huge arguments." (WG11).

57 The limits to the borrowing capacities of the Scottish Government were set at 15 per cent of an overall borrowing cap of £3 billion for capital expenditure (HM Government and Scottish Government 2016). The Scottish Government argues that the borrowing limits cannot compensate adequately for the volatility of the Fiscal Framework (SG9).

58 In June 2020 during the Corona pandemic, the Scottish Government again called for a higher borrowing limit of £500 million per year and more flexibility in the handling of its capital borrowing powers to support economic recovery (BBC 2020g).

59 The land transaction tax (former stamp duty land tax) and the landfill disposals tax (former landfill tax) came into effect from 2018/19 and the powers over Welsh business rates from 2019/2020 on.

60 Air passenger duty came into effect in 1994 as a levy on passenger flights from UK airports (Welsh Affairs Committee 2019a, 4).

61 A report issued by UK Government concluded that reducing air passenger duty would have detrimental effects on Bristol airport, which was challenged by a report commissioned by the Welsh Government (Northpoint 2017).

62 "In the case of APD devolution, the UK government remains concerned about the competitive impact of introducing tax competition within a single aviation market. We consider Cardiff and Bristol airports to serve the same market. This is consistent with State aid guidelines which consider airports to operate in the same market if they are within 63 miles of each other. Cardiff and Bristol are within 60 miles of each other by road. While it would be for the Welsh Government to decide whether to reduce rates if the power was devolved, previous statements from Welsh ministers have indicated that they

consider control of APD as an opportunity to promote Cardiff airport. This will naturally have an impact on Bristol airport, Cardiff's closest competitor, and to a lesser extent other English airports. [...] In the case of APD, the aviation markets in Northern Ireland and Scotland are fundamentally different to that in Wales, and as such warrant a different approach to devolution. [...] The merits of the case for devolution of APD in Wales should therefore be considered independently of the case in the other nations. [...] Our primary concern is to ensure the best outcome for businesses and consumers on both sides of the border. We do not believe introducing tax competition in this market will be beneficial overall and therefore have no current plans to change APD policy." (Welsh Affairs Committee 2019b).

63 Of course, not every policy team within DEFRA is equally engaged in devolved affairs.

64 See letter from Fergus Ewing, Scottish Cabinet Secretary for the Rural Economy (2018), to the UK Secretary of State for Environment, Food and Rural Affairs, Michael Gove.

65 As large quantities of Scottish and Welsh beef and sheep are processed in England, the levy is collected and distributed by the UK Agriculture and Horticulture Development Board instead of by the Meat Promotion Wales and Quality Meat Scotland.

66 The Constitutional and Legislative Affairs Committee reported (Welsh Parliament 2020i):

> "33.[...] The position arrived at with clause 28 – and the Bill as a whole – presents a significant transfer of power which prevents the National Assembly from holding the Welsh Government to account in a way that is constitutionally appropriate. The Bilateral Agreement, negotiated by the Minister, would not be our chosen model for the future and we do not believe it is a good outcome.
>
> 34. In our view, the Bilateral Agreement appears to provide the UK Government with all the power. Despite the processes for co-operation and consultation set out in the Bilateral Agreement, the Secretary of State will have the final say on draft regulations. In making Part 7 regulations, it is the UK Parliament that will discharge the scrutiny duty, despite it not having done so in the area of Welsh agriculture policy for 20 years, whereas the National Assembly does not have a role. As stated in our first report, the National Assembly's scrutiny function is being bypassed, which is a situation we find constitutionally unacceptable."

67 When the head of Food and Drink of the Scottish Government gave evidence to the UK Parliament (2020), he expressed his concern about the powers given to the UK Secretary of State in relation to livestock information provision, organic products, the WTO agreement on agriculture and fair dealing in supply chains, which would interfere in devolved matters.

68 The clause on organic products was changed to refer not only to the Secretary of State as the authority to make regulations but also to Scottish and Welsh ministers and DAERA (Department of Agriculture, Environment and Rural Affairs) of the Northern Ireland Executive (Clause 41(1)). The Secretary of State can now only make regulations on organic products that affect the devolved administration with their consent (Clause 41(2)).

69 The Scottish and UK Governments could also resolve the outstanding issues the identification and traceability of animals (Clause 32(1)) (Scottish Parliament 2020d). The former also successfully pointed out that WTO reports could be managed by existing provisions, as the devolution settlements already covered reporting duties on international obligations (UKG2).

70 These concerned amendments tabled by the UK Government on the identification and traceability of animals (Clause 32) and the regulation of organic products (Clause 37). In addition, in the House of Lords, provisions were changed in regard to the WTO classification of domestic support (Clause 42) and commencement (Clause 53). Provisions under Schedule 5 of the previous bill to replace direct payments with payments for public goods were also dropped for Wales.

71 Schedule 6 of the Agriculture Bill extended similar powers that apply in England to Northern Ireland to ensure the continuity of agriculture support payments, and to regulate intervention in agricultural markets; collection and sharing of data; and marketing standards, organic products and carcass classification (Coe and Finlay 2020, 75). The Northern Ireland Assembly gave it consent to the Bill in March 2020.

72 For instance, the UK Government controls energy efficiency in public procurement, the energy infrastructure and licensing for oil and gas, coal mining and nuclear energy (SG8, SP3, UKG8). Devolved powers include the promotion of renewable energy and energy efficiency, onshore oil and gas licensing, and nuclear waste storage. The Scottish Government is responsible for building and maintenance of energy infrastructure and can refuse the building of new nuclear power plants. For a detailed overview see Cairney et al. (2019, 460–462).

73 This includes Clauses 17 to 19 on policy statement on environmental principles; Clauses 50 and 51 on producer responsibility; Clauses 52 and 53 on resource efficiency; Clauses 74 to 77 on the recall of motor vehicles; Clauses 89 and 93 on water quality and Clause 92 on the Solway Tweed river basin district. There are a series of Clauses that apply to England and Wales but not to Scotland.

74 The bill provides specific provisions for environmental governance, managing waste and water quality in Northern Ireland. Under Clauses 45, 56, 58, 62, 64, 68 and 83 and Part 2 of the bill, the UK Government took on board the request of the Permanent Secretary of Northern Ireland's Department for Agriculture, Environment and Rural Affairs (DAERA) to extend the scope of the Environment Bill to Northern Ireland (Smith and Priestley 2020, 19–20). The bill also established the Office for Environmental Protection (OEP) to operate in England and Northern Ireland.

75 As well as with the Northern Ireland Civil Service and Executive.

76 The Northern Ireland Assembly gave its consent on 30 June 2020 and again on 20 September 2021.

77 Such 'forest risk commodities' include foods such as beef, soya, palm oil and cocoa. The provisions are based on a recommendation of the Global Resource Initiative Taskforce commissioned by the UK Government in 2019.

78 In the supplementary memorandum of 9 July 2021, the Scottish Government "believe[s] that the UK Government's proposed amendments on environmental principles do not simply address a purported gap, which in any case we do not believe exists. The UK Government's amendments also change the previously agreed approach by disapplying the Scottish guiding principles on the environment when UK Ministers are acting in reserved areas in Scotland, and replacing them with the principles set by UK Government Ministers." (Net Zero, Energy and Transport Committee 2021).

79 Including the European Union (Continuity) (Scotland) Bill and Law Derived from the European Union (Wales) Bill.

80 Respondents from Scotland and Wales said: "All of them have an element of Scotland and UK responsibility or at least political interest, and there's quite often some fuzzy areas where Scottish responsibility and UK responsibility starts and stops." (SG14).

"The economies of Wales and England are heavily interlinked. Some of the stuff the Welsh Government does on its own but a lot of the stuff is either jointly with the UK Government or is a response to working ahead of the UK Government policy." (WP3).

81 In the absence of the Northern Ireland Assembly, city and growth deals followed only at a late stage in Northern Ireland during March 2019. The Belfast City Region Deal consists of 22 projects across innovation and digital, Tourism-led regeneration, and infrastructure funded by a total amount of £850 million. While the UK Government spends £350 million over 15 years on innovation and digital pillar, Northern Ireland Executive uses the same amount to fund tourism led regeneration and infrastructure projects (Ward 2020, 17). In February 2021, the heads of terms of Derry and Strabane City Region Deal were signed to provide a total investment of up to £250 million (Northern Ireland Office 2021).

82 The Borderlands Inclusive Growth Deal stretches across the South of Scotland and the North of England (Dumfries and Galloway, Scottish Borders, Carlisle City, Cumbria, Northumberland) and cover digital, energy, place, destination, mountain biking, business infrastructure, knowledge exchange, land and marine, and transport.

83 In comparison to the Scottish deals, in Wales the separation between reserved and devolved responsibilities has not informed the allocation of funding for different elements of the projects (except for the Cardiff deal). It was also mentioned that the Welsh local authorities within a designated area were not always in agreement amongst themselves about the focus of their deals (WG6).

84 The ten local authorities are Blaenau Gwent; Bridgend; Caerphilly; Cardiff; Merthyr Tydfil; Monmouthshire; Newport; Rhondda Cynon Taff; Torfaen and Vale of Glamorgan. £734 million of a total of £1.2 billion are designated for a new metro network for South East Wales. However, the UK and Welsh Governments had not signed off on every project of the Cardiff Deal and a large part of the funding will only be released after five years when the city region has passed the gateway review process.

85 Whereas the Cardiff Deal was driven by the vision of a modernised metro system, the Swansea Bay Deal presents a collection of individual projects (WG6). The four local authorities had started some of the projects even during the negotiation phase without guarantees that the UK and the Welsh Governments would fund them. Unlike for Cardiff, the Swansea Deal also does not require a gateway review but the whole funding was granted from the start without an allocation according to devolved and reserved responsibilities (WP7).

86 Joint Committee of all six local authorities, two Colleges, two Universities and the Private Sector in North Wales.

87 The seven programmes focus on low-carbon energy; advanced manufacturing; land-based industries and tourism; land and property; skills and employment; digital; strategic transport.

88 This covers public service vehicle operator licensing, safety issues, roadworthiness, vehicle excise duty (road tax), licensing and registration, main road traffic offences and transport accessibility.

89 In 2005, Transport Scotland was established as an executive agency, and merged with the Transport Directorate of the Scottish Government in 2010. Ten years later, the Welsh Government set up Transport for Wales to give support and advice on transport projects (Butcher 2017, 4; 14).

90 While many aspects of transport are similar for Wales and Scotland, Northern Ireland is fairly self-contained for geographical reasons and the Department for Infrastructure of the Northern Ireland Executive enjoys more autonomy over transport policy and planning, including the railway (UKG9) (Butcher 2017, 16).

91 Rail services that operate across Scotland and England are tendered by the UK Government in consultation with the Scottish Government (UKG9). Since 2013, the UK and the Scottish Governments have worked together in the identification of potential high-speed rail routes to Scotland as part of the High Speed 2 North network. In the course of the cooperation, both governments agreed to develop a joint Business Case for High Speed Rail infrastructure in Scotland adding a short high-speed link between Glasgow and Edinburgh (SG15) (Transport Scotland 2016). In 2017, the Scottish Government CP6 rail settlement offered a grant of £3.75 billion to the Scottish Government for investments in rail infrastructure (which was raised from the initial offer of £1.5 billion) (HM Treasury 2017).

92 Managing the implication of the Coronavirus on public transport also led to an exceptionally intense exchange at official and ministerial levels, for instance to ensure some consistency in the transport guidance for passengers.

93 For policy priorities see Transport for Wales (2017) and Welsh Government (2019d).

94 Article 12 of the agreement also sets out the establishment of a Joint Strategic Board to discuss and cooperate on the operation and development of the franchise.

95 Estimated costs in 2018 were at £1.4 billion, which would have exhausted the Welsh Government's borrowing capacities.

96 These included the reduction of car emissions, as well as the protection of the Gwent Levels nature reservoir.

97 "Cabinet concluded that, in light of the cost of the Project, other demands and potential demands on the Welsh Government's capital budget, and uncertainty as to the financial position of the Welsh Government, the cost of the Project, and its consequential impact on other capital investment priorities, was not acceptable. Accordingly, the Welsh Government's position is that it will not provide funding for the Project." (First Minister of Wales 2019, 5.1).

98 Northern Ireland has its own Health and Safety Executive (SG7).

99 The Scotland Office played an important role in encouraging the Cabinet Office and other UK Government Departments to work with the Scottish Government to get their expertise and consent (UKG5).

100 For an overview of the different provisions, see Haddon et al. (2020).

101 In 2018, the Welsh and UK Governments (together with NHS England and NHS Wales) produced a non-binding Joint Statement of Values and Principles on how the two health services should work together: "the principles set out in this document and recognise that English and Welsh residents are legally entitled to be treated in accordance with the rights of their country of residence." (Welsh Government 2018).

102 The annual number of 20,000 patients from northeast Wales treated in the Countess of Chester hospital makes up about one-fifth of the hospital's workload (BBC 2019).

103 Clauses 1 and 2 relate to payments and arrangements for payments to be made in respect of the cost of healthcare provided outside the UK. Clause 4 provides a basis for facilitating data processing to support the making of payments or provision for payments to be made.

104 In contrast to the UK Government, the Welsh Government also believed that Clause 5 would require consent because it provided the UK Government with powers to amend, repeal or revoke primary legislation of the devolved legislatures and to confer functions to the UK Secretary of State.

105 In the Legislative Consent Memorandum of 18 November, the Cabinet Secretary for Health and Social Services reported: "There are therefore outstanding concerns about the extent to which the Welsh Government will be involved

in informing and shaping the healthcare agreements to be delivered under the Bill which will impact on the NHS in Wales. Whether or not legislative consent should be given, therefore, needs to be considered in light of legislative and non-legislative assurances given by the UK Government to ensure that the Welsh Government is involved in matters that affect devolved areas in Wales." (Welsh Parliament 2020m).
106 Previously Clause 5(3).
107 Due to its suspension, the Northern Ireland Assembly did not pass a Legislative Consent Motion but the Northern Ireland Department of Health "signified its support for the provisions in the Act in so far as they related to devolved matters."
108 The situation is similar in Northern Ireland.
109 In 2018, Scotland counted over 1,136 alcohol-specific deaths and 1,187 drug-related deaths (Scottish Government 2019d).
110 For instance, the classification and control of 'controlled drugs' is reserved.
111 See the Scottish Government's strategy to improve health by preventing and reducing alcohol and drug use, harm and related deaths (Population Health Directorate 2018).
112 The first report was published in July 2019 (Ministry of Justice 2019).
113 The Independent Expert Advisory Committee for Ongoing Review of the Operation of Justice in Wales (2019, 5) also stated: "Justice is perhaps one of the areas with greatest level of interaction between devolved and reserved matters. For example, not only must healthcare and education be provided to those in prison or other forms of detention, but often devolved matters have a significant bearing on the root causes of offending at an early stage: family and social life, substance misuse and other health issues as well as education. Similarly, most devolved policies rely on the justice system in order to ensure they work effectively: from the civil disputes over housing to criminal offences relating to devolved matters, Assembly legislation is likely to impact the justice system to some degree and legal professionals, the judiciary and the general public will need to be aware of the different approaches taken in Wales and in England."
114 To consider the administrative and practical implications of legislation by the Welsh Assembly, MoJ and the Wales Office established the Justice in Wales Working Group within the UK Government.
115 Cardiff, Parc near Bridgend, Swansea Usk/Prescoed in Monmouthshire, and the Berwyn 'super prison' in Wrexham.
116 For an overview of committees, boards and groups of the criminal justice system in Wales see Commission on Justice in Wales (2019, 137–139).
117 The Youth Justice Blueprint was based on the Social Services and Well-being (Wales) Act 2014 and the Well-being of Future Generations (Wales) Act 2015.
118 Named after the former Lord Chief Justice, Lord Thomas.
119 "In criminal justice there is no overall alignment of policy and spending which is essential if the criminal justice system is to be effective in reducing crime and promoting rehabilitation. Instead the arrangements for coordination between devolved and non-devolved bodies are overly complex, are expensive and do not provide transparent accountability for effective performance."

Bibliography

Adam, Elisenda C. (2021) *Brexit and the Mechanisms for the Resolution of Conflicts in the Context of Devolution: Do We Need a New Model?* In: Doyle, Oran, McHarg, Aileen and Murkens, Jo (eds.) *The Brexit Challenge for Ireland and the United Kingdom: Constitutions Under Pressure*. Cambridge: Cambridge University Press, pp. 43–63.

Ambrose, Jillian (2020) *UK Government Lifts Block on New Onshore Windfarm Subsidies*. 2 March. The Guardian. https://www.theguardian.com/business/2020/mar/02/uk-government-lifts-block-on-new-onshore-windfarm-subsidies

Andrews, Leighton (2021) *The Forward March of Devolution Halted – and the Limits of Progressive Unionism*. The Political Quarterly, Volume 92, Issue 3, pp. 512–521.

Anthony, Chloe (2021) *Mind the Gap: The Fragmentation of UK Environmental Governance Post-Brexit*. Commentary. 28 May. UK in a Changing Europe. https://ukandeu.ac.uk/mind-the-gap-the-fragmentation-of-uk-environmental-governance-post-brexit/

Arts, Bas and Verschuren, Piet (1999) *Assessing Political Influence in Complex Decision-Making: An Instrument Based on Triangulation*. International Political Science Review, Volume 20, Issue 4, pp. 411–424.

Attorney General's Office (2018) *Devolved Brexit Legislation Referred to the Supreme Court*. Press release. 17 April. UK Government. https://www.gov.uk/government/news/devolved-brexit-legislation-referred-to-the-supreme-court

BBC (2018) *Severn Bridges: M4 Severn Crossing Reopens Toll Free*. News. 17 December. https://www.bbc.com/news/uk-wales-46539184

BBC (2020a) *Boris Johnson 'Called Scottish Devolution Disaster'*. News. 17 November. https://www.bbc.com/news/uk-politics-54965585

BBC (2020b) *Devolution Not a Disaster, Says Senedd Tory Leader*. News. 17 November. https://www.bbc.com/news/uk-wales-politics-54973382

BBC (2020c) *Brexit: PM Defends Planned Changes to Withdrawal Agreement*. News. 9 September. https://www.bbc.com/news/uk-politics-54003483

BBC (2020d) *Brexit: UK to Unveil Planned Changes to Withdrawal Agreement*. News. 9 September. https://www.bbc.com/news/uk-politics-54081211

BBC (2020e) *Welsh Tory Quits Senedd Frontbench over Prime Minister's Union Stance*. News. 9 September. https://www.bbc.com/news/uk-wales-politics-54090332

BBC (2020f) *UK Immigration Plans 'Devastating' for Scotland, Says Sturgeon*. News. 19 February. https://www.bbc.com/news/uk-scotland-scotland-politics-51558830

BBC (2020g) *Coronavirus: Scottish Government Calls for New Borrowing Powers*. News. 25 June. https://www.bbc.com/news/uk-scotland-scotland-politics-53178108

BBC (2020h) *M4 Relief Road: UK Ministers 'Could Bypass Welsh Government'*. News. 10 October. https://www.bbc.com/news/uk-wales-politics-54469828

BBC (2020i) *Drug Consumption Rooms Are a 'Distraction' Says UK Minister*. News. 27 February. https://www.bbc.com/news/uk-scotland-5164478

Bell, David, Eiser, David and Phillips, David (2016) *Scotland's Fiscal Framework: Assessing the Agreement*. Working Paper W16/05, March. The Institute for Fiscal Studies. https://ifs.org.uk/uploads/publications/wps/wp201605.pdf

Birrell, Derek (2012) *Comparing Devolved Governance*. Basingstoke: Palgrave Macmillan.

Blackall, Molly (2020) *Boris Johnson Insists He Is Not Opposed to Devolution after 'Disaster' Comment*. 21 November. The Guardian. https://www.theguardian.com/politics/2020/nov/21/boris-johnson-insists-he-is-not-opposed-to-devolution-after-disaster-comment

Boffey, Emma (2019) *Case Comment: The UK Withdrawal from the European Union (Legal Continuity) (Scotland) Bill – A Reference by the Attorney General and the Advocate General for Scotland [2018] UKSC 64*. Blog, 11 January. UK Supreme Court. http://ukscblog.com/case-comment-the-uk-withdrawal-from-the-european-union-legal-continuity-scotland-bill-a-reference-by-the-attorney-general-and-the-advocate-general-for-scotland-2018-uksc-64/

Bolleyer, Nicole (2009) *Intergovernmental Cooperation: Rational Choices in Federal Systems and Beyond*. Oxford: Oxford University Press.

Bradbury, Jonathan (2021) *Constitutional Policy and Territorial Politics in the UK. Volume 1: Union and Devolution 1997–2007*. Bristol: Bristol University Press.

Brand, Anna and Atherton, Sarah (2020) *Revised UK Agriculture Bill 2020*. SPICe Briefing SB 20-28. 27 March. Scottish Parliament. https://sp-bpr-en-prod-cdnep.azureedge.net/published/2020/3/27/Revised-UK-Agriculture-Bill-2020/SB%2020-28.pdf

Brien, Philip (2022) *The UK Shared Prosperity Fund*. Briefing Paper Number 08527. 26 April. House of Commons. https://researchbriefings.files.parliament.uk/documents/CBP-8527/CBP-8527.pdf

Brooks, Libby (2015) *Scotland Calls for Consultation over Windfarm Subsidies*. 14 June. The Guardian. https://www.theguardian.com/environment/2015/jun/04/scotland-calls-for-consultation-over-windfarm-subsidies

Butcher, Louise (2017) *Transport in Scotland, Wales & Northern Ireland*. Briefing Paper Number SN03156. 12 June. House of Commons. https://researchbriefings.files.parliament.uk/documents/SN03156/SN03156.pdf

Cabinet Office (2011) *JMC Agreement on 2012 Olympics Consequential Funding*. Press release. 22 December. UK Government. https://www.gov.uk/government/news/jmc-agreement-on-2012-olympics-consequential-funding

Cabinet Office (2012) *Devolution: Memorandum of Understanding and Supplementary Agreement*. Policy paper. 1 October. https://www.gov.uk/government/publications/devolution-memorandum-of-understanding-and-supplementary-agreement

Cabinet Office (2018a) *Intergovernmental Agreement on the European Union (Withdrawal) Bill*. Policy paper. 25 April. UK Government. https://www.gov.uk/government/publications/intergovernmental-agreement-on-the-european-union-withdrawal-bill

Cabinet Office (2018b) *UK and Welsh Governments Reach Agreement on EU Withdrawal Bill*. Press release. 25 April. UK Government. https://www.gov.uk/government/news/uk-and-welsh-governments-reach-agreement-on-eu-withdrawal-bill

Cabinet Office (2019a) *Common Frameworks Update*. Guidance. 3 July. UK Government. https://www.gov.uk/government/publications/common-frameworks-update

Cabinet Office (2019b) *Revised Frameworks Analysis: Breakdown of Areas of EU Law That Intersect with Devolved Competence in Scotland, Wales and Northern Ireland*. April. UK Government. https://assets.publishing.service.gov.uk/government/uploads/system/uploads/attachment_data/file/792738/20190404-Frameworks Analysis.pdf

Cabinet Office (2020a) *Frameworks Analysis 2020 Breakdown of Areas of EU Law That Intersect with Devolved Competence in Scotland, Wales and Northern Ireland*. UK Government. https://www.gov.uk/government/publications/frameworks-analysis

Cabinet Office (2020b) *The European Union (Withdrawal) Act and Common Frameworks: 26 June to 25 September 2020*. December. UK Government. https://assets.publishing.service.gov.uk/government/uploads/system/uploads/attachment_data/file/941711/The_European_Union__Withdrawal__Act_and_Common_Frameworks.pdf

Cabinet Office (2021a) *Review of UK Government Union Capability*. Independent report. 24 March. UK Government. https://www.gov.uk/government/publications/the-dunlop-review-into-uk-government-union-capability

Cabinet Office (2021b) *Communiqués from the Joint Ministerial Committee (EU Negotiations)*. Collection. UK Government. https://www.gov.uk/government/collections/communiques-from-the-joint-ministerial-committee-eu-negotiations

Cabinet Office and Department for Levelling Up, Housing and Communities (2022) *Review of Intergovernmental Relation*. Policy paper. 13 January. UK Government. https://www.gov.uk/government/publications/the-review-of-intergovernmental-relations

Cabinet Secretary for Finance and the Constitution (2016) *Fiscal Framework – Response to Issues Raised in Session 4 Finance Committee Letter to the Devolution (Further Powers) Committee (7 March 2016)*. 7 March. Scottish Government. https://archive2021.parliament.scot/S5_Finance/Cabinet_Secretary_to_Finance_Committee_-_Fiscal_Framework.pdf

Cabinet Secretary for the Constitution, Europe and External Affairs (2020a) *UK Internal Market*. Letter to the Convener of the Finance and Constitution Committee. 8 July. Scottish Parliament. https://archive2021.parliament.scot/S5_Finance/General%20Documents/2020.07.14_Binder_1.pdf

Cabinet Secretary for the Constitution, Europe and External Affairs (2020b) *Internal Market Bill: Statement by the Cabinet Secretary for the Constitution, Europe and External Affairs*. Publication – Speech/statement. 16 December. Scottish Government. https://www.gov.scot/publications/statement-internal-market-bill/

Cabinet Secretary for the Rural Economy (2018) *Letter to the UK Secretary of State for Environment, Food and Rural Affairs*. 24 October. Scottish Government. https://www.gov.scot/binaries/content/documents/govscot/publications/correspondence/2018/10/proposed-amendments-to-the-uk-agriculture-bill/documents/letter-from-mr-ewing-to-mr-gove—24-oct-2018/letter-from-mr-ewing-to-mr-gove—24-oct-2018/govscot%3Adocument/Letter%2Bfrom%2BMr%2BEwing%2Bto%2BMr%2BGove%2B-%2B24%2BOct%2B2018.pdf

Cairney, Paul (2011) *The Scottish Political System Since Devolution: From New Politics to the New Scottish Government*. Exeter: Imprint Academic.

Cairney, Paul, McHarg, Aileen, McEwen, Nicola, and Turner, Karen (2019) *How to Conceptualise Energy Law and Policy for an Interdisciplinary Audience: The Case of Post-Brexit UK*. Energy Policy, Volume 129, pp. 459–466.

Cameron, David (2015) *Welsh Devolution – St David's Day Agreement: Prime Minister's Speech*. Speech. 27 February. UK Government. https://www.gov.uk/government/speeches/welsh-devolution-st-davids-day-agreement-prime-ministers-speech

Cardiff University (2021) *Video: Counsel General on Internal Market Act and UK future*. News. 22 January. https://www.cardiff.ac.uk/news/view/2490834-video-counsel-general-on-internal-market-act-and-uk-future

Chappell, Elliot (2020) *Mark Drakeford Slams Boris Johnson as "Greatest Threat to the Union"*. 20 October. LabourList. https://labourlist.org/2020/10/mark-drakeford-slams-boris-johnson-as-greatest-threat-to-the-union/

Cheung, Aron (2020) *Barnett Formula*. Explainer. 25 November. Institute for Government. https://www.instituteforgovernment.org.uk/explainers/barnett-formula

Coe, Sarah and Finlay, Jonathan (2020) *The Agriculture Act 2020*. Briefing Paper Number CBP 8702. 3 December. House of Commons. https://researchbriefings.files.parliament.uk/documents/CBP-8702/CBP-8702.pdf

Commission on Justice in Wales (2019) *Justice in Wales for the People of Wales*. Report. October. https://gov.wales/sites/default/files/publications/2019-10/Justice%20Commission%20ENG%20DIGITAL_2.pdf

Committee for the Scrutiny of the First Minister (2019) Meeting 05/04/2019. *The Record*. Welsh Parliament. https://record.assembly.wales/Committee/5676

Constitution and Cabinet Directorate (2018) *Strengthening the Sewel Convention: Letter from Michael Russell to David Lidington*. Publication – Correspondence. 12 September. Scottish Government. https://www.gov.scot/publications/strengthening-the-sewel-convention-letter-from-michael-russell-to-david-lidington/

Constitution and Cabinet Directorate (2020) *UK Internal Market: Initial Assessment of UK Government Proposals*. Publication – Factsheet. 12 August. Scottish Government. https://www.gov.scot/publications/uk-internal-market/pages/introduction/

Constitution and Cabinet Directorate (2021) *After Brexit: The UK Internal Market Act and Devolution*. Publication – Strategy/plan. 8 March. Scottish Government. https://www.gov.scot/publications/brexit-uk-internal-market-act-devolution/pages/5/

Constitutional and Legislative Affairs Committee (2016) *Report on the UK Government's Wales Bill*. October. National Assembly for Wales. https://senedd.wales/laid%20documents/cr-ld10771/cr-ld10771-e.pdf

Constitutional and Legislative Affairs Committee (2019a) *The Welsh Government's Legislative Consent Memorandum on the Healthcare (International Arrangements) Bill*. January. National Assembly for Wales. https://senedd.wales/laid%20documents/cr-ld12062/cr-ld12062-e.pdf

Constitutional and Legislative Affairs Committee (2019b) *Meeting 07/01/2019*. The Record. Welsh Parliament. https://record.assembly.wales/Committee/5026

Corbyn, Cloe (2021) *The Future of Railways in Wales*. Senedd Research. 27 May. Welsh Parliament. https://research.senedd.wales/2019/01/31/the-future-of-railways-in-wales/

Cowie, Graeme (2018a) *Brexit: Devolution and Legislative Consent*. Briefing Paper Number 08274. 29 March. House of Commons. https://researchbriefings.files.parliament.uk/documents/CBP-8274/CBP-8274.pdf

Cowie, Graeme (2018b) *Last Chance for Compromise? Devolution and the EU (Withdrawal) Bill*. Insight. 11 June. UK Parliament. https://commonslibrary.parliament.uk/last-chance-for-compromise-devolution-and-the-eu-withdrawal-bill/

Cowie, Graeme, Mars, Sylvia de, Kelly, Richard and Torrance, David (2020) *Constitutional Implications of the Withdrawal Agreement Legislation*. Briefing Paper Number 08805. 20 February. House of Commons. https://researchbriefings.files.parliament.uk/documents/CBP-8805/CBP-8805.pdf

Curtis, John, Mars, Sylvia de, Fella, Stefano, Ferguson, Daniel, Finlay, Jonathan, Hinson, Suzanna, Jozepa, Ilze, Keep, Matthew, Seely, Anthony, Torrance, David and Webb, Dominic (2019) *The October 2019 EU-UK Withdrawal Agreement*. Briefing Paper Number CBP 8713, 17 October. House of Commons. https://researchbriefings.files.parliament.uk/documents/CBP-8713/CBP-8713.pdf

Delegated Powers and Regulatory Reform Committee (2018) *Fisheries Bill Healthcare (International Arrangements) Bill Divorce (Financial Provision) Bill [HL] Prisons (Interference with Wireless Telegraphy) Bill*. 39th Report of Session 2017–19. HL Paper 226. 15 November. House of Lords. https://publications.parliament.uk/pa/ld201719/ldselect/lddelreg/226/226.pdf

Delegated Powers and Regulatory Reform Committee (2019) *Healthcare (International Arrangements) Bill, Healthcare (International Arrangements) Bill: Government Response, Financial Services (Implementation of Legislation) Bill [HL]: Government Response, Legislative Reform (Horserace Betting Levy) Order 2018*. 47th Report of Session 2017–19. HL Paper 289. 14 February. House of Lords. https://publications.parliament.uk/pa/ld201719/ldselect/lddelreg/289/289.pdf

Department for Business, Energy and Industrial Strategy (2017) *Industrial Strategy: Building a Britain Fit for the Future*. Policy paper. 27 November. UK Government.

Department for Business, Energy and Industrial Strategy (2020) *UK Internal Market*. Policy paper. 16 July. UK Government. https://www.gov.uk/government/publications/uk-internal-market

Department for Education (2020) *New Turing Scheme to Support Thousands of Students to Study and Work Abroad*. Press release. 26 December. UK Government. https://www.gov.uk/government/news/new-turing-scheme-to-support-thousands-of-students-to-study-and-work-abroad

Department for Environment, Food and Rural Affairs (2018) *Health and Harmony: The Future for Food, Farming and the Environment in a Green Brexit – Policy Statement*. Policy paper. 14 September. UK Government. https://www.gov.uk/government/publications/the-future-for-food-farming-and-the-environment-policy-statement-2018/health-and-harmony-the-future-for-food-farming-and-the-environment-in-a-green-brexit-policy-statement

Department for Environment, Food and Rural Affairs (2019) *Draft Environment (Principles and Governance) Bill 2018 Policy Paper*. Policy paper. 23 July. UK Government. https://www.gov.uk/government/publications/draft-environment-principles-and-governance-bill-2018/environment-bill-policy-paper

Department for Environment, Food and Rural Affairs (2020) *30 January 2020: Environment Bill 2020 Policy Statement*. Policy paper. 21 October. UK Government. https://www.gov.uk/government/publications/environment-bill-2020/30-january-2020-environment-bill-2020-policy-statement

Department for Environment, Food and Rural Affairs (2021) *Protected Geographical Food and Drink Names: UK GI Schemes*. Guidance. 4 January. UK Government. https://www.gov.uk/guidance/protected-geographical-food-and-drink-names-uk-gi-schemes

Department for Environment, Food and Rural Affairs and Welsh Government (2019) *UK and Welsh Government Bilateral Agreement on WTO Provisions within the Agriculture Bill*. Policy paper. 21 March. UK Government. https://www.gov.uk/government/publications/agriculture-bill-progress-with-devolved-administrations/uk-and-welsh-government-bilateral-agreement-on-wto-provisions-within-the-agriculture-bill

Department for Exciting the European Union (2018) *The Future Relationship between the United Kingdom and the European Union*. Policy paper. 17 July. UK Government. https://www.gov.uk/government/publications/the-future-relationship-between-the-united-kingdom-and-the-european-union/the-future-relationship-between-the-united-kingdom-and-the-european-union-html-version

Department for International Trade (2019) *Processes for Making Free Trade Agreements Once the UK Has Left the EU*. Policy paper. 28 February. UK Government. https://www.gov.uk/government/publications/processes-for-making-free-trade-agreements-once-the-uk-has-left-the-eu

Department for International Trade (2021) *UK Trade Agreements with non-EU Countries*. Guidance. 19 July. UK Government. https://www.gov.uk/guidance/uk-trade-agreements-with-non-eu-countries

Department for Levelling Up, Housing and Communities (2022a) *Intergovernmental Relations Annual Report – Reporting Period 1 January – 31 December 2021*. CP 655. March. UK Government.

Department for Levelling Up, Housing and Communities (2022b) *UK Shared Prosperity Fund: Prospectus.* Guidance. 19 July. UK Government. https://www.gov.uk/government/publications/uk-shared-prosperity-fund-prospectus/uk-shared-prosperity-fund-prospectus

Department for Levelling Up, Housing and Communities and Cabinet Office (2021) *The European Union (Withdrawal) Act and Common Frameworks: 26 June to 25 September 2021.* Policy paper. 9 December. UK Government. https://www.gov.uk/government/publications/the-european-union-withdrawal-act-and-common-frameworks-26-june-to-25-september-2021

Department for Levelling Up, Housing and Communities and Cabinet Office (2022) *The European Union (Withdrawal) Act and Common Frameworks: 26 September to 25 December 2021.* Policy paper. 10 March. UK Government. https://www.gov.uk/government/publications/the-european-union-withdrawal-act-and-common-frameworks-26-september-to-25-december-2021

Department for Transport (2018) *Wales and Borders Rail Franchise 2018: Devolution Agreements.* Guidance. 11 September. UK Government. https://www.gov.uk/government/publications/wales-and-borders-rail-franchise-2018-devolution-agreements

Department of Health and Social Care (2020a) *Nutrition Labelling Composition and Standards Provisional Common Framework Command Paper.* Policy paper. 9 October. UK Government. https://www.gov.uk/government/publications/nutrition-labelling-composition-and-standards-provisional-common-framework-command-paper

Department of Health and Social Care (2020b) *Food and Feed Safety and Hygiene: Provisional Common Framework.* Policy paper. 27 November. UK Government. https://www.gov.uk/government/publications/food-and-feed-safety-and-hygiene-provisional-common-framework

Department of Health and Social Care (2020c) *Coronavirus (COVID-19) Action Plan.* Policy paper. 3 March. UK Government. https://www.gov.uk/government/publications/coronavirus-action-plan

Deputy Prime Minister's Office, HM Treasury and Ministry of Housing, Communities and Local Government (2011) *Unlocking Growth in Cities.* Policy paper. 8 December. UK Government. https://www.gov.uk/government/publications/unlocking-growth-in-cities-5

Dougan, Michael, Hayward, Katy, Hunt, Jo, McEwen, Nicola, McHarg, Aileen and Wincott, Daniel (2020) *UK Internal Market Bill, Devolution and the Union.* Reports & Briefings. Centre on Constitutional Change. https://www.centreonconstitutionalchange.ac.uk/publications/uk-internal-market-devolution-and-union

Drakeford, Mark (2020) *Written Statement: Intergovernmental Relations.* Cabinet Statement. 26 October. Welsh Government. https://gov.wales/written-statement-intergovernmental-relations

Drakeford, Mark (2022) *Written Statement: Review of Intergovernmental Relations.* Cabinet Statement. 13 January. Welsh Government. https://gov.wales/written-statement-review-intergovernmental-relations-0

Eccleston, Richard, Hortle, Robert and Krever, Richard (2017) *The Evolution of Intergovernmental Financial Relations in the 21st Century.* In: Eccleston, Richard and Krever, Richard (eds.) *The Future of Federalism – Intergovernmental Financial Relations in an Age of Austerity.* Cheltenham: Edward Elgar Publishing, pp. 1–12.

Economic Development Directorate (2017) *Scotland's International Framework 2017*. Publication – Strategy/plan. 8 December. Scottish Government. https://www.gov.scot/publications/scotlands-international-framework-9781788514033/

Eiser, David and Roy, Graeme (2019) *The Fiscal Framework: 2021 Review*. Economic Commentary, June. Fraser of Allander Institute, University of Strathclyde. https://www.strath.ac.uk/media/1newwebsite/departmentsubject/economics/fraser/vol43no2/Fiscal-Framework-2021.pdf

Energy and Climate Change Directorate (2020) *Climate Change*. Policy. Scottish Government. https://www.gov.scot/policies/climate-change/

Environment, Climate Change and Land Reform Committee (2020) *Legislative Consent Memorandum – UK Environment Bill*. 7th Report of Session 5. SP Paper 765. 19 June. Scottish Parliament. https://sp-bpr-en-prod-cdnep.azureedge.net/published/ECCLR/2020/6/19/Legislative-Consent-Memorandum—UK-Environment-Bill/ECCLR-S5-20-7R.pdf

Nice, Alex (2018) *European Structural Funds after Brexit: The UK Shared Prosperity Fund*. Explainer. 4 September. Institute for Government. https://www.instituteforgovernment.org.uk/explainers/european-structural-funds-after-brexit

Evans, Rebecca (2019) *Written Statement: UK Response to the Welsh Affairs Committee Report into the Devolution of Air Passenger Duty to Wales*. Cabinet statement. 6 September. Welsh Government. https://gov.wales/written-statement-uk-response-welsh-affairs-committee-report-devolution-air-passenger-duty-wales

Evans, Rebecca (2020a) *Written Statement: Welsh Government Response to the Chancellor of the Exchequer's UK Spending Review*. Cabinet statement. 25 November. Welsh Government. https://gov.wales/written-statement-welsh-government-response-chancellor-exchequers-uk-spending-review

Evans, Rebecca (2020b) *Written Statement: Update on Welsh Government's Formal Request to UK Government for Devolution of Further Tax Competence to Senedd Cymru*. Cabinet statement. 8 September. Welsh Government. https://gov.wales/written-statement-update-welsh-governments-formal-request-uk-government-devolution-further-tax

Ewing, Fergus (2018a) *Coverage on UK Agriculture Bill*. Blog, Rural and Environment. 13 November. Scottish Government. https://blogs.gov.scot/rural-environment/2018/11/13/coverage-on-uk-agriculture-bill/

Ewing, Fergus (2018b) *In the News: Red Meat Levy Success*. Blog, Rural and Environment. 16 November. Scottish Government. https://blogs.gov.scot/rural-environment/2018/11/16/in-the-news-red-meat-levy-success/

External Affairs and Additional Legislation Committee (2020) *UK Internal Market Bill Legislative Consent*. Report. November. Welsh Parliament. https://senedd.wales/laid%20documents/cr-ld13860/cr-ld13860-e.pdf

External Affairs Directorate (2019) *International Offices: Strategic Objectives*. Publication – Strategy/plan. 28 August. Scottish Government. https://www.gov.scot/publications/international-offices-strategic-objectives/

External Affairs Directorate (2020a) *Coronavirus (COVID-19): Letter to UK Government about Future Borders and Immigration System*. Publication – Correspondence. 17 May. Scottish Government. https://www.gov.scot/publications/coronavirus-covid-19-future-borders-and-immigration-system-letter/

External Affairs Directorate (2020b) *Migration: Helping Scotland Prosper*. Publication – Strategy/plan. 27 January. Scottish Government. https://www.gov.scot/publications/migration-helping-scotland-prosper/

First Minister of Wales (2019) R*e: Various Schemes and Orders in Relation to the M4 Corridor Around Newport*. Letter. 4 June. Welsh Government. https://gat04-live-1517c8a4486c41609369c68f30c8-aa81074.divio-media.org/M4-Newport/decision.pdf

Gallagher, Jim (2012) *Intergovernmental Relations in the UK: Co-Operation, Competition and Constitutional Change*. British Journal of Politics and International Relations, Volume 14, Issue 2, pp. 198–213.

Gallagher, Jim (2016) *Where Next for Scotland and the United Kingdom?*. In: Bailey, David and Budd, Leslie (eds.) *Devolution and the UK Economy*. London: Rowan and Littlefield.

Gallagher, Jim (2020) *Intergovernmental Relations: Two Decades of Co-Operation, Competition, and Constitutional Change*. Keating, Michael (ed.) *The Oxford Handbook of Scottish Politics*. Oxford: Oxford University Press, pp. 565–583.

Gething, Vaughan (2022a) *Written Statement: Confirmation of Welsh Government's Position on the UK Government's Shared Prosperity Fund Prospectus*. Cabinet statement. 7 June. https://gov.wales/written-statement-confirmation-welsh-governments-position-uk-governments-shared-prosperity-fund

Gething, Vaughan (2022b) *Written Statement: The UK Shared Prosperity Fund*. Cabinet statement. 13 April. https://gov.wales/written-statement-uk-shared-prosperity-fund

Gove, Michael (2021) *Letter from the Chancellor of the Duchy of Lancaster to Lord*. 24 March. UK Government. https://assets.publishing.service.gov.uk/government/uploads/system/uploads/attachment_data/file/973001/L_Dunlop_Letter.pdf

Griffiths, Lesley (2018) *Written Statement – Introduction of the UK Agriculture Bill*. Cabinet statement. 12 September. Welsh Government. https://gov.wales/written-statement-introduction-uk-agriculture-bill

Griffiths, Lesley (2020) *Written Statement: UK Agriculture Bill*. Cabinet statement. 16 January. Welsh Government. https://gov.wales/written-statement-uk-agriculture-bill

Health, Social Care and Sport Committee (2019) *Legislative Consent Memorandum: Healthcare (International Arrangements) Bill*. January. National Assembly for Wales. https://senedd.assembly.wales/documents/s83606/Health%20Social%20Care%20and%20Sport%20Committee%20-%20Report%20on%20the%20Legislative%20Consent%20Memorandum%20for%20the%20Healt.pdf

HM Government (2015) *Scotland in the United Kingdom: An Enduring Settlement*. Presented to Parliament by the Secretary of State for Scotland by Command of Her Majesty. Cm 8990. January. UK Government. https://assets.publishing.service.gov.uk/government/uploads/system/uploads/attachment_data/file/397079/Scotland_EnduringSettlement_acc.pdf

HM Government and Scottish Government (2016) *The Agreement between the Scottish Government and the United Kingdom Government on the Scottish Government's Fiscal Framework*. Independent report. February. UK Government. https://www.gov.uk/government/publications/the-agreement-between-the-scottish-government-and-the-united-kingdom-government-on-the-scottish-governments-fiscal-framework

HM Government and Welsh Government (2016) *The Agreement between the Welsh Government and the United Kingdom Government on the Welsh Government's Fiscal Framework*. December. Welsh Government. https://gov.wales/sites/default/files/publications/2018-11/agreement-on-welsh-government-fiscal-framework.pdf

HM Treasury (2015) *Statement of Funding Policy: Funding the Scottish Parliament, National Assembly for Wales and Northern Ireland Assembly.* November. 7th edition. UK Government. https://www.gov.uk/government/publications/spending-review-and-autumn-statement-2015-documents

HM Treasury (2017) *Scottish Government CP6 Rail Settlement.* Correspondence. 8 December. UK Government. https://www.gov.uk/government/publications/scottish-government-cp6-rail-settlement

HM Treasury (2020a) *Statement of Funding Policy: Funding the Scottish Parliament, National Assembly for Wales and Northern Ireland Assembly.* November. 8th edition. UK Government. https://assets.publishing.service.gov.uk/government/uploads/system/uploads/attachment_data/file/943689/Statement_of_Funding_Policy_2020.pdf

HM Treasury (2020b) *Spending Review 2020 Documents.* Policy paper. 25 November. UK Government. https://www.gov.uk/government/publications/spending-review-2020-documents

Hogarth, Raphael (2020) *The Internal Market Bill Breaks International Law and Lays the Ground to Break More Law.* Comment. 9 September. Institute for Government. https://www.instituteforgovernment.org.uk/blog/internal-market-bill-breaks-international-law

Holyrood (2020) *Scottish Government 'Very Surprised' by Announcement of Glasgow Drugs Summit.* News. 24 January. https://www.holyrood.com/news/view,scottish-government-very-surprised-by-announcement-of-glasgow-drugs-summit_15016.htm

Home Office (2018) *The UK's Future Skills-based Immigration System.* Policy paper. 19 December. UK Government. https://www.gov.uk/government/publications/the-uks-future-skills-based-immigration-system

Home Office (2020) *The UK's Points-based Immigration System: Policy Statement.* Policy paper. 19 February. UK Government. https://www.gov.uk/government/publications/the-uks-points-based-immigration-system-policy-statement/the-uks-points-based-immigration-system-policy-statement

Home Office, Department of Health and Social Care, Jo Churchill MP, and The Rt Hon Kit Malthouse MP (2020) *Ministerial Meeting to Discuss Key Drugs Issues.* News story. 17 September. UK Government. https://www.gov.uk/government/news/ministerial-meeting-to-discuss-key-drugs-issues

Howorth, Fransesca (2021) *Relief at Last? M4 Decision Looms.* Senedd Research. 27 May. Welsh Parliament. https://research.senedd.wales/2018/11/20/relief-at-last-m4-decision-looms/

Hunt, Jo (2017) *The Supreme Court Judgement in Miller and Its Implication for the Devolved Nations.* Commentary, 1 February. UK in a Changing Europe. https://ukandeu.ac.uk/the-supreme-court-judgment-in-miller-and-its-implications-for-the-devolved-nations/

Hunt, Jo (2021) *Subsidiarity, Competence, and the UK Territorial Constitution.* In: Doyle, Oran, McHarg, Aileen and Murkens, Jo (eds.) *The Brexit Challenge for Ireland and the United Kingdom: Constitutions Under Pressure.* Cambridge: Cambridge University Press, pp. 21–42.

Hunt, Jo and Minto, Rachel (2017) *Between Intergovernmental Relations and Paradiplomacy: Wales and the Brexit of the Regions.* The British Journal of Politics and International Relations, Volume 19, Issue 4, pp. 647–662.

Hutt, Jane (2015) *Written Statement – Joint Statement from the Finance Ministers of the Devolved Administrations*. Cabinet statement. 7 August. Welsh Government. https://gov.wales/written-statement-joint-statement-finance-ministers-devolved-administrations

Independent Expert Advisory Committee for Ongoing Review of the Operation of Justice in Wales (2019) *First Report*. July. https://assets.publishing.service.gov.uk/government/uploads/system/uploads/attachment_data/file/819728/independent-expert-advisory-committee-first-report-web.pdf

International Trade and Investment Directorate (2019) *Scotland: A Trading Nation. A Plan for Growing Scotland's Exports*. Publication – Strategy/plan. 1 May. Scottish Government. https://www.gov.scot/publications/scotland-a-trading-nation/

Jack, Maddy T. (2017) *EU Withdrawal Act 2018*. Explainer. 16 January. Institute for Government. https://www.instituteforgovernment.org.uk/explainers/eu-withdrawal-act

James, Julie (2021) *Written Statement: UK Environment Bill*. Cabinet statement. 25 October. Welsh Government. https://gov.wales/written-statement-uk-environment-bill

JMC Joint Secretariat (2018) *Report of the Joint Ministerial Committee: 2015–2018*. Policy paper. 14 March. UK Government. https://www.gov.uk/government/publications/joint-ministerial-committee-communique-14-march-2018

Keating, Michael (2012) *Intergovernmental Relations and Innovation: From Co-Operative to Competitive Welfare Federalism in the UK*. British Journal of Politics and International Relations, Volume 14, Issue 2, pp. 214–230.

Keating, Michael (2020a) *The Scottish Continuity Bill. Will It Work?* Opinion. 5 November. Centre on Constitutional Change. https://www.centreonconstitutionalchange.ac.uk/news-and-opinion/scottish-continuity-bill-will-it-work

Keating, Michael (2020b) *Scotland as a Political Community*. Keating, Michael (ed.) *The Oxford Handbook of Scottish Politics*. Oxford: Oxford University Press, pp. 1–19.

Keating, Michael (2021) *State and Nation in the United Kingdom: The Fractured Union*. Oxford: Oxford University Press.

Kellam, Jack (2018) *The Welsh and Scottish Continuity Bills Have Been Published, But Challenges Remain*. Comment. 6 March. Institute for Government. https://www.instituteforgovernment.org.uk/blog/welsh-and-scottish-continuity-bills-published-challenges-remain

Kenealy, Daniel and Parry, Richard (2018) *Devolution Commissions in the Shadow of Whitehall: the Smith Commission and the Creation of a 'Powerhouse Parliament'*. British Politics, Volume 13, Issue 4, pp. 484–504.

Kenny, Michael, Rycroft, Philip and Sheldon, Jack (2021) *Union at the Crossroads: Can the British State Handle the Challenges of Devolution*. Report by the Bennett Institute for Public Policy Cambridge. The Constitution Society.

Kenny, Michael and Sheldon, Jack (2022) *Green Shoots for the Union? The Joint Review of Intergovernmental Relations*. The Constitution Unit Blog. 19 January. The Constitution Unit Blog. https://constitution-unit.com/2022/01/19/green-shoots-for-the-union-the-joint-review-of-intergovernmental-relations/

Kenyon, Wendy (2019) *A Review of Convergence Funding for Agriculture in Scotland*. SPICe Briefing. 25 June. SB19-40. Scottish Parliament. https://sp-bpr-en-prod-cdnep.azureedge.net/published/2019/6/25/A-review-of-convergence-funding-for-agriculture-in-Scotland/SB%2019-40.pdf

Lee, Simon (2017) *The Gathering Storm: Federalization and Constitutional Change in the United Kingdom*. In: Eccleston, Richard and Krever, Richard (eds.) *The Future of Federalism – Intergovernmental Financial Relations in an Age of Austerity*. Cheltenham: Edward Elgar Publishing, pp. 124–144.

Local Government and Communities Committee (2017) *Official Report: City Region Deals*. 22 November. Scottish Parliament. https://archive2021.parliament.scot/parliamentarybusiness/report.aspx?r=11222

Local Government and Communities Committee (2018) *Official Report: City Region Deals*. 13 June. Scottish Parliament.

Mandal, Ruma (2020) *Breaching International Law Comes at a Price*. Expert Comment. 21 October. Chatham House. https://www.chathamhouse.org/2020/10/breaching-international-law-comes-price

Haddon, Catherine, Hogarth, Raphael, Marshall, Joe, Nice, Alex and Tasneem, Ghazi (2020) *Coronavirus Act 2020*. Explainer. 20 March. Institute for Government. https://www.instituteforgovernment.org.uk/explainers/coronavirus-act

McEwen, Nicola (2017) *Still Better Together? Purpose and Power in Intergovernmental Councils in the UK*. Regional and Federal Studies, Volume 27, Issue 5, pp. 667–690.

McEwen, Nicola, Kenny, Michael, Sheldon, Jack and Brown Swan, Coree (2018) *Reforming Intergovernmental Relations in the United Kingdom*. Edinburgh: Centre on Constitutional Change and Cambridge: Bennett Institute for Public Policy.

McEwen, Nicola and Petersohn, Bettina (2015) *Between Autonomy and Interdependence: The Challenges of Shared Rule after the Scottish Referendum*. The Political Quarterly, Volume 86, Issue 2, pp. 192–200.

McHarg, Aileen (2018) *The Scottish Continuity Bill Reference*. Opinion. 18 December. Centre on Constitutional Change. https://www.centreonconstitutionalchange.ac.uk/opinions/scottish-continuity-bill-reference

Miles, Jeremy (2018) *Written Statement: Supreme Court Reference: UK Withdrawal from the European Union (Legal Continuity) (Scotland) Bill*. Cabinet statement. 20 December. Welsh Government. https://gov.wales/written-statement-supreme-court-reference-uk-withdrawal-european-union-legal-continuity-scotland-bill

Miles, Jeremy (2019) *Written Response by the Welsh Government to the Report of the EAAL Committee Report: Changes to Freedom of Movement after Brexit – The Implications for Wales*. 20 December. Welsh Government. https://senedd.wales/laid%20documents/gen-ld12963/gen-ld12963%20-e.pdf

Miles, Jeremy (2020a) *Written Statement: Welsh Government Amendments to the United Kingdom Internal Market Bill*. Cabinet statement. 15 October. Welsh Government. https://gov.wales/written-statement-welsh-government-amendments-united-kingdom-internal-market-bill

Miles, Jeremy (2020b) *Written Statement: Possible Legal Challenge to the UK Internal Market Bill*. Cabinet statement. 16 December. Welsh Government. https://gov.wales/written-statement-possible-legal-challenge-uk-internal-market-bill

Miles, Jeremy (2020c) *Written Statement: Welsh Government's Analysis of the UK Government's Negotiating Mandate for the Future Relationship with the EU*. Cabinet statement. 28 February. Welsh Government. https://gov.wales/written-statement-welsh-governments-analysis-uk-governments-negotiating-mandate-future-relationship

Minister for Business, Trade, Tourism and Enterprise (2020) *Scottish Replacement for EU Structural Funds*. Publication – Strategy/plan. 19 November. Scottish Government. https://www.gov.scot/publications/scottish-replacement-eu-structural-funds/

Minister for Just Transition, Employment and Fair Work (2021) *Cities and Regions. Policy.* Scottish Government, Economic Development Directorate. https://www.gov.scot/policies/cities-regions/regional-growth-deals/

Ministry of Housing, Communities and Local Government (2020) *Hazardous Substances: Provisional Planning Framework*. Policy paper. 23 November. UK Government. https://www.gov.uk/government/publications/hazardous-substances-provisional-planning-framework

Ministry of Justice (2018) *Concordat between the Ministry of Justice and the Welsh Government*. Policy paper. 25 June. UK Government. https://www.gov.uk/government/publications/concordat-between-the-ministry-of-justice-and-the-welsh-government

Ministry of Justice (2019) *Justice in Wales: First Report of the Independent Advisory Committee on Justice in Wales*. Independent report. 23 July. UK Government. https://www.gov.uk/government/publications/justice-in-wales-first-report-of-the-independent-advisory-committee-on-justice-in-wales

Ministry of Justice and Welsh Government (2019a) *Female Offending Blueprint for Wales*. UK Government. https://gov.wales/sites/default/files/publications/2019-05/female-offending-blueprint_3.pdf

Ministry of Justice and Welsh Government (2019b) *Youth Justice Blueprint for Wales*. UK Government. https://gov.wales/sites/default/files/publications/2019-05/youth-justice-blueprint_0.pdf

Morgan, Eluned (2020) *Written Statement: The UK's Approach to Trade Negotiations with the US*. Cabinet statement. 4 March. Welsh Government. https://gov.wales/written-statement-uks-approach-trade-negotiations-us

Morris, Steven and Brooks, Libby (2020) *Welsh Government Calls PM's Devolution Remarks 'Shocking'*. 17 November. The Guardian. https://www.theguardian.com/politics/2020/nov/17/welsh-government-calls-pms-devolution-remarks-shocking

Muthumala, Aruni and Keep, Matthew (2018) *Confidence and Supply: Northern Ireland's £1 billion*. Insight. 19 November. UK Parliament. https://commonslibrary.parliament.uk/confidence-and-supply-northern-irelands-1-billion/

Net Zero, Energy and Transport Committee (2021) *Supplementary Legislative Consent Memorandum (LCM) on the UK Environment Bill*. SP Paper 20 (Session 6). 29 September. Scottish Parliament. https://sp-bpr-en-prod-cdnep.azureedge.net/published/NZET/2021/9/29/fc6720ce-36a7-4688-b3b1-f5962dd18f07-3/NZETS062021R1.pdf

Northern Ireland Office (2021) *UK Government Signs Agreement for £250m Investment in the North West*. Press release. 24 February. UK Government. https://www.gov.uk/government/news/uk-government-signs-agreement-for-250m-investment-in-the-north-west

Northpoint (2017) *Evolution of Air Passenger Duty to Wales*. Report to the Welsh Government. June. Welsh Government. https://llyw.cymru/sites/default/files/publications/2017-11/datganoli-toll-teithwyr-awyr-i-gymru.pdf

O'Neill, Michael (2004) *Devolution and British Politics*. London: Routledge.

Office of the Secretary of State for Scotland and HM Treasury (2021) *Further £1.1 billion Boost for Scotland's Response to COVID-19*. News story. 15 February. UK Government. https://www.gov.uk/government/news/further-11-billion-boost-for-scotlands-response-to-covid-19

Office of the Secretary of State for Wales (2020) *Mid Wales Growth Deal Reaches Key Milestone*. Press release. 22 December. UK Government. https://www.gov.uk/government/news/mid-wales-growth-deal-reaches-key-milestone

Office of the Secretary of State for Wales and HM Treasury (2021) *Further £650 million Funding Boost for Covid-19 Response in Wales.* Press release. 16 February. UK Government. https://www.gov.uk/government/news/further-650-million-funding-boost-for-covid-19-response-in-wales

Orford, Katy and Henderson, Elfyn (2020) *UK Agriculture Bill 2019–21 Bill Summary.* Senedd Research. 8 May. Welsh Parliament. https://senedd.wales/research%20documents/20-19%20uk%20agriculture%20bill%202019-21/agriculture%20bill%20v2%20-%20eng-%20web.pdf

Owen, Gruffydd and Valsamidis, Lucy (2020) *Internal Market Bill Becomes Law – How Has the Act Changed?* Senedd Research. 22 December. Welsh Parliament. https://research.senedd.wales/research-articles/internal-market-bill-becomes-law-how-has-the-act-changed/

Paun, Akash, Klemperer, David and Sargeant, Jess (2017) *Devolution: Common Frameworks and Brexit.* Explainer. 13 October. Institute for Government. https://www.instituteforgovernment.org.uk/explainers/devolution-joint-ministerial-committee

Paun, Akash and Nice, Alex (2021) Alun Davies. Interview, Ministers Reflect. 12 October 2021. https://www.instituteforgovernment.org.uk/ministers-reflect/person/alun-davies/

Paun, Akash and Nice, Alex (2022) Michael Russell. Interview, Ministers Reflect. 26 January 2022. https://www.instituteforgovernment.org.uk/ministers-reflect/person/michael-russell/

Paun, Akash, Sargeant, Jess, Shuttleworth, Kelly and Nice, Alex (2020) *Coronavirus and Devolution.* Explainer. 26 March. Institute for Government. https://www.instituteforgovernment.org.uk/explainers/coronavirus-and-devolution

Petersohn, Bettina, Behnke, Nathalie and Rhode, Eva Maria (2015) *Negotiating Territorial Change in Multinational States: Party Preferences, Negotiating Power and the Role of the Negotiation Mode.* Publius, Volume 45, Issue 4, pp. 626–652.

Population Health Directorate (2018) *Rights, Respect and Recovery: Alcohol and Drug Treatment Strategy.* Publication – Strategy/plan. 28 November. Scottish Government. https://www.gov.scot/publications/rights-respect-recovery/documents/

Powell, Thomas (2019) *Healthcare (International Arrangements) Bill 2017–19.* Research Briefing Number 08435. 17 January. House of Commons. https://commonslibrary.parliament.uk/research-briefings/cbp-8435/

Public Administration and Constitutional Affairs Committee (2018a) *Devolution and Exiting the EU: Reconciling Differences and Building Strong Relationships.* Eight Report of Session 2017–19. HC 1485. 31 July. House of Commons. https://publications.parliament.uk/pa/cm201719/cmselect/cmpubadm/1485/1485.pdf

Public Administration and Constitutional Affairs Committee (2018b) *Devolution and Exiting the EU. Oral Evidence.* HC 484. 20 June. House of Commons. https://data.parliament.uk/writtenevidence/committeeevidence.svc/evidencedocument/public-administration-and-constitutional-affairs-committee/devolution-and-exiting-the-eu/oral/85914.html

Rawlings, Richard (2017) *Brexit and the Territorial Constitution: Devolution, Reregulation and Inter-Governmental Relations.* London: The Constitution Society.

Sargeant, Jess and Stojanovic, Alex (2021) *The United Kingdom Internal Market Act 2020.* Analysis, Brexit and Devolution report, February. Institute for Government. https://www.instituteforgovernment.org.uk/sites/default/files/publications/internal-market-act.pdf

Scharpf, Fritz (1997) *Games Real Actors Play – Actor-Centered Institutionalism in Policy Research.* Boulder: Westview Press.

Scharpf, Fritz (2000) *Interaktionsformen – Akteurzentrierter Institutionalismus in der Politikforschung.* Wiesebaden: Springer VS.

Schiavon, Jorge A. (2019) *Comparative Paradiplomacy.* London: Routledge.

Scottish Affairs Committee (2015) *The Implementation of the Smith Agreement.* Fourth Report of Session 2014–15. HC 835. 19 March. House of Commons. https://publications.parliament.uk/pa/cm201415/cmselect/cmscotaf/835/835.pdf

Scottish Affairs Committee (2019a) *The Relationship between the UK and Scottish Governments.* Eighth Report of Session 2017–19. HC 1586. 7 June. House of Commons. https://publications.parliament.uk/pa/cm201719/cmselect/cmscotaf/1586/1586.pdf

Scottish Affairs Committee (2019b) *Oral Evidence: Problem Drug Use in Scotland.* HC 1997. 4 June. House of Commons. https://data.parliament.uk/writtenevidence/committeeevidence.svc/evidencedocument/scottish-affairs-committee/problem-drug-use-in-scotland/oral/102845.html

Scottish Affairs Committee (2019c) *Problem Drug Use in Scotland.* First Report of Session 2019. HC 44. 4 November. House of Commons. https://publications.parliament.uk/pa/cm201919/cmselect/cmscotaf/44/44.pdf

Scottish Affairs Committee (2020) *Problem Drug Use in Scotland: Government Response to the Committee's First Report of Session 2019.* First Report of Session 2019. 22 July. House of Commons. https://publications.parliament.uk/pa/cm5801/cmselect/cmscotaf/698/69802.htm

Scottish Government (2018) *Scotland's Population Needs and Migration Policy: Discussion Paper on Evidence, Policy and Powers for the Scottish Parliament.* February. https://www.gov.scot/binaries/content/documents/govscot/publications/consultation-paper/2018/02/scotlands-population-needs-migration-policy/documents/00531087-pdf/00531087-pdf/govscot%3Adocument/00531087.pdf

Scottish Government (2019a) *Scottish Government Overview of 'No Deal' Preparations. Laid before the Scottish Parliament, October.* SG/2019/204. October. https://www.gov.scot/binaries/content/documents/govscot/publications/progress-report/2019/10/scottish-government-overview-no-deal-preparations/documents/scottish-government-overview-no-deal-preparations/scottish-government-overview-no-deal-preparations/govscot%3Adocument/scottish-government-overview-no-deal-preparations.pdf

Scottish Government (2019b) *Building a Fairer Immigration System.* News. 13 July. https://www.gov.scot/news/building-a-fairer-immigration-system/

Scottish Government (2019c) *Spring Statement Must Stop Scotland being 'Short Changed'.* News. 10 March. https://www.gov.scot/news/spring-statement-must-stop-scotland-being-short-changed/

Scottish Government (2019d) *Alcohol and Drugs.* Policy. https://www.gov.scot/policies/alcohol-and-drugs/

Scottish Government (2020a) *Continuing CAP for Scotland's Farmers.* News. 26 August. https://www.gov.scot/news/continuing-cap-for-scotlands-farmers/

Scottish Government (2020b) *Parliament Asked to Back European Union Continuity Bill.* News. 19 June. https://www.gov.scot/news/parliament-asked-to-back-european-union-continuity-bill/

Scottish Government (2021a) *Brexit.* Topics. https://www.gov.scot/brexit/

Scottish Government (2021b) *Budget 2021/22: Supporting the COVID-19 Recovery - Analysis of Consultation Responses.* Publication – Consultation analysis. 26 January. https://www.gov.scot/publications/budget-2021-22-supporting-covid-19-recovery-analysis-consultation-responses/pages/4/

Scottish Government (2022) *EU Replacement Funding £151 million Less in First Year.* News, 13 April. https://www.gov.scot/news/eu-replacement-funding-gbp-151-million-less-in-first-year/

Scottish Parliament (2018a) *Trade Bill.* Parliamentary Business. https://archive2021.parliament.scot/parliamentarybusiness/bills/107243.aspx

Scottish Parliament (2018b) *Legislative Consent Memorandum – Healthcare (International Arrangements) Bill 2017–19.* Parliamentary Business. https://archive2021.parliament.scot/parliamentarybusiness/currentcommittees/110506.aspx

Scottish Parliament (2018c) *Debate: Safe Injection Services.* 19 April, 1.30 pm. https://www.scottishparliament.tv/meeting/debate-safe-injection-services-april-19-2018?clip_start=14:30:00&clip_end=17:05:27

Scottish Parliament (2019) *Legislative Consent Memorandum – Healthcare (International Arrangements) Bill 2017–19.* Parliamentary Business. https://archive2021.parliament.scot/parliamentarybusiness/currentcommittees/110506.aspx

Scottish Parliament (2020a) *UK Withdrawal from the European Union (Continuity) (Scotland) Bill [2020].* Bills and Laws. https://www.parliament.scot/bills-and-laws/bills/uk-withdrawal-from-the-european-union-continuity-scotland-bill-2020

Scottish Parliament (2020b) *United Kingdom Internal Market Bill.* Parliamentary Business. https://archive2021.parliament.scot/parliamentarybusiness/bills/116127.aspx

Scottish Parliament (2020c) *Trade Bill.* Parliamentary Business. https://archive2021.parliament.scot/parliamentarybusiness/bills/115814.aspx

Scottish Parliament (2020d) *Agriculture Bill.* Parliamentary Business. https://archive2021.parliament.scot/parliamentarybusiness/Bills/115054.aspx

Scottish Parliament (2020e) *Environment Bill.* Parliamentary Business. https://archive2021.parliament.scot/parliamentarybusiness/Bills/115187.aspx

Scottish Parliament (2020f) *European Union (Withdrawal Agreement) Bill.* Parliamentary Business. https://archive2021.parliament.scot/parliamentarybusiness/bills/113984.aspx

Scottish Parliament (2021) *Meeting of the Parliament (Hybrid).* Official Report (Draft). 5 October, Session 6. https://archive2021.parliament.scot/parliamentarybusiness/report.aspx?r=13345

Scottish Parliament (2022) *Meeting of the Parliament (Hybrid).* Official Report. 2 March, Session 6. https://www.parliament.scot/chamber-and-committees/official-report/what-was-said-in-parliament/meeting-of-parliament-02-03-2022?meeting=13609&iob=123538

Secretary of State for Environment, Food and Rural Affairs (2018) *Letter to Cabinet Secretary for the Rural Economy.* 18 November. Department for Environment, Food and Rural Affairs, UK Government. https://assets.publishing.service.gov.uk/government/uploads/system/uploads/attachment_data/file/903152/letter-from-sos-to-fergus-ewing-agriculture-bill.pdf

Select Committee on the Constitution (2020) *United Kingdom Internal Market Bill.* 17th Report of Session 2019–21. HL Paper 151. 16 October. House of Lords. https://publications.parliament.uk/pa/ld5801/ldselect/ldconst/151/151.pdf

Smith, Louise (2021) *Environment Bill 2019–21 and 2021–22: Report on committee and remaining stages in the Commons.* Briefing Paper Number CBP 09119. 21 June. House of Commons. https://commonslibrary.parliament.uk/research-briefings/cbp-9119/

Smith, Louise and Priestley, Sara (2020) *Commons Library analysis of the Environment Bill 2019–20.* Briefing Paper Number CBP 8824. 18 February. House of Commons. https://commonslibrary.parliament.uk/research-briefings/cbp-8824/

Strickland, Pat and Pepin, Sarah (2018) *Merger of British Transport Police Scottish Division with Police Scotland.* Debate Pack Number CDP-2018-0058. 5 March. House of Commons. https://researchbriefings.files.parliament.uk/documents/CDP-2018-0058/CDP-2018-0058.pdf

Sturgeon, Nicola (2020) 16 November. Twitter. https://twitter.com/NicolaSturgeon/status/1328437520313487363?ref_src=twsrc%5Etfw%7Ctwcamp%5Etweetembed%7Ctwterm%5E1328437520313487363%7Ctwgr%5E%7Ctwcon%5Es1_&ref_url=https%3A%2F%2Fwww.theguardian.com%2Fuk-news%2F2020%2Fnov%2F16%2Fscotland-devolution-a-disaster-north-of-the-border-says-boris-johnson

Supreme Court (2018) *The UK Withdrawal from the European Union (Legal Continuity) (Scotland) Bill – A Reference by the Attorney General and the Advocate General for Scotland (Scotland) [2018] UKSC 64.* Press Summary. 13 December. https://www.supremecourt.uk/cases/docs/uksc-2018-0080-press-summary.pdf

Tatham, Michael (2016) *With, Without, or Against the State? How European Regions Play the Brussels Game.* Oxford: Oxford University Press.

Thom, Iain (2020) *The UK's Trade Bill 2019–21 and Devolved Consent.* SPICe Spotlight. 3 September. Scottish Parliament. https://spice-spotlight.scot/2020/09/03/the-uks-trade-bill-2019-21-and-devolved-consent/

Thomas, Gareth and Thomas, Alys (2019) *Trade Bill: Bill Summary.* Senedd Research. March. National Assembly for Wales. https://senedd.wales/research%20documents/19%20-%20015%20-%20trade%20bill/015%20-%20web%20-%20english.pdf

Tipples, Christian (2021) *How Effective Is the Welsh Fiscal Framework?* Senedd Research. 24 March. Welsh Parliament. https://research.senedd.wales/research-articles/how-effective-is-the-welsh-fiscal-framework/

Torrance, David (2019) *Withdrawal Agreement Bill: Implications for Devolved Institutions.* Insight. 23 October. UK Parliament. https://commonslibrary.parliament.uk/withdrawal-agreement-bill-implications-for-devolved-institutions/

Torrance, David, Hutton, Georgina, Cowie, Graeme, Jozepa, Ilze, Curtis, John, Keep, Matthew, Butchard, Patrick, Brien, Philip and Fella, Stefano (2020) *UK Internal Market Bill: Lords Amendments Explained.* Briefing Paper Number 9051. 4 December. House of Commons. https://commonslibrary.parliament.uk/research-briefings/cbp-9051/

Transport for Wales (2017) *Rail Franchise and Metro: Policy Priorities.* Policy and strategy. 1 March. Welsh Government. https://gov.wales/rail-franchise-and-metro-policy-priorities

Transport Scotland (2021) *ScotRail Franchise.* Rail. Scottish Government. https://www.transport.gov.scot/public-transport/rail/scotrail-franchise/#

UK Parliament (2020) *Agriculture Bill (Fourth Sitting).* Debate. 13 February. Hansard. https://hansard.parliament.uk/commons/2020-02-13/debates/fe1488df-5930-4f99-86a3-b795ea0cd89f/AgricultureBill(FourthSitting)

Ward, Matthew (2020) *City Deals*. Briefing Paper Number 7158. 22 July. House of Commons. https://researchbriefings.files.parliament.uk/documents/SN07158/SN07158.pdf

Welsh Affairs Committee (2019a) *Devolution of Air Passenger Duty to Wales*. Fifth Report of Session 2017–19. HC 1575. 11 June. House of Commons. https://publications.parliament.uk/pa/cm201719/cmselect/cmwelaf/1575/1575.pdf

Welsh Affairs Committee (2019b) *Devolution of Air Passenger Duty to Wales: Government Response to the Committee's Fifth Report*. Fifth Report of Session 2017–19. 6 September. House of Commons. https://publications.parliament.uk/pa/cm201719/cmselect/cmwelaf/2634/263402.htm

Welsh Affairs Committee (2019c) *City Deals and Growth Deals in Wales*. Second Report of Session 2019. HC 48. 1 November. House of Commons. https://publications.parliament.uk/pa/cm201919/cmselect/cmwelaf/48/48.pdf

Welsh Affairs Committee (2019d) *Prison Provision in Wales*. Fourth Report of Session 2017–19. HC 742. 17 May. House of Commons. https://publications.parliament.uk/pa/cm201719/cmselect/cmwelaf/742/742.pdf

Welsh Affairs Committee (2020a) *Brexit and Trade: Implications for Wales*. Fifth Report of Session 2019–21. HC 176. 11 December. House of Commons. https://committees.parliament.uk/publications/3940/documents/39434/default/

Welsh Affairs Committee (2020b) *Brexit and Trade: Implications for Wales: Government Response to the Committee's Fifth Report of Session 2019–21*. Fifth Report of Session 2019–21. HC 1223. 16 February. House of Commons. https://committees.parliament.uk/publications/4708/documents/47283/default/

Welsh Government (2017a) *Joint Statement from First Ministers of Wales and Scotland in Reaction to the EU (Withdrawal) Bill*. Press release. 13 July. https://gov.wales/joint-statement-first-ministers-wales-and-scotland-reaction-eu-withdrawal-bill

Welsh Government (2017b) *Brexit and Fair Movement of People: Securing Wales' Future*. Policy and strategy. 7 September. https://gov.wales/brexit-and-fair-movement-people

Welsh Government (2018) *Cross Border Healthcare Services*. Guidance. 5 November. https://gov.wales/cross-border-healthcare-services

Welsh Government (2019a) *Reforming Our Union: Shared Governance in the UK*. Policy and strategy. 10 October. https://gov.wales/reforming-our-union-shared-governance-in-the-uk

Welsh Government (2019b) *Brexit and Devolution*. Speech by Jeremy Miles, Counsel General and Brexit Minister at the Wales Governance Centre. 17 June. https://gov.wales/brexit-and-devolution-speech-17-june-2019

Welsh Government (2019c) *Preparing for a No Deal Brexit*. Publication. 11 September. https://gov.wales/sites/default/files/publications/2019-09/preparing-for-a-no-deal-brexit_0.pdf

Welsh Government (2019d) *A Railway for Wales: Meeting the Needs of Future Generations*. https://gov.wales/sites/default/files/publications/2019-10/a-railway-for-wales-the-case-for-devolution.pdf

Welsh Government (2020a) *Providing Inter-governmental Information to the National Assembly: Annual Report 2019 to 2020*. Report. 26 October. https://gov.wales/providing-inter-governmental-information-national-assembly-annual-report-2019-2020

Welsh Government (2020b) *The Future UK/EU Relationship: Negotiating Priorities for Wales. Welsh Government Analysis of the UK Government Political Declaration*. Policy and strategy. 23 January. https://gov.wales/the-future-uk-eu-relationship-negotiating-priorities-for-wales-html#section-35339

Welsh Government (2020c) *International Strategy for Wales*. Report. 14 January. https://gov.wales/international-strategy-for-wales

Welsh Government (2020d) *International Action Plans*. Policy and strategy. 14 December. https://gov.wales/international-action-plans

Welsh Government (2020e) *Welsh Government International Office Remits*. Policy and strategy. 6 November. https://gov.wales/welsh-government-international-office-remits-html

Welsh Government (2020f) *We Need a Migration System That Works for Wales*. Press release. 9 March. https://gov.wales/we-need-a-migration-system-that-works-for-wales

Welsh Government (2020g) *Wales Position Paper on Migration*. Policy and strategy. 9 March. https://gov.wales/wales-position-paper-migration

Welsh Government (2020h) *Welsh Government to Take Rail Franchise under Public Control*. Press release. 22 October. https://gov.wales/welsh-government-take-rail-franchise-under-public-control

Welsh Government (2021a) *International Trade Policy*. Collection. 21 February. https://gov.wales/international-trade-policy

Welsh Government (2021b) *Inter-institutional Relations Agreement between the National Assembly for Wales and the Welsh Government: Annual Report 2020 to 2021*. Report. 28 September. https://gov.wales/providing-inter-governmental-information-national-assembly-annual-report-2020-2021-html

Welsh Parliament (2020a) *Interparliamentary Forum on Brexit*. Senedd Business. 9 July. https://business.senedd.wales/mgIssueHistoryHome.aspx?IId=22530

Welsh Parliament (2020b) *UK Government's Wales Bill*. Senedd Business. 15 June. https://business.senedd.wales/mgIssueHistoryHome.aspx?IId=15009

Welsh Parliament (2020c) *Legislative Consent: European Union (Withdrawal) Bill*. Senedd Business. 26 September. https://business.senedd.wales/mgIssueHistoryHome.aspx?IId=19908

Welsh Parliament (2020d) *Law Derived from the European Union (Wales) Act 2018*. Senedd Business. 7 March. https://business.senedd.wales/mgIssueHistoryHome.aspx?IId=21280

Welsh Parliament (2020e) *Legislative Consent: European Union (Withdrawal Agreement) Bill*. Senedd Business. 9 January. https://business.senedd.wales/mgIssueHistoryHome.aspx?IId=27420

Welsh Parliament (2020f) *Common UK Policy Frameworks*. Senedd Business. 11 January. https://senedd.assembly.wales/mgIssueHistoryHome.aspx?IId=23807

Welsh Parliament (2020g) *Legislative Consent: United Kingdom Internal Market Bill*. Senedd Business. 2 October. https://business.senedd.wales/mgIssueHistoryHome.aspx?IId=29782&Opt=0

Welsh Parliament (2020h) *Legislative Consent: Trade Bill 2020*. Senedd Business. 16 April. https://business.senedd.wales/mgIssueHistoryHome.aspx?IId=28240&Opt=

Welsh Parliament (2020i) *Legislative Consent: Agriculture Bill*. Senedd Business. 23 October. https://senedd.assembly.wales/mgIssueHistoryHome.aspx?IId=23015

Welsh Parliament (2020j) *Legislative Consent: Agriculture Bill 2020*. Senedd Business. 13 February. https://business.senedd.wales/mgIssueHistoryHome.aspx?IId=27736

Welsh Parliament (2020k) *Legislative Consent: Environment Bill*. Senedd Business. 2 July. https://business.senedd.wales/mgIssueHistoryHome.aspx?IId=37509

Welsh Parliament (2020l) *Legislative Consent: Environment Bill 2020.* Senedd Business. 26 February. https://business.senedd.wales/mgIssueHistoryHome.aspx?IId=27737

Welsh Parliament (2020m) *Legislative Consent Memorandum on the Healthcare (International Arrangements) Bill.* Senedd Business. 23 January. https://business.senedd.wales/mgIssueHistoryHome.aspx?IId=23365

Wincott, Daniel, Murray, C. R. G. and Gregory Davies (2021) *The Anglo-British Imaginary and the Rebuilding of the UK's Territorial Constitution after Brexit: Unitary State or Union State?* Territory, Politics, Governance, Volume 10, Issue 5, pp. 696–713.

6 Comparing Scotland and Wales

With the 2010 General Election, a turbulent decade began for intergovernmental relations with different parties in power across Westminster, Holyrood, Cardiff Bay and Stormont.[1] Subsequently, more responsibilities were devolved, and the Welsh and Scottish legislatures and executives became more autonomous; though not as self-reliant as they would like to be. In the aftermath of the 2016 EU referendum, territorial representation at the centre has gained ever more relevance, as the devolved governments were severely at odds with Westminster over the future alignment with the EU, the repatriation of powers from the EU to the UK, and over the constitutional implications of Brexit for the devolution settlement. Without the EU's supranational regulatory framework, the UK Government has become increasingly interested in interfering in the devolved jurisdictions, and in turn the devolved governments have sought to influence policies and decisions at Westminster and Whitehall. These issues caused not only severe intergovernmental tensions but also led to examples of intensive cooperation. The following will closely compare the institutions and practices; the political influence of the Scottish and Welsh Governments on central decisions and policies and the nature of their interactions with the UK Government for Scotland and Wales as a 'within-case analysis' of two territorial administrations within the UK's unitary polity.

Intergovernmental institutions and practices for Scotland and Wales

Constitutional and institutional design shapes how multilevel states operate and governments interact, which is why many studies have investigated federations with constitutional and legally binding arrangements to enable the participation of substate entities in central decision-making (cf. Wright 1988; Watts 2008; Bolleyer 2009; Hueglin and Fenna 2010; Broschek 2011; Bolleyer and Thorlakson 2012; Poirier et al. 2015). The devolution of political, legislative and fiscal authority to Scotland, Wales and Northern Ireland did not alter Westminster's unitary framework. To preserve Parliament's supremacy consecutive UK Governments have preferred the flexibility of

DOI: 10.4324/9781003349952-6

ad hoc coordination over a formalisation of intergovernmental relations. As a result, neither the Scottish nor the Welsh Governments can rely on intra-institutional arrangements at the centre through which they are integrated and socialised within state-wide decision-making. There are only formal provisions with intergovernmental relevance, whereby those located in Whitehall have failed to provide consistent guidance in the interaction between the central and the devolved administrations. Initiatives, such as the Number 10 Union Unit and the Union Directorate in the Cabinet Office, could not ensure coherent leadership on devolution within the core executive. The Cabinet Office struggles to coordinate intergovernmental business across Government, and individual departments have a mixed record of expertise and proactive engagement with devolution issues (Cabinet Office 2021, 14; Kenny et al. 2021, 22–23). The Wales Office is the smallest Whitehall department with less than 50 members of staff, followed by the Scotland Office with approximately 75 civil servants. They liaise with the devolved executives and facilitate exchanges between the different governments. But due to their limited size, powers and political weight, they often struggle to assert themselves vis-à-vis other departments and in Cabinet meetings. Despite their regular and beneficial working relations with the Scotland and Wales Office, the Scottish and Welsh Governments have questioned the necessity of these territorial departments and prefer to directly approach the Cabinet Office and other Whitehall departments and ministers.

Without commanding the same authority as constitutional courts in federal polities, the Supreme Court has evolved into a significant arbitrator to clarify disputes over the different devolution settlements and the allocation of competences. A prominent example hereof was the judgement on *Miller v Secretary of State for Exiting the European Union*, which rejected the appeal of the Scottish and Welsh Governments that triggering Article 50 TEU would require their legislative consent. The Supreme Court also disapplied the UK Withdrawal from the European Union (Legal Continuity) (Scotland) Bill upon referral by the UK Attorney General and the Advocate General for Scotland. Its rulings are only legally binding for the devolved administrations but not for the UK Parliament, which means that by default its judgements favour the centre. While governments typically seek to resolve potential challenges before the enactment of statutes, the judges have adopted rather a cautious and text-bound approach to the interpretation of cases and avoid resolving political or constitutional matters (Brouillet and Mullen 2018, 63–74). Nevertheless, on some occasions, the Supreme Court has ruled in favour of the devolved institutions, decisions which the UK Government has accepted and even led it to redefine the allocation of powers to the Senedd, when the Wales Act 2017 subsequently replaced the conferred with a reserved power model.

In the absence of formal intergovernmental institutions, governments have to rely on informal, non-binding *inter-institutional* means, which enable governments to flexibly enter or exit any joint negotiations (cf. Broschek 2011,

545; Hueglin 2013, 39). The existing informal institutions and practices are neither *complementing*,[2] *accommodating*,[3] nor *competing*,[4] but they are *substantive* for the interaction between governments (cf. Helmke and Levitsky 2004, 728–731). Until the 2022 review of intergovernmental relations, the institutional depth of all intergovernmental arrangements was *weak*, except for the British-Irish Council.[5] The most important informal institution is the Sewel Convention according to which the devolved legislatures need to give their legislative consent to Westminster bills that impact on areas within their competences. The requirement of Legislative Consent Motions is meant to provide a constitutional guarantee for territorial self-rule and in practice works as a political device for intergovernmental scrutiny and negotiations. In particular, when the UK Government relies on devolved legislation to implement laws in reserved areas, Sewel can be a source of cooperation and political influence. The convention was codified in the Scotland Act 2016 and in the Wales Act 2017 but remains legally non-binding for Westminster. During the first two decades of the devolution settlement over 200 consent motions were passed (155 in the Scottish Parliament, 61 in the Senedd and 65 in the Northern Ireland Assembly). By 2020, only 13 out of 350 times was consent fully or partially withheld, mostly by the Welsh Assembly under the conferred powers model (Paun and Shuttleworth 2020, 11). The Sewel Convention was then the primary reason why the UK Government initiated the turn to the reserved powers model and introduced the Wales Act 2017. However, on exceptional occasions when constitutional guarantees are needed most have exposed the flaws of an informal convention. When the EU (Withdrawal) Act 2018 finally received Royal Assent, it was the first but not the only time when the UK Government acknowledged the need for legislative consent but decided to ignore the veto of the Scottish Parliament. While this time the Welsh Government had negotiated terms for which it recommended giving consent, subsequently the EU (Withdrawal Agreement) Act 2020 and the UK Internal Market Act 2020 did not get the approval of any of the three devolved legislatures but nevertheless received Royal Assent. Although this has seriously undermined trust in the effectiveness of Legislative Consent Motions, at the time, the Welsh Government (2019a, 8) took a slightly more positive outlook on the future of Sewel than the Scottish Government. (WG11). Despite proposals from both executives (Constitution and Cabinet Directorate 2018; Welsh Government 2019a, 8) to formalise the convention, the review of intergovernmental relations left it untouched. Meanwhile, other bills continued to receive consent from the Scottish and Welsh Parliaments, including the Coronavirus Act 2020.[6]

An opaque network of informal multilateral and bilateral compacts, concordats and protocols supports engagement between the different governments. Most visibly, at the top sits the general Memorandum of Understanding (MoU), which sets out the main principles of communication, consultation, cooperation and the exchange of information. The MoU also provides a protocol on dispute avoidance and resolution, albeit in practice the official resolution procedure was only triggered five times. Governments typically try to avoid the "cumbersome, time-consuming, resource intensive" procedure with its uncertain outcomes by resolving arguments before they escalate (SG12). While in the past, only the UK Government could decide whether it acknowledged an issue raised by the devolved administrations as a legitimate dispute, the 2022 review of intergovernmental relations updated the dispute resolution mechanism now allowing all governments as a last resort to refer disagreements to impartial IGR Secretariat, which is designated to decide whether an issue is a legitimate dispute.[7] Leaving the EU has led to an expansion of informal intergovernmental provisions, often to complement statutes.[8] The UK Common Frameworks programme adds a significant array of multilateral agreements with varying purposes in terms of operational coordination and joint policy development. Before the passage of the UK Internal Market Act undermined the cooperative spirit of the Common Frameworks, the Scottish and Welsh Governments sought them as a promising initiative, which yet need to stand up to examination.

The MoU also contains a supplementary agreement establishing the Joint Ministerial Committee (JMC), which represented the highest intergovernmental forum to debate constitutional and political issues in a confidential private space without external scrutiny. The JMC was only *weakly* institutionalised, not a decision-making body, and, except for the former sub-committees JMC Europe, meetings took not place frequently. In October 2016, JMC European Negotiations (JMC EN) was installed as the only sub-committee with terms of references that were in principle favourable to the devolved administrations, but to the frustration of the Scottish and Welsh Governments in reality they did not provide opportunities for effective consultation and joint decision-making on the EU withdrawal process. Besides the JMC structures, there were some task-oriented bilateral groups, such as the Scottish and the Welsh Joint Exchequer Committees that worked on the devolution of tax, borrowing and social security powers under the Scotland Acts of 2012 and 2016 and the Wales Acts of 2014 and 2017. While the British-Irish Council used to be the only *medium* institutionalised intergovernmental body with statutory functions, its own resources, collectively financed staff and a standing secretariat, most interactions between the Scottish and Welsh administrations and the UK Government happen elsewhere. The review of intergovernmental relations, however, introduced the new three-tier structure to replace the JMC with the Prime Minister and Heads of Devolved Governments Council (third tier), the Interministerial Standing Committee and Finance Interministerial Standing Committee[9] (second tier).[10] It also established a standing IGR Secretariat hosted by the Cabinet Office. This provides a *medium* institutional depth to the new committee structure.

Considering the limits of the existing informal institutions, informal practices cover an essential part of intergovernmental interactions to facilitate regular exchanges via fluid and task-oriented networks of working groups and quadrilateral meetings between individual departments. At ministerial level, the review of intergovernmental relations added a more coherent structure to previous quadrilateral formats[11] and created new Interministerial Groups (IMGs).[12] It also highlights that the portfolio engagement (first tier) and the resolution of disputes should be by and large take place at official level. Whether for Scotland or Wales, without the engagement between civil servants beneath the ministerial level the UK's multilevel polity would hardly function. The innumerable informal and personal relations between directors, deputy directors, policy teams and other officials are at the heart of intergovernmental relations and help to resolve any issues that occur at an early stage (SG8, WG12) (Scottish Affairs Committee 2019, 6). While all officials are technically employed by the UK Government, their political accountability is separated for each administration and their mutual engagement depends on the need to cooperate on common policies and the goodwill of ministers and permanent secretaries. Their engagement is widely perceived as trustworthy and professional, without any systematic differences across Scotland and Wales. Among the best-established links are bilateral senior officials' groups between HM Treasury and each devolved administration; between the Department for Work and Pensions and the Scottish Government; the Justice in Wales Strategy and for the delivery of English-Welsh border health services. In response to Brexit, Whitehall's devolution coordinating teams have generally grown, and more senior officials' and working groups, pioneered by DEFRA and the Welsh Government, have emerged and also as part of the Common Frameworks programme. In particular, the Senior Officials' Group has become a central hub between the ministerial and official levels of engagement.

Lastly, there are some interparliamentary practices between the different legislatures; though as in most multilevel systems, these relations are marginal and ad hoc (Public Administration and Constitutional Affairs Committee 2016, 26). The Welsh Affairs Committee can conduct joint meetings with the Senedd but has only sporadically (less than ten times) made use of the possibility to hold joint sessions and inquiries. Such authorised interparliamentary practices are not laid down for Scotland or Northern Ireland. The Scottish Affairs Committee can invite committees of the Scottish Parliament to give evidence (Birrell 2012a, 222–223), and occasionally Westminster and Holyrood held joint evidence sessions on specific inquiries. In addition, the Speakers and Presiding Officers of the four UK legislatures met regularly without producing publicly available outcomes (Public Administration and Constitutional Affairs Committee 2016, 26; Evans 2019, 102). In 2017, the Interparliamentary Forum on Brexit was established to provide for a collective scrutiny of EU-related legislation and policies, but towards the end of 2019 following the General Election and the COVID-19 pandemic the forum "appears to have lost momentum" (UK Parliament 2020a). Despite new calls for the institutionalisation of interparliamentary cooperation (Evans 2019; UK Parliament 2020b), as long as the

UK Government is unwilling to loosen its grip over Parliament, the different parliaments lack political incentives to cooperate with each other on a systematic basis.

Political influence of Scotland and Wales

In the absence of intra-institutional and *highly* institutionalised intergovernmental arrangements, which would enable the devolved administrations to participate in central policy- and decision-making by majority vote, an examination of political influence beyond a merely legalistic approach is essential to get a satisfying idea of their territorial power. Based on extensive in-depth research, the *EAR instrument* by Arts and Verschuren (1999) provided a valuable tool to triangulate multiple sources and perspectives for a systematic analysis of a wide range of policies and decisions. To examine the extent to which the devolved governments could modify the behaviour and outcomes of the UK Government, their *political influence* was assessed the multiplication of their *goal-achievement* (GA), *ascription* of the outcome to either through their direct or anticipated intervention (AS); and the *political relevance* of the policy outcome (PR):[13] PI = GA × AS × PR.[14]

Though there are issues which the devolved administrations could not influence according to their interests, looking at Table 6.1, there are plenty of examples where the UK Government accommodated their preferences. Considering the big constitutional matters, albeit the UK Government did not meet all demands,[15] during the preparations within the Smith Commission, in the direct negotiations and later through the implementation of the statute, the Scottish Government impacted substantially on the Scotland Act 2016. Under different circumstances and on a more modest scale, the Welsh Government was also successful in feeding its priorities into the Wales Act 2017. As mentioned earlier, the Sewel Convention provided an important source of influence, as the Senedd withheld legislative consent to the initial bill, which was not viewed as guaranteeing sufficient and lasting autonomy. Overall, the Scottish and the Welsh Governments exercised *substantial* political influence on both of their respective constitutional reform acts, as well as on the review of intergovernmental relations.

Over the course of Brexit, new constitutional issues have arisen within various statutes that de facto interfered with devolved competences. Throughout 2017, the Scottish and Welsh Governments lobbied Whitehall and prevent a re-centralisation of retained EU power and a freezing of devolved powers. It took them a concerted and hard-fought campaign that included various actors, such as a coalition of Conservative, Labour, LibDem and Crossbencher peers in the House of Lords, to ensure that most retained competences went to the devolved instead of the central level. Both governments also introduced their own continuity bills for the purpose of ensuring the continuation of and dynamic alignment with EU rules, as well

Table 6.1 Summary of political influence

Policy/decision	Devolved government	Goal-achievement	Ascription	Political relevance	Political influence
Scotland Act 2016	SG	Substantial (2)	Substantial (2)	Great (3)	Substantial (12)
Wales Act 2017	WG	Substantial (2)	Substantial (2)	Great (3)	Substantial (12)
Intergovernmental review	SG	Substantial (2)	Some (1)	Great (3)	Substantial (6)
	WG	Substantial (2)	Substantial (2)	Great (3)	Substantial (12)
EU (Withdrawal) Act 2018	SG	Substantial (2)	Substantial (2)	Great (3)	Substantial (12)
	WG	Substantial (2)	Great (3)	Great (3)	Great (18)
EU (Withdrawal Agreement) Act 2020	SG/WG	No (0)	No (0)	Great (3)	No (0)
UK Common Frameworks	SG/WG	Substantial (2)	Great (3)	Great (3)	Great (18)
UK Internal Market Act 2020	SG	No (0)	No (0)	Great (3)	No (0)
	WG	No (0)	Substantial (2)	Great (3)	No (0)
Shared Prosperity Fund	SG/WG	No (0)	No (0)	Great (3)	No (0)
Trade Act 2021	SG/WG	Some (1)	Some (1)	Great (3)	Some (3)
Immigration and Social Security Co-ordination Act 2020	SG/WG	No (0)	No (0)	Substantial (2)	No (0)
Statement of Funding Policy	SG	Substantial (2)	Some (1)	Great (3)	Substantial (6)
	WG	Some (1)	Some (1)	Great (3)	Some (3)
Fiscal Framework for Scotland	SG	Great (3)	Substantial (2)	Great (3)	Great (12)
Fiscal Framework for Wales	WG	Substantial (2)	Substantial (2)	Great (3)	Substantial (12)
Agriculture Act 2020	SG/WG	Substantial (2)	Substantial (2)	Substantial (2)	Substantial (8)
Environment Act 2021	SG/WG	Some (1)	Substantial (2)	Substantial (2)	Substantial (4)
City and growth deals	SG/WG	Substantial (2)	Substantial (2)	Substantial (2)	Substantial (8)
Rail franchise for Scotland	SG	Great (3)	Substantial (2)	Substantial (2)	Substantial (12)
Rail franchise for Wales	WG	Great (3)	Great (3)	Substantial (2)	Great (18)
Healthcare (EEA and Switzerland Arrangements) Act 2019	SG	Substantial (2)	Some (1)	Substantial (2)	Substantial (4)
	WG	Substantial (2)	Substantial (2)	Substantial (2)	Substantial (8)
Drug use and crime prevention	SG	No (0)	Some (1)	Some (1)	No (0)
Criminal justice	WG	Some (1)	Substantial (2)	Substantial (2)	Substantial (4)

as of pressuring the UK Government. Whereas the Welsh Government was pleased with amendments and passed a non-binding Intergovernmental Agreement on the EU (Withdrawal) Bill in April 2018, the Scottish Government was not satisfied and did not recommend giving legislative consent. The UK Government passed EU (Withdrawal) Act 2018 anyway and for the first time ignored the Sewel Convention. In December, the Scottish Continuity Bill was suspended by the Supreme Court on the grounds that the Scottish Parliament cannot constrain the UK Parliament by legislating on the same objective. The UK's Attorney General withdrew his reference of the European Union (Wales) Bill to the Supreme Court after the UK and Welsh Governments reached their intergovernmental agreement. Because the goal-achievement can be more ascribed to the Welsh than the Scottish Government, the former's overall political influence was rated as *great*. At the same time, both were eager to stay economically and politically closely aligned with the EU and had *no* political influence to affect the UK's negotiation position. Looking at the Withdrawal Agreement with the EU, the Trade and Cooperation Agreement of 30 December 2020 between the EU and the UK, and in particular the subsequent passing the EU (Withdrawal Agreement) Bill, their priorities diverged too strongly from those of the UK Government.

The UK Government has worked closely with the Scottish and Welsh Governments on the development of the UK Common Frameworks programme, during which they exerted at least *substantial* political influence across the different policy areas. Whether the Common Frameworks have established effective joint governance structures for policy development, decision-making and conflict resolution remains to be seen. Yet, there was *no* political influence exercised by the Scottish and Welsh Governments over the UK Internal Market Act 2020, which undermined the framework's purpose of managing potential policy divergence in agreement with the devolved administrations. The Welsh Government again collaborated with the House of Lords and subsequently challenged the act before the High Court without success.[16] Regardless of the Scottish and Welsh vetoes, the UK Government enforced the act, which it can use to set binding standards for goods and services on the devolved jurisdictions, to establish a UK-wide scheme to control state aid, and to make direct payments in devolved areas. The Scottish and the Welsh Governments also had *no* political influence over the Shared Prosperity Fund, which replaced the EU's Cohesion Policy. Having managed the EU's Structural Funds in the past, both wanted to be equivalently and directly compensated by the UK Government. Instead, the UK Government set up a new programme that allocates less funding for Scotland and Wales, targets local authorities and only involves the devolved administrations as stakeholders rather than as decision-makers. The UK Internal Market Act further empowers the centre to promote the Union by funding projects across the UK, which may even be at odds with the policy objectives of the Scottish and Welsh Governments.

Both devolved governments exerted *some* political influence on the UK's trade policies and the Trade Act 2021 giving UK and devolved ministers powers to make subordinate legislation for the implementation of trade agreements by removing non-tariff barriers. Even though control over foreign affairs and international treaties is a prerogative power of the UK executive, the Scottish and Welsh Governments were, among other stakeholders, consulted in the development of the bill and ministers and officials have subsequently worked together on trade priorities. While they lobbied successfully for amendments giving similar powers to UK ministers, the devolved administrations only achieved non-binding instead of binding consultation rights if UK ministers were to legislate on devolved matters. They also aimed for a closer alignment with the European Single Market and have continued to criticise their lack of influence on international obligations. Immigration policy has been another highly relevant issue for all governments. The Scottish and Welsh Governments had *no* influence by proposing tailored immigration rules for their jurisdictions, such as post-study work visas, lowering the financial thresholds, ending the net migration target and the immigration skills charge, allowing for shortage occupation lists and extending rights in family migration. Since the UK Government needed to deliver its manifesto promises, it passed the Immigration and Social Security Co-ordination (EU Withdrawal) Act 2020, which introduced a point-based immigration system.

Funding decisions have been deliberately depoliticised and kept out of public negotiations or disputes (Bradbury 2021, 288–289). Although the UK Government tends to announce its allocation of public budgets without prior consultation, and in theory the Barnett formula is supposed to reflect territorial needs, the distribution of resources indicates asymmetrical levels of political influence. Scotland and Wales enjoy relatively generous block grants, which they can spend autonomously, whereby the share per capita is comparatively more favourable to the former than to the latter. Hence, the Scottish and Welsh executives can claim *substantial* and *some* political influence on the Treasury in advance to the Statement of Funding Policy.[17] The Fiscal Frameworks for Scotland and Wales, which were agreed to manage the devolution of tax and borrowing authority under the Scotland Act 2016 and the Wales Act 2014, further demonstrate a *substantial* political influence of the respective devolved government. The Scottish Government could secure more funding than the UK Government initially proposed but in turn had to accept lower borrowing limits than it wanted.[18] Welsh ministers did not receive higher borrowing limits and all the tax powers that they asked for, including vacant land tax and air passenger duty, but they were still pleased with the outcome.

Agriculture and food is an area characterised by long-standing cooperation and consultation between the different governments. Some clauses of the Agriculture Bill 2017–2019 required the legislative consent of the Scottish and Welsh Parliaments, and provided executive powers for Scottish and Welsh ministers to ensure the continuation of payments to farmers post-Brexit.[19] The Scottish Government was strongly opposed to potential interference in its devolved responsibilities, asked for a series of amendments, and passed its own Agriculture (Retained EU Law and Data) (Scotland) Bill. The Welsh Government was generally fine with the scope of the bill but due to the concerns of the Senedd gained some important changes and consultation rights. After the first Agriculture Bill was stopped by the dissolution of Parliament in 2019, the newly elected UK Government introduced the Agriculture Bill 2019–2021 and controversial issues were resolved, including clauses that would have enabled the UK Government to exercise powers that are devolved. Both the Scottish and Welsh Governments had *substantial* political influence in reshaping the bill and subsequently recommended giving legislative consent to the Agriculture Act 2020.

The Johnson administration also relaunched the Environment Bill 2019–2021 to introduce a new domestic framework for environmental governance, which established a range of concurrent powers held by UK and devolved ministers.[20] Except for two last-minute amendments added after Holyrood had already given its consent, the Scottish Government felt content with the bill. The UK Government subsequently committed to informally consult the Scottish Government when its policies would impact on Scotland. For some time, the Senedd withheld its consent due to concerns over the transfer of its primary legislative powers to the UK and Welsh executives. The Welsh Government still accepted an informal consultation and a non-binding informal agreement to resolve the dispute with the UK Government over legislative competence in relation to forest risk commodities. Overall, the Scottish and Welsh Governments had exercised *substantial* political influence over the Environment Act 2021, though their goal-achievement was fairly low. While both passed their own legislation to stay closely aligned to the EU's environmental regulations, the UK Internal Market Act and international trade agreements enable central legislation to undermine the effectiveness of their environmental policies.

With regard to economic policies and development, the city and growth deals across Scotland[21] and Wales[22] have been a joint collaboration that also includes local authorities. Even though the UK Government consulted neither the Scottish and Welsh Governments when it announced its first funding initiatives nor intended to cooperate closely with them, the latter sought to seize the extra financial opportunity and were supported by the Scotland and Wales Offices. Both devolved governments negotiated the heads of terms for each deal and worked together on the delivery of each project, which gave them *substantial* political influence. They were further able to gain executive control over the rail franchises within their jurisdictions and enjoyed *substantial* (Scotland) and *great* (Wales) political influence over the UK Government's transport decisions. It took the Welsh Government longer with more compromises, but in 2018 the UK Welsh Ministers (Transfer of Functions) (Railways) Order and the Cooperation and Collaboration Agreement between the Secretary of State for Transport and the Welsh Ministers empowered the Welsh executive to design the rail franchise for 15 years. Due to the low number of passengers during the COVID-19 pandemic, Wales eventually received the ability to use public providers and was the first nation to renationalise its railway services under the publicly owned company Transport for Wales Rail Limited in February 2021. The Scottish Government announced its takeover of the Scottish franchise in 2022 as the operator of last resort under the COVID-19 emergency measures.

The Healthcare (European Economic Area and Switzerland Arrangements) Act 2019 was another example of *substantial* political influence, although the Welsh Government was more proactive in shaping the outcome. The bill was about reciprocal funding and the implementation of international healthcare schemes post-Brexit, and it permitted UK ministers to amend, repeal or revoke devolved legislation. Together with the Scottish Government, which had recommended consent fairly early in the legislative process, the Welsh Government did not get legally binding guarantees, but achieved amendments made in the House of Lords, and signed a memorandum of understanding on the consultation procedure for the development of international healthcare agreements. The final examples analysed were in the area of justice and policing. In 2018, the UK Government did not allow the Scottish Government to introduce a pilot scheme for safe injection facilities and services by the Glasgow City Council, nor to change reserved legislation (the Misuse of Drugs Act 1971) to remove legal barriers to safe injection facilities, or to approve a general devolution of criminal justice sanctions for drugs and other drug-related laws. Consequently, the Scottish Government had *no* political influence. The Welsh Government lost battles over the establishment of Police and Crime Commissioners and Panels, financial support for legal aid services and the building of new prisons. Whereas it has also unsuccessfully pushed for a devolution of justice, it cooperates closely with the UK Government on criminal justice matters and its overall political influence on justice-related matters is *substantial*.

To some extent, Bulpitt's (2008, 62–67) idea of a dual polity of *high politics* (e.g. foreign affairs, trade and immigration) for which the centre claims sole responsibility and *low politics* (e.g. agriculture, environment, transport, healthcare) handed down to the periphery still applies today. Originally published in 1983, John's (2008, 7) introduction to the reprint of Bulpitt's *Territory and Power* states: "The book informs the reader about the complicity and arrogance of the elites at the centre; their false sense of grandeur about their international role; the lack of planning; the tendency to move from crisis to crisis; the propping up of reactionary elites in Northern Ireland; and the underlying instability of the system." Since then, meaningful resources that supported central dominance pre-devolution have eroded; including its control over the decentralised party system, bureaucratic territorial elites, interest groups and citizens. Largely indifferent (hands-off) towards devolved politics, Whitehall has only occasionally pursued promotional (hands-on) strategies to gain support during elections and referendums.

Though a more hegemonic unionist approach may ensure the centre's autonomy over high politics, it has become more difficult to coerce the periphery to simply accept unpopular decisions. Constitutional matters require the consent of the devolved legislatures, powers overlap and decisions by one government have mutual implications. Even though the Sewel Convention cannot provide an absolute protection against interference by the UK Government, it is a source of territorial power. The Scottish and Welsh Governments have forwarded arguments as well as threatened to withhold consent, whereby the former has been more likely to make gains by threatening to withdraw from negotiations. Except when the stakes are too high for the centre to accept territorial disruptions or divergence, the requirement to receive legislative consent from the devolved legislatures is generally taken seriously by the UK Government.

As Table 6.1 shows, there are certainly issues where the devolved administrations had *no* political influence, primarily in relation to EU withdrawal, foreign affairs, international trade and immigration rules, matters over which the UK Government commands reserved or prerogative authority. The assessment of the various policy examples and areas also reveals a remarkable range of central decisions that were affected by either the Scottish or the Welsh Governments. And yet, the Scottish and Welsh Governments appear generally sceptical that they can impact decisions in Whitehall (SG11, SG12, SG14, WG9), while respondents from the UK Government equally struggled to give concrete examples of devolved influence. An official from the Scottish Government expressed it:

> One complaint that our ministers have is that the consultation of the devolved administrations appears to be a tick box exercise. We're consulted, we say what we think, and nothing changes, ever. If we could be in an environment where we could be sure that our views have been considered sometimes, if we could see where the policy positions have changed as a result of the consultation, then maybe we would feel in a much more amicable space. Part of the problem is that consultation happens generally at a very last stage.
>
> (SG12)

While psychologically, experiences of not being heard on especially grave matters may skew the perception of political influence, there are also possible strategic motives to downplaying one's impact on Whitehall. Claiming influence on the centre may trigger sovereignty reflexes, and also take away opportunities to shift blame onto the UK Government. Further, if the Scottish Government was seen to be warmly welcomed and heard in Whitehall, it would undermine arguments for further territorial autonomy.

Although in the UK's unitary state, the centre is not bound by majority vote and can legislate and allocate financial resources unilaterally and by hierarchical direction, its actions are still shaped and constrained by strategic constellations. There is a widespread perception that the Welsh Government cannot unfold the same political influence as its Scottish counterpart (cf. Public Administration and Constitutional Affairs Committee of the House of Commons 2016, 16; Hunt and Minto 2017; Rawlings 2017, 22). Due to its larger size and greater thirst for political autonomy Scotland has secured more legislative and financial competences and resources. Still, relative to their objectives and the ascription of successful outcomes, the empirical analysis reveals that the Scottish and Welsh Governments have a similar record in influencing the UK Government. In regard to EU (Withdrawal) Act 2018 and the devolution of the rail franchises, for instance, the Welsh were even more effective in shaping the outcome according to their preferences. The examples presented in this study further indicated that administrations are less likely to exercise *great* political influence on politics at the centre. Even the strong impact of the Welsh Government on the EU (Withdrawal) Act 2018 was partly mitigated by subsequent statutes. When different governments only engage reactively rather than by positively coordinating their actions or developing joint policies as like-minded, trusting partners, the political influence of the devolved administrations can hardly be *great*. Political influence is then mostly exercised as part of negative coordination to ensure that UK bills permit the devolved institutions to rule on the same issues or to prevent a disruptive impact from the centre on devolved policies or competences.

Interactions of Scotland and Wales with the centre

In addition to the comparison of intergovernmental institutions and practices, as well as political influence, the third investigation focuses on the devolved governments' patterns of interaction with the centre. Based on research by Tatham (2016, 16 et seq.), Chapter 5 examined the extent to which functional and political interdependence (IV1), preference intensity (IV2), party congruency (IV3) and strategic power (IV4) determined whether the Scottish and Welsh Governments either do not interact (DV1), cooperate (DV2) or engage in conflict (DV3) with the UK Government. There are some caveats to a symmetrical analysis of the patterns of interactions. First, the examples of policy- and decision-making depended on the availability of empirical data and on the insights of respondents. Second, by 2010, the devolved and the central governments were all run by different parties, which means that within the timeframe of this study there is not a direct comparison of the impact of party congruency (IV3) on the patterns of interaction. Third, and related to this, during the last decade, and particularly since the 2016 EU referendum, the political relations between the

Scottish and Welsh Governments on the one hand and the UK Government on the other have become increasingly strained.

Functional and political interdependence

Examples from different policy areas indicate that low functional and political interdependence (IV1) is a strong predictor for non-interaction (DV1). Yet, non-interaction (DV1) itself can stem from tensions when governments refuse to cooperate and instead act unilaterally, even though their powers and policy problems are interdependent (UKG8). In loosely coupled multilevel polities, functional and political interdependence (IV1) may therefore not always lead to interaction, but cooperation (DV2) and conflict (DV3) would hardly take place without the mutual implications of overlapping responsibilities in policy areas. The dual allocation of legislative authority did not incentivise a great deal of intergovernmental exchange, and before the EU referendum intergovernmental relations were largely seen as niche (SP2). Whitehall departments have a reputation to "devolve and forget" and to act only for England without caring for the further implications of policy divergence unless an overlap of devolved and reserved powers presents an unpredicted challenge for its policy delivery (UKG1, UKG3, WG8). In areas, like education or local government, where the devolved administrations enjoy a great deal of legislative autonomy, the different governments hardly coordinate their agendas and policies (SG12, UKG1, WG8, WP3).[23] Although the devolution of more legislative and fiscal authority by the Scotland Acts 2012 and 2016 and the Wales Acts 2014 and 2017 has not integrated the UK's loosely coupled multilevel polity, actions of one government have become more likely to affect other jurisdictions leading governments to cooperate (DV2) (SP2, WG7).

The EU membership obscured the coupling of different jurisdictions, which has become all too obvious during the withdrawal process. It was in fact only EU matters and the implementation of European legislation in which the different governments most frequently and productively cooperated (DV2), as a civil servant from the Welsh Government put it:

> With the exception of the EU, there's not been a lot of need for shared governance, because generally the allocation of responsibility is fairly clear. But it's only fairly clear in a way that only makes sense within the context of operating within the EU. [...] Apart from that there's been relatively little need for the governments to interact. For a quite a long time there were virtually no formal meetings of the JMC. That wasn't a sign that relations had broken down. It just wasn't really needed. We knew what we were doing, they knew what they were doing, and it sort of worked.
>
> (WG11)

Nevertheless, in the words of a former Welsh minister: "The reality is geography dictates that the four nations of these isles have to work together. They have no choice. You can't just pretend that England isn't over there any more than Northern Ireland can pretend that the EU is across the road. Territorial cooperation is inevitable." (WP5) In light of the high political and functional interdependence (IV1) between European, national and regional levels, agriculture and food are typically referred to as areas where consultation and joint policymaking between governments are most advanced. Further examples include the planning, building and maintaining cross-border transport infrastructure and services, as well as the devolution of the rail franchises the Scottish and Welsh executives, have required ongoing cooperation (DV2) between governments. Because of their geographical proximity with a long-shared border, the functional and political interdependence (IV1) is significantly stronger for Wales than for Scotland (UK7) and governments cooperate (DV2) on relevant legal initiatives in Whitehall. A Welsh official therefore said:

> If we're talking about the development of new legislation, then there's a regular dialogue between Whitehall and Cardiff about the terms of new UK legislation, which potentially could apply in Wales. The question is repeatedly asked: 'Do you want this to apply in Wales? Do you want the powers that we are taking for UK ministers in respect of England also to be made available by this bill to the Welsh ministers? Does the bill impinge on matters which the assembly could legislate about for Wales and if it does, are you happy nevertheless for Parliament to legislate?'
> (WG8)

Although healthcare services are clearly separated across jurisdictions, they have substantial cross-border implications, in particular between Wales and England, which are dealt with largely at an operational rather than a policy level (WG8). The UK and Welsh Governments have to coordinate the treatment of English and Welsh patients in the other jurisdiction, and together with NHS England and NHS Wales, they produce cross-border protocols concerning access to and costs of medical services and the treatment of patients. Except when there is an (inter-)national health crisis, the Scottish and UK Governments show significantly less interaction (DV1). Due to different approaches to limit the spread of the virus and the lack of inner-party communication channels, even the initial cooperation (DV2) during the COVID-19 pandemic did not last long.

Non-interaction (DV1) is also the predominant pattern of interaction between the Scottish and the UK Governments in the area of justice and policing. Since Scotland retained its own legal system throughout the centuries, there are only very few occasions when both have cooperated (DV2) on related matters.[24] In contrast, justice and policing is not devolved to Wales, and "is perhaps one of the areas with greatest level of interaction between devolved and reserved matters." (Independent Expert Advisory Committee for Ongoing Review of the Operation of justice in Wales 2019, 5). As justice is linked to a wide range of policy areas, including healthcare, education, rehabilitation measures and prison services, the UK and Welsh Governments are in regular contact to deal with the corresponding political and functional interdependence (IV1). Both governments maintain good working relations and policy teams discuss the potential implications of legal measures on each other.[25] Different approaches towards the sentencing, imprisonment and rehabilitation of criminals, however, have complicated their intergovernmental relations, as the prisoner population in both territories consists of Welsh and English inhabitants.[26] While policing, the overall imprisonment strategy, infrastructure planning and maintenance of prisons,[27] and probation services fall under the remit of the Ministry of Justice (MoJ), the Welsh Government has prioritised crime reduction through education, drug prevention, and social, health and rehabilitation services (Commission on Justice in Wales 2019). Despite their disagreement over the need for and usefulness of new prisons in Wales, the UK and the Welsh Governments still closely coordinated the building of HM Prison Berwyn in North Wales, which was opened in 2017. In 2018, the Ministry of Justice (2018) and the Welsh Government also published a concordat providing working-level guidance for intergovernmental consultation and cooperation (DV2), and set up integrated project teams, working groups, committees or meetings, including the Justice in Wales Strategy Group. Other coordination agreements include the Blueprints for Female Offending and Youth Justice. In light of their diverging policies, the Welsh Government would like justice and policing to become devolved to Wales, which is opposed by the UK Government on the grounds that crime is a cross-border concern and policies were not sufficiently diverging to justify a transfer of competence.

Despite the high relevance of functional and political interdependence (IV1) for interactions, it has not always been a reliable predictor on its own. Even though it is widely and internationally acknowledged that environmental, climate change and energy policy require joint measures to be effective, central and devolved governments have acted not interacted (DV1) on these matters without coordinating their policies. All governments passed their own targets and legislation to reduce greenhouse gas emissions.[28] Except for some discussions on renewable energies and green infrastructure, environmental protection remains largely territorial, and energy policy has not played a major role for their intergovernmental relations.[29] Similar dynamics apply to areas of economic policy and development, which are separated between macro-responsibilities reserved to Westminster and devolved micro-levers. With the exception of the city and growth deals, ministers rely by and large on their own economic agendas without consistently coordinating their approaches. As the economies of Wales and England are perhaps more interlinked, the Welsh Government tends to look more closely to the policy of the UK Government than the Scottish Government (WP3).

Preference intensity

The preference intensity (IV2) of the issues at stake needs to be high, at least for one government, to seek to cooperate (DV2) with their counterparts. Issues around the constitutional allocation of powers, fiscal relations, agriculture, the economy, transport and justice were characterised by an interplay of political tensions and pragmatic engagement across governments. During state-wide health crises, for instance, functional and political interdependence (IV1) and preference intensity (IV2) are especially high and draw governments together (SP1). During the first outbreak of the Coronavirus in March and April 2020, ministers and officials worked well together (UKG2, UKG5, UKG7, UKG8, UKP2); established the Civil Contingencies Committee (COBR), in which all heads of government met, and five ministerial implementation groups (MIGs); produced a joint Coronavirus Action Plan (Department of Health and Social Care 2020); agreed on lockdown measures for the whole of the UK (Kenny et al. 2021, 31–32); and fast-tracked the Coronavirus Act 2020 through all legislatures. After this initial period of remarkable cooperation (DV2), disagreements started to reappear in late spring 2020, and the four governments largely stopped their interaction (DV1) and acted unilaterally on the lockdown restrictions and reopening of schools.

If an issue is salient for both sides and their priorities diverge, they may likely end up in conflict (DV3) with each other. EU withdrawal with its constitutional implications for the devolution settlement has without a doubt been a matter of high functional political interdependence (IV1) and preference intensity (IV2). When Prime Minister Theresa May intended to reallocate the competences returning from the EU to the centre, allowing UK ministers to alter repatriated EU law by secondary legislation by UK ministers, the Scottish and Welsh Governments vehemently insisted that those powers belong within their remits. After intensive battles, the UK Government only gradually altered its initial approach under the Withdrawal Bill 2018 (previously named the Great Repeal Bill), which included 'freezing' certain devolved powers in areas of retained EU law to ensure that the UK would adhere to its international obligations (Cowie et al. 2020, 73).[30] The different governments also needed to prepare for the event of a no-deal Brexit in order to avoid the detrimental effects of regulative and legislative uncertainty. The political disputes were therefore set aside, and behind the scenes and largely unreported the different governments cooperated (DV2) thoroughly to close potential legislative loopholes. Scottish and Welsh ministers gave consent to around 150 statutory instruments by the UK Parliament (Scottish Government 2019; Welsh Government 2019b). As Kenny et al. (2021, 29) put it:

> This extended episode of more functional, informal collaboration highlights one of the enduring paradoxes of intergovernmental relations in

the UK context during the extended Brexit crisis. While there were clear political incentives for the devolved governments to express and demonstrate their disagreement with the May government's approach to the mandate supplied by the referendum, the requirements of good administrative order at times impelled these different partners to co-operate, even if on occasions through gritted teeth.

Despite some improvement from early 2017 on, when Boris Johnson became Prime Minister in July 2019, his idea of a minimal economic trade agreement with the EU was not reconcilable with the Scottish and Welsh Governments' preferences for a close alignment with the European Single Market. In a historically unprecedented move the UK Government ignored the Sewel Convention, as neither of the devolved legislatures gave their consent to the EU (Withdrawal Agreement) Act 2020.[31] Notwithstanding the period of collaboration under Theresa May to prepare for a potential no-deal Brexit and towards the development of the UK Common Frameworks programme, after winning a clear absolute majority in the 2019 General Election, the UK Government's political leverage increased dramatically. Equipped with a strong political mandate 'to get Brexit done,' the Johnson administration's approach to maintaining the integrity of a UK-wide market through hierarchical direction by statute was fundamentally opposed by the Scottish and Welsh Governments. The UK Internal Market Act also did not receive the consent of the devolved legislatures, yet was enacted on 17 December 2020 allowing other governments to impose lower requirements for the selling of goods and services on other jurisdictions (Paun et al. 2020). The act enables the UK Government to bypass, constrain and overrule the devolved legislatures without prior consultation, and to provide direct financial assistance across the UK, which means a de facto recentralisation of powers and caused an even more serious dispute than that over the EU (Withdrawal) Act 2018 (Andrews 2021, 3).

Party congruency

Governments made-up of different parties are less likely to cooperate, share information and make concessions but rather compete with each other (McEwen 2017, 670). When governments are run by the same party, they share not only common ideologies, agendas and policy objectives, but can also rely on convenient and effective opportunities and access points to coordinate their positions (McEwen et al. 2012, 323; Weissert and Fahey 2018, 345). Even though the investigated decade was never marked by the same party in power at different levels, various issues provided valuable insights into the impact of party congruency (IV3) on patterns of interaction. The combination of functional and political interdependence (IV1) and party congruency (IV3) has proven to be particularly strong in conditioning cooperation (DV2) as well as conflict (DV3). Prior to 2007, intra-party channels compensated for the lack of an effective intergovernmental structure did not require the official conflict resolution mechanism, and facilitated cooperation (DV2) across the Scottish, Welsh and UK Governments (WP5, SG12, UKG7). As a former Scottish minister remembered:

> There was a natural ease about the communications, that was a lot more informal, over the phone, email, party to party, not just through the civil service. There were connections with people who wanted to make a new institution work, and some of them had been in politics together for a long, long time – that was helpful.
> (SP1)

Agreements between the Scottish and UK Governments were easier because they wanted to make devolution work, and the latter tended to smooth political tension with extra funding for Scotland (SG13). Also, when the Welsh Government needed Westminster to pass primary legislation for Wales, its relationships with the UK Government were especially close (WP5).[32] Still, while parties sought to avoid open disputes and handled these behind the scenes (SG3, SP2, WG6, WP6), every now and again tensions between the devolved administrations and the UK Government would publicly surface pre-2007 (SG6). For instance, former Prime Minister Tony Blair and the then First Minister for Wales Rhodri Morgan did not maintain the best relationship (UKG7, WP3). In his famous speech in 2002, Morgan openly attacked New Labour's public sector reforms and spoke of the "clear red water" between the UK Government's market-oriented approach to health and education and the Welsh Assemblies support for universal public service delivery (BBC 2002).

After the SNP formed a minority government in Scotland in 2007 and the Conservatives became the major force in Westminster in 2010, Sewel motions were passed slightly more reluctantly, and disagreements were discussed more publicly (Cairney 2012, 245). Yet, in the early days of party incongruency (IV3), governments behaved less confrontational than the public discourse may have indicated (cf. Mitchell 2010, 65; Cairney 2012, 232 et seq., McEwen et al. 2012, 324; Deacon 2012, 244). A few interviewees further believed that the party constellation had a more modest impact on intergovernmental relations than one would expect (SG2, SG5, SG12, SP2). Former Welsh minister, Alun Davies, for instance, described a state of constructive engagement under the Coalition Government:

> And, for most of the time, we had a very good relationship with the UK government. I think one of the things we forget today, in the disaster that is intergovernmental relations in the UK, is how good the relationship could be and has been. I dealt with UK ministers who were mostly Conservative – there were a few Lib[eral] Dem[ocrat]s in the mix, but mostly Conservative. And when the door is closed and when the

cameras are switched off and when there's no microphones around, you have a good and rich interaction with UK ministers.

(Paun and Nice 2021)

Without intra-party links governments have fared well by not interacting (DV1) with each other unless political and functional interdependence (IV1) and preference intensity (IV2) required them to do so (SP2).[33] Due to the different political outlooks, however, policy objectives have either become difficult to reconcile across governments or governments have competed for electoral support rather than making concessions from which they have little to gain. If they do not belong to the same political community, ministers do not share the same kind of social relationships and meet less frequently (WG7, WP6) (Scottish Affairs Committee 2019, 6–7). A civil servant of the Welsh Government described the constellation as the following:

A Welsh Labour minister is not naturally going to meet a UK Tory minister anywhere apart from if they have formal meetings. Whereas when you're in the same party, you will come across each other in party bodies. You can pick up the phone to each other and you can have conversations which bypass the civil servants; and that doesn't happen between different parties. […] quite often conflicts happen when they don't really want them. Those channels are really useful to stop things blowing up. But they don't exist, and they don't exist with the Scots and London either. It's a shame that we can't have those backroom conversations with the government in London at that level.

(WG11)

As governments struggle to build trust with each other (UKG7), the state of party incongruency (IV3) has created a competitive, and even adversarial environment, in which intergovernmental conflict (DV3) could thrive. Majoritarian democracies in particular create strong pressures for parties to compete with each other for electoral support and foster an adversarial culture of blame-shifting between single-party governments, which are unlikely to have to work together in coalitions (cf. Scharpf 1997, 183 et seq.; Bolleyer 2009, 35–37; 2018, 51; Poirier and Saunders 2015, 451).[34] The fact that the Conservative Party has never formed a government in Scotland, Wales or Northern Ireland may then explain its lack of support for the devolution settlement (SG9, WG2, WG6, WG11, WP5). At the same time, the continuous demand for an expansion of powers for the Scottish Parliament has affected the relations between the UK and the Scottish Governments (SG14). According to a Scottish official: "After 2007, the SNP Government has been extremely active in terms of messaging and public engagement. The intensity and expectation have increased every year." (SG8) The relations worsened remarkably in the course of the 2014 independence referendum and the 2016 EU referendum (SP4). Whereas conflicts (DV3) over the allocation of powers were rare and could be solved in frequent exchanges between officials and legal advisors (Adam 2021, 51–52), policy disagreement and mutual suspicion resulted in an unwillingness to share information and strained the relationship. The constitutional struggles have not only boosted the popularity of independence in Scotland but also in Wales. Welsh ministers have become less hesitant to openly criticise the Conservative-led government over the lack of consultation, representation and influence within UK policy-making (Wyn Jones and Royles 2012, 263–264). In principle, the Welsh Government continues to support remaining part of the Union, but it has started to openly question the legitimacy of Westminster's sovereignty over the devolved legislatures (WG6, WG11, WP5).

Intergovernmental relations turned especially difficult between 2017 and 2019, when the UK Government could neither command an absolute parliamentary majority nor a unified position over the future relationship with the EU. Instead of reaching out to the devolved administrations to deliver its policies, Westminster's centralisation reflexes and the lack of transparency over Whitehall's policies have limited political cooperation (SG4, SG8, SG11). When Boris Johnson won an outright majority in the 2019 General Election, the position of the UK Government towards Brexit became clearer, though also more in contrast to those of the devolved administrations (WG9), which has caused high levels of distress reaching deep into many related policy areas. As the reciprocal willingness and recognition between governments have eroded over the last decade, competitive dynamics have trumped a positive coordination of policies. The continuous tensions have also trickled down to the official level negatively affecting their ability to share information across different administrations (SG2, SG11, UKG3, UKG8, UKG10, WP3). Looking at the examples of environmental and economic policies, it seems likely that the different governments would have cooperated (DV2), if they were led by the same party. And yet, as the empirical findings have demonstrated, despite the lack of party congruency (IV3) all governments manage to work together when their objectives converge, which makes this variable not an absolute determinant of either cooperation or conflict.

Strategic power

While the first three variables offer fairly straightforward causal explanations and similar patterns of interactions for Scotland and Wales, the insights from the fourth variable are more complex and diverse. On its own strategic power (IV4) is an ambivalent predictor of the pattern of interaction. The various conflicts (DV3) between the different levels are typically characterised by high political and functional interdependence (IV1), preference intensity (IV2), and party incongruency (IV3). The political leaderships prioritise their objectives, reflect on their opposites' interests, and evaluate possible outcomes (cf. Scharpf 1997, 44). Although de jure, the centre ultimately has the upper hand, different actor constellations strengthen or weaken the strategic power (IV4) of the periphery. For actors from the Scottish and Welsh Governments intergovernmental relations then become a strategic game between cooperation (DV2) and conflict (DV3) that is shaped by their *strategic preferences, negotiation power* and the *mode of interaction*.[35] The devolved administrations generally resort to cooperative approaches (DV2) when they lack strategic power (IV4), but this does not necessarily provide them with political influence, nor does it prevent tensions. Public disagreements are often not an intentional choice for the Scottish, and even more so for the Welsh Governments, but rather the result of the unresponsiveness of the centre.

The previous chapter analysed a number of unresolved disputes between the different administrations, among which EU withdrawal has often been at the core. The centre did not consider the devolved governments to have a legitimate say over leaving the EU, and therefore acted largely unilaterally when it triggered Article 50 TEU and negotiated the terms of withdrawal and future alignment. Despite their outspoken disagreement with the UK Government's positions, the Scottish and Welsh Governments hoped to cooperate (DV2) with Whitehall and to promote their preferences for the future alignment with the EU in a non-conflictual way (SG11) – though unsuccessfully. The making and implementation of international trade agreements post-Brexit together with the negative implications for territorial autonomy have been a further source of severe tensions between the governments. The Scottish and Welsh Governments presented arguments and information to the UK Government to ensure their interests fed into the international negotiations, but the latter has only reluctantly listened to them and passed the UK Internal Market Act to legally bind the former to implement international obligations that apply in England. Both the Scottish and Welsh executives also expressed a strong preference for a more open immigration regime since the ending of freedom of movement for EU citizens and sought to argue with Whitehall by presenting evidence and statistical modelling to achieve regional exemptions. Yet, because immigration is a reserved matter and limiting it was a key promise of the Vote Leave campaign during the EU referendum, they held little strategic power (IV4) and the centre did not respond to their calls. Even though the block grant system is intended to depoliticise fiscal relations between the governments, conflict (DV3) has often revolved around the allocation of financial resources.[36] The amount of money allocated through the Barnett formula is decided by HM Treasury through hierarchical direction leaving the devolved administrations little strategic power (IV4) in fiscal negotiations. While the devolved government seek to cooperate (DV2) and gain more resources, they may also highlight disagreement when it reflects the interests of their supporters and electorate. In the aftermath of the 2008 financial crisis, for instance, governments diverged in their views on how to restore the fiscal and economic balance, and the Scottish and Welsh

Governments strongly opposed the austerity agenda of the coalition government (SG9, WG2, WG6, WG11, WP5).

While both enjoy strong electoral and public support for their parties and causes, which makes conflict (DV3) more affordable (cf. Benz 2009, 168), they still need to deliver positive outcomes to maintain their favourable electorate. The SNP is often thought of as manufacturing a politics of grievance (SP1, WP4, UKG9). But Scottish ministers cannot afford to be solely confrontational but rather consider carefully any potential negative implications of not cooperating with Whitehall (SG2, SG11). Even though blaming the UK Government for unfavourable developments in Scotland has been used as an argument for Scottish independence, constantly losing political disputes would shed a bad light on any devolved administration (SP2, WG1). Adam and Hepburn (2019, 564) referred to this as a fundamental dilemma: successful cooperation undermines claims for territorial autonomy, but refusing to engage in joint policy solutions can be perceived as bad governance and legitimises a re-centralisation of competences. While the Scottish Government has a strong interest in making policies work for Scotland, openly confronting the centre is an unlikely tactic to secure any concessions but rather will provoke Whitehall to assert its authority (SP1, UKG9). Hence, it generally acts pragmatically and seeks to anticipate which objectives they can achieve by cooperating (DV2) with the UK Government, what the costs of not interacting (DV1) would be and whether emphasising political conflict (DV3) can rally public support for their causes (SG1, SG2, SG5, SG6, SG12). The following responses are exemplary of this:

> Some of it will be for political reasons because the party in government in Scotland will have a different view over the policy being pursued than by the party in government at UK level, and vice versa as well. So some of it will be taken and play to the political supporters. Some of it will be to create a bit of a fuss and a bit of a row. Some of it will be genuinely for politicians to make an argument. So there will be a whole range of reasons why ministers choose to make points and sometimes very strongly about certain aspects of policies.
>
> (SG10)

> In any circumstance we look at what route is more likely to get the right result. That can either try to be cooperative and generally our stance would be that we're trying to cooperate, at very least at official level. It would be very rare that the first thing that we would do is reach for the send-out-a-press-release-button. Generally, we start with cooperation and see how that's going. So it's probably more an escalation of engagement. [...] There will be issues at times where our minister will send letter to the UK Government minister to make a particular point. Sometimes that correspondence will be used if there is a desire to put the issue into the public domain. So ministers can say in parliament or

present to the press: here is the letter I've sent [...], see how I'm fighting on your behalf.' There are times when it's mega-phoned diplomacy and you're writing the letter not expecting an answer but to make a point. There are other times when it's actually putting forward a case and looking for hopefully agreement or at least debate on a particular subject.

(SG3)

Whereas the Scottish and Welsh Governments exercise fairly similar political influence over the centre, they do not enjoy the same strategic power (IV4). The Public Administration and Constitutional Affairs Committee (2016, 16) of the House of Commons emphasised that the respective influence wielded by governments shapes the nature of intergovernmental relations. According to the JMC Joint Secretariat (2018, 7) both administrations have gained "very different experiences and perspectives" when dealing with the UK Government, and "[c]ommentators have highlighted the perceived lack of 'leverage' of Wales/the Welsh Government, particularly relative to Scotland/the Scottish Government". A UK official further acknowledged: "Politically, you don't have to please Wales in the same way as you have to please Scotland." (UKG9) The Welsh Government is well aware that it carries the least political weight among the three devolved administrations (WG2, WG11, WP5, WP6).[37] Notwithstanding that it is the only devolved executive fully supportive of the Union, it needs to demonstrate that it stands up for preserving the Senedd's autonomy and respond to the rising support for Welsh independence and the challenges of competitors, like Plaid Cymru. Welsh politicians have therefore become more assertive of their legitimacy and powers, and started to articulate disagreements more clearly with the UK Government. Disputes and disruptions however bear costs and risks, which is why the Welsh Government has sought to constructively feed its views into UK-wide policies and pushed for a more formalised system of intergovernmental relations (UKG2, UKG8, WG2, WG5, WG7, WG10, WG11, WP4):

We don't have an obvious threat to the UK. The only way we can persuade them is by the force of reason, making sure that we have a lot of evidence, that we marshal our arguments, that we keep on battering at the door of 'this is the reasonable thing to do', and that sometimes works and sometimes doesn't. We have less influence than the Scots for both questions of size but also questions of what we threaten in terms of disruption or what are prepared to threaten in terms of disruption.

(WG11)

We don't 'throw our toys out of the pram' as the Scots do. There's an element of the fact that we don't have as much leverage. If we're just going to be awkward with them and difficult. But it isn't just that. There's a genuine view that we want the Union to work. And also because frankly our ministers just take the view even regardless of how much or how little leverage we've got, regardless of what the political situation is, actually you're probably going to get more done by trying to be positive and constructive than difficult and uncooperative. There's an element of the leverage thing but there's other things that probably weigh more heavily in influencing in the general approach we generally take.

(WG2)

When the Welsh Government has felt like it has relatively high strategic power (IV4), because it is acting within its legitimate rights and enjoys electoral support; it has defended its interests more vehemently. The Police Reform and Social Responsibility Bill 2011 was the first bill to which the Welsh Assembly withheld consent.[38] The building of a relief road for the M4 motorway has been another example of public conflict (DV3).[39] On another occasion, the UK Government changed the tariff system for healthcare services in England without prior consultation, and thereby implicitly increased the costs for the Welsh health boards when accessing services in England. The Welsh Government refused to accept the new system and stopping compensatory payments. Because of the UK Government's dependency on the Welsh Government to provide healthcare for English patients, both governments were motivated to reach an agreement over the funding.

How the governments interact depends in particular on the needs or goodwill of the UK Government. The centre may find it easier to act unilaterally and could simply direct hierarchically, and benefits of making concessions to the devolved administrations are limited (SG9). And yet, it is also subject to wider strategic constellations shaping its behaviour and has an interest "not to end up in pitch battle with the devolved institutions" (WG11). Being perceived as entirely dismissive to the other governments can cost its MPs crucial votes in Scotland and Wales (SG3, SG8), as a Conservative MS suggested:

Sometimes for a Conservative government to intervene in Wales that takes a lot of political expenditure unless you really compromise about your own priorities and future relationships, you might stand apart and say 'it's not worth a fight'.

(WP6)

The devolved administrations can be forced to implement policies, but due to their functional and political interdependence (IV1) for measures to be effective and in accordance with the different territorial systems and practices, central government still relies on a spirit of constructive engagement. The lack of mutual trust and willingness to develop common policies means that joint problems are mostly solved by negative coordination to prevent the detrimental impact of actions by other governments. On various issues, the UK Government started to improve its engagement with the devolved governments after it realised that not working together would come at functional and political costs. On a number of occasions, the UK Government engaged in informal self-organising networks *(voluntary negotiation systems)* with terms of references setting out participating actors, objectives and procedures.[40] When unilateral actions were legally or practically not possible, the different governments even committed themselves to formalised normative regimes *(compulsory negotiation systems)* based on consensus (cf. Scharpf 2000, 241–245). Although these negotiation systems do not bind the centre to decisions taken by majority vote, they raise the strategic power (IV4) of the devolved government significantly.

When the Scottish Government asked for new powers to be devolved to Scotland, negotiations with the UK Government were tough but also cooperative (DV2) because the issue had a high-preference intensity (IV2) on both sides.[41] All five main parties from Scotland unanimously agreed on the devolution of new welfare and fiscal powers (HM Government 2015, 11; Scottish Affairs Committee 2015, 6), which provided a strong political mandate and strategic power (IV4). Within a compulsory negotiation system, the two governments produced a negotiated agreement to transfer new legislative tax and borrowing authority to the Scottish Parliament. Wales is smaller and calls for Welsh independence, though growing, have not yet become a serious threat to the UK Government. Nevertheless, following two defeats before the Supreme Court, the UK Government had a strong interest in realising its commitment made in the St David's Day Agreement and in changing the conferred into a transferred powers model. Both governments also entered a compulsory negotiation system resulting in a negotiated agreement supported by both the Senedd and Westminster. The Wales Act 2017 was followed by a period of difficult, yet constructive, engagement in which the Welsh Government held meaningful strategic power (IV4). The interactions towards the Fiscal Frameworks for Scotland and Wales were also characterised by considerable strategic power (IV4) for the devolved governments, which led the UK Government to change its initial approach of hierarchical direction.

Despite the severe tensions over the terms of leaving the EU, all governments recognised the need for some form of joint mechanisms to deal with policy and law divergence after having left the European Single Market. Because the UK Government relied on the support of the devolved governments to restructure their functional and political interdependence (IV1), it entered a voluntary negotiation system and provided the Scottish and Welsh Governments with notable strategic power (IV4). Their cooperation (DV2) towards the UK Common Frameworks programme was close and consensual, and by the end of 2021, 29 provisional frameworks were agreed4). Leaving the EU's regulatory regime and the Common Agriculture Policy (CAP) has also required a systematic approach of engagement between governments to develop and implement common standards[42]. Regardless of their different outlooks,[43] the Scottish and Welsh Governments had some strategic power (IV4) and the exchange with the UK Government improved subsequently to resolve controversial issues.

Conclusion

Considering the differences in the powers of the Scottish and Welsh legislatures and executives, the political ambitions of the ruling parties, and the population sizes, landmass and economies, variations in their intergovernmental relations in terms of institutions and practices, political influence and patterns of interactions are not as strong as one might expect from the outset. The availability and usage of intergovernmental forums and channels differ only moderately across Scotland and Wales, mostly in the space of bilateral working groups for specific policy issues. The starkest contrast can be found in their preferences for intergovernmental reforms. Whereas the Welsh Government seeks to make the Union work for all territories by introducing a system of formalised shared governance and some form of joint decision-making, albeit potentially benefitting from such reforms, the Scottish Government is cautious to support any arrangements that would bind itself closer to the centre. There is also little incentive for the UK Government to commit to any formal institutions, it cannot be forced to listen to the devolved administrations, and it can pass statutes that the devolved institutions are legally bound to follow. Depending on the issue at hand and the UK centre's need and willingness to find compromise, the devolved governments can still exert substantial political influence on decisions in Whitehall and Westminster.

Functional and political interdependence (IV1), preference intensity (IV2) and party congruency (IV3) together are likely to trigger either cooperation (DV2) or conflict (DV3). Due to their geographical position and the more incremental and less comprehensive devolution of powers, functional and political interdependence (IV1) and thus cooperation (DV2) between the Welsh and the UK Governments are higher than is the case for Scotland. While converging interests around issues of high priority are likely to lead to cooperation (DV2), diverging objectives of high preference intensity (IV2) for both the centre and devolved governments is a probable cause of conflict (DV3). When preference intensity (IV2) is high for one side but low for the other, cooperation (DV2) and non-interaction (DV1) rather than conflict (DV3) are expected outcomes. Depending on the first two variables, party congruency (IV3) facilitates cooperation (DV2), while party incongruency strains the relations across governments it but does not necessarily lead to non-interaction (DV1) or conflict (DV3).

Notwithstanding the desolate state of the political relations between the UK and the devolved governments at the beginning of the 2020s, research on the UK's intergovernmental relations tends to focus on the discord rather than on the cooperation. All governments consider the costs and risks of non-interaction (DV1) and conflict (DV3). When issues reach the public, however, the ability to find a compromise is constrained as governments do not want to appear weak by stepping back from their initial position (SG1, SG12, SP1). As a Scottish official said, "Once things get into the public space, then general positions are set and there will not be a huge amount of compromise. If we publicly take very different positions, then we will not have a lot of influence in where that goes." Hence, open disputes are typically neither desired by the different governments nor expected to lead to a favourable outcome, and disagreements often do not escalate to the ministerial level. In many cases, functional and political interdependence (IV1) has kept all governments trying to find pragmatic solutions for the delivery of policies and services that have a mutual impact on each jurisdiction. At least at official level, interactions have therefore never completely broken down, and this research presented a range of examples of governments cooperating (DV2) to solve disputes (SG2, SG4, SG11, SP1, UKG10, WG10). Multiple Scottish civil servants confirmed this:

> I've also been struck though by the professional way in which the ministers and civil servants in particular have conducted themselves during that period. There's always been political rows and disagreements of course, but in my area of work all the ministerial team understand that a good working relationship with Conservative ministers both in DWP and Scotland Office is important to making the programme of devolution a success.
>
> (SG10)

> At official level our colleagues in Westminster will always generally be professional. I hope we are as well. We will have more conversations that need either to go into a political space to be discussed and agreed, or we can't always find a way through. But at official level it works reasonably well.
>
> (SG2)

> Our inclination is always for more dialogue rather than putting the shutters up, if two ministers disagree very publicly. It's only something that we would really ever advise ministers as a last resort because very public disagreements don't tend to solve matters.
>
> (SG5)

Conflicts (DV3) rather are often an expression of frustration when the different positions are simply irreconcilable and the UK Government shows no intention of accommodating a high preference intensity (IV2) of the Scottish and Welsh Governments (SG2). Whereas the centre's indifference towards the devolved governments has resulted in conflict (DV3), when governments are interdependent (IV1) and share similar objectives of high preference intensity (IV2) they are likely to cooperate (DV2). The prospect of independence makes conflict (DV3) an alternative option for the Scottish Government increasing its strategic power (IV4). In essence, when the centre has a strong interest in finding consensus and consequently in cooperation (DV2), the strategic power (IV4) of both devolved administrations is at its highest. So rather than understanding strategic power (IV4) as a determinant of conflict (DV3), it can help to get the centre to cooperate (DV2) and find workable solutions in case of disagreement. These dynamics are remarkably similar for Scotland and Wales.

Notes

1 For reasons of comparability (not at least due to suspension of the Northern Ireland Assembly and Executive between 2017 and 2020) but also due to the travel restriction during the COVID-19 pandemic in 2020, Northern Ireland was only marginally considered in this study.
2 Enhancing the efficiency of formal institutions.
3 Altering the intention and effects of ineffective formal institutions without violating them.
4 Violating ineffective formal institutions.
5 In the absence of formal intergovernmental bodies, the existing procedures are not *highly* institutionalised, which would require at least two of four criteria: (a) majority rule which deviates from unanimity; (b) an internal differentiation of the coordinating body into offices and organs with policy-specific tasks; (c) the legal status to produce binding agreements and (d) the formulation of precise arrangements (Bolleyer 2009; 2013, 324–325; 2018, 48).
6 In 2021, a total of 19 Legislative Consent Motions were passed (Department for Levelling Up, Housing and Communities 2022, 46).
7 Policy decisions on funding are exempted and subject to separate mechanism for the Finance Interministerial Standing Committee.
8 E.g. the EU (Withdrawal) Act 2018; the Healthcare (European Economic Area and Switzerland Arrangements) Act 2019; the Agriculture Act 2020 and the Environment Act 2021.
9 The Finance Interministerial Standing Committee institutionalised the Finance Ministers Quadrilateral as the format responsible for economic and financial matters.
10 Timely limited Interministerial Committees (ICs) can be set up for issues that required in-depth discussions.
11 The Joint Ministerial Working Group on Welfare is an important bilateral group between the Scottish and the UK governments that continues to exist.
12 For instance, IMGs for Business and Industry; Education; Elections and Registration; Environment; Food and Rural Affairs; Housing, Communities and Local Government; Net Zero, Energy and Climate Change; Tourism; Trade and Transport Matters.
13 The political relevance is either 'high' or 'low' depending on whether a decision is perceived as a key or trivial issue, the extent to which it is binding or merely symbolic on stakeholders, and the level of controversy of the issue.
14 0 means *no*; 1 means *some*; 2 means *substantial* and 3 means *great*, which produce overall scores of 0 (*no* political influence); 1, 2 or 3 *(some)*; 4, 6, 8, 9 or 12 *(substantial)* and 18 or 27 *(great)*.
15 For instance, in regard to the permanency of the Scottish Parliament and Scottish Government.

16 The Welsh Government pushed to include consultation rights on the usage of delegated powers by the UK ministers, to remove centralised funding and state aid powers in devolved areas, and to prevent the bill from becoming a 'protected enactment' that cannot be altered by the devolved legislatures.
17 The block grants they receive are fairly generous. Spending per head was 125 per cent higher in Northern Ireland, 121 per cent higher in Scotland and 115 per cent higher in Wales than in England in 2018/2019 (Cheung 2020). During the COVID-19 between spring 2020 and February 2021, an extra total of £9.7 billion for Scotland and £5.85 billion for Wales were allocated through the Barnett formula.
18 Upon request, the UK Government increased borrowing limits to provide additional money to deal with the impact of the COVID-19 pandemic.
19 These cover provisions on financial assistance and support to replace CAP; the collection and sharing of data; interventions in agricultural markets; marketing standards and carcass classification; fairness in the supply chain; World Trade Organisation (WTO) obligations and on the Red Meat Levy.
20 The concurrent powers relate to waste and resource efficiency and producer responsibility, including electronic waste tracking, as well as cross-border river basin districts and the regulation of chemicals.
21 Glasgow and the Clyde Valley in 2014; Aberdeen and Aberdeenshire in 2016; Inverness and Highlands in 2016; Edinburgh and South East Scotland in 2017; Stirling and Clackmannanshire in 2018 and Tay Cities in 2018; Ayrshire Growth Deal, the Borderlands Inclusive Growth Deal, Moray Growth Deal and the Argyll and Bute Growth Deal in 2019; the Falkirk Growth Deal and the Islands Growth Deal in 2020.
22 Cardiff Capital Region in 2016; Swansea Bay in 2017; North Wales Growth Deal in 2020 and Mid Wales Growth Deal in 2020.
23 Decisions by one government can still have repercussions for the other territories. For instance, Scotland abolished university tuition fees for students from Scotland and the EU, but not for Welsh and English students (WG8). In theory, the Senedd could adopt a different higher education policy than for England. However, because the majority of students at Welsh universities are from England, and Welsh students by and large go to study outside of Wales, policy divergence would cause a great deal of complication (WG11). In the light of Brexit, quadrilateral meetings of ministers responsible for education took place throughout 2019 but interactions between them, in general, remain ad hoc (Drakeford 2020).
24 For instance, in regard to national security, counter-terrorism or the Human Rights Act 1998.
25 Although the financial consequences caused by actions of one administration need to be compensated for, so far the Welsh Government has refused to make such payments for the costs of Welsh legislation to the UK Ministry of Justice.
26 For instance, Wales lacks certain prison facilities, such as high security or female-only prisons.
27 The five prisons located in Wales are run by the UK Government.
28 The Welsh Assembly passed the Environment (Wales) Act 2016 and sets 2050 as a target date for net-zero emissions; the Scottish Parliament passed the Climate Change (Emissions Reduction Targets) (Scotland) Act 2019 and aims for 2045 for net-zero emissions; and the UK Government amended the Climate Change Act 2008 by the (2050 Target Amendment) Order 2019 also aiming for net-zero emissions by 2050.
29 When the UK Government introduced the first Environment Bill 2019, which was stopped by the dissolution of Parliament in autumn 2019, it had not engaged with the devolved administrations even though the bill affected their

responsibilities. The Environment Bill 2019–2021 was subsequently re-introduced in January 2021 to establish a framework for environmental governance including a range of shared or concurrent powers. While cooperation (DV2) improved and both the Scottish and Welsh Governments recommended giving consent, the bill was not a jointly driven endeavour, as subsequent conflicts (DV3) over the allocation of responsibilities demonstrate. International trade agreements and the UK Internal Market Act 2020 further enable the UK Government to undermine the environmental standards set by the devolved legislatures.

30 The UK Government did not use the EU (Withdrawal) Act to freeze devolved legislation and announced the repeal of Section 12 (Department for Levelling Up, Housing and Communities and Cabinet Office 2022).

31 The Welsh Government (2020) simultaneously issued its own negotiation priorities for a closer alignment with the EU as well as their desire for a strong role for the devolved governments in the negotiations with the EU. In June 2020, the Scottish Government introduced the UK Withdrawal from the European Union (Continuity) (Scotland) Bill, which was enacted on 31 January 2021, to stay aligned with the EU law after the end of the transition period on 31 December 2020 (Scottish Parliament 2020).

32 For Northern Ireland, in turn, party incongruency with Westminster is the norm, as the consociational arrangement produces a coalition of Republicans and Unionists within the Northern Ireland Executive (Birrell 2012b, 272–273). While between 2017 and 2019 the DUP, which was close to the Conservative Party, at least provided confidence and supply for the minority government under May, Sinn Fein does not recognise the legitimacy of the UK Parliament to rule for Northern Ireland and therefore does not take the seats it wins in General Elections.

33 Interactions in European affairs were dealt with through the JMC Europe.

34 Proportional election and power-sharing systems, in turn generate more stable interest configurations and a continuous need to work together through government coalitions at different levels.

35 Scharpf's (1997, 46–49) four modes of interaction are unilateral action, negotiated agreement, majority vote and hierarchical direction.

36 For instance, the allocation of £1 billion to Northern Ireland outside of the Barnett formula in return for the DUP's support of Theresa May's minority government in 2017 was not recognised as a legitimate matter for the dispute resolution mechanism to the great frustration of the Scottish and the Welsh Governments. The UK Government argued that Northern Ireland received funding for specific purposes, and therefore the Barnett consequentials for departmental spending would not apply.

37 As a former Welsh minister commented: "We've tried all years, as a government that was in favour of keeping the Union, that it was more reasonable to be flexible with us than with Scotland or Northern Ireland. And in fact it was the other way: if you threaten conflict, you get money; if you threaten independence, you get money; if you're reasonable you get nothing. That unfortunately is the message, that's now being received. You can't just be reasonable, because they won't take notice of you. We're always forceful but it's got to be a threat that they recognise is real." (WP5)

38 The Welsh Government opposed the introduction of Police and Crime Commissioners and advisory committees (Police and Crime Panels) in local authorities across England and Wales, arguing that the requirement for local authorities to set up the advisory committees was a devolved responsibility. However, the UK Government amended the bill so that the Police and Crime Commissioners and Panels would be appointed by the UK Home Secretary and not by local authorities (Cowie 2018, 47).

39 Though the road network is a devolved competence and the Welsh Government has decided its own measures to resolve traffic congestion in the area, the UK Government has continuously expressed its commitment to the relief road and even indicated it will use the Shared Prosperity Fund and bypass the Welsh Assembly.
40 These are more prone to exit strategies and autonomous actions, and therefore only provide loose structural coupling (Benz 2009, 87).
41 The UK Government needed to deliver on its promise made over the course of the 2014 Scottish independence referendum.
42 Intergovernmental cooperation included the no-deal preparations, agriculture subsidies, geographical indications for food, drinks and agricultural products, and the UK Common Frameworks programme.
43 Whereas the Welsh Government was also in consultation with the UK Government in the making of the Agriculture Bills 2017–2019 and 2019–2021, the Scottish Government criticised the lack of early engagement from the UK Government and initiated its own Agriculture (Retained EU Law and Data) (Scotland) Bill.

Bibliography

Adam, Elisenda C. (2021) *Brexit and the Mechanisms for the Resolution of Conflicts in the Context of Devolution: Do We Need a New Model?* In: Doyle, Oran, McHarg, Aileen and Murkens, Jo (eds.) *The Brexit Challenge for Ireland and the United Kingdom: Constitutions Under Pressure.* Cambridge: Cambridge University Press, pp. 43–63.

Adam, Ilke and Hepburn, Eve (2019) *Intergovernmental Relations on Immigrant Integration in Multi-Level States. A Comparative Assessment.* Regional & Federal Studies, Volume 29, Issue 5, pp. 563–589.

Andrews, Leighton (2021) *The Forward March of Devolution Halted – and the Limits of Progressive Unionism.* The Political Quarterly, Volume 92, Issue 3, pp. 512–521.

Arts, Bas and Verschuren, Piet (1999) *Assessing Political Influence in Complex Decision-Making: An Instrument Based on Triangulation.* International Political Science Review, Volume 20, Issue 4, pp. 411–424.

BBC (2002) *New Labour 'attack' under fire.* News. 11 December. http://news.bbc.co.uk/2/hi/uk_news/wales/2565859.stm

Benz, Arthur (2009) *Politik in Mehrebenensystemen.* Wiesbaden: Springer VS.

Birrell, Derek (2012a) *Comparing Devolved Governance.* Basingstoke: Palgrave Macmillan.

Birrell, Derek (2012b) *Intergovernmental Relations and Political Parties in Northern Ireland.* British Journal of Politics and International Relations, Volume 14, Issue 2, pp. 270–284.

Bolleyer, Nicole (2009) *Intergovernmental Cooperation: Rational Choices in Federal Systems and Beyond.* Oxford: Oxford University Press.

Bolleyer, Nicole (2013) *Paradoxes of Self-Coordination in Federal Systems.* In: Benz, Arthur and Broschek, Jörg (eds.) *Federal Dynamics: Continuity, Change, and the Varieties of Federalism.* Oxford: Oxford University Press, pp. 321–342.

Bolleyer, Nicole (2018) *Challenges of Interdependence and Coordination in Federal Systems.* In: Detterbeck, Klaus and Hepburn, Eve (eds.) *Handbook of Territorial Politics.* Cheltenham: Edward Elgar Publishing, pp. 45–60.

Bolleyer, Nicole and Thorlakson, Lori (2012) *Beyond Decentralization – The Comparative Study of Interdependence in Federal Systems.* The Journal of Federalism, Volume 42, Issue 4, pp. 566–591.

Bradbury, Jonathan (2021) *Constitutional Policy and Territorial Politics in the UK. Volume 1: Union and Devolution 1997-2007.* Bristol: Bristol University Press.

Broschek, Jörg (2011) *Conceptualizing and Theorizing Constitutional Change in Federal Systems: Insights from Historical Institutionalism.* Regional and Federal Studies, Volume 21, Issue 4–5, pp. 539–559.

Brouillet, Eugénie and Mullen, Tom (2018) *Constitutional Jurisprudence on Federalism and Devolution in UK and Canada.* In: Keating, Michael and Laforest, Guy (eds.) *Constitutional Politics and the Territorial Question in Canada and the United Kingdom: FedEralism and Devolution Compared.* Cham: Palgrave Macmillan, pp. 47–77.

Bulpitt, Jim (2008) *Territory and Power in the United Kingdom: An Interpretation.* Colchester: ECPR Press (first published in 1983).

Butcher, Louise (2017) *Transport in Scotland, Wales & Northern Ireland.* Briefing Paper Number SN03156. 12 June. House of Commons. https://researchbriefings.files.parliament.uk/documents/SN03156/SN03156.pdf

Cabinet Office (2021) *Review of UK Government Union Capability.* Independent report. 24 March. UK Government. https://www.gov.uk/government/publications/the-dunlop-review-into-uk-government-union-capability

Cairney, Paul (2012) *Intergovernmental Relations in Scotland: What Was the SNP Effect?* British Journal of Politics and International Relations, Volume 14, Issue 2, pp. 231–249.

Cheung, Aron (2020) *Barnett Formula.* Explainer. 25 November. Institute for Government. https://www.instituteforgovernment.org.uk/explainers/barnett-formula

Constitution and Cabinet Directorate (2018) *Strengthening the Sewel Convention: Letter from Michael Russell to David Lidington.* Publication – Correspondence. 12 September. Scottish Government. https://www.gov.scot/publications/strengthening-the-sewel-convention-letter-from-michael-russell-to-david-lidington/

Corbyn, Cloe (2021) *The Future of Railways in Wales.* Senedd Research. 27 May. Welsh Parliament. https://research.senedd.wales/2019/01/31/the-future-of-railways-in-wales/

Cowie, Graeme (2018) *Brexit: Devolution and Legislative Consent.* Briefing Paper Number 08274. 29 March. House of Commons. https://researchbriefings.files.parliament.uk/documents/CBP-8274/CBP-8274.pdf

Cowie, Graeme, Mars, Sylvia de, Kelly, Richard and Torrance, David (2020) *Constitutional Implications of the Withdrawal Agreement legislation.* Briefing Paper Number 08805. 20 February. House of Commons. https://researchbriefings.files.parliament.uk/documents/CBP-8805/CBP-8805.pdf

Deacon, Russell (2012) *Devolution in the United Kingdom.* Edinburgh: Edinburgh University Press.

Delegated Powers and Regulatory Reform Committee (2018) *Fisheries Bill Healthcare (International Arrangements) Bill Divorce (Financial Provision) Bill [HL] Prisons (Interference with Wireless Telegraphy) Bill.* 39th Report of Session 2017–19. HL Paper 226. 15 November. House of Lords. https://publications.parliament.uk/pa/ld201719/ldselect/lddelreg/226/226.pdf

Department for Levelling Up, Housing and Communities (2022) *Intergovernmental Relations Annual Report – Reporting Period 1 January – 31 December 2021.* CP 655. March. UK Government.

Department for Levelling Up, Housing and Communities and Cabinet Office (2022) *The European Union (Withdrawal) Act and Common Frameworks: 26 September to 25 December 2021*. Policy paper. 10 March. UK Government. https://www.gov.uk/government/publications/the-european-union-withdrawal-act-and-common-frameworks-26-september-to-25-december-2021

Department of Health and Social Care (2020) *Coronavirus (COVID-19) Action Plan*. Policy paper. 3 March. UK Government. https://www.gov.uk/government/publications/coronavirus-action-plan

Drakeford, Mark (2020) *Written Statement: Intergovernmental Relations*. Cabinet Statement. 26 October. Welsh Government. https://gov.wales/written-statement-intergovernmental-relations

Evans, Adam (2019) *Inter-Parliamentary Relations in the United Kingdom: Devolution's Undiscovered Country?* Parliaments, Estates and Representation, Volume 39, Issue, 1, pp. 98–112.

Helmke, Gretchen and Levitsky, Steven (2004) *Informal Institutions and Comparative Politics: A Research Agenda*. Perspectives on Politics, Volume 2, Issue 4, pp. 725–740.

HM Government (2015) *Scotland in the United Kingdom: An Enduring Settlement*. Presented to Parliament by the Secretary of State for Scotland by Command of Her Majesty. Cm 8990. January. UK Government. https://assets.publishing.service.gov.uk/government/uploads/system/uploads/attachment_data/file/397079/Scotland_EnduringSettlement_acc.pdf

Hueglin, Thomas O. (2013) *Comparing Federalism: Variations or Distinct Models?* In: Benz, Arthur and Broschek, Jörg (eds.) *Federal Dynamics: Continuity, Change, and the Varieties of Federalism*. Oxford: Oxford University Press, pp. 27–47.

Hueglin, Thomas O. and Fenna, Alan (2010) *Comparative Federalism: A Systematic Inquiry*. Peterborough: Broadview Press.

Hunt, Jo (2017) *The Supreme Court Judgement in Miller and Its Implication for the Devolved Nations*. Commentary, 1 February. UK in a Changing Europe. https://ukandeu.ac.uk/the-supreme-court-judgment-in-miller-and-its-implications-for-the-devolved-nations/

Hunt, Jo and Minto, Rachel (2017) *Between Intergovernmental Relations and Paradiplomacy: Wales and the Brexit of the Regions*. The British Journal of Politics and International Relations, Volume 19, Issue 4, pp. 647–662.

Independent Expert Advisory Committee for Ongoing Review of the Operation of Justice in Wales (2019) *First Report*. July. https://assets.publishing.service.gov.uk/government/uploads/system/uploads/attachment_data/file/819728/independent-expert-advisory-committee-first-report-web.pdf

Paun, Akash and Nice, Alex (2021) *Alun Davies*. Ministers Reflect. 12 October 2021. https://www.instituteforgovernment.org.uk/ministers-reflect/person/alun-davies/

JMC Joint Secretariat (2018) *Report of the Joint Ministerial Committee: 2015–2018*. Policy paper. 14 March. UK Government. https://www.gov.uk/government/publications/joint-ministerial-committee-communique-14-march-2018

John, Peter (2008) *New introduction: Territory and Power and the Study of Comparative Politics*. In: Bulpitt, Jim (eds.) *Territory and Power in the United Kingdom: An Interpretation*. Colchester: ECPR Press (first published in 1983), pp. 1–16.

Kenny, Michael, Rycroft, Philip and Sheldon, Jack (2021) *Union at the Crossroads: Can the British State Handle the Challenges of Devolution*. Report by the Bennett Institute for Public Policy Cambridge. The Constitution Society.

McEwen, Nicola (2017) *Still Better Together? Purpose and Power in Intergovernmental Councils in the UK*. Regional and Federal Studies, Volume 27, Issue 5, pp. 667–690.

McEwen, Nicola, Swenden, Wilfried and Bolleyer, Nicole (2012) *Intergovernmental Relations in the UK: Continuity in a Time of Change?* British Journal of Politics and International Relations, Volume 14, Issue 2, pp. 323–343.

Mitchell, James (2010) *Two Models of Devolution: A Framework for Analysis.* In: Stolz, Klaus (ed.) *Ten Years of Devolution in the United Kingdom: Snapshot at a Moving Target.* Augsburg: Wißner-Verlag, pp. 52–71.

Paun, Akash and Shuttleworth, Kelly (2020) *Legislating by Consent: How to Revive the Sewel Convention.* IfG Insight. September. Institute for Government.

Paun, Akash, Sargeant, Jess and Klemperer, David (2020) *Devolution: Common Frameworks and Brexit.* Explainer. 5 October. Institute for Government. https://www.instituteforgovernment.org.uk/explainers/devolution-joint-ministerial-committee

Poirier, Johanne and Saunders, Cheryl (2015) *Conclusion: Comparative Experience of Intergovernmental Relations in Federal Systems.* In: Poirier, Johanne, Saunders, Cheryl and Kincaid, John (eds.) *Intergovernmental Relations in Federal Systems.* Oxford: Oxford University Press, pp. 440–498.

Poirier, Johanne, Saunders, Cheryl and Kincaid, John (2015) *Intergovernmental Relations in Federal Systems.* Oxford: Oxford University Press.

Public Administration and Constitutional Affairs Committee (2016) *The Future of the Union, Part Two: Inter-institutional Relations in the UK.* Sixth Report of Session 2016–17. HC 839. 8 December. House of Commons.

Rawlings, Richard (2017) *Brexit and the Territorial Constitution: Devolution, Reregulation and Inter-Governmental Relations.* London: The Constitution Society.

Scharpf, Fritz (1997) *Games Real Actors Play – Actor-Centered Institutionalism in Policy Research.* Boulder, CO: Westview Press.

Scharpf, Fritz (2000) *Interaktionsformen – Akteurzentrierter Institutionalismus in Der Politikforschung.* Wiesebaden: Springer VS.

Scottish Affairs Committee (2015) *The Implementation of the Smith Agreement.* Fourth Report of Session 2014–15. HC 835. 19 March. House of Commons. https://publications.parliament.uk/pa/cm201415/cmselect/cmscotaf/835/835.pdf

Scottish Affairs Committee (2019) *The Relationship between the UK and Scottish Governments.* Eighth Report of Session 2017–19. HC 1586. 7 June. House of Commons. https://publications.parliament.uk/pa/cm201719/cmselect/cmscotaf/1586/1586.pdf

Scottish Government (2019) *Scottish Government Overview of 'No Deal' Preparations.* Laid before the Scottish Parliament, October. SG/2019/204. October. https://www.gov.scot/binaries/content/documents/govscot/publications/progress-report/2019/10/scottish-government-overview-no-deal-preparations/documents/scottish-government-overview-no-deal-preparations/scottish-government-overview-no-deal-preparations/govscot%3Adocument/scottish-government-overview-no-deal-preparations.pdf

Scottish Parliament (2020) *UK Withdrawal from the European Union (Continuity) (Scotland) Bill [2020].* Bills and Laws. https://www.parliament.scot/bills-and-laws/bills/uk-withdrawal-from-the-european-union-continuity-scotland-bill-2020

Tatham, Michael (2016) *With, Without, or Against the State? How European Regions Play the Brussels Game.* Oxford: Oxford University Press.

UK Parliament (2020a) *Written Evidence Submitted by Jack Sheldon, University of Cambridge and Hedydd Phylip, Cardiff University.* TTC 02. November. https://committees.parliament.uk/writtenevidence/14593/html/

UK Parliament (2020b) *Committee Launch New Major Inquiry on House of Commons Procedure and the Territorial Constitution.* News article. 24 September. https://committees.parliament.uk/committee/126/procedure-committee/news/119460/committee-launch-new-major-inquiry-on-house-of-commons-procedure-and-the-territorial-constitution/

Watts, Ronald L. (2008) *Comparing Federal Systems.* Montreal and Kingston: McGill-Queen's University Press.

Weissert, Carol S. and Fahey, Kevin (2018) *Actor-Centered or Institutional Approaches in Europe and the US: Moving towards Convergence.* In: Detterbeck, Klaus and Hepburn, Eve (eds.) *Handbook of Territorial Politics.* Cheltenham: Edward Elgar Publishing, pp. 341–353.

Welsh Government (2019a) *Reforming Our Union: Shared Governance in the UK.* Policy and Strategy. 10 October. https://gov.wales/reforming-our-union-shared-governance-in-the-uk

Welsh Government (2019b) *Preparing for a No Deal Brexit.* Publication. 11 September. https://gov.wales/sites/default/files/publications/2019-09/preparing-for-a-no-deal-brexit_0.pdf

Welsh Government (2020) *The Future UK/EU Relationship: Negotiating Priorities for Wales. Welsh Government Analysis of the UK Government Political Declaration.* Policy and Strategy. 23 January. https://gov.wales/the-future-uk-eu-relationship-negotiating-priorities-for-wales-html#section-35339

Welsh Parliament (2020) *Legislative Consent Memorandum on the Healthcare (International Arrangements) Bill.* Senedd Business. 23 January. https://business.senedd.wales/mgIssueHistoryHome.aspx?IId=23365

Wright, Deil S. (1988) *Understanding Intergovernmental Relations.* 3rd edition. Belmont, TN: Brooks/Cole Publishing.

Wyn Jones, Richard and Royles, Elin (2012) *Wales in the World: Intergovernmental Relations and Sub-State Diplomacy.* British Journal of Politics and International Relations, Volume 14, Issue 2, pp. 250–269.

7 Lessons from and for Comparative Federalism

While the study of intergovernmental relations provides meaningful insights about the practical workings of a multilevel polity, comparative federalism offers a systematic perspective in relation to the constitutional and institutional framework, the allocation of political, legislative and fiscal authority, as well as wider political dynamics. In return, the extensive empirical analysis of a devolved unitary state as a critical case enables us to draw theoretical conclusions and to contribute the scholarship of federalism. In order to reflect on the UK's multilevel dynamics and its comparative merit for federal studies, this last chapter will examine the linkages between the allocation of legislative and fiscal authority (self-rule), the intergovernmental architecture (shared rule) and the constitutional doctrines of sovereignty. It will then continue with the discussion of the UK's federalisation before it draws a series of conclusions that can help to analyse other multilevel polities in the future.

Self-rule, shared rule and sovereignty

During the second half of the 20th century, economic and political disparities drove calls for greater autonomy from England and national movements represented by the SNP and Plaid Cymru increasingly won electoral ground, which eventually led the New Labour Government under Blair to introduce fundamental reforms by devolving legislative authority to newly created territorial legislatures (Becker 2002, 63–64; Schieren 2010, 133–136; Deacon 2012, 5 et seq.). The devolution of political, legislative and fiscal authority in 1998 was a concession to the growing demands for self-government guided by pragmatism rather than by a federal idea (Tierney 2018, 106; Dickson 2019, 85) or long-term thinking over the consequences for the UK's unitary constitution. Lulled by "a sense of false security" (Hazell 2015, 6), politicians at the centre did not foresee that the new "multi-layered constitution" (Leyland 2011, 252) and the growing dispersion and pluralism of competences (Keating 2004, 326) would clash with the sovereignty of Westminster and its majoritarian principle. Until today, the UK Parliament retains exclusive legislative authority over any policy matter and can overrule the devolved

DOI: 10.4324/9781003349952-7

legislatures. Over the last two decades, responsibilities over *residual powers* were gradually devolved to the Scottish and Welsh Parliaments, while an explicit list of *enumerated powers* is reserved by the centre.[1] In federations, it is common to specify the enumerated powers of the substate units and leave the centre exclusively in control of the residual authority over the remaining policy areas (typically over international affairs, defence, international trade, monetary and economic policies, major taxes, major infrastructure and pensions). Under the *conferred powers* model, this logic applied only to the Welsh Assembly, which received enumerated powers over secondary legislation and statutory instruments but was not given full legislative authority without approval by the UK Parliament. The Wales Act 2017 then established the same *reserved powers* model for both Scotland and Wales, which is the opposite method to that common in federal polities.

In regard to the devolution of fiscal authority, similarly to federations, the UK Government holds *exclusive fiscal authority* over major taxes, including customs, corporation tax, VAT and income tax and then redistributes resources, in order to provide internal coherence. Income tax has implicitly turned into a *shared* tax, but the potential for divergence from the rest of the UK is limited, since an increase of the income tax rate in Scotland would reduce the amount of the block grant for the Scottish Government (Bell 2016, 43). Unlike *fiscal federalism* (cf. Lee 2017, 127–128), the devolved administrations can autonomously decide how to spend the funding given by the centre but hold only limited powers to decide over revenues. Ad hoc grants are an additional source of revenues assigned for specific, ring-fenced purposes, which the UK Government awards to meet an urgent need or political rationale rather than to promote central policies, as it is the case under *coercive federalism* (cf. Eccleston et al. 2017, 20). In the course of the UK's withdrawal from the EU, bypassing the devolved governments to directly fund initiatives of the UK Government has become a controversial practice.

The duality of the initial devolution settlement provided a high degree of self-rule over legislation, policymaking and implementation instead of a functionally integrated approach, which has determined how governments interact with each other. In *loosely coupled* multilevel states, the different levels have little incentive to cooperate or to engage in joint decision-making (Scharpf 2000, 289; Broschek 2011, 545; Bolleyer and Thorlakson 2012, 571–573; Poirier and Saunders 2015b, 446; Behnke 2018, 38). And yet, thinking of devolution as a 'layer cake' (Entwistle et al. 2014), in which the exercise of legislative authority is neatly separated between levels of government, is misleading. Mitchell (2010, 53) argued that dual polities with separate jurisdictions are characterised by in-built tensions and "the reality of interdependence" is obscured by debates around autonomy and sovereignty. In practice, devolution has been closer to interdependent than to dual federations than is typically acknowledged (op. cit., 57–64). Already in 2007, Rhodes (2007, 1258) suggested that the British government is "interlocked into power-dependent relations", and indeed, the UK's governments have found themselves increasingly in situations where they have to work together or face the negative impact of not cooperating. Meanwhile, the devolution of more and more competences has implicitly and explicitly created more concurrent legislative powers not exclusively assigned to one level but either overlapping or complementarily exercised. As policy problems and the capacities to solve them have become increasingly interconnected beyond the remits of individual levels of government, the 'marble cake' metaphor has come closer to reflecting the blurring of jurisdictions without manifesting in an integrated or tightly coupled system. Gallagher (2020, 582) thus suggested that the UK has evolved towards a federal-like system between competition and cooperation.[2]

Paradoxically, the different levels of government were more interwoven during the UK's EU membership. For most of the last two decades, the UK Government did not engage with any framework legislation, common standards or policy objectives for the whole of the UK – except for some specific financial grants. According to an MS:

> What has happened, being part of the EU created a constitutional framework that allowed for those disfunctions to continue without the massive effect that they have once you take away that constitutional umbrella. If you take away that constitutional umbrella you can find that there is no proper framework for what you have left.
>
> (WP1)

The need for a UK-wide regime to prevent the disruptive effects of policy divergence has only become obvious in the course of leaving the EU, which provides a system of concurrent powers within its Member States and shared powers at the supranational level (Gallagher 2012, 200). Statutes, such as the EU (Withdrawal) Act 2018, the EU (Withdrawal Agreement) Act 2020 and the UK Internal Market Act 2020, have been introduced to maintain the UK's political and economic integrity but they were imposed on the devolved jurisdictions rather than subject to shared governance. Territorial autonomy of substate units is conditional on the extent to which the higher authority interferes in decentralised affairs (Dickovick 2005, 186; Bolleyer 2018, 47). The centre is not meant to interfere in the primary responsibilities of the devolved administrations. The Sewel Convention represents a source of territorial power that can under most circumstances protect them from such interventions, but there are no complete guarantees that the devolved administrations will not be overruled by Westminster and Whitehall. The UK Government has shown a growing interest in promoting its policies in Scotland and Wales and has not refrained from using Brexit-related legislative and financial decisions to recentralise political authority and ignored when legislative consent was withheld by the devolved legislatures.

As territorial autonomy cannot be absolute (cf. Rodden 2004, 486; Cheema and Rondinelli 2007), or else they would be independent, it is not only determined by the self-rule capacities but also by institutions through which governments work together for their mutual benefit (cf. Bolleyer and Thorlakson 2012, 566–567). Leaving the EU has uncovered the lack of a robust intergovernmental structure and the flaws of informal inter-institutional forums and institutions. Federal systems rely on constitutionalised stability, but federalism is perhaps, first of all, an idea to balance self-rule and embodied by a variety of institutional arrangements (cf. Tierney 2018, 106). Preserving territorial sovereignty and autonomy against higher authorities is thereby a fundamental principle of federal constitutions (Hueglin and Fenna 2010, 31–33; Hueglin 2013, 44). Whereas the genius of a federal mindset takes this a step further and aims at sharing power for common purposes (Watts 2008, 23; Benz 2013, 72), UK Governments have been unwilling to give up power to other parties in Parliament, the Supreme Court (or the European Court of Justice) or the devolved administrations. Instead, they responded to calls for more territorial power with a devolution of competences without adopting any form of shared governance. Westminster's majoritarian power-hoarding reflexes have endured until today meaning that including other governments in their decision-making is not regarded as an opportunity to increase the legitimacy and effectiveness of outputs but rather as a loss of control and leadership. A Scottish official said:

> Westminster doesn't have many set rules, you can do almost anything, if you get the numbers right in the House of Commons. This is making it quite difficult for everybody. The instinct in that time is for Westminster and Whitehall to turn in on themselves. They are culturally quite secretive.
>
> (SG4)

Even if the political positions of the different parties in power were closer to each other, the political culture in Westminster and Whitehall would struggle to come to terms with the idea of sharing power on a systematic basis (UKG1, UKG5). Remarkably, over two decades of devolution the political thinking in Westminster and Whitehall has remained unitary and centralised in the UK Cabinet, which thinks of consultations with the devolved administrations as mere box-ticking exercises (SG6, SG8, SG12, UKG3, UKG10). Intergovernmental affairs have remained marginal on the agenda of many Whitehall departments (Anderson and Gallagher 2018, 32), some of which have become predominantly responsible for policies in England rather than for the whole of the UK (Keating 2021, 81). It has become harder to ignore the Scottish and Welsh Governments' voices and to impose central policies and decisions against their will. But, their attempts to influence the UK Governments still often resemble a form of interest representation rather than of cooperative partnership.

The federalisations of a devolved unitary state?

Considering the formation of the UK through the Acts of Union between England and Wales in the 16th century, with Scotland in 1707, and with Ireland throughout the 19th century, scholars like Loughlin (2011, 3), have rejected a unitary-federal terminology based on a historical reading of the British constitution. A notable range of recent publications from within the UK has engaged with the state of the British Union (Andrews 2021; cf. Bradbury 2021; Keating 2021; Kenny et al. 2021; Martin 2021; Wincott et al. 2021). As Keating (2020, 4) describes it, "a union is a polity formed from the merger of distinct entities, which have preserved and developed elements of their pre-union structures." Unlike federations, political unions are forged by pragmatic statecraft rather than by long-term constitutional design, which leaves opportunities for ongoing negotiations and disputes over the relationships between the centre and the constituent units (Keating 2021, 19; 50).[3] Presenting the UK as a union is linked to the political discussions and arguments about territorial sovereignty (Mitchell 1997, 199), and is clearly more sensitive to the different nations than thinking of the UK as a hierarchical unity (Requejo 2011, 9). To emphasise their voluntary membership in the UK, the Scottish and Welsh Governments have also come to adopt the idea of a union over the unitary conception of the UK (Wincott et al. 2021, 698).[4] While they perceive themselves as a union of consent dependent on their support rather than a union by law (Keating and Laforest 2018, 7), under Boris Johnson, the UK Government kept referring to the UK as a unitary state.[5] The notion of a union may disguise the fundamental asymmetries in the power relations between the centre and the devolved parts, but de jure the devolved nations are not sovereign and Westminster remains the political authority for England and the whole state. While Prime Ministers, such as Margaret Thatcher and later David Cameron, recognised the right of Scotland to leave the UK if supported by a referendum majority, there are no explicit constitutional provisions granting the right to secession. The fact that it can refuse to grant another independence referendum to Scotland demonstrates that the Union is ultimately one by legal force (Martin 2021, 7–18). The UK's unitary nature is further reflected by the fact that the devolved administrations have no general competence and cannot act ultra vires beyond the powers provided by statutes of the UK Parliament (Mitchell 1997, 197).

Without a codified constitution, sovereign constituent states and territorial representation in a bicameral legislature, the UK lacks defining criteria that would qualify it as a federal polity. The principle argument against a federalisation of the UK brought forward by politicians and scholars points to the principle of parliamentary sovereignty, which would be constrained by a strong horizontal and vertical division of executive, legislative and judicial powers. A fully-fledged federal polity would also require a meso-level of government with a separate legislature in England, which would further reduce the power of Westminster – though producing a positive-sum rather than a zero-sum game. However, English MPs have little to gain from providing the devolved nations with a greater say over English matters (SP2), nor from sharing their realm of influence with members of a parliament or assembly for England. Although the Conservative Government's reassertion of parliamentary sovereignty vis-à-vis the EU and the devolved legislatures (Andrews 2021, 7; Wincott et al. 2021, 708), the devolution referendums in 1997, 2011 (in Wales) and 2014 (in Scotland) marked an expression of popular sovereignty that acknowledges the national identities and the administrations of the devolved nations (Horgan 2004, 114; Schütze 2018, 22).[6] By contesting the idea of a fully sovereign Parliament to rule the whole of the UK, the UK has shifted towards a more federal polity (Tomkins 2018, 73), which is why academics and politicians have frequently engaged with a federal perspective to discuss the UK's multilevel polity.

Comparative federalism provides an "instructive" frame to study the challenges of balancing centralisation and decentralisation dynamics in the UK (Hunt 2021, 23–26). Federations serve distinct purposes and evolve under different ideational contexts legitimising their political order, which is reflected in the allocation of authority and the nature of intergovernmental relations (Benz and Broschek 2013, 2). A main objective of federal constitutions is to ensure the sovereignty of different territorial identities under one collective political community (Burgess 2006, 156; Hueglin and Fenna 2010, 31–37). Federations are not static or immune to transformation (Rodden 2004, 289; Benz 2013, 73), but "permanently in motion or exposed to pressure for change caused by social developments or internal tensions." (Benz and Broschek 2013, 3). Like federalism, devolution is a work in progress to manage the distribution and exercise of authority. By pragmatically adopting federal elements without fundamentally altering its unitary set-up (Tomkins 2018, 73), the UK can nowadays be understood as a federal-like hybrid that has evolved in response to functional and political demands from different levels (cf. Benz 2013, 73). The Scotland Act 2016 and the Wales Act 2017 have moved the UK further in the direction of federalism not only by transferring more powers downwards, but also by confirming the permanence of the devolved institutions dependent upon a referendum. This highlights the constitutional rank of the devolution legislation and comes close to a de facto constitutional entrenchment of territorial autonomy (Tierney 2018, 109–114). As Schütze (2018, 24) put it:

> A political understanding of federalism may portray the United Kingdom as a federation 'in normal times', while – still – a unitary state 'in crisis times'. And indeed, from a 'political' point of view, many of the 'legal' phenomena within the history of the United Kingdom can fruitfully be seen through a federal lens. [...] even from a legal perspective some relationships within and without the United Kingdom are potentially 'federal' in nature.

The asymmetrical transfer of political, legislative and fiscal authority compares to the idea of a 'territorial federation' to represent the political communities living within a geographical area (cf. Benz 2009, 24–25). Apart from enabling subnational governments to act autonomously, federation can also respond to political and functional demands by providing opportunities for collaboration, joint decision-making and conflict resolution that balance central dominance and glue the different parts together (O'Neill 2004, 179; Watts 2008, 135; Benz and Broschek 2013, 7). In *integrated* or *cooperative federations*,[7] multilateral negotiations are channelled through intra-governmental institutions that mediate individual and collective interests, generate a distinct federal loyalty and bind the devolved governments to the centre (cf. Benz 2013, 82; Poirier and Saunders 2015a, 6–7; 2015b, 446). In contrast, the UK represents something in between *cooperative intergovernmentalism* (Flinders 2009, 181) and *divided* or *interstate federalism*, where intergovernmental relations take the form of diplomatic negotiations *inter-institutional* arrangements, which the governments can exit and act unilaterally without being constrained by another level (cf. Broschek 2011, 545; Hueglin 2013, 39; Behnke 2018, 38).

If we want to comprehend, why the UK has so far resisted the formalisation of an intergovernmental architecture and instead produced an increasingly complex, yet opaque web of non-binding institutions and practices, we need to account for the fundamentally different perspectives not only in London but also in Edinburgh and Cardiff, which are hard to reconcile. Whereas in the past the centre responded to calls for decentralisation with pragmatic statecraft to provide territorial stability (Bulpitt 2008, 67–68), devolution could not ease the calls of independence but rather created unintended effects and tensions (WP6). Economic and political competition between different governments is typically high in states with secessionist movements, such as in Québec and Catalonia, and in the UK has spread to taxation, welfare and public services (Gallagher 2020, 567; 579). More severely, devolution has not only led to policy divergence but also challenged the idea of an integrated unitary state (cf. Sturm 2017, 44–45). People's national identities have diverged across the UK (Henderson and Wyn Jones 2021, 136 et seq.) and undermined the sense of a common British identity (UKG10, WP6). Over the course of EU withdrawal, the power asymmetries between England and the other territories have become painfully obvious. Many people in Scotland and a rising share of the Welsh population have come to question the purpose of a state that works largely to the advantage of southern England and have ceased to support a union that cannot reconcile their own national identities under a shared polity (WG1, WP1). In the words of a former senior official from the UK Government:

> We're yet to find a happy medium where that Britishness can be expressed in a way that accepts essentially at heart that the people in

Scotland, Wales and England are sovereign and it's through their sovereign choice and Northern Ireland that they stay in this union. But that concept is not well articulated and there's certainly nothing like agreement or consensus on how you might find a long-term institutional infrastructure that would find expression for that sort of Britishness. It is now very late in the day, because in order for that to become a binding factor for the union, it needs to have an emotional appeal and you can't build something with emotional appeal overnight.

(UKG10)

Nationalists in Scotland and Wales have their reasons not to support a system of power-sharing, in which all devolved nations were treated as more or less equal partners. When territorial autonomy is the primary goal, governments resist institutionalised forms of cooperation and coordination (Benz 2009, 36). A functioning system, in which all devolved nations were treated as equal partners, would challenge the necessity to leave the Union. In the words of an official in Scotland: "The Scottish Government are in a slight Janus position because our ministers want to be independent. To put to them a proposition that would make the UK work really well isn't necessarily in their interest." (SG4) A federalisation of intergovernmental relations to integrate and hold states together stands in stark contrast to their objective of breaking away from the Union. As Keating (2021, 51) put it, the SNP-led Scottish Government "tended to prefer bilateral relationships with Westminster rather than federalizing reforms that could enhance their influence but bring them more within the embrace of Westminster." This leaves the Labour-led Welsh Government as the only administration that proactively promoted fundamental intergovernmental reforms and a vision of shared governance (Welsh Government 2019).[8] A Labour Member of the Senedd brought the Welsh Government's position to the point:

The Welsh Government's view at the moment, certainly a view I endorse, is that we need to move to a constitutional system of a union of nations, which raises all sorts of issues because it means we're moving away from the concept of traditional Westminster sovereignty and the role of the monarchy, which also includes the right to secede from the Union. Providing a new constitutional framework for the UK also raises the issue of England itself. [...] The bit that cumulate in crisis, politically and constitutionally, is the what is the role of the UK Parliament and Westminster. Until you start defining that, you can't really define all the others as well. But the reality is unless this process happens, we're moving to a situation where the UK will disintegrate and break up into its component parts eventually, probably a very dysfunctional and very damaging way; and that's all the consequence of Brexit.

(WP1)

As parts of the Conservative Party have shown a growing, or perhaps resurfacing, resentment towards devolution (SG6), the UK Government has sought to reinstate and centrally impose its authority onto the devolved jurisdictions (cf. Andrews 2021, 5; Kenny et al. 2021, 4).[9] Unsurprisingly, this strategy has not calmed the relations between the different governments but exacerbated further centrifugal dynamics. The success of the incumbent parties in Scotland and Wales during their national elections in May 2021[10] indicates that undermining the devolved administrations has hardly been effective in holding the Union politically together. The Scottish Government has planned to hold a second independence referendum in October 2023, and in a pre-emptive move referred the Scottish Independence Referendum Bill to the Supreme Court to clarify the lawfulness of the bill before introducing it to the Scottish Parliament. If the Supreme Court decides that the bill is outside of the Scottish Parliament's legislative competence, and the UK Government continues to refuse its approval for a referendum, the SNP has also announced a contingency plan to interpret a win at the next UK General Election as a mandate to negotiate Scotland's secession (Salamone 2022). Regardless of the outcome, Westminster would still need to agree to an independent Scotland and the terms of departure.

In the midst of the political turmoil this research also pointed towards extensive and ongoing cooperation on day-to-day issues as well as on the policymaking, often behind the scenes. The rise in overlapping powers has led to more arrangements between governments to coordinate policies and legislations across different jurisdictions. Brexit in particular has not only fostered the creation of new concurrent powers to be exercised by the central and devolved executives but also of new informal institutions and practices to deal with policy areas that were previously operating under the European system of governance. A complex and hardly transparent web of informal agreements has evolved to guide the engagement between the different governments. Especially, the UK Common Frameworks programme introduced a wide range of concordats, memorandums of understanding,[11] and working groups[12] for coordination, consultation, joint decision-making, conflict resolution and even policy-development. Statutes, such as the EU (Withdrawal) Act 2018, the Healthcare (European Economic Area and Switzerland Arrangements) Act 2019, the Agriculture Act 2020 and Environment Act 2021, require the UK Government to consult with the devolved authorities and to resolve disputes when it legislates in devolved areas where their powers are affected. Beneath the eruptive debates across London, Edinburgh and Cardiff, officials play a key role in making policies and legislation work across the different jurisdictions. They have continued to build their informal and personal networks and relationships and to cooperate pragmatically to prevent the escalation and disruptive effects of disputes (SG8, WG12). As Behnke (2019) suggested, their expertise and *neutrality* allow them to *bond* with other

Lessons from and for Comparative Federalism 295

administrations; to anticipate and mediate between different outlooks and to *bridge* potential divisions – often before intergovernmental matters get signed off or need interventions by ministers.

While the bulk of intergovernmental business takes place in a depoliticised space away from the public, the different levels are more integrated than is commonly assumed. The 2022 review of intergovernmental relations has introduced a new framework with the potential to integrate policy- and decision-making across the different jurisdictions by consensus. Through the rotation of chairing and hosting meetings between London, Edinburgh, Cardiff and Belfast, and the standing IGR Secretariat, the devolved governments gain a greater role in setting the agenda. In addition, the reformed dispute resolution mechanism enables all governments to submit a dispute for independent arbitration and cannot be denied by the UK Government as easily anymore – though it cannot produce legally binding solutions. The review demonstrates a remarkable recognition that good governance for the whole of the UK requires the centre to share control and constructively engage with the devolved governments on more and more substantive policy challenges (Kenny and Sheldon 2022). In light of the UK Governments' attitude towards devolution and the de facto decentralisation of power through statutes, such as the UK Internal Market Bill, intergovernmental relations may continue to be the pragmatic muddle-through statecraft that has led to the current political divisions and instabilities. The informality of the intergovernmental system means that effective change will depend on the willingness and commitment of all governments, as Sargeant (2022) stated:

> While there always be some degree of political posturing in public, the new intergovernmental structure could help the four governments to navigate these challenges, to discuss policies, find solutions, and settle issues behind closed doors. But a change in structures is not sufficient. There will need to be a change in attitudes too. The UK government will need to more away from its competitive approach to the Union – asserting its place as the government of the whole of the UK at the expense of devolution – and seek to cooperate with the devolved administrations [...]. The devolved administrations too must accept that only by working with, not against, the UK government to have the opportunity to shape and influence key programmes.

Even though the evolution of intergovernmental linkages reflects the "essence of the federal matrix" (Elazar 1987, 13), only thorough future analyses will be able to tell how effectively the new intergovernmental institutions and practices can integrate the UK's unitary polity. If the UK intents to effectively soften the secessionist movements, rebuild loyalties towards a common polity maintaining the integrity of the whole, it can learn from 'holding-together federalism' (cf. Eccleston et al. 2017, 17–19). This would involve recognising and strengthening the territorial sovereignty of the different nations by constitutional guarantees, moving from a state of substate lobbying to joint decision-making, and a formalisation of the intergovernmental architecture to overcome the structural bias manifested in the supremacy of Parliament (UKG10, WG4, WP6). Without an adjustment of the devolution settlement and the evolution of the constitutional relationship between the different governments, the frequency and intensity of intergovernmental disputes may only grow rather than diminish (Lazarowicz and McFadden 2018, 163). As governments have begun to share responsibilities for policy outcomes, they may become more *tightly coupled*, but this requires common ideational frameworks as well as supporting actor constellations (cf. Benz and Broschek 2013, 4–8).

Comparative federalism from a devolved unitary perspective

As evolving multilevel polities, such as the UK, have blurred the clear-cut dichotomy between unitary and federal states (cf. von Beyme 2010, 208; cf. Broschek 2016, 338; Behnke 2018, 30; Keating and Laforest 2018, 2–3), studies of federalism has turned from classical cases to decentralised non-federal multilevel polities and federal-like hybrids (Behnke 2015, 9). So what insights can comparative federalism take from studying intergovernmental relations in a devolved unitary state? First of all, this study has shown how values and norms inform the interactions of governments (cf. Bolleyer 2009, 1; Bolleyer and Thorlakson 2012, 569). Understanding territorial politics and (quasi-)federalism depends not only on the distribution of powers but on the different perceptions of the multilevel constitution across central and decentralised jurisdictions (Gallagher 2020, 582). Any multilevel polity relies on ideational constructs and interpretative frameworks to legitimise the exercise of authority by different governments (Benz and Broschek 2013, 6). For Elazar's (1987, 5): "[...] a federal arrangement is one of partnership, established and regulated by a covenant, whose internal relationships reflect the special kind of sharing that must prevail among the partners, based on a mutual recognition of the integrity of each partner and the attempt to foster a special unity among them." In contrast, governments of centralised states, which are not used to relying on the consent of substate units, tend to ignore dynamics within their territorial parts and favour their own institutional interests over those who are also affected by their decisions and policies (Kropp 2010, 21). The majoritarianism inherent in the UK's democratic system promotes the concentration of power in single-party executives, rather than sharing it with other parties, institutions and governments. Because the UK Government remained the central authority for England, the political thinking in Westminster and Whitehall has struggled to come to terms with the existence of other legislatures and executives. The lack of mutual engagement and trust is further exacerbated by the adversarial nature of the party competition in the UK (cf. Scharpf 1997, 183 et seq.; Bolleyer 2009, 35–37; 2018, 51; Poirier and Saunders 2015b, 451). Unitarism is then an expression of a political culture that is manifested in the constitutional and institutional configuration of the authority relations within a state.

In the absence of legally binding intra- and inter-institutional mechanisms, informal institutions and practices become substantive (cf. Helmke and Levitsky 2004, 728–731). Yet, if governments can flexibly enter or exit negotiations and the centre can disregard vetoes from lower tiers and overrule them, informal provisions are not definite guarantees for top-down interventions in substate affairs or intergovernmental cooperation. Depending on the given strategic constellations, informal institutions and practices can still be important channels for interactions and enable decentralised governments to exercise substantial political influence vis-à-vis the centre, especially if it needs them for its policies to be effective. If the centre commands the exclusive authority over a policy issue, such as foreign affairs, trade and immigration, it is more likely to jealously guard its authority and act unilaterally than if the authority over a matter is decentralised. Unless the central authority hierarchically claims competence over decentralised affairs, which may come at considerable political costs, issues that require the consent of the substate legislators can hardly be solved without intergovernmental coordination, cooperation or agreement. If the substate tiers are highly dependent on the centre and have little legal leeway, they are most effective in engaging constructively in negotiations and providing plausible arguments to support their positions. Without strong institutional and political incentives to cooperate, civil servants play a fundamental role in making policies work across jurisdictions and preventing severe disruptions in the operation of the state. The elected ministers rely on civil servants to ensure the working of essential day-to-day operations, engage in consultations and smooth political tensions, often before they get themselves involved. As highlighted by Benz (2009, 85–86) and Behnke (2019), the networks of officials are instrumental for maintaining a flow of information and reciprocal recognition between different administrations. In addition to ad hoc exchanges, flexible and task-oriented working groups and regular meetings are a vital part of intergovernmental practices.

The combination of intergovernmental informality and a dual allocation of power does not provide strong incentives for political dialogue and common policy development. Still, any multilevel polity is characterised by implicit interdependencies that in practice require some form of coordination (Benz 2009, 17–23). Whereas functional and political interdependence and cooperation are inevitable in tightly coupled or integrated federations, in loosely coupled states they are also a precondition, though not necessarily sufficient reason for governments to interact. If the preference intensity of the issues at stake is high, governments seek to cooperate unless their interests diverge too strongly, in which case conflict (also in the form of a refusal to interact) is a likely outcome. Party congruency determines whether governments are sympathetic and cooperative with each other or do not interact and end up in conflict over diverging policies. Under a state of party incongruency, governments have little to gain from making concessions or granting other governments positive results. As a result, cooperation is largely driven by negative coordination to prevent damaging effects rather than by shared political ambitions. This is naturally different when the same party is in control of different executives and they share policy objectives. In combination with party congruency, functional and political interdependence and preference intensity, the strategic power of governments informs whether they cooperate or engage in conflict. Although in general politicians may seek to avoid open confrontations (Scharpf 2000, 292), if territorial governments pursue competing goals, in particular, if they seek to pull away from the centre, and at the same time they enjoy strong public support for their agenda, conflict becomes a lot more affordable and even a means to increase their political leverage. High functional and political interdependence and preference intensity create a context in which the centre may find it difficult to act unilaterally or by hierarchical direction and instead commits to voluntary or mandatory negotiation systems. This makes finding consensus almost imperative, in particular for mandatory negotiation systems, which increases the strategic power of the substates to work through disagreements.

Lastly, empowering substate entities creates new functions, competences and complex structures that affect the role of the centre (cf. Pasquier 2021, 60). New modes of shared governance can compensate for the loss of some authority and can turn decentralisation into a positive-sum game (Jensen, Koop and Tatham 2014, 1249). Perhaps the most obvious lesson of this study is that decentralising an increasing number of competences unaccompanied by a formal intergovernmental framework and shared-rule mechanisms does not lead to a balanced integration of different jurisdictions but drives them further apart. Supranational regulatory regimes, such as the EU, can complement state-wide legislative and policy frameworks or provide an effective substitute. Yet, without a system of concurrent powers, multilevel systems are hardly functional. Meanwhile, substate governments develop their own rationales for either supporting or resisting a pull towards the centre. For government to effectively cooperate on a political level, they rely at least on goodwill or a federal-like mindset accustomed to power-sharing, but ultimately only a solid intergovernmental architecture can provide long-term stability regardless of personal relations and party politics. In order to make this work for all administrations, create a common sense of loyalty and promote solidarity as a collective political community, territorial governments need binding assurances that the central authority will not abuse its power but rather acts on their behalf.

Conclusion

To get a comprehensive picture of territorial power and politics, it is essential to place the self-rule capacities in the context of shared rule. The theoretical and empirical insights gained from the analysis of intergovernmental institutions and practices shed light on the variety and effectiveness of mechanisms and arrangements through which governments engage with each other in a devolved unitary polity. These interactions are more complex than implied by the constitutional and legal framework, and they are also typically unrecorded. While the bulk of existing studies of multilevel polities focus on formal provisions and institutions, examining the informal dynamics has thus provided a different perspective and delivered new findings. Foremost, the devolved governments have more impact on the centre than political and academic discourses usually account for. Despite the growing tensions between governments, in the course of the UK's withdrawal from the EU and the rise of concurrent powers, new arrangements, frameworks, forums and groups have emerged at ministerial and official levels integrating the different jurisdictions on a more systematic basis. Whichever direction the UK's multilevel constitution and institutions take, a future research agenda includes ongoing studies of the UK to see how the recent review of intergovernmental relations and informal institutions and practices will affect and potentially transform the unitary state. Beyond the UK, this study has sought to contribute to the ongoing development of comparative federalism, as a guiding perspective to engage with a wide range of constitutional, legal, political, social, economic, cultural and ideological questions (Burgess 2006, 1). Future research will be necessary to consolidate our knowledge about the relations between functional and political interdependence, preference intensity, party congruency and strategic power and patterns of interaction, and to see how they apply in other multilevel polities. More investigations into the political influence of substate units on central decision-making will support our knowledge of territorial power within states that lack formal shared rule arrangements. Eventually, further in-depth case studies of informal intergovernmental relations in decentralised unitary states, loosely coupled or divided federations, and tightly coupled or integrated federations will provide exciting opportunities for international comparisons.

Notes

1 *Emergency overriding powers* that enable the UK Government to intervene in devolved areas under exceptional circumstances are not explicitly assigned but are inherent in the sovereignty of Westminster.
2 Sturm (2020, 23–25) compared the relationship between the central and the devolved administrations partly with competitive federalism characterised by territorial divergence rather than solidarity with each other. According to economic theories, competition between decentralised territories is a source of innovative problem-solving and enhances the efficiency and effectiveness of

3. policies. Yet, due to the different socio-economic conditions across geographies competition also fosters disparities rather than cohesion within a federation (Benz 2009, 74–75; Kropp 2010, 45–46).
3. Andrews (2021, 5–6) suggests that in contrast to a *passive* unionism associated with a 'devolve and forget' approach, an *activist* unionism promoting the UK Government in the devolved parts, or a *progressive* unionism to reform the constitutional settlements to the benefit of all administration, as pursued by the Welsh Government.
4. The conception of the UK as a unitary state was also rejected by the Calman Commission in 2009 and House of Lords' Select Committee on the Constitution in 2016.
5. Paragraph 16 of the UK Government's policy paper on the UK Internal Market states: "The UK is a unitary state with powerful devolved legislatures, as well as increasing devolution across England. The Scottish Parliament, the Senedd Cymru/Welsh Parliament, and the Northern Ireland Assembly are powerful democratic institutions acting within a broad set of competences. Each reflects the unique history of that part of the UK, and their history within the Union of the United Kingdom. This is a history to be celebrated and the Government's approach set out here will ensure that devolution continues to work well for all citizens." (Department for Business, Energy and Industrial Strategy 2020).
6. Referendums are not legally binding on the Westminster Parliament, but their results are widely regarded as irrevocable (Sturm 2015, 326). The legitimacy of people's sovereignty over parliamentary sovereignty was also accepted by many politicians in the context of the EU referendum.
7. Whereas cooperative operates on an informal basis allowing governments to act autonomously if they cannot agree on a common approach (Kropp 2010, 12–13; 2011, 15–16; Sturm 2020, 17–18), in integrated federalism competences to legislative or implement policies are allocated functionally to interdependent jurisdictions (Bolleyer 2018, 47–48). Germany is considered to be the ideal case of an integrated federalism *(Verbundsföderalismus)* with a high degree of functional interdependence and shared rule laid down in the constitution (Hueglin 2013, 44; Lauth 2014, 7–8). The interdependence between German *Bund* and *Länder* provides negative and positive incentives to effectively work together but also locks them into a 'joint decision-making trap' *(Politikverflechtungsfalle)* (Kropp 2010, 9–10; 27–28; Kropp 2011, 18).
8. See Reforming Our Union (Welsh Government 2019).
9. Examples hereof are the UK Internal Market Act 2020, the Shared Prosperity Fund, the city and growth deals, and the M4 relief road in Wales.
10. The SNP won 64 of 129 seats in the Scottish Parliament, and Labour gained 30 of 60 seats in the Senedd.
11. The Food Compositional Standards and Labelling Provisional Common Framework is supported by a concordat to set out governance arrangements around "commonality in approach and minimum standards." Similar concordats guiding the communication and cooperation between governments are part of the Common Frameworks on Organs, Tissues and Cells (apart from embryos and gametes) Provisional; Nutrition Related Labelling, Composition and Standards Provisional; Blood Safety and Quality; and the Food and Feed Safety and Hygiene; and Public Health Protection and Health Security.
12. Examples hereof are the Food Compositional Standards and Labelling Officials Group; the Food and Feed Safety and Hygiene Frameworks Management Group and the Food and Feed Safety and Hygiene Four Nations Director Group; the Nutrition Related Labelling, Composition and Standards Policy Group; and the UK Health Protection Committee and the Four

Nations Health Protection Oversight Group, both which require decisions to be made by unanimity a minimum 75 per cent of its permanent membership and a minimum of one representative from each nation to be present at the meeting.

Bibliography

Anderson, George and Gallagher, Jim (2018) *Intergovernmental Relations in Canada and the United Kingdom*. In: Keating, Michael and Laforest, Guy (eds.) *Constitutional Politics and the Territorial Question in Canada and the United Kingdom*. Cham: Palgrave Macmillan, pp. 19–46.

Andrews, Leighton (2021) *The Forward March of Devolution Halted – and the Limits of Progressive Unionism*. The Political Quarterly, Volume 92, Issue 3, pp. 512–521.

Becker, Bernd (2002) *Politik in Großbritannien: Einführung in das politische System und Bilanz der ersten Regierungsjahre Tony Blairs*. Paderborn: Ferdinand Schöningh.

Behnke, Nathalie (2015) *Stand und Perspektiven der Föderalismusforschung*. Aus Politik und Zeitgeschichte, Volume 65, pp. 28–30.

Behnke, Nathalie (2018) *Federal, Devolved or Decentralized State: On the Territorial Architecture of Power*. In: Detterbeck, Klaus and Hepburn, Eve (eds.) *Handbook of Territorial Politics*. Cheltenham: Edward Elgar Publishing, pp. 30–44.

Behnke, Nathalie (2019) *How Bureaucratic Networks Make Intergovernmental Relations Work: A Mechanism Perspective*. In: Behnke, Nathalie, Broschek, Jörg and Sonnicksen, Jared (eds.) *Configurations, Dynamics and Mechanisms of Multilevel Governance*. Cham: Palgrave Macmillan, pp. 41–59.

Bell, David (2016) *The Aftermath of the Scottish Referendum: A New Fiscal Settlement for the United Kingdom?* In: Bailey, David and Budd, Leslie (eds.) *Devolution and the UK Economy*. London: Rowan and Littlefield, pp. 37–56.

Benz, Arthur (2009) *Politik in Mehrebenensystemen*. Wiesbaden: Springer VS.

Benz, Arthur (2013) *Dimensions and Dynamics of Federal Regimes*. In: Benz, Arthur and Broschek, Jörg (eds.) *Federal Dynamics: Continuity, Change, and the Varieties of Federalism*. Oxford: Oxford University Press, pp. 70–90.

Benz, Arthur and Broschek, Jörg (eds.) (2013) *Federal Dynamics: Introduction. Federal Dynamics: Continuity, Change, and the Varieties of Federalism*. Oxford: Oxford University Press, pp. 1–23.

Beyme, Klaus von (2010) *Vergleichende Politikwissenschaft*. Wiesbaden: Springer VS.

Bolleyer, Nicole (2009) *Intergovernmental Cooperation: Rational Choices in Federal Systems and Beyond*. Oxford: Oxford University Press.

Bolleyer, Nicole (2018) *Challenges of Interdependence and Coordination in Federal Systems*. In: Detterbeck, Klaus and Hepburn, Eve (eds.) *Handbook of Territorial Politics*. Cheltenham: Edward Elgar Publishing, pp. 45–60.

Bolleyer, Nicole and Thorlakson, Lori (2012) *Beyond Decentralization – The Comparative Study of Interdependence in Federal Systems*. The Journal of Federalism, Volume 42, Issue 4, pp. 566–591.

Bradbury, Jonathan (2021) *Constitutional Policy and Territorial Politics in the UK. Volume 1: Union and Devolution 1997–2007*. Bristol: Bristol University Press.

Broschek, Jörg (2011) *Conceptualizing and Theorizing Constitutional Change in Federal Systems: Insights from Historical Institutionalism*. Regional and Federal Studies, Volume 21, Issue 4–5, pp. 539–559.

Broschek, Jörg (2016) *Staatsstrukturen in der Vergleichenden Politikwissenschaft: Förderal- und Einheitsstaat.* In: Lauth, Hans-Joachim, Kneuer, Marianne and Pickel, Gert (eds.) *Handbuch Vergleichende Politikwissenschaft.* Wiesbaden: Springer VS, pp. 331–343.

Bulpitt, Jim (2008) *Territory and Power in the United Kingdom: An Interpretation.* Colchester: ECPR Press (first published in 1983).

Burgess, Michael (2006) *Comparative Federalism: Theory and Practice.* London: Routledge.

Cheema, G. Shabbir and Rondinelli, Dennis A. (2007) *Decentralizing Governance: Emerging Concepts and Practices.* Washington, DC: Brookings Institution Press.

Deacon, Russell (2012) *Devolution in the United Kingdom.* Edinburgh: Edinburgh University Press.

Department for Business, Energy and Industrial Strategy (2020) *UK Internal Market.* Policy paper. 16 July. UK Government. https://www.gov.uk/government/publications/uk-internal-market

Dickovick, J. Tyler (2005) *The Measure and Mismeasure of Decentralisation: Subnational Autonomy in Senegal and South Africa.* The Journal of Modern African Studies, Volume 43, Issue 2, pp. 183–210.

Dickson, Brice (2019) *Writing the United Kingdom Constitution.* Manchester: Manchester University Press.

Eccleston, Richard, Krever, Robert and Smith, Helen (2017) *Fiscal Federalism in the 21st Century.* In: Eccleston, Richard and Krever, Richard (eds.) *The Future of Federalism – Intergovernmental Financial Relations in an Age of Austerity.* Cheltenham: Edward Elgar Publishing, pp. 15–45.

Elazar, Daniel J. (1987) *Exploring Federalism.* Tuscaloosa, AL: University of Alabama Press.

Entwistle, Tom, Downe, James, Guarneros-Meza, Valeria and Martin, Steve (2014) *The Multi-Level Governance of Wales: Layer Cake or Marble Cake?* British Journal of Politics and International Relations, Volume 16, Issue 2, pp. 310–325.

Flinders, Matthew (2009) *Democratic Drift: Majoritarian Modification and Democratic Anomie in the United Kingdom.* Oxford: Oxford University Press.

Gallagher, Jim (2012) *Intergovernmental Relations in the UK: Co-Operation, Competition and Constitutional Change.* British Journal of Politics and International Relations, Volume 14, Issue 2, pp. 198–213.

Gallagher, Jim (2020) *Intergovernmental Relations: Two Decades of Co-Operation, Competition, and Constitutional Change.* Keating, Michael (ed.) *The Oxford Handbook of Scottish Politics.* Oxford: Oxford University Press, pp. 565–583.

Hazell, Robert (2015) *Devolution and the Future of the Union.* London: The Constitution Unit.

Helmke, Gretchen and Levitsky, Steven (2004) *Informal Institutions and Comparative Politics: A Research Agenda.* Perspectives on Politics, Volume 2, Issue 4, pp. 725–740.

Henderson, Alisa and Wyn Jones, Richard (2021) *Englishness: The Political Force Transforming Britain.* Oxford: Oxford University Press.

Horgan, Gerard W. (2004) *Inter-Institutional Relations in the Devolved Great Britain: Quiet Diplomacy.* Regional and Federal Studies, Volume 14, Issue 1, pp. 113–135.

Hueglin, Thomas O. (2013) *Comparing Federalism: Variations or Distinct Models?* In: Benz, Arthur and Broschek, Jörg (eds.) *Federal Dynamics: Continuity, Change, and the Varieties of Federalism.* Oxford: Oxford University Press, pp. 27–47.

Hueglin, Thomas O. and Fenna, Alan (2010) *Comparative Federalism: A Systematic Inquiry.* Peterborough: Broadview Press.

Hunt, Jo (2021) *Subsidiarity, Competence, and the UK Territorial Constitution.* In: Doyle, Oran, McHarg, Aileen and Murkens, Jo (eds.) *The Brexit Challenge for Ireland and the United Kingdom: Constitutions under Pressure.* Cambridge: Cambridge University Press, pp. 21–42.

Jensen, Mads Dagnis, Koop, Christel and Tatham, Michael (2014) *Coping with Power Dispersion? Autonomy, Co-Ordination and Control in Multilevel Systems.* Journal of European Public Policy, Volume 21, Issue 9, pp. 1237–1254.

Keating, Michael (2004) *The United Kingdom as a Post-Sovereign Polity.* In: O'Neill, Michael (ed.) *Devolution and British Politics.* London: Routledge, pp. 319–332.

Keating, Michael (ed.) (2020) *Scotland as a Political Community. The Oxford Handbook of Scottish Politics.* Oxford: Oxford University Press, pp. 1–19.

Keating, Michael (2021) *State and Nation in the United Kingdom: The Fractured Union.* Oxford: Oxford University Press.

Keating, Michael and Laforest, Guy (eds.) (2018) *Federalism and Devolution: The UK and Canada. Constitutional Politics and the Territorial Question in Canada and the United Kingdom.* Cham: Palgrave Macmillan, pp. 1–18.

Kenny, Michael and Sheldon, Jack (2022) *Green Shoots for the Union? The Joint Review of Intergovernmental Relations.* The Constitution Unit Blog. 19 January. The Constitution Unit Blog. https://constitution-unit.com/2022/01/19/green-shoots-for-the-union-the-joint-review-of-intergovernmental-relations/

Kenny, Michael, Rycroft, Philip and Sheldon, Jack (2021) *Union at the Crossroads: Can the British State Handle the Challenges of Devolution.* Report by the Bennett Institute for Public Policy Cambridge. The Constitution Society.

Kropp, Sabine (2010) *Kooperativer Föderalismus und Politikverflechtung.* Wiesbaden: Springer VS.

Kropp, Sabine (2011) *Politikverflechtung – und kein Ende? Zur Reformfähigkeit des deutschen Föderalismus.* In: Gagnon, Alain-G. and Sturm, Roland (eds.) *Föderalismus als Verfassungsrealität Deutschland und Kanada im Vergleich.* Baden-Baden: Nomos, pp. 15–37.

Lauth, Hans-Joachim (ed.) (2014) *Analytische Konzeption für den Vergleich politischer Systeme. Politische Systeme im Vergleich: Formale und informelle Institutionen im politischen Prozess.* Oldenbourg: De Gruyter, pp. 3–50.

Lazarowicz, Mark and McFadden, Jean (2018) *The Scottish Parliament – Law and Practice.* Edinburgh: Edinburgh University Press.

Lee, Simon (2017) *The Gathering Storm: Federalization and Constitutional Change in the United Kingdom.* In: Eccleston, Richard and Krever, Richard (eds.) *The Future of Federalism – Intergovernmental Financial Relations in an Age of Austerity.* Cheltenham: Edward Elgar Publishing, pp. 124–144.

Leyland, Peter (2011) *The Multifaceted Constitutional Dynamics of U.K. Devolution.* International Journal of Constitutional Law, Volume 9, Issue 1, pp. 251–273.

Loughlin, John (2011) *Political and Administrative Asymmetries in a Devolving United Kingdom.* In: Requejo, Ferran and Nagel, Hans-Jürgen (eds.) *Federalism beyond Federations.* London: Routledge, pp. 37–60.

Martin, Ciaran (2021) *Resist, Reform or Re-Run? Short- and Long-Term Reflections on Scotland and Independence Referendums. Research and Practitioners' Insight.* April. Blavatnik School of Government Oxford. https://www.bsg.ox.ac.uk/research/publications/resist-reform-or-re-run-short-and-long-term-reflections-scotland-and

Mitchell, James (1997) *Conceptual Lenses and Territorial Government in Britain*. In: Jordan, Ulrike and Kaiser, Wolfram (eds.) *Political Reform in Britain, 1886–1996: Themes, Ideas, Policies.* Bochum: Universitätsverlag Dr. N. Brockmeyer, pp. 193–226.

Mitchell, James (2010) *Two Models of Devolution: A Framework for Analysis*. In: Stolz, Klaus (ed.) *Ten Years of Devolution in the United Kingdom: Snapshot at a Moving Target.* Augsburg: Wißner-Verlag, pp. 52–71.

O'Neill, Michael (2004) *Devolution and British Politics.* London: Routledge.

Pasquier, Romain (2021) *Devolution, Functional Decentralisation or Recentralisation? Convergence and Divergence in the European Territorial Governance.* In: Callanan, Mark and Loughlin, John (eds.) *A Research Agenda for Regional and Local Government.* Cheltenham: Edward Elgar Publishing, pp. 49–62.

Poirier, Johanne and Saunders, Cheryl (2015a) *Comparing Intergovernmental Relations in Federal Systems: An Introduction.* In: Poirier, Johanne, Saunders, Cheryl and Kincaid, John (eds.) *Intergovernmental Relations in Federal Systems.* Oxford: Oxford University Press, pp. 1–13.

Poirier, Johanne and Saunders, Cheryl (2015b) *Conclusion: Comparative Experience of Intergovernmental Relations in Federal Systems.* In: Poirier, Johanne, Saunders, Cheryl and Kincaid, John (eds.) *Intergovernmental Relations in Federal Systems.* Oxford: Oxford University Press, pp. 440–498.

Requejo, Ferran (2011) *Decentralisation and Federal and Regional Asymmetries in Comparative Politics.* In: Requejo, Ferran and Nagel, Hans-Jürgen (eds.) *Federalism beyond Federations.* London: Routledge, pp. 1–12.

Rhodes, Roderick Arthur William (2007) *Understanding Governance: Ten Years On.* Organization Studies, Volume 28, Issue 8, pp. 1243–1264.

Rodden, Jonathan (2004) *Comparative Federalism and Decentralization – On Meaning and Measurement.* Comparative Politics, Volume 36, Issue 4, pp. 481–500.

Salamone, Anthony (2022) *The Scottish Government's Independence Referendum Strategy: A Last Roll of the Dice?* European Politics and Policy. 26 July. London School of Economics. https://blogs.lse.ac.uk/europpblog/2022/07/26/the-scottish-governments-independence-referendum-strategy-a-last-roll-of-the-dice/

Sargeant, Jess (2022) *New UK Intergovernmental Structures Can Work, But Only with Political Will.* Comment. 28 January. Institute for Government. https://www.instituteforgovernment.org.uk/blog/new-intergovernmental-structures-can-work-only-political-will

Scharpf, Fritz (1997) *Games Real Actors Play – Actor-Centered Institutionalism in Policy Research.* Boulder, CO: Westview Press.

Scharpf, Fritz (2000) *Interaktionsformen – Akteurzentrierter Institutionalismus in der Politikforschung.* Wiesebaden: Springer VS.

Schieren, Stefan (2010) *Großbritannien.* Schwalbach: Wochenschau Verlag.

Schimmelfennig, Frank, Leuffen, Dirk and Rittberger, Berthold (2015) *The European Union as a System of Differentiated Integration: Interdependence, Politicization and Differentiation.* Journal of European Public Policy, Volume 22, Issue 6, pp. 764–782.

Schütze, Robert (2018) *Introduction: British 'Federalism'?* In: Schütze, Robert and Tierney, Stephen (eds.) *The United Kingdom and the Federal Idea.* Oxford: Hart Publishing, pp. 1–26.

Sturm, Roland (2015) *Die britische Westminsterdemokratie – Parlament, Regierung und Verfassungswandel.* Baden-Baden: Nomos.

Sturm, Roland (2017) *Das politische System Großbritanniens*. Wiesbaden: Springer VS.

Sturm, Roland (2020) *Föderalismus*. Baden-Baden: Nomos.

Tierney, Stephen (2018) *Drifting towards Federalism? Appraising the Constitution in Light of the Scotland Act 2016 and Wales Act 2017*. In: Schütze, Robert and Tierney, Stephen (eds.) *The United Kingdom and the Federal Idea*. Oxford: Hart Publishing, pp. 101–121.

Tomkins, Adam (2018) *Shared Rule: What the UK Could Learn from Federalism*. In: Schütze, Robert and Tierney, Stephen (eds.) *The United Kingdom and the Federal Idea*. Oxford: Hart Publishing, pp. 73–99.

Watts, Ronald L. (2008) *Comparing Federal Systems*. Montreal and Kingston: McGill-Queen's University Press.

Welsh Government (2019) *Reforming Our Union: Shared Governance in the UK*. Policy and strategy. 10 October. https://gov.wales/reforming-our-union-shared-governance-in-the-uk

Wincott, Daniel, Murray, C. R. G. and Gregory Davies (2021) *The Anglo-British Imaginary and the Rebuilding of the UK's Territorial Constitution after Brexit: Unitary State or Union State?* Territory, Politics, Governance, Volume 10, Issue 5, pp. 696–713.

Index

A Trading Nation 177
Act of Union 50
actor-centred institutionalism 7, 31, 221n5
additional-member-system 52
Advocate General 86, 92, 132n4, 158, 171, 251
Agreement on Government Procurement 225n51
Agreement on the Joint Ministerial Committee 100, 110
Agricultural Advisory Panel 77n33, 91, 97
Agricultural Holdings (Scotland) Act 91
Agricultural Wages Board 91, 97, 77n33
Agriculture (Retained EU Law and Data) (Scotland) Bill 196, 259, 281n43
Agriculture Act; Agriculture Bill 193–197, 222n15, 227n71, 256, 259, 278n8, 281n43, 294
Agriculture Sector (Wales) Act 91, 97
APD (air passenger duty) 71, 73, 191, 192, 225n60, 225n62, 258
Alcohol (Minimum Pricing) (Scotland) Act 133n15
All Wales Criminal Justice 137n66
Alliance Party of Northern Ireland (APNI) 55
Anglo-Irish Treaty 50
Antisocial Behaviour, Crime and Policing Bill 95
Anti-Terrorism, Crime and Security Act 133n25
Antoniw, Mick 135n43
Arenenkopplung *see* interlocked federalism
Article 50 Treaty on European Union, TEU 92, 97, 105, 162, 251, 271
Australia 21, 78n42, 179

AXA General Insurance v The Lord Advocate and others 133n15

Belfast Agreement 75n7, 115, 117, 132n8; *see also* Good Friday Agreement
Belgium 138n75
Blair, Tony 51, 149, 221n1, 268, 287
Brexit and Devolution 153
British-Irish Council 9, 36, 37, 93, 110, 115–118, 129, 153, 252, 253
British-Irish Parliamentary Assembly; British-Irish Parliamentary Body Assembly 136n46
Brown, Gordon 136n47
Brown, Keith 204
Bundestreue 49n27
Burns, Conor 135n43
Business and Industry Quadrilateral 119

Cadder v Her Majesty's Advocate 133n14
Calman Commission 40n28, 300n4
Cameron, David 3, 57, 70, 151, 208, 290
Canada 20, 21, 26, 27, 78n42, 138n75
Catalonia 292
Catholic 51, 54
Chancellor of the Duchy of Lancaster 85, 86
Channel Islands; Guernsey; Jersey 115–117, 136n46, 136n50
Chequers Plan (Future Relationship between the United Kingdom and the European Union) 163
Children (Abolition of Defence of Reasonable Punishment) (Wales) Act 216
Children and Family Courts Advisory and Support Service 216
city and growth deal 69, 202–206, 228n81, 256, 259, 265, 300n9

Index 307

Civil Contingencies Committee (COBR) 211, 266
Clegg, Nick 85
Climate Change (Emissions Reduction Targets) (Scotland) Act 198, 199, 279n28
Climate Change Act 198, 279n28
Climate Change, Environment and Rural Affairs Committee 196
Coalition Government 25, 27, 54, 57, 70, 85, 105, 121, 183, 268, 272
coercive federalism 63, 287
Cohesion Policy 174, 257
Commission on Devolution in Wales 59, 72, 127
Commission on Justice in Wales 217–219
Common Agriculture Policy (CAP) 192–196, 276, 279n19
Competition and Markets Authority (CMA) 223n36, 224n38
Concordat on Co-ordination of European Union Policy Issues 100
Concordat on Financial Assistance to Industry 100
Concordat on International Relations 100, 176
concurrent legislative authority 55, 59, 74
Constitution Committee 126
Constitution Group 86
Constitutional and Legislative Affairs Committee 127, 196, 226n66
Constitutional Reform Act 90
Continuity Bill *see* UK Withdrawal from the European Union (Legal Continuity) (Scotland) Bill
cooperative federalism 40n25
Corbyn, Jeremy 22
Coronavirus Act 99, 211, 252, 266
Coronavirus Action Plan 211, 266
Corporation Tax (Northern Ireland) Act 73
Council of the EU; Council of Ministers 155, 137n58, 198
Counsel General 76n10, 91, 108, 135, 158, 166
Court of Justice of the EU; European Court of Justice 224n37, 289
Courts and Tribunal Service 137n66
COVID-19; Corona; Coronavirus; pandemic 4, 9, 37, 38, 68, 84, 102, 128, 135n41, 136n48, 168, 187, 192, 202, 206, 209, 211, 225n52, 225n58, 229n92, 255, 260, 264, 266, 278n1, 279n18

Criminal Proceedings etc. (Reform) (Scotland) Act 133n14
Cross Border Healthcare with Wales Statement of Values and Principles 134n34
Crossbench; crossbencher 158, 256
Crown Estate 57
Czech Republic 39n3

d'Hondt formula 76n13
DAERA (Department of Agriculture, Environment and Rural Affairs) 226n68, 227n74
Damages (Asbestos-related Conditions) (Scotland) Act 133n15
Davies, Alun 133n12, 155, 268
Davies, David 198, 162
Delegated Powers and Regulatory Reform Committee 212
Democratic Unionist Party (DUP) 54, 55, 76n16, 111, 138n76, 185, 186, 280n32, 280n36
Department for Business, Energy and Industrial Strategy (BEIS) 123, 135n37, 137n62, 170, 202, 223n30, 223n35, 224n39, 300n5
Department for Communities and Local Government 137n64
Department for Constitutional Affairs 85
Department for Environment, Food and Rural Affairs (DEFRA) 120, 123, 124, 135n37, 137n56, 137n57, 137n62, 138n69, 166, 178, 179, 192–201, 223n28, 226n63, 254
Department for Exiting the EU 107, 163
Department of Health and Social Care 123, 135n37, 213, 214, 223n30
Department for International Trade (DIT) 123, 124, 178, 179
Department for Transport (DfT) 123, 134n34, 137n63
Department for Transport and Rail Network 134n34
Department for Work and Pensions (DWP) 57, 123, 254, 277
Devolution and You 121, 130
Devolution Committee 85, 132n3
Devolution Guidance Note 100, 126
Downing Street 221n1
Drakeford, Mark 10n5, 22, 131, 135n43, 152, 153
Dunlop Review 86, 132n1, 132n3, 132n9, 222n14

Edinburgh Agreement 150
emergency overriding powers 55, 56, 299n1
Energy and Climate Change Quadrilateral 119
Enterprise and Regulatory Reform Bill 77n33, 97, 134n26
enumerated powers 55–58, 74, 287
Environment (Wales) Act 199, 279n28
Environment Act; Environment Bill 63, 199–201, 227n74, 256, 259, 278n8, 279n29, 294
Erasmus+ 162, 173
EU (Notification of Withdrawal) Act 98
EU Emissions Trading System 135n37
European Commission 224n37
European Communities Act 56, 77n35, 156
European Convention on Human Rights 75n6, 78n39, 133n14
European Council 97, 105, 155
European Exit and Trade (Domestic Preparedness, Legislation and Devolution) Cabinet sub-committee and working groups 160
European Single Market 63, 169, 258, 267, 275
European Union (Wales) Bill 133n19, 158, 161, 228n79, 257
European Union (Withdrawal) Act, European Union (Withdrawal) Bill, EU (Withdrawal) Act, EU (Withdrawal) Bill, EU Withdrawal Bill, Withdrawal Bill 92, 98, 133n19, 155–161, 165, 169–171, 196, 222n23, 223n29, 252, 256, 257, 262, 266, 267, 280n30, 288, 294
European Union (Withdrawal Agreement) Act, European Union (Withdrawal Agreement) Bill, EU (Withdrawal Agreement) Act, EU (Withdrawal Agreement) Bill, Withdrawal Agreement Act, Withdrawal Agreement Bill 98, 99, 162–166, 221, 222n23, 252, 256, 257, 267, 278n8, 288
Evans, Rebecca 174, 191
Ewing, Fergus 193, 195, 226n64
exclusive legislative authority 55–61, 74, 76n18, 287

Female Offending Blueprint 134n34, 219, 230n117, 265

Finance Ministers' Quadrilateral 115, 118
Fiscal Framework; Fiscal Framework Agreement 69, 72, 112–115, 136n45, 189–192, 225n57, 256, 258, 275
Food Standards Act 133n25
Food Standards Agency 134n25, 223n30
Foreign and Commonwealth Office (FCO); Foreign Office 105, 117, 176
Foster, Arlene 54
France 39n3
Fraser v Her Majesty's Advocate 133n14

Geographical Indication Scheme (UKGI) 193
Germany 115, 138n75
Gething, Vaughan 139n82, 176
Good Friday Agreement 54, 55, 76n7, 76n15; *see also* Belfast Agreement
Gove, Michael 86, 135n43, 195, 226
Government of Wales Act 52, 53, 58, 73, 207
Great Repeal Bill 256, 266
Green Party; Greens 53, 55
Griffith, Lesley 196, 197

Hart, Simon 132n12, 135n43, 210
Health and Harmony 193, 210
Health and Safety Executive 229n98
Healthcare (European Economic Area and Switzerland Arrangements) Act; Healthcare (International Arrangement) Bill 212–214, 222n15, 260, 278n8, 294
Helping Scotland Prosper 181
Henry VIII 50; Henry VIII powers 164, 165
High Court 172, 257
High Speed 2 North; High Rail 229n91
Higher Education Quadrilateral 119
Home Rule Bill 50
Home Secretary 134n27, 217, 225n52, 280n38
Horizon Europe 162
Housing and Planning Bill 134n26
Human Rights Act 59, 77n35, 215, 279n24

IGR Secretariat 85, 86, 110, 112, 116, 125, 132, 253, 295
Immigration and Social Security Co-ordination (EU Withdrawal) Act 182, 258

Index 309

Imperial Tobacco Limited v The Lord Advocate 133n15
Independence Referendum Bill 93, 294
Independent Expert Advisory Committee for Ongoing Review of the Operation of Justice 216, 230n113
India 78n42
integrated federalism; integrated federations; intrastate federalism 22, 40n25, 297, 299, 300n7
interlocked federalism 41n37
Interministerial Committees 110, 278n10
Interministerial Group (IMG) 85, 110, 119, 120, 135n44, 138n74, 139n82, 278n12
Interministerial Group for Environment, Food and Rural Affairs (IMG EFRA) 120, 124, 137n57, 193, 197
Interministerial Standing Committee (IMCS); Finance Interministerial Standing Committee (F:ISC) 85, 110–118, 186, 202, 253, 278n7, 278n9
Internal Market Act; Internal Market Bill 69, 99, 103, 156, 169–178, 201, 221, 223n35, 252–259, 267, 271, 280n29, 288, 295, 300n9
International Action Plans 177
International Criminal Court Act 133n25
International Trade Strategy for Wales 177
Interparliamentary Forum on Brexit 127, 130, 254
INTERREG 162
interstate federalism; interstate federations; divided federations 21, 292, 299
Ireland Act 50
Irish Parliament 50, 136n46
Irish Republican Army (IRA) 76n16
Isle of Man 115–117, 136n46, 136n50
Italy 39n3

Jack, Alister 135n43
James, Julie 200
Japan 179
Johnson, Boris 10, 55, 86, 108, 148, 163, 164, 169, 170, 181, 182, 219, 223n34, 259, 267, 270, 290
Joint Exchequer Committee 9, 93, 112–115, 129, 189, 190, 253
Joint Ministerial Working Group on Welfare 119, 123, 150, 278n11
Judicial Committee 90

Justice Act 77n36
Justice in Wales Strategy Group 123, 137n66, 218, 265

Law Derived from the European Union (Wales) Bill 133n19, 158, 227n79
Law Officer 67, 77n29, 92, 132n4, 158, 171
Legislation, Justice and Constitution Committee 197
Legislative Competence Orders 58, 191
Liberal Democrats; LibDem peers 53, 158, 255
Liddell, Helen 132n10
Lidington, David 157, 160
Local Audit and Accountability Bill 95
Local Autonomy Index 39n8
Local Government and Communities Committee 203, 204
Local Government Byelaws (Wales) Bill 91
Localism Act 202
Lochhead, Richard 176
loosely coupled 6, 22, 263, 287, 298, 299

M4 209, 210, 274, 300n9
Major, John 51
Mandelson, Peter 76n16
Marine Scotland Directorate 150
Martin v Most 133n14
Matheson, Michael 200, 201
May, Theresa 55, 97, 111, 132n1, 162, 163, 170, 185, 223n34, 266, 267, 280n32, 280n36
McGuiness, Martin 54
Medical Costs for Asbestos Diseases (Wales) Bill 91, 92
Medical Innovations Bill 134n28
Melding, David 171
Miles, Jeremy 108, 158, 166, 171, 172
Miller case (Miller v Secretary of State for Exiting the European Union) 92, 97, 99, 162, 222n21, 251
Ministerial Forum (European Negotiations) 108
Ministerial Forum for Trade 178
Ministry of Justice (MoJ) 85, 123, 132n2, 134n34, 137n62, 137n65, 216–220, 230n113, 265, 279n25
Misuse of Drugs Act 216, 260
mode of interaction, negotiation mode 7, 31–33, 41n40, 149, 161, 173, 271
Morgan, Rhodri 268

Index

National Health Service (NHS) 92, 123, 177, 212, 224n49, 229n101, 230n105, 264
National Health Service Act 134n34
National Loans Fund 73, 74, 79n60
negotiation power 7, 31–33, 149, 271
negotiation systems, voluntary, compulsory 7, 31–33, 149, 275, 298
neo-institutionalism 41n32
Network Rail Reclassification 134n34
New Deal 184
New Decade New Approach 69
New Zealand 179
North Wales Economic Ambition Board 206
Northern Ireland Act 52, 59, 60, 73, 74, 77n35, 77n36
Northern Ireland Affairs Committee 126, 138n79
Northern Ireland Office; Northern Ireland Department 56, 137n7, 138n79
Northern Ireland Protocol 55, 164, 222n23, 223n36, 224n38
Number 10 Union Unit 86, 128, 251

Ofcom 57
Office for Environmental Protection 227n74
Office for the Internal Market (OIM) 224n38
Olympics; Olympic Games 69, 185

Personal Independence Payment 95
Plaid Cymru 51, 76n11, 222n17, 273, 286
Poland 39n3
Police and Crime Commissioners and Panels 95, 217, 220, 260, 280n38
Police Reform and Social Responsibility Bill 95, 217, 274
Politikverflechtung *see* integrated federalism
Portugal 39n3
Prime Minister and Heads of Devolved Governments Council 85, 109, 253
Prison and Probation Service 138n66, 219
Privy Council 90
Procedure Committee 128
Proceeds of Crime Act 133n25
Protestant 51–54
Protocol on Dispute Resolution 93, 110–112, 114, 129, 136n55
Public Administration and Constitutional Affairs Committee 126, 221n14, 273

Public Bodies Act 97
Public Service Pensions Bill 96

Québec 292

Radical Federalism group 22
Railway Policing Scotland Act 207
Railways Act 207
Red Meat Levy 194–197, 279n19
Reforming our Union 153, 154, 221n13
Regional Authority Index 17–19, 64, 77n18
Reid, John 132n10
residual powers, residual authority 55–63, 74, 287
Revenue and Customs 67, 71
Revenues Scotland 71
Russell, Michael 172, 139n81, 223n34

Salvesen v Riddell 91
Scotland Act 52–61, 71, 73, 78n46, 79n53, 88, 94, 112, 114, 119, 123, 127, 129, 150–152, 187–190, 207, 208, 221n9, 222n20, 252–258, 263, 291
Scotland Office; Scottish Office 56, 75n1, 85–89, 121, 128, 132n10, 203, 229n99, 251, 277
Scotland's International Framework 177
Scottish Affairs Committee 108–111, 126, 127, 139n80, 215, 221n14
Scottish Health and Social Care Committee 139n80
Scottish Independence Referendum Bill 93, 294
Scottish Whiskey Association v Lord Advocate 133n15
Secretary of State for Exiting the EU 105, 108, 162
Secretary of State for Northern Ireland 59, 132n8
Secretary of State for Scotland 56, 77n29, 88, 112, 132n10, 135n43, 136n54
Secretary of State for Wales 88, 122, 132n12, 135n43, 208, 210
Select Committee on the Constitution 17, 40n28, 300n4
Senior Officials Programme Board 123, 124, 197
shared authority 55, 60, 61, 71
Shared Prosperity Fund 69, 156, 174, 175, 210, 256, 257, 281n39, 300n9
Silk Commission *see* Commission on Devolution in Wales
Sinn Féin 54, 55, 76n16, 138n76, 280n32

Index

Smith Commission 57, 66, 71, 114, 151, 189, 190, 208, 221n11, 255
Social Democratic and Labour Party (SDLP) 55
Social Services and Well-being (Wales) Act 230n117
Spain 2, 39n3, 138n75
Spending Review 65–67, 174
St Andrews Agreement 54, 76n16, 77n36
St David's Day Agreement 152, 275
Standing Scottish Grand Committee 75n1
Starmer, Keir 22
Statement of Funding Policy 65–69, 112, 119, 183–186, 225n54, 256, 258
strategic preferences 7, 31–33, 149, 271
Structural Funds; EU Structural Funds; European Structural Funds 69, 105, 174–176, 24n40
Sturgeon, Nicola 88, 135n43, 148, 171, 181, 182
Swinney, John 135n43
Switzerland 78n42, 138n75, 212, 214, 222n14, 256, 260, 278n8, 294

Taoiseach 136n47
Terrorism, Prevention and Investigatory Measures Act 133n25
Thatcher, Margaret 51, 64, 290
Thomas Commission *see* Commission on Justice in Wales
tightly coupled 22, 288, 296–299
Tobacco and Primary Medical Services (Scotland) Act 133n15
Trade Act; Trade Bill 179, 180, 222n15, 225n51, 256, 258
Trade and Cooperation Agreement 166, 179, 257
Trade Remedies Authority (TRA) 224n51
Trade Union (Wales) Act 77n33, 97
Trade Union Bill 77n33, 97, 134n29
Trade Working Group 136n56
Transport for Wales 209, 228n89, 260
Transport Scotland 137n63, 228n89
Trimble, David 76n16

UK Drug Summit; UK Drugs Ministerial Meeting 215
UK Governance Group 86, 88, 104, 128
UK Industrial Strategy 202
UK Internal Market Act; UK Internal Market Bill 103, 169–178, 201, 221, 223n35, 252–259, 267, 271, 280n29, 288, 295, 300n9
UK Withdrawal from the European Union (Legal Continuity) (Scotland) Bill 92, 133n17, 133n19, 157–161, 251, 256, 257
Ulster Unionist Party (UUP) 76n16
Union Advisory Group 86
Union Directorate 86, 251
Union Strategy Committee 86
United Arab Emirates 40n26
United States (US) 19, 27, 75n2, 138n75
Universal Credit 57, 78n40, 95, 221n9
Unlocking Growth in Cities 202

Venezuela 40n26
Verbundsföderalismus *see* integrated federalism
Vote Leave 271

Wales Act 59, 72–74, 76n9, 77n32, 79n55, 91, 94, 97, 112, 114, 129, 138n76, 152, 187, 191, 207, 216, 251–258, 263, 275, 287, 291
Wales and Borders Rail Franchise 208
Wales Office; Welsh Office 56, 57, 75n1, 85–90, 121, 128, 230n114, 251, 275, 287, 291
Wallace, Lord 132n10
War of Independence 50
Welfare Reform (Further Provision) (Scotland) Act 95
Welfare Reform Act; Welfare Reform Bill 95
Well-being of Future Generations (Wales) Act 230n117
Welsh Affairs Committee 10n5, 126, 127, 130, 138n78, 192, 206, 218, 254
White Paper on the UK Internal Market 170
Withdrawal Agreement 155, 163–166, 171, 257
World Trade Organisation (WTO) 194–197, 226n67, 227n69, 227n70, 279n19
World War I 50

Youth Justice Blueprint 134n34, 219, 230n117, 265

Zwangsverhandlungssystem *see* integrated federalism